CW01337899

CLIPPER SHIPS
to OCEAN GREYHOUNDS

H. C. de Mierre

CLIPPER SHIPS

to

H35965

910.4

OCEAN GREYHOUNDS

Harold Starke
LIMITED

© H. C. DE MIERRE 1971

First published April 1971

All rights reserved. No part of this publication may be reproduced, stored in a retrieval system,
or transmitted, in any form or by any means, electronic, mechanical, photocopying, recording
or otherwise, without the prior permission of Harold Starke Limited.

ACKNOWLEDGEMENTS

The illustrations on the following pages are reproduced from drawings and etchings by the
author: 35, 130, 161, 171, 172, 175, 199, 201 and 202.

The author is grateful to the following companies and individuals for permission to reproduce
their illustrations:
D. Marshall Brown (page 20)
Brown, Son & Fergusson Ltd. (pages 41 and 209)
Captain H. J. Chubb (pages 123 and 128)
The National Maritime Museum, Greenwich (pages 90, 207, 231, 237 and 318)
The Nautical Photo Agency (pages 102, 213, 288 and 292)

ISBN 0 287 66986 6
Harold Starke Limited
14 John Street, London, W.C.1
Printed in Great Britain by
Fletcher and Son Limited, Norwich

Contents

vi

List of Illustrations

viii

Oh, most magnificent the youthful sea!
There are many seas, friend;
As many as there are men, as many as there
Are times and periods in a man's life.
But the sea of all is the sea of the young heart . . .
Not the sea of him to whom the ocean
Is but a road of traffic.

MORLEY ROBERTS

1 *The End of a Long Voyage*

In August 1908 I left the ship *Main* in Hamburg. She was a fine, full-rigged ship and in her I had served the first three years of my apprenticeship to the sea. The voyage had taken us to most of the romantic-sounding places whose names had filled my head when I was at school and should have been thinking of other things: Demerara, Cape Town, Calcutta, Dutch Guiana, Barbados, St. Helena, Guadeloupe, New York and Rangoon. We had known the steady thrust of the trade winds through seas of smiling blue and we had ghosted through the baffling cat's-paws, squalls and cloud-bursts of the doldrums. We had raced before the giant seas and wild, westerly winds of the roaring forties; we had known the frustration of flat, glassy calms in the Indian Ocean—with days of burning sun and nights of utter stillness, so black that sky and sea were as one and only the reflection of the stars showed that we were not floating in space. In the West Indies we had sailed our ship up the Surinam River to the little town of Paramaribo—a distance of twenty-five miles from the lightship outside the bar—and great was the pride of the local pilot when he dropped the port anchor, gave the ship a small sheer to starboard and allowed the tide to take her alongside the old wooden wharf where she came to rest so gently that there was not even a creak from its ancient timbers. He was a skilful pilot and it was not at all his fault that, when we cast off from the wharf, the tide planted us firmly on the mud with our jibboom only a monkey's jump from the jungle. In the North Atlantic we had beat through blinding snow and struggled with a fierce hurricane that did disastrous damage to our heavy spars and came within an ace of sending us to the bottom.

It had been a long voyage but a happy one. Now came the greatest happiness of all. I had left home a schoolboy, barely fifteen years old, and was going back a sea-toughened sailor of eighteen. In fine, summer weather but against a stiff north-westerly breeze the small steamer splashed and pitched her way across the North Sea to land us in Grimsby at a very early hour on a Saturday morning. My joy and excitement were beyond describing as the little train wound its way through the pleasant countryside. With its smoke and dust lit by the early sunshine, even Manchester looked very beautiful. My arrival at my father's office brought the wheels of commerce to a momentary halt. A grinning office-boy led me down an aisle between the high desks where clerks sat with their pens poised as they stared at me in wonder or astonishment. My uniform was the same that I had worn so proudly three years earlier; its brass buttons were now green with salt and no amount of blacking could subdue the brine which forced its way to the surface on my shoes and defied all attempts to raise a polish. The young men who watched my progress towards my father's office were such models of clerkly neatness that I was very conscious of the defects in my own appearance. My father, however, did not seem to notice that anything was amiss. He jumped to his feet, threw his arms about me and then held me at arm's length, his face so alight with happiness that my joy in this day of homecoming was redoubled. He introduced me to his colleagues who greeted me with typical Lancashire heartiness.

"Eh lad, but it's good to see you looking so well. Look at the brown face. Anyone could see that you have not spent the last three years slaving away in Manchester."

Their welcome was so warm and they plied me with so many questions about my life in a sailing-ship that, since I was a little self-conscious, I was glad when it was time for lunch.

My last meal had been aboard the steamer before docking in Grimsby so I ate a good lunch with great appetite and drank a large tankard of ale. This made my father chuckle with delight. Then we took the train to Cleveleys where the family was in residence for the summer holidays. We settled in the comfort of a first-class compartment. My father was smoking one of his favourite Turkish cigarettes and I, feeling very contented after such a meal, reached in my breast pocket and pulled out one of my Hamburg cigars. I bit the end off and lit it. I was looking for somewhere to put the spent match, when I realised that my father was shaking with laughter. To see me relish a tankard of ale had been jolly but that I should so casually light and enjoy a cigar seemed to be the supreme joke. He slapped his knee exclaiming, "Good boy! Good boy!" to the amusement of the other passengers who lowered their newspapers and gave us a friendly smile.

Every detail of that wonderful day is still vivid in my memory: how we rejoiced to see each other again. Dorothy, Olga and young Max all met us at Cleveleys. How we found the youngest whom we called "Tommy Golly Ugly Mug"—because her real name was Irmintrude and she was rather a pretty child—digging sand-castles on the beach, and how at first she did not realise who I was.

Then there was the bath. For the last thirty-seven months whenever I had taken a bath—"washed myself all over", as we called it—it had been from a bucket of cold water, standing naked in the lee scuppers on the main deck. So, as soon as we got indoors, I filled the bath and revelled in the warm water and the luxurious feeling of complete cleanliness. I was really "washed all over". Nothing could be missed when you lay with the water lapping your lips. Then I saw that my bath-towel was missing; I gave a hail and young Max came running in with it. But, as soon as he saw me sitting upright in the bath, he let out an excited yell, dropped the towel and ran from the room. He had seen the tattooing on my left arm.

Then came the long happy evening: the delicious meal and everyone full of eager questions about my adventures, my shipmates and the other apprentices. And, finally, to bed; not to a narrow bunk with its thin mattress spread on hard unyielding wooden boards, with its straw-filled pillows and rough blankets; but to lie in a wide soft bed between clean, white sheets. How blissfully I closed my eyes.

The week's frolicking on the beach and in the sea passed quickly. Early in September came the time to go home; the school holidays were nearly over. Wilmslow, in Cheshire, is only a short twelve miles from the city of Manchester but in those days, almost sixty years ago, it was still a pretty country village. Our house was at the end of a lane, among old trees of beech and ash. Over the hawthorn hedge, across the road, beautiful grasslands dropped steeply down to the River Bollin and rose on the other side of the valley to wide pastures dotted with woods and farms. It was a time of the year as lovely as Spring. The full-blown beauty of Summer, now rather blowzy, was passing to the spirited bluster of Autumn. I wandered about the countryside, relishing the earthy scent of ploughed fields, the keen, sudden gusts of wind that sent clouds of multicoloured leaves swirling aloft, and the fitful bursts of sunshine that turned the roadside puddles into fathomless pools of deepest blue. Plover and peewit tumbled about the air in jerky flight. In the woods, the rooks chattered noisily in the swaying treetops and then fell silent as the sky darkened and a sudden sharp shower of stinging rain swept through the leafless branches. The water ran down the smooth grey trunks of the old beeches until they shone, as though refreshed. A shaft of sunlight came out of the clouds and they glistened. The rain squall had gone, the sun was bright again. The rooks flapped the raindrops from their wings, made chuckling noises as though clearing their throats in unison and then let out a raucous scream of joy. It must have been joy; it had the same spontaneous triumphant ring that comes from the crowd at a football match when the home side has scored a winning goal.

On Sunday mornings my sisters went to church with Max who sang in the choir and my father and I took long walks, sometimes covering as much as six miles. On our way home we usually stopped at *The Bull;* after so much exercise it was pleasant to rest a while and drink a pot of ale. The company was also as pleasant as it was varied; we usually found old Ned Bower and the local solicitor sitting in the parlour waiting for us. The solicitor, a man with the same scholarly tastes as my father, shared his interest in the Classics and in the origins of words and their roots. In his own way, Ned Bower was just as learned; he knew all there was to know about moles, voles, stoats, badgers, weasels, rabbits and hares and, of course, partridge and pheasant. He was a little man, about seventy years old; and his bright-eyed face was the colour of a russet apple. Now, in his old age, he made his living breaking stones by the roadside for the highway authorities but he had been a farm labourer and ploughman all his working days and, as he confessed with a twinkle, a poacher all his working nights. There was a nice friendship between the three men and old Ned enjoyed their meetings without any tinge of subservience on his part or patronage on theirs. I suppose this was because, regardless of their different stations in life, all three were gentlemen.

With the near prospect of cold weather my father had given Ned a warm greatcoat. That is, he had sent it to the landlord of *The Bull* who promised to deliver it. On the following Sunday, as we were about to pass Ned's cottage, he came running down its garden path to meet us at the gate. His normally red face was an even deeper colour and he was holding a large bunch of flowers.

"Good morning, sir. Eee, but it's a grand day. I've got ee a few flowers from my garden . . . if t'young sailor doan't mind carrying them."

Before my father could make any reply, Ned turned and went quickly back into his cottage. There had been no mention of the overcoat, no "thank you", but much more than Ned or anybody else could have said, was carried in the flowers.

Before going to sea I had been at Manchester Grammar School, during the reign of two High Masters. There was a short, painful period under John Edward King and the rest of the time was spent under John Lewis Paton. He was not only a schoolmaster of country-wide fame; he also had the wonderful gift of attracting the affectionate loyalty of all the boys at the school (even though there were between eight and nine hundred of them). He got to know many of them personally, even including some of the drones—such as I—who were not in any way shining scholars. My head was frequently in the clouds, dreaming of ships and sailors, of coral islands, copra and coconuts; and I was often in trouble. Discipline was strict and there were many kinds of punishment; for boisterous behaviour or fighting in the corridors the prefects could cane you on the hand and the form masters could do the same for mischief or bad conduct in the classroom. If your work in class was unsatisfactory or if you were stupid, you could be sent up into the attic to Punishment School, after school had closed for the day, there to continue for an extra hour the subject in which you had been found deficient. If you were a persistent back-slider, you could be sent to Punishment Drill which meant going to the gymnasium when all the other boys had gone home and there enduring a rugged forty-five minutes of exercise with an iron bar-bell, under the stern eye of Drill Sergeant Naden.

For more serious misdemeanours you were sent for punishment to the High Master's study. Here the ritual was as precise as it was painful. With a master's old silk gown hanging from your shoulders, you knelt on the seat of a low chair, lowered your trousers, leant over the back of the chair and grasped the rung between its legs. Then came the swish of the cane, leaving its burning stripes on your backside until the punishment was deemed sufficient. When it was over, you very gingerly pulled up your trousers, dropped the old gown across the chair and made slowly towards the door. There was no sermonising by the High Master, which was just as well for that surely would have brought the tears that had been suppressed with such difficulty. He stood there at the door with a small, wistful smile on his pale face, saying, "Go boy. I hope I don't have to do that again." The door closed and you took to your heels and ran as fast as you could to get away from the place so that no one should know that you had been in there or what you had been in there for. You ran out to Long Millgate to dash to the station, pause to wipe your eyes and swallow hard. You stood up in the train, gently rubbing your bottom, all the way home. That is how it had been under Mr. King.

My last day at school did not go smoothly. Knowing that it was my last day I had not done my homework for the bull-throated drawing master "Slimy" Jackson. It did not work.

"Oh, so you have not done your brushwork and you know that because there will be no school tomorrow I can't tell you to bring me three copies in the morning. That's it. Isn't it? All right. Then you'll go to P.D. instead."

At the end of the day those of us who were leaving school met in the High Master's study to receive his farewell greeting and bid him good-bye in our turn. Mr. Paton's speech was very simple and forthright and he did not mince his words. He told us of the things that could give us comfort and courage, and of those which could help us to success. He also warned us of the evils and temptation which could bring us miserably down. Then came the leavetaking. When my turn came to grasp his hand he looked at me very kindly.

"So you're going to sea, de Mierre. No strawberries and cream there."

"No, sir," I replied. And then, thinking that the moment was propitious, I went on, "Please, sir, I have a punishment drill against me. May I be excused?"

The blue eyes twinkled as he said, "Well, de Mierre, if you walk out I can't stop you. But don't leave a fag-end behind. Good-bye."

So I went down to the gymnasium and did my drill. Then I left the school for ever, feeling very happy and lighthearted. A fag-end had suddenly become a very important thing.

I had written to Mr. Paton once or twice during the voyage and received very kind replies. Now, he had invited me to tea in his study and again I found myself walking down Long Millgate which seemed to have lost the severe air that I had sometimes found so daunting in the past. But I was not carrying a school satchel heavy with books and unfinished homework. I was wearing a new uniform, my shoes were brightly polished and my badge-cap was perched on my head, "flat aback". The street was full of boys who came pouring out of the school and they stared at me—not in astonishment but, I felt sure, with envy—and I am afraid that my gait took on a more pronounced nautical roll. Mr. Paton received me with a warmth so sincere that I was immediately at my ease. There was another guest, an elderly American lady who was principal of one of the large women's colleges in Massachusetts. She was delighted that I had such happy memories of the weeks I had spent in New York and, for me at least, the time passed very pleasantly for upwards of an hour, eating muffins and drinking tea, occasionally cocking an eye over to the far corner where, behind the life-sized nude statue of the young David, the low chair—the stool of repentance—was concealed, with the old silk gown hanging on the wall beside it. When I took my leave of Mr. Paton I mentioned the last occasion and how he had taught me not to go leaving a fag-end behind. He listened, smiling. When I had finished, he exclaimed, "Did I indeed! Well, well, my boy. Even if you had learned nothing else here, you took something away with you that is rather precious. Good-bye, my boy. God Bless you!"

Two months went by very quickly and we were well into October when at last my orders came. Every day I had feared, hoped and expected them. I knew that it could not be much longer before my glorious holiday came to an end and it was this that I feared and expected. I knew that the ship *Main* was still in Hamburg and I hoped that I would be instructed to join her again. But, no, I was to go to the ship *Arno*, joining her in London. It was blowing a real live gale when the last post of the day brought the letter from James Nourse Ltd., the owners. The wind howled around the chimneys causing the cosy fire to burn more merrily and the hard squalls of hail and rain drumming on the glass roof of the conservatory emphasized our warmth and comfort. They also brought me sharply back to earth with a quick glimpse of the weeks ahead

16

when a freezing wind would be shrieking through the rigging and the rain and hail beating on our oilskins. My face must have shown my disappointment because my father immediately asked, "What is it, my boy? Don't you want to go?"

"Oh yes," I replied. "But I did hope that it would have been the *Main*. She was such a happy ship and a lucky one. But, ah, no!" I punned clumsily.

"Ah, yes," cried young Max. "I'm sure that you will make yourself as happy in the *Arno* as you did in the *Main*."

"Three cheers and Amen to that," said my father. "Good boy Max. Give us some more sherry and get a small glass for yourself and Dorothy and Ollie."

"And me too," cried little Tommy.

So the glasses were filled—a very small one for Tommy—and we all drank to the *Arno* and wished her fair winds and good weather.

2   *The Full-rigged Ship* Arno

The policeman at the gate of the South-West India Docks fingered his chin, repeating meditatively, "*Arno . . . Arno*", then stepped into his hut, ran his finger down a blackboard and, in a moment, was out again. "There she is, mate," he said, waving an arm, "number five jetty . . . west side . . . one 'uv them ships, yer can't miss 'er. Ye'll find a watchman aboard . . . but that's about all."

The ships were a couple of hundred yards away; there were half a dozen of them, their masts and rigging lost in the dark of the misty October evening. We pulled up alongside the *Arno* and the watchman, carrying a lantern, came down the gangway. The fat, good-natured cabby helped us to get my gear aboard and stowed in the half-deck which was in the after deckhouse. Then he seated himself on my sea-chest, mopping his brow. He gazed, wide-eyed, about him—at the simple, empty wooden bunks and at the bare deck, all very comfortless and gloomy in the limited, feeble light of the watchman's lantern. His eyebrows rose in astonishment.

"Yer goin' to live 'ere! Where're yer goin' to eat?—'ere! What! All the bleedin' way to 'Orstrailia'! An' go up into all thet mess o' ropes 'n spars!" He slowly shook his head. I was holding out four shillings, but he gave me sixpence change. "Three an' a tanner we said. Didn' we? Well three an' a tanner it is." He got to his feet and, wagging his head, he went over the gangway.

I was the first to join. The ship had not started loading and it would be some weeks before we had a crew and would be ready for sea. In the meantime, the owners had arranged that we apprentices would be fed at a workmen's coffee rooms, just outside the dock gates. The watchman hung his lantern at the head of the gangway and then took me the short distance to Pullfords' restaurant. There, we went through to the back room where I was introduced to the family: Pa and Ma and a son and daughter. Pa sat smoking a short, black clay pipe, stacking up before him the day's takings. Ma, spruced up for the evening, had her hair done in a pile of curls, like Queen Alexandra. She wore a black bombazine dress with a high neck, and necklaces and bangles of jet. She dimpled and smiled a welcome and readily agreed that the watchman should have his supper with us.

I had been many hours in the train, delayed by fog, coming up from Cheshire, and I was hungry. Whatever the watchman had been doing, he was hungry also. We ate poached finnan haddock, several slices of fried ham with eggs, platefuls of bread and butter and slabs of fruit cake, washed down with cups of tea. And my bill for my guest was only ten pence!

Back on board, I took the lantern from the gangway to provide some light in the half-deck, made up my bunk and was soon under the blankets, wriggling about, trying to induce some warmth into the straw pallet and make it and the wooden bunk boards as accommodating to my bones as the soft bed had been at home. Nine wonderful weeks had passed since I had left the ship *Main*. She was still at Hamburg, tied up, waiting to be sold.

Of the twelve fine full-rigged sailing-ships owned by James Nourse Ltd. when I had joined the company only three were still in commission: the *Ems* making her last passage, homeward-bound from Demerara, the *Forth* waiting for the rice harvest in Rangoon, and the *Arno*, now to load a general cargo for Australia. Steam was the thing now.

Outside, a cold easterly wind carried patches of wet fog before it. Up aloft, ropes and wires chattered in the breeze and tinkled against the steel masts. The empty ship rolled gently against her fenders, the mooring-lines strained and creaked drowsily at the bitts on the quarter-deck and I was soon asleep.

Next morning, the watchman brought me a bucket of cold water which he had kindly pumped at the main fife rail. It was still grey dawn and I shivered as I washed and got into working clothes—dungaree trousers and a heavy blue woollen jersey—and went ashore. On my way back from breakfast I wandered about looking at the ships which had been barely visible the night before. At the first jetty lay the auxiliary barque *Discovery*, the three-masted barque *Loch Trool* and the full-rigged ship *Loch Garve*. They were laid up, uncared for and lifeless; the *Discovery* discarded after her return from the Antarctic expedition in 1904, the others waiting to be sold.

Sharing the *Arno*'s jetty was a three-masted barque, the *Amulree*, also bound for Australia. At the other wharves, up the dock, were the ships *Macdiarmid* of Castletown, Isle of Man, loading for Sydney, New South Wales, and three barques: the *Pharos* belonging to Shaw Savill, for Launceston, Tasmania, the Norwegian *Sara* which began life as the *Firth of Stronsa* of Glasgow, loading for the Cape, and the British barque *Sussex*, up for sale. There was only one steamer to be seen, a rusty-looking old-timer tied up in a corner of the dock, with a dirty rag of tarpaulin made fast across the top of her funnel to keep the rain from pouring down below. She invited no second glance. The sailing-ships were a fine sight—a forest of masts! Well, anyhow, a copse of withering old timber. Steam! Steam was the thing now!

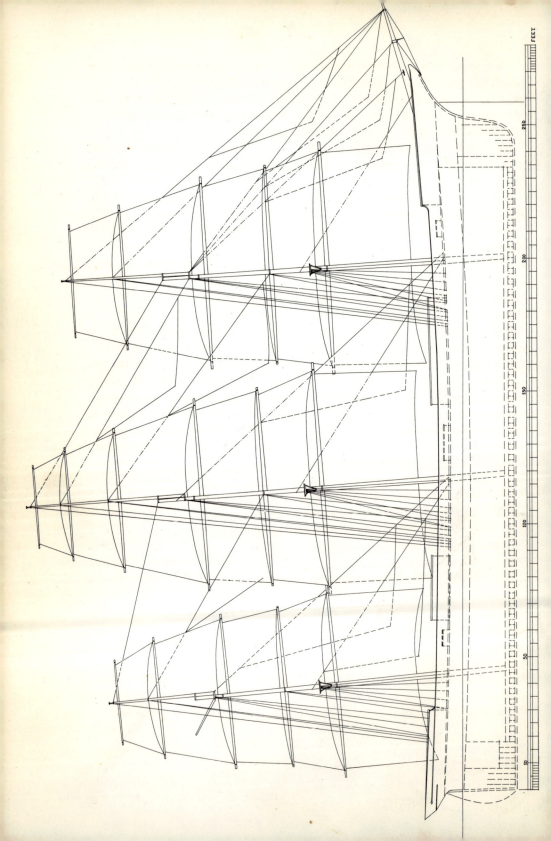

FEET

That day Banbury and Isdale joined—I had been shipmates with them in the *Main*—also Mr. Fowler, the Mate. He was a well-made, ruddy-faced man in his mid-forties, quiet spoken, with the lilt of County Cork on his tongue, but now very taciturn as he went about his new ship with an appraising eye, which also took our measure as he questioned us.

"Ye were in the *Main* . . . the one voyage three years. Aye. We were together with ye in New York when I was in the *Forth*, ye mind. An' we heard of the trouble ye had afterwards off Hatteras. Lucky ye didn't lose the ship . . . so ye were." He paused, his attention held by a crash aboard the *Macdiarmid*, across the dock, where the boss stevedore let fly a flood of lurid language. Mr. Fowler smiled and remarked, "That would be a sling of liquor they dropped. They'd have been more careful with anything else." Then he went on, "Alright, let's get the hatches off and see what she's like down below. We'll be loading ourselves one of these days."

We turned back the tarpaulins, lifted off a few hatches, fore and aft, and got down into the holds where we found a mess of dunnage wood, burlap and bamboo matting, scattered about as they had been left when the last of the cargo had been discharged. Our job was to get the ship ready for her next cargo and we spent the following ten days sorting out the mess, stacking the dunnage wood and mats ready for the stevedores, then sweeping the hold and 'tween-decks and getting rid of all the unserviceable stuff. The days passed pleasantly. At Pullfords' the family had taken us to their bosom and on many evenings we would be invited upstairs where pretty Miss Pullford played the piano and we sang the favourite songs of the day, such as *Love me and the world is mine*. We fairly raised the roof with that!

By the middle of November the ship was deep in the water and had almost finished loading a most diverse general cargo for Adelaide and Melbourne. It consisted of light plantation railway sections for transhipment to the South Sea Islands, barrels of Portland cement, coils of fencing wire, rolls of barbed wire, cases of hardware, barrels of printing ink, rolls of newsprint, bales of dry goods, barrels of beer and stout, cases of bottled beer, canned goods, sausages, tongues, herrings, sardines and the like.

When loading commenced Captain Edwin German joined us. His last ship, the *Elbe*, in which he had made so many smart passages, was now rigged down as a hulk in Martinique. He was a good fifteen years younger than the men who had commanded the *Main* during our voyage—Captains William Stuart Smith and Newbery George Hatch—and was of a completely different generation and background.

Captain German hailed from Swansea and had been twenty-eight years at sea. He served his apprenticeship, from the age of sixteen, in a little wooden barque, the *San José* and sailed in her for six years as apprentice, able seaman, Bos'n and Second Mate, making short voyages with coal out to Cape Town and bringing copper ore from Port Nolloth back to Swansea; or, occasionally, with coal to Cadiz and salt from there to Newfoundland, and home with a cargo of lumber. The *San José* was only 130 feet long, just about half the length of the *Arno*, and it must have been a hard and monotonous life.

When he had passed for Master he joined a Dundee company which owned a fleet of ten ships and at the age of thirty-six was appointed Master of the *Glenogle*, a three-masted barque of 914 tons net. Sailing from Liverpool in February, 1900, he took her to Brisbane where he arrived after a rather long passage, having experienced heavy gales in the Southern Ocean which damaged his bulwarks. Then, down to Newcastle, New South Wales, where she loaded a cargo of coal for Valparaiso. Again he was unlucky. He made an average passage of sixty-six days but the weather was so bad that on one occasion the little barque was thrown on her beam-ends and arrived with bulwarks smashed and decks strained which necessitated repairs costing £400.

Then to Caleta Buena for a cargo of nitrate and round the Horn home to Ardrossan. The homeward passage of 132 days was poor. The *Glenogle* was evidently not a fast ship. Or perhaps the young Captain had been rapped over the knuckles and was afraid to press the ship when he had the wind. There had been plenty of time for correspondence while the ship was on the coast of Chile and the thrifty gentlemen in Dundee would not have taken kindly to a repair bill which probably absorbed most of the profits of the voyage.

One can imagine the tone of their letters. Why had the ship been thrown on her beam-ends? Could he not have shortened down and hove her to, in good time to avoid such an extremity? Or did she go over on her beam-ends because the cargo shifted? If this were so, it would not have happened if the hold had been properly prepared for a bulk cargo of loose coal, with adequate shifting boards, carefully secured. Yes, the ship had paid for shifting boards but had they been supplied and fitted? Had they?

The *Glenogle* arrived in Ardrossan on July 1st, 1901. Her voyage of sixteen months had taken her around the world. It was the end of Captain German's first voyage in command and, whatever the reason, it was also the end of his service with the Dundee *Glens*. When the *Glenogle* left Ardrossan for Table Bay, again with a coal cargo, a Scot, Captain Ramsay, walked her poop.

Captain Ramsay took her on her last passage. When she was still 1,500 miles from Cape Town—out in the middle of the South Atlantic, about 240 miles north of Tristan da Cunha—fire broke out in the cargo by spontaneous combustion. The crew worked at the pumps, night and day, for four days and during this time a number of explosions occurred which burst the decks and injured several of the men. Then the full-rigged ship *Ardencraig* came along and stood by until it was certain that the ship could not be saved. She took the crew aboard and landed them in Cape Town on September 30th.

The *Glenogle* sank, burnt out. Perhaps it was she that carried the bad luck. Captain German could be forgiven if he thought so when he read of it and remembered all the worry and trouble she had given him when she was in his charge.

In June 1902 Captain German joined Nourse's ship *Elbe* as Mate. Three years later he was given command of her; and when he came to us in the *Arno* he had had a further three years' experience as Master.

In appearance Captain German was tall, wiry and broad-shouldered. Because of his habit of standing as though he were perpetually on a heaving deck—feet well apart, knees slightly bent, thumbs hooked into his belt, elbows out like stunsails—one had the impression of very long arms and legs. As soon as he came aboard he changed his bowler for a peaked cap which he wore well off his forehead; it made his bony seaman's face look as massive as the rest of him. He spent the first morning looking around the ship, walking around the lower hold and 'tween-decks to satisfy himself that they were in good shape for the cargo. Then we had to open the door of the sail locker and he stuck his head inside.

"Smells sweet and dry, Mr. Fowler," he said. "They'll be sending a crowd of riggers aboard to bend sail for us next week."

"Yes, sir," Mr. Fowler replied. "I got a chit about it from the office. Well, we'll be ready for them. There's all the rovins they'll be needing in the sail locker. An' tacks and sheets for fore, main and cro'jack, an' head sheets, we've got stowed, all handy, in the fo'c's'le. An' now there's nothing more for these young fellows to do down below, they can bend skys'l, royals, head sails and spanker an', maybe, their own mizzen to'gal'nts'l an' we'll be that much ahead. So we will."

Captain German gave us a quick, quizzical glance. Mr. Fowler gave us a wink and a small smile and away we went forward, for block and gantline, glad to have done with dirt and brooms and polishing brass on poop and quarter-deck. We soon had the block fast at the main mast-head and the gantline rove; we dragged the skysail from the locker and hove it aloft with the main deck capstan, Mr. Fowler heaving around with Isdale and me, while Banbury sat on the deck taking in the slack. Then the three of us went up to bend the sail to the yard, reeve off its burnt-lines and shackle on sheets and clew-lines.

It was a brisk November morning with a touch of frost in the breeze. From the skysail yard, 150 feet above the deck, the whole of dockland was spread before us, all the square miles of roofs and smoking chimneys of Poplar, Canning Town, Rotherhithe and Millwall. Near by was the busy river with its tugs and lighters, barges in tow and under sail, steamers puffing plumes of steam at their funnels, blowing their whistles, and threading a cautious way among the small craft. The whole scene, sometimes grey, sombre and cold, sometimes sparkling—when shafts of sunlight pierced the clouds, danced on the roof tops and glittered gaily on the river.

We got the skysail and the three royals up to the yards and snugly furled before the end of the day. The following morning we bent the spanker, jibs and mizzen topgallantsail, leaving the rest of the heavier sails for the riggers. Coming down from aloft, that day, I was reminded of myself three years earlier; standing on the dock, abreast the mizzen shrouds, was a youngster of about seventeen, his eager face alight as he watched us drop from the sheer pole to the deck. His father was with him and, when we had finished taking up the slack of the topgallant sheets, clew-lines and bunt-lines and hanging them up in coils at the belaying pins in the rail, he stood at the edge of the wharf and spoke to us. His boy, Sam, could think of nothing else but going to sea in a sailing-ship—our ship—and he had spent most of the previous day standing about in the cold, frosty weather, watching us working aloft. The father was glad to be able to speak to boys who had the same urge and he was evidently easier in his mind when he learned that we had already had three years of the life.

The company's ship *Ems* arrived at Dieppe from Demerara on November 14th; three of her apprentices—Morris, Mantell and Le Patourel—came to join us after only a few hours at home. We had already met Le Patourel, "Paddy" as we called him, when the *Ems* lay in the berth ahead of us in Calcutta in April 1906. She had her topgallant yards down, lying on a lighter alongside, and Paddy had joined her to make his first voyage.

One Saturday evening when Banbury, Isdale and I were in the Eden Gardens listening to the military band, we had come across little Charles Le Patourel. With a heavy nautical roll, and very proud of his new uniform, he walked up and down the greensward and amused us with his sailorly talk. The climax of the conversation was his remark, "We're going to have a 'sonofabitch' of a job on Monday, crossing those bloody to'gal'nt yards." He spoke as though, in a large measure, the success of the job depended on him, an old sailor of only a few days' standing. And he certainly had learned sailor's language in short order.

Now we reminded him of that meeting and the six of us enjoyed a good laugh, Paddy most of all.

On November 19th our crew joined and we warped through the lock into the river where a tug gave us her line. Mrs. Pullford and her pretty daughter were among those waving from the dock-head, Ma alternately smiling and wiping her eyes. I was with Mr. Fowler, working with the far from sober sailors, hauling the lines aboard as they were cast off from the bollards ashore. When we were clear of the dock, forward, I waved my cap, thinking of all the kindness the old lady had shown for us. Then I saw Sam's father, smiling wanly, bareheaded in the breeze. Alongside me, a slim youngster in blue trousers and jersey stood on the fore bitts, waving good-bye. He jumped down and turned to me with a happy grin, his hand outstretched, "My name's Sam Bullock. I'm a boy in the fo'c's'le now." He chuckled diffidently. "My father said I should get to know you chaps in the half-deck." We shook hands and gave his father a final wave and soon he was out of sight as we headed down river.

After the long weeks of living in the ship while she lay desolate, still and empty in the South-West India Docks it was good to see her alive again. Four small black and white pigs squealed and grunted in the sheep pens and a cheerful young cook was busy with his pots and pans. He had come aboard stone cold sober the night before, had settled his gear in his cabin in the forward deck-house and then gone ashore. At midnight he came back, very happy, telling the night in a rich and lusty baritone, "I'm cook aboard the *Arno*, the finest ship sailing out o' the London river, an' me name's Jack Desborough." And that really was his name. As I passed the galley door I noticed another new member of the ship's company: a fat, middle-aged tom cat, a tabby, obviously an old sailor, sitting on the seat locker opposite the stove, his tail curled around his ankles, blinking with contentment.

On the quarter-deck the steward, just a little drunk, stood frowning at a sheaf of papers which he clutched in both hands. He was surrounded by an assortment of parcels, cases and light wooden barrels of cabin biscuits—cabin stores which had been put aboard at the last moment—and, as I came aft, Captain German hailed me from the poop with scarce concealed ill humour, "Away there, de Mierre, get your half-deck crowd along here and help the steward stow all this mess of stores in the lazaret." We put Morris and Paddy down the lazaret hatch, under the deck of the saloon; the rest of us passed the stuff along and we had it down there and stowed while the steward was still goggling over his lists. While we replaced the small hatch, Morris and Paddy nipped into the half-deck to unload their jerseys which they had stuffed with cabin bread and a couple of tins of salmon.

Amidships, a gang of carpenters from the shore was busy sawing and hammering, building a magazine in the 'tween-deck, in the square of the main hatch, using clean, white timber and copper nails. When we anchored at

Gravesend, a tug brought a covered lighter alongside with twenty tons of gunpowder, in little wooden kegs. These we took aboard, passing them from hand to hand, and stowed them carefully in the magazine, well chocked off to avoid any motion or friction. Then the carpenters went ashore, the hatch was covered and battened down, we hung out riding lights and swung to our anchors thoughout the night.

A couple of hours before sunrise, sparks were coming from the galley funnel. The cook was still strange to the ship but we got our coffee, steaming hot and very welcome for the morning was as black as midnight and bitingly raw and cold. We put on oilskins and went on to the quarter-deck where the Mate and Second Mate were standing. There was a light north-easterly breeze and a drizzle of rain. Already, the Captain and Pilot were on the poop, looking about them, watching for the tugs which shortly came out from the bank, moving crab-wise across the ebb tide. We made them fast, one on each side, for a compass adjuster had come with them.

The *Arno* had been lying for four months in the docks, heading the whole time in the same direction and acquiring by induction from the earth's magnetism changes in the magnetism inherent in her steel hull which consequently exerted an influence on the compass needle different from that previously known. So, as soon as there was enough daylight, the ship would be turned, "swung", through a complete circle. As she moved round, her steel hull and superstructure would move over a series of changing positions in relation to the stationary compass needle, and with different effects on it. The adjuster, by comparing the bearings taken with our compass with the known bearings of his transit marks on shore, would determine its error, or deviation. By moving the short magnetic rods which were housed in the binnacle stand, he would reduce the deviation to a minimum and leave a record of it, for each heading of the compass, with the Captain.

"Alright, sir," said the Pilot, addressing the Captain but speaking so heartily that the Mate could also hear, "You can heave short, if you please. Let me know when the chain's up, and down on your riding anchor; then, before we break it out, the tug can swing us round and this gentleman can do his work on your compass."

"Alright, Mr. Fowler?" the Captain asked.

"Aye aye, sir," replied the Mate and we trailed after him to man the capstan on the fo'c's'le head. We had made a running moor the previous day, with forty-five fathoms of chain on each anchor. We hove the starboard chain smartly in as the carpenter at the windlass slacked away on the port cable. A few lusty heaves broke the starboard anchor out of the mud and we hove it

26

up to the hawse pipe. Then began the long heave to the riding anchor. Mr. Fowler, like the rest of us, was all muffled up in oilskins, the rain dripping from his sou'wester and from the end of his red nose but his eyes twinkled from his ruddy face as he urged us on.

"Heave with a song, lads," he cried, "come on wid ye . . . cheerily now. You there, Flynn," he pointed to a burly, middle-aged shellback, "come on now, for the pride o' County Cork, or sure an' it's meself'll be startin' ye."

Flynn's weatherbeaten face turned a still deeper red but, after glancing nonchalantly right and left, he let out a yell that settled down to his own version of an old capstan chanty. He had a good, rich Irish voice and we all took up the chorus with a will.

> *"We're outward bound for Adelaide town,*
> *Good-bye, fare ye well, good-bye, fare ye well,*
> *The girls of Limehouse are all cast down,*
> *Good-bye, my dears, we're outward bound.*
>
> *Their manners were easy, their talk was so gay,*
> *Good-bye, fare ye well, good-bye, fare ye well,*
> *They drank all the liquor an' took all our pay,*
> *Good-bye, my dears, we're outward bound.*
>
> *And now, me lads, they're looking roun',*
> *Good-bye, fare ye well, good-bye, fare ye well,*
> *For some other poor sailors who've just come to town,*
> *Good-bye, my dears, we're outward bound.*
>
> *But down where we're goin' we'll come to no harm,*
> *Good-bye, fare ye well, good-bye, fare ye well,*
> *The Adelaide girls are so kind and so warm,*
> *Hurray, me boys, we're outward bound.*
>
> *For the girls we are leaving we'll have no regret,*
> *Good-bye, fare ye well, good-bye, fare ye well,*
> *We'll up with the anchor, our sails we will set,*
> *Hurray, me boys, we're outward bound."*

With the tugs alongside moving us up to the anchor, the pawls clanked merrily as we walked around the capstan. Sam Bullock, heaving around next to me, broke into a delighted grin when Flynn started the chanty and he shouted the chorus as heartily as the rest of us until a bellow came from the Mate.

"Heave a pawl," he cried, "'vast heaving."

"'Vast heaving, sir," we all echoed, puffing and blowing, well warmed up with our exertions.

"Screw her up, Chips," the Mate hailed down the fo'c's'le skylight. He blew his whistle to let the Captain know we were all ready, then turned to me and said, "Nip along to the poop, de Mierre, and tell the Old Man I've got the fifteen fathom shackle on the windlass. And then go to the wheel."

"Aye aye, sir," I replied. I reported to the Captain and then stood by at the wheel while the compass adjuster took charge. Day was just breaking and he could pick out his marks against the grey, lightening sky. It seemed a slow business; there was not much for me to do, and the Old Man was inclined to be impatient.

"Just about low water, slack," he was saying. "We'll have the flood against us all the way down river, dammit! I'd like to get around the Foreland while the wind holds in the north-east."

"No use worrying, Cap'n," replied the Pilot. "The flood won't bother us more than a knot, . . . and I'll be glad of the water with your draught. He paused and looked up and around at the sullen, heavily clouded sky, then went on, "This north-easterly is dying away, anyhow, and if it goes round to the sou'west we'll not get further than the Downs."

The Captain's only response was a look of disgust and a shrug of his shoulders.

It was 8.30 a.m. before the adjuster had finished and we were under way. One of the A.B.s had relieved me at the wheel and, after breakfast, I stood with Paddy and Mantell looking at the dreary expanse of mud and marshland away to port as we swung into the Lower Hope Reach. In the narrows, off the Mucking Buoy, an inward-bound Orient liner passed us close by; her bright yellow funnels billowed black and tawny coal smoke. With her black hull and gleaming white deck-houses and the string of gaily-coloured flags, she was a lively contrast to the grey of the November day and the drab, muddy Thames water which splashed noisily between us. She looked splendid, towering above us, and so did her Captain and officers gazing down from her bridge. We probably looked as handsome to them, with our lofty white masts, black yards and snugly furled sails. They were certainly looking down on the days of their youth and perhaps there was among them a lump in the throat and a pair of wistful eyes as they watched us heading for the sea, our flags flying just as gaily as theirs.

By the end of the afternoon watch the North Foreland light was four points on our starboard bow, shining steady and bright three miles off, for when I went to the wheel again at 4.00 p.m. the sun had just set.

Steering to follow the sternlight of the tug was easy. We were deep in the water but she kept us going at about six knots. The Old Man was gloomy but reconciled to the obvious, for the north-east wind had gone, the sky had cleared in the west, and as we headed south, round the buoy off the North Foreland, we met the first mild puffs of a westerly which was to hold us wind-bound for the next eight days.

We anchored in the Downs, about a mile and a half from the beach, between Deal and Walmer. As soon as the ship was brought up and lying securely to her anchor, the tug came alongside for our Pilot and went with him into Dover, about eight miles to the south'ard. We were finished with them. For all practical purposes, we were at sea. The voyage had begun. All we needed was a wind that we could use to get down Channel.

All we needed was a leading wind, one that would serve even though we had to beat our way down Channel. But it held to the west and south of west and the anchorage was soon crowded with all kinds of rigs and sizes of outward-bounders, from little wooden barques and barquentines of Norway, Sweden and the Baltic, deep laden, with their grace hidden beneath high, square deck-loads of timber, to a taut and trim, grey-painted German four-masted barque. Steamers great and small passed close to seaward at all states of wind and tide. The only effect the head wind had on them was to provoke an extra outpouring of their filthy black smoke.

Nor were the coastal craft consisting of ketches, schooners and topsail schooners—fore and afters—worried by the westerly. They beat or reached their way past the Downs and only put in for shelter on one day when for twenty-four hours it blew a hard gale with a dense, blinding rain. Then a fleet of them came running back round the South Foreland, to take up a quiet berth in smooth water inshore, "rounding to", head to wind, as headsails and fore-sail came down, with anchors splashing, chain cables rattling and their small oilskin-clad crews of two men and a couple of boys tending sheets, downhauls and halliards and making all snug and secure.

We were at anchor, windbound, but by no means idle. Eight days with all hands available for work from six in the morning until 5.30 in the evening were a godsend for the Mate and he made full use of them. It blew and it rained, we put on oilskins and seaboots and washed the ship down, fore and aft—tops of deck-houses, boats, fo'c's'le head and poop; we scrubbed bulwarks and rails, swilling the cold, clear Channel water around until all traces of London's grime had gone. Then we looked over all the gear up aloft, to see that the riggers, when bending sail, had securely shackled sheets and clew-lines to the clews of the sails and that all was rove with clear leads.

At night we kept anchor watches: an ordinary seaman and one A.B. forward and the Mate or Second Mate and one apprentice aft. I was in the port watch with the Mate. While we lay in the South-West India Docks he had been very quiet and short-spoken, a man of few words. This was largely due to his concern for the ship, watching the riggers bending sail and overseeing the loading of a cargo so varied that it was a challenge for any conscientious Mate to achieve good stowage and the best distribution of weight for safe and sea-kindly stability. Now, all that was done with. We had left the dockside bar-parlours behind. They, too, had had something to do with his taciturnity. The cargo was well stowed under hatches which were well battened down and when it was my turn for a two-hour watch on the poop I found him to be genial and talkative.

The many lights marking the Goodwin Sands flashed brightly to seaward; in the chart-house a large-scale chart was spread on the table under the oil lamp, with parallel rulers and dividers, and Mr. Fowler let me go to the compass to take bearings of the South Goodwin and East Goodwin light-vessels and then compare them with those which had previously been set down on the chart, to make sure that the ship lay securely to her anchor. With this and his talk of earlier ships the watches passed quickly.

Mr. Fowler had been twenty-eight years at sea. He had served his apprenticeship in a wooden ship called the *Prince Louis*. She sailed wherever she could find a cargo: Penarth to Rio de Janeiro, round the Horn to San Francisco, San Francisco to Le Havre. That was his first voyage.

After completing his apprenticeship he spent six years as Second Mate of five different sailing-ships trading out of the Bristol Channel, down to Rio, across the Atlantic, or out to Bombay. He was a carefree young sailor, gaining experience. Then he tried steam and for three years sailed as Second Mate and Mate, out of Cardiff with coal for Port Said, on to the Black Sea, in ballast, and home with grain. It was a disagreeable life and he must have been full of joy when he got the chance to join the beautiful little *Orari* as Mate. A full-rigged ship, she had been built for the New Zealand Shipping Company in 1875.

From the time of joining as Mate, he was seven years in the ship, six of them as Master, and made the west to east passage six times around Cape Horn. The *Orari* was a busy ship and smart, too. She made the passage from New York to Dunedin in only eighty-six days, and from Lyttleton, New Zealand, to Falmouth in ninety-six days. The seven years were free from trouble. Fowler had handled her well. There had been no loss of spars or serious heavy-weather damage, no repair bills out of the ordinary. The ship was never idle. She must have made money for her owners.

But when she was twenty-six years old the *Orari* was sold and on her next voyage she had a new Master.

It was July 1901. Fowler had lost his command, to get another was difficult and he was a married man. In September, he was outward bound again, back as Mate, in a three-masted steel barque, the *Dalrymple*, sailing from the Bristol Channel with a cargo of coal for Montevideo. Then came the long run in ballast to Newcastle, N.S.W., to take another coal cargo across the South Pacific to Iquique and, finally, home with nitrate; a voyage of fifteen months.

Then he spent three years as Mate of a small wooden barque, the *Charles E. Lefurgey*, of Charlottetown, Prince Edward Island, eventually arriving in Fleetwood in August 1905 with a cargo of lumber from New Brunswick. The following February, Mr. Fowler joined our company's ship *Forth* as Mate.

He spoke of it all without bitterness as he puffed at his pipe in the darkness of the night watch. But, after commanding his own ship for six years, it must have been a bitter test of character and endurance to have to ship as Mate of the *Dalrymple*; to go back to four-hour watches, to find himself no longer in dry comfort up on the poop but once more down on the main deck, at the weather fore braces, up to his waist in icy water as the ship drove homeward around the Horn.

Before joining the *Arno*, Mr. Fowler had served in twelve different sailing-vessels. He had been raised in the kind of ships that made fine seamen. The ring of command in his voice was born not of mere self-assurance. It was founded on the sure seamanlike instinct which came of a lifetime's experience of wind and canvas, of ships, of sailors and of the sea. And, if there had been any especial reason why he had not been able to get another ship of his own, as Master, when the *Orari* was sold, it could have nothing to do with his competence. He was the completely capable sailor.

Sometimes, during the anchor watches, the Bos'n would come aft to the poop and, at a hint from Mr. Fowler, I would nip along to the galley, where the kettle was always on the boil, and make three mugs of tea—a special brew of China tea which I had brought from home and which had cost ten shillings the pound, a fantastic price for those days. But it was a fantastic tea and the Bos'n fair smacked his lips when he first got its steaming perfume under his nose. We all did. It was such an exotic and extreme change from the stuff that bubbled away for the crew.

So the night watches passed agreeably and, for the whole ship's company, with the exception of Captain German who was impatient to get away, the days at anchor were an unusual boon. We were setting out on a voyage of which the first passage to Adelaide would be about 13,500 miles and here was our chance to get to know each other and our ship.

We were twenty-nine, all told; Captain, two Mates, six apprentices, Carpenter, Steward, Cook, Sailmaker, fourteen able seamen including the Bos'n, and two ordinary seamen. The Second Mate, George Raad, was thirty-four years old and all of his nineteen years at sea had been spent in sailing-ships, mostly before the mast or as Bos'n. He had spent many years in Nova Scotia ships and, although he was born in Lancashire he spoke with a pronounced "down east", nasal drawl, heavily interlarded with "Jesus H. Christ" and "sonofabitch". At least, it was so for the first twenty-four hours. Then, as senior apprentice, I spoke to him about it.

"Look, Mister Raad, sir," I said, "if you call me or any of my shipmates a son of a bitch again, we'll have to do something about it. We don't talk to each other like that in these ships."

He was a short, thickset man. He looked up at me astonished, purple in the face, then guffawed, "Well, I'm a sonofa . . . ," broke off, and went on, "Ah, hell! There's no harm meant." And that was the last of it. In due course, his speech even reverted to its homely native accent.

The carpenter was a Finn. The sailmaker was a Chileno, a little elfin-like man with a shaven upper lip and a short, grey, spade beard. He was seventy-three years old and had been many years in the ship. Of the fourteen able seamen nine were British, two Swedes, one American, one German and one Norwegian. Their average age was forty-three years and ten of them were between forty and sixty years old. The oldest was the sixty-year-old Norwegian who had signed on as "John Smith". The American, J. Connor of Boston was fifty-three and Hans Hanssen, the German, was fifty-two. We had a good crew of seasoned seamen. These were the days when there were still many men who would only go to sea in sailing-ships, where they could exercise their craft as sailors, although they never thought of it that way. The sailing-ship gave them the kind of life they were accustomed to, plus a long voyage and a correspondingly fat pay-day; in 1908 there were still plenty of them—both ships and men.

The day had not yet arrived when the square-rigged sailing-ship was so scarce that she was eagerly welcomed as wonderful "box-office" material for a glamorous colour film, or written up with strident dramatic treatment, with all the vibrato stops pulled out, as a "Cape Horner". How the old shellbacks in the Arno's fo'c's'le would have laughed. And what of Captain German and his shipmates of the Swansea copper-ore trade? What would they have thought of the exaggerated epics and heroics which describe the last great steel sailing-ships fighting their way—frequently from west to east with a fair gale behind them—around Cape Horn? The same Cape Horn that they had doubled voyage after voyage in little wooden barques only 130 feet long.

3 An Early Disaster

The *Arno* was built of steel by Connell of Glasgow in 1893. When I joined her she was only fifteen years old, ten years younger than my last ship the *Main*. Her steel lowermasts and topmasts were in one piece and her topgallant, royal and skysail masts were also of steel. She was 270 feet long with the same deck arrangement and rigging as all Nourse's ships. She had a fine hull with good, clean lines, but the robes of the white lady of her figurehead terminated abruptly on the dense black of the bows. They did not flow into a yellow tracery or ornamental scroll-work as they had in the *Main* and, aft, the deck of the poop extended to the ship's side. There was no good, old-fashioned, but rather impractical, half-round.

She was a modern sailing-ship, stout as they could be built, as she had proved on the homeward passage of her second voyage when she was only two years old.

From Calcutta she had carried coolies to Jamaica and then gone to New York. There, instead of the usual case-oil for India or Australia, she loaded wheat in bulk for Liverpool. Grain poured from the spouts of the elevator into the hold. Down there, the dust of Kansas and Oklahoma swirled in blinding dense clouds which drove the ship's officers up on deck, choking and gasping for breath. It would have been impossible for them to supervise the stowage and trimming of the grain and the secure erecting of shifting-boards, even if they had had previous experience of grain cargoes which might have made their supervision authoritative and worthwhile. Actually, none of them had been with a grain cargo before. This was their first experience. But the ship was being loaded under the supervision of a surveyor appointed by the Board of Underwriters of New York, so they had no reason for misgivings.

Most of the 'tween-deck cargo was in bags and there, also, wooden trunk-ways or bins were built over the open hatches of the lower hold and filled with grain which would feed into the lower hold as the cargo settled during the voyage. This was supposed to keep the lower hold full and so ensure that the cargo could not shift.

The *Arno* sailed from New York on March 21st, 1895, under command of Captain Newham, who had his wife and child with him. When they were seven days out, the ship was shortened down to three lower topsails, main upper topsail and fore topmast staysail, running before a hard westerly gale. The high seas thrust under her stern, raced forward and curled inboard, filling her decks waist deep, as she rolled her rails under. But all was going well, it was a fair gale and they were homeward bound.

Then, in the middle of a black night, there was a sudden rumbling below and the noise of splintering wood. The *Arno* rolled heavily to port and failed to rise. She lay there in the trough of the seas. The cargo had shifted and the force of wind and sea held the ship down on her beam-ends. Sheets and halliards were let fly, to take the pressure off masts and rigging. The sails were hauled up in the clew-lines and bunt-lines and were left hanging in their gear. Then the weather side of the main hatch was opened and all hands got below.

They found that the feeders had collapsed under the strain of the rolling. In addition, all their store of grain, the loose grain and the bags of the 'tween-deck cargo had fallen bodily over to the port side. For forty-eight hours the hands laboured, carrying the bags and shovelling the grain up to windward—from Thursday night until Saturday night—and at last they succeeded in trimming the ship upright and she continued on her voyage.

However, March is a bad month in the North Atlantic and the weather had not eased. By Sunday morning, March 31st, it was blowing harder than ever. Under her reduced canvas, as she ran before the gale, the heavy following seas threw the *Arno*'s stern high, put her bows down and then rushed forward, balancing her for an instant on their crests. For that fraction of time, the ship was borne on a body of water that was travelling even more swiftly than she was. At such moments there was no grip on the water either of hull or rudder and the ship would yaw widely to either side of her course and roll heavily. These were conditions under which the prudent shipmaster would brace his yards sharp up, watch his chance and wait for a "smooth". Then he would put his helm down and heave to with the wind and sea comfortably on the starboard bow.

But swinging around meant deliberately bringing the wind abeam, putting the ship broadside on to wind and sea. With a cargo of such proven instability it was understandable that Captain Newham was reluctant to do so. As it turned out, he was left no choice; in one of her wilder rolls to windward, the ship again fell heavily over on her side. The cargo in the lower hold had shifted. The ship lay on her starboard beam-ends. Up aloft her sails thrashed about in the gale and flogged themselves to ribbons.

Now her position was much more serious than before because all the 'tween-deck cargo that had been shifted so laboriously over to starboard was also bearing her down. She lay on her side with her starboard bulwarks entirely

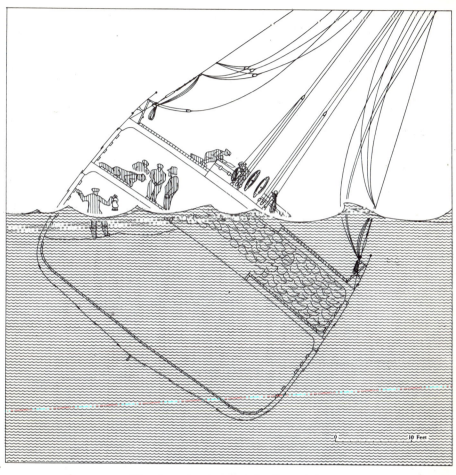

The *Arno*, abandoned, on her beam ends

submerged and her yards dipped deep in the sea every time she lurched still further over to windward. Her decks and hatches were exposed to the full fury of the seas. The waves swept the decks of everything moveable, including all the life-boats which were smashed to matchwood. To have opened the hatches to go below would have been to invite instant disaster. Until the weather moderated, there was nothing could be done to get the ship under control again. But, so far from easing, the weather became worse until it was blowing a very heavy gale with tremendous seas which pounded with their full weight on her decks, threatening to smash in her hatches and flood the hold. If that happened, in an instant the *Arno* would sink to the bottom like a stone.

It was a desperate situation and it seemed hopeless until, at 1.00 p.m., a steamer was sighted and Captain Newham decided to abandon the ship rather than expose his crew to the apparent certainty that she would be overcome by the seas at any moment and founder with the loss of all on board.

So they hoisted signals of distress, reporting that the cargo had shifted and all boats washed away; that they could not navigate the ship and wished to leave her; and that they needed immediate help. The steamer was the *Normannia*, a German vessel of the Hamburg-America Line. She went as close as possible to the *Arno* and replied that, although it was very dangerous in such a sea, they would do their best. One of the *Normannia*'s large boats was launched. However, the steamer was rolling so heavily that the boat broke away from the davits and fell into the water. She was manned by an officer and seven men but they could not manage her and she was drifting away. The *Normannia* bore down on her, gave her a lee. They succeeded in getting the crew aboard but had to abandon the boat.

A second, smaller boat, under the command of the Second Officer was launched and got safely away. The *Arno* was listing so heavily, with her starboard side under water, that it was impossible for the boat to get alongside. So they worked astern of her and threw a line aboard her poop where the crew were gathered. Twenty-eight men jumped into the sea, one by one, and were hauled into the boat. Then the Captain dropped first his child and then his wife over the stern, and at last jumped himself.

One can picture the *Arno*'s men, the water still streaming from their clothing, sitting on the thwarts next to the German sailors, double-banking on the oars with all their weight. And, in the sternsheets, sitting on the floorboards, the Captain's wife, shivering with cold and the reaction from her terrifying ordeal, wet and miserable, clutching the child, frightened by the shrieking of the wind, the violent motion of the boat and the water dashing over its gunnel. With what deep thankfulness she must have found refuge on the steamer.

The rescue, a very gallant rescue, took seven hours. It was nearly dark when they made the perilous passage in the heavily laden boat. At 8.00 p.m. the *Normannia* was put on her course again and one can imagine the feelings of the *Arno*'s crew as the steamer turned eastwards. All of them standing silent, looking across the fury of the sea at the ship they had abandoned lying there deserted and lifeless. The wild Atlantic combers swept over her deck-houses. The flying rags of her sails whipped and cracked, screaming a dirge in the dusk. She was doomed, just as surely as darkness was falling and hiding her from their sight.

Or so it seemed.

36

But two days later the *Arno*, still lying on her beam-ends, was still afloat. She had drifted 180 miles before the gale. She was as sound as a bell for her masts were of steel, right up to the trucks. Her decks and hatches were tight as a bottle.

The weather had moderated and she was in latitude 45·22 North and 41·40 West when the Elder Dempster steamer *Merrimac* came along and found her. A boat was sent away and came back bringing the ship's log-book from which it was seen that she was carrying a grain cargo which, it was concluded, had shifted. So Captain Morgan of the *Merrimac* sent his boat back to sound the ship to see if there was any water down below, to find out the condition of the cargo and see if there was room for men to go into the hold and trim. All this was done. The result was satisfactory and the well was dry. They could not do more that day because it came on to blow again, so they stood by throughout the night.

Next day, April 3rd, as the wind and sea were moderating, the Chief Officer, Mr. Howel Williams, and eight men were put aboard to try and trim her up. They got down the hatch with their shovels and, after some hours, Captain Morgan saw such a marked change that he decided to take the ship in tow and trim her upright while towing. They took the *Arno*'s hawser aboard but, after towing for some time, it broke owing to the heavy seas. Then the *Merrimac*'s thirteen-inch hawser was shackled to one of the *Arno*'s wire pendants which, in turn, was shackled to her anchor cable which was hove out until the length of the tow was about 130 fathoms. Again towing was commenced but again the weight of the weather was too much. *Merrimac*'s hawser parted and the seas were so bad that any idea of towing had to be abandoned for that day.

How they must have worked! Think of the Chief Officer and those eight men from the steamer struggling aboard the *Arno*, scarcely able to keep their feet on her steeply inclined decks, the ship labouring, the heavy seas still smashing furiously over her rails, the water swirling about their waists. Think of them rooting about down in the dark of her unfamiliar forepeak, looking for hauling lines, shackles and wires and manhandling her heavy sixteen-inch coir hawser. Then, after it parted, getting the end aboard and out of the way. Then looking for the wire towing-pendant, shackling it on to the end of the *Arno*'s anchor cable at the windlass, inside the fo'c's'le, unplugging the hawse-pipe and passing the other end of the wire pendant through while the water gushed through the hawse-pipe with the force of a fire-hose, flooding the fo'c's'le, every time the ship put her nose down. Then fishing for the pendant outside and hauling it up on the fo'c's'le-head. Picking up and then hauling hand over hand on the small line that was floated down to them by a lifebuoy from the steamer, taking the bigger line (to which it was made fast) to the capstan and with it heaving the end of the *Merrimac*'s heavy thirteen-inch hawser aboard, over the bows, shackling on the wire pendant, pushing it all overboard and, at last, walking around the windlass capstan on the fo'c's'le-head which sloped like the roof of a house, heaving out thirty fathoms of chain.

And that after hours of shovelling wheat in the black gloom of the hold. What a bitter disappointment it must have been when, for the second time, the hawser parted and they had to put their backs into it again to get their end of it, the chain cable and the wire back on board.

But there was no thought of giving in. "No! Indeed to Goodness! To hell 'withth' the 'weathther'!" one can hear Captain Morgan saying, as he looked over the canvas dodger of the *Merrimac*'s bridge. There she was, a fine ship, practically new, with around three thousand tons of wheat in her. He sent another six men aboard the *Arno* to help in trimming—that made fourteen men in all. There must have been stokers as well as deck-hands and they included the carpenter. But they were all good seamen and the sailors must have been good watermen.

Then a dense fog came down and, by midnight, Captain Morgan had lost sight of his prize, with his Chief Officer and fourteen of his men!

They, apparently, were not worried by either the fog or the steamer's disappearance. Probably did not even notice it. They were too busy down below. Mr. Williams had come to the conclusion that the main shift of cargo had taken place in the lower hold so he had the carpenter cut a hole in the planking of the 'tween-deck. He lowered himself down there and found that he could stand upright on the grain without touching the beams that supported the 'tween-deck, over his head. He had found the answer; now he cut holes in the 'tween-deck planks at intervals all along the port side and he and his men poured all the grain from the bags, and shovelled all the loose grain of the 'tween-deck cargo through the holes into the lower hold. He had men down there trimming and levelling the grain as it came down. They must have been at it all through the night for when the *Merrimac* found them again next day the ship was upright, within five or six degrees. How they must have worked! When first sighted, the *Arno* had a list of about forty degrees and within twenty-four hours, due to the courage and leadership of Howel Williams, they had trimmed her upright.

So the Captain gave orders to check the quantity and quality of provisions on board, to see if there was sufficient water and if the ship was well provided with sails and other gear. The answer was that there was plenty of everything. Even the chronometers were still going when they first boarded her and it is probable that Mr. Williams, like a good officer, instinctively wound them up while his men were getting the tarpaulins off a corner of the main hatch.

Having restored the ship to a thoroughly seaworthy condition Captain Morgan left his Chief Officer and ten men aboard to bring her home to England while he went on his way to Le Havre.

I like to think of the *Arno* at that moment. She was alive again and on an even keel, with one of the *Merrimac*'s boats hanging at the lee davits, a healthy plume of smoke streaming from her galley funnel. I see her already under easy sail, the big foresail set, three new lower topsails and fore topmast staysail bent. A brand-new ensign flies bravely from her gaff, and Mr. Williams and his men, one of them at the wheel, one at the signal halliards, stand on the poop waving their caps and sou'westers while the ensign is dipped in response to the parting blasts of the steamer's whistle. Cheers surely rang out across the water.

Now they were on their own. Only eleven of them. A very small crew compared with the twenty-nine who were taken off by the *Normannia*. But these men were sailors, not just seafarers, and I am sure that their eyes gleamed with excitement and determination as they watched the *Merrimac* going on her way. Then, led by the resourceful Mr. Williams, they would have left the poop and gone to the sail locker, to find a new main upper topsail. Before the end of the day the *Arno* would be under comfortable canvas, perhaps topgallant sails set, homeward bound.

On April 20th, sixteen days after the *Merrimac* had left her, the *Arno* was twenty miles west of the Fastnet Rock, off the Irish coast. The wind was south by east, it was coming on to blow and it was hazy weather. She was on the port tack, under reduced canvas, heading west-south-west, uncertain of her position, when at 1.00 p.m. the Cunarder *Umbria* came along, bound for Queenstown and Liverpool. Signals were exchanged and, as the *Arno* put up a hoist asking for "the course to steer"—the flags M-D-F—the *Umbria*'s Captain reported, on arrival at Queenstown, that he believed that the officer in charge of her either had no charts or did not know the coast.

There must have been charts in plenty aboard the *Arno*. What is more probable is that Mr. Williams had not been getting good observations and had run into soundings of sixty fathoms and less. The weather being hazy it is likely that he had not even seen the coast. And he could have had the same depth of water off the Scilly Isles or in the approaches to the Bristol Channel. He would only have to be 120 miles out in his reckoning, that much further east, to be in either place. This was not by any means impossible after a passage of 1,300 miles in a strange ship, perhaps uncertain of the accuracy or the daily rate of gain or loss of his chronometers; they had been nearly run down when he wound them up. So, in putting her head off the land until, after speaking the *Umbria*, he was sure of his position, Williams did the prudent thing.

Then it really piped up a gale of wind and, on April 22nd, Queenstown wired Nourse in London, "No further news of *Arno*. Blowing hard, S.S.E, thick and rain." The *Arno* probably remained hove to throughout the night of April 20th. Then, with daylight, she wore round on to the starboard tack and, with a fair wind on the beam, she ran for Tuskar. Then she carried the south-easterly gale on her quarter up the St. George's Channel.

Luckily—or with foresight, because he was undoubtedly a fine seaman—Williams had his anchors ready. It was blowing hard, and raining; when, after running some eighty miles from Tuskar, land and lights were seen right ahead and on both bows, he brought his ship to the wind and anchored. He realised that he had been set in to the Welsh coast for, after the run from Tuskar, he could not be anywhere else.

He could have hauled off the land when it was first sighted, brought the wind abeam for a short reach until he picked up the South Stack light and then put her before it to run round the Skerries. But that would have meant a lot of heavy work at the braces, hauling the yards around, and his little crew must have been very tired. Of his ten men, one acted as Mate and another would be working in the galley, cooking, leaving eight including the carpenter. So each watch would consist only of the officer in charge and four seamen. The ship, with all the cargo in the lower hold, was no longer in any danger of falling on her beam-ends, she was stable but she must have rolled heavily and violently. The weather had been continuously bad and we can be sure that for any work at sheets and braces, to drag those heavy yards around with their thousands of square feet of canvas, both watches were on deck most of the time. There would have been very few hours of unbroken rest for any of them and the carpenter, who was hale and hearty when he went on board, died of exposure and exhaustion. And then they were only nine.

Nine weather-worn sailors, one at the wheel, the other eight kneeling on the black tarpaulins of the main hatch, to be for the moment clear of the water which rushed about the decks, while one of them sewed "Chips" up in sail-cloth; then rising to their feet, bare heads reverently lowered, while Howel Williams read the simple words of the burial service. And, finally, carrying their shipmate to the ship's side, watching their chance and, as the rail rose clear of the water, passing him gently into the sea.

Yes, they were very tired when the anchor was let go and they went aloft to make the sails fast. Mr. Williams was very thankful when at last the *Arno* was "brought up", lying steadily to her anchor, and he could see the lights of the houses ashore, flickering through the darkness and the rain. He was on a lee shore but his ground tackle was good and he knew that it was good holding ground. It was his own Welsh land.

Next morning he found that he was anchored two miles off the little town of Barmouth. A telegram was sent to Liverpool and one of Nourse's Masters, Captain Rock of the ship *Mersey*, went down in a salvage tug to see the position of the ship. He found it to be satisfactory. On April 24th, the *Arno* got under way at 10.00 p.m. in tow of the tug *Reaper* and twelve hours later arrived in Liverpool, twenty-five days after being abandoned and twenty-one days after the *Merrimac* had left her in the middle of the Atlantic.

She berthed in the Wapping Dock and her cargo turned out very well, only twenty-four tons being damaged.

In the meantime, the *Normannia* had landed the *Arno*'s crew in Southampton on April 5th. Six days later, the *Merrimac* arrived in Le Havre with the report that she had found the ship and that it was being sailed home. This must have been staggering news for Captain Newham. His discomfiture would have been the more acute when, on May 3rd, anticipating the findings of an official enquiry, before all the circumstances had been given expert consideration, a leading shipping journal referred to the *Arno* as "yet another case of premature abandonment".

The official Board of Trade Inquiry was concluded at Liverpool on June 19th before a judge and two nautical assessors. They found that although the

The *Mersey*, one of the *Arno*'s sister-ships, under full sail

ship had been loaded under the supervision of a surveyor appointed by the Board of Underwriters of New York, the cargo was badly stowed in badly constructed feeders, also that the ship had not been properly prepared for a grain cargo. The shifting-boards in the lower hold were inadequate and ineffective and none had been erected in the 'tween-deck. It was also brought out that when the *Arno* fell on her beam-ends the second time, the weather becoming worse and the *Normannia* being sighted, the crew had declined to do anything further. The Court decided that the *Arno* was not abandoned prematurely and that neither Master nor officers were in default.

So Captain Newham was absolved from blame. But he did not resume command of the *Arno*. His place was taken by a Captain Mullen.

The services of the *Normannia* and her boats' crews were duly recognised by the Board of Trade. Captain H. H. Berends was presented with a gold watch. The Second Officer, W. H. Hauer, who went away in the boats, was awarded a silver medal and a pair of binoculars. The seven seamen who manned the first boat received silver medals and four of them who manned the second, smaller boat each received the sum of £2 in addition. That was perhaps the equivalent of a month's pay in the German Merchant Service at the time.

There were also financial penalties and rewards resulting from the abandonment and salvage of the *Arno*.

When James Nourse learned that the ship had been found and was on her way home, he obtained an undertaking from the owners of the *Merrimac*, after giving them security in respect of their salvage claim, that she and her cargo would be handed over to him.

The owner of the cargo, however, contended that as the ship had been abandoned so had the contract of affreightment and that he was entitled to delivery of the cargo without payment of freight, and this he demanded. The case was tried on May 15th when the judge gave a decision in favour of the cargo-owner with right of appeal to the shipowner.

The appeal by James Nourse was heard before Lord Esher, Master of the Rolls, at the end of June. The previous decision was upheld and the appeal dismissed with costs.

In the Salvage Court the value of the *Arno*, including freight and cargo, was considered to be £24,000. The judge made awards totalling £7,810: to the owners of the *Normannia* £600; to her Master and crew £420; total £1,020.

The owners of the *Merrimac* were awarded £3,500, her Master £800, her Second Officer £150, and her crew £550. The salvage crew received a total of £1,440 of which £750 went to Howel Williams, £150 to the man who acted as his Mate, £100 to the widow of the carpenter and £440 to the remaining eight seamen. The tug was paid £350.

The owners of the *Normannia* would only accept £90 to cover their expenses, so Master and crew received £930. This generosity on the part of the Hamburg-America Line was applauded in the British shipping press and it is interesting to notice that in the year 1895 seven hours' manoeuvring and delay of a medium-sized passenger-liner in an Atlantic gale plus the value of the large lifeboat that was lost seem to have cost only £90.

The award to Mr. Williams and his crew was criticized by one of the shipping journals as insufficient. The hardships they underwent were terrible. The judge (it was said) should have awarded more than £1,440—which represented less than £1 per mile of the distance that they sailed the ship.

However, for those days, compared with their normal earnings it is likely that the salvage crew were well satisfied. Mr. Williams as Chief Officer of the *Merrimac* was probably paid about £9 per month, the carpenter £5 and the seamen £3. So Mr. Williams was given the equivalent of about seven years' pay, the A.B. who acted as his Mate, fifty months' pay; and, since the eight seamen would each get £55, they received about eighteen months' pay. Only the carpenter's widow was poorly compensated for the loss of her husband.

4 *Fair Wind for the Outward-bounder*

At last, after three days of light westerlies, the wind shifted to the south and, although it was still a head wind, Captain German seemed more cheerful. He stood on the quarter-deck, puffing at a blackened clay pipe, talking to Mr. Fowler and keeping his weather eye on the goings-on at the gangway. A Deal lugger lay alongside and a couple of us were helping the steward and the cook to take aboard the fish, meat and vegetables that she had brought off. We had been seven days at anchor and had used up the stock of fresh food which normally would have fed us during the first week at sea. It was a case of getting more from the shore or going on to hard tack and salt provisions which would have been "contrary to the Act". The Articles of Agreement for the voyage provided that in port, when procurable at a reasonable cost, each man should have a daily allowance of a pound of soft bread, a pound and a half of fresh meat (which could include three-quarters of a pound of fresh fish) and a pound of fresh vegetables.

I was in the lugger and, when the last basket of stuff had been passed over the rail, I stood on her gun'ale ready to climb aboard when the boatman beckoned me. So I got down again and went to where he stood in the sternsheets, by the tiller, keeping his boat, riding to her painter, sheered off a foot or so.

"That's the last lot I'll be bringing off to you, son," he said. His weather-beaten face crinkled in a grin. "D'ye think th'Ole Man 'ud be good fer a plug o' baccy, a lump o' salt pork and mebbe an ole piece o' canvas? Ye'll be away tonight."

"What!" I exclaimed, "with this southerly wind!"

"Aye, that's what I said," he replied. "Wind's south now but it'll be round to the nor'ard before long. That's the last fresh grub ye'll be eatin' till ye gets to Orstralia."

I got over the bulwarks and went towards the Captain where he stood by the mizzen rigging, still talking to the Mate.

"Sir."

"Yes, de Mierre boy. What is it?"

"The boatman says we'll be getting a northerly wind, sir, and that we'll be away tonight."

"I know that," Captain German exclaimed. "Wind's south, but the glass is rising. Is that all?"

"Well, sir. He says he'll not be coming off again, unless you need something more from the shore. He's been coming and going every day and he'd thank you if you could spare a piece of old sailcloth and a lump of salt pork and maybe a plug or two of tobacco. That's what he said, sir."

I passed the bundle over the side and after profuse thanks the old chap pushed off and set his two lugsails. The smart breeze sent him scurrying shorewards, on a broad reach, his lee gun'ale nearly down to the water. They were wonderful boats and we never lost our admiration for the skill with which they were handled, the way they raced out in all kinds of weather and rounded to alongside us, as well as the ease and unhurried smoothness with which they got their sails down and hitched their painter to our guest warp.

Lying in the Downs at the end of November was a dreary round of leaden skies and clouds of rain. We were never out of oilskins and seaboots. There was no heat; we had no stoves. And, no matter which point of the compass the wind came from, it was bitterly cold, too cold to encourage much personal hygiene. Bedding and everything else, including ourselves, in half-deck, officers' cabins and fo'c's'le was damp and fusty-smelling. We had done everything that could be done to make the ship clean and trim and we were just as anxious as the Old Man to pick up our "hook" and be gone.

That night, at two bells in the middle watch—one o'clock in the morning—as we swung to the first of the flood, the wind came along with the tide, out of the north. As though he had heard or felt its coming, at the same moment, Captain German came up the companion-way on to the poop, still blind from the light of his cabin.

"Ye there, Mr. Fowler?" he bellowed.

"Aye, aye, sir," replied the Mate, almost as heartily and almost in his ear. He had been on the point of going down below to call him.

The Captain jumped, startled, and continued in a quieter tone, "Alright, Mister, ye can back your fore yards, lay the main and mizzen square and we'll get under way. Soon as we can."

I called the Second Mate and turned out the half-deck crowd, while the Bos'n went forward to call the hands. As soon as we had finished trimming the yards, some were sent aloft and out on the jibboom to loose topsails, staysail and jibs while the rest manned the windlass capstan up on the fo'c's'le head. We hove around with freezing hands thrusting against the capstan bars, the night was pitch dark, with no stars. Our riding light, hanging from the fore stay, threw the black circular shadow of its lantern-bottom over us and, beyond that, was a yellow mist through which the lights of the shore, other vessels and Channel buoys shone but feebly. Only the figure of the Mate seemed solid and real. Like the rest of us, he was in oilskins and seaboots; his hands were bare and red, like ours, even more so as we were warmed at our work. But, as at Gravesend, he was as cheerful as though it had been sunny noonday.

"Come on now! Where's that Irishman with the fine voice from Cork? Or isn't there a Yankee among ye? Sure, there is, now. Come on, Connor, from Boston; give us *Shenandoah*. Let the folks ashore know we're leaving them."

It was impossible to remain sleepy and withdrawn, not to become alert and wide awake in the face of such good humour. Flynn and Connor were aloft, so a fat, cheerful East Anglian named Brown piped up with a lusty, anatomical version of the *Maid of Amsterdam* of which we shouted the chorus: *No more I'll go a-roving with you, fair maid* so vigorously that perhaps we were, indeed, heard by the folks ashore, although the German barque showed no sign of life.

When we were hove short, I was sent to the wheel. "A good sailor and helmsman" said my reference from Captain Hatch of the *Main*. Now it was standing me in good stead. Fore topsail and headsails were set; the anchor left the ground and the ship's head swung smartly to starboard as wind and tide took hold of her.

"Midships y'r hellum."

"Midships it is, sir."

She had a little sternway. The fore yards were swung round, the men yo-hoing at the braces; the sails filled and she gathered headway.

"Port y'r hellum. Steady her on sou' b'west."

"Port, sir. South by west it is, sir."

Main and mizzen lower topsails were sheeted home and the *Arno* slipped quietly through the water of the Downs past the sleeping German barque, although by that time both watches were stamping along our decks with the main upper topsail halliards, singing and making enough noise to waken Rip van Winkel himself. We had the upper topsails and topgallants on her in short order. By six bells, three o'clock, with a fair wind and a two-knot tide under our counter, the South Foreland was just before the beam. The South Goodwin light-vessel flashed close to port, and the lights of Dover were some four points on our starboard bow. Ahead and all about us the darkness was crowded with red and green side-lights, white masthead- and stern-lights. There were steamers coming and going in all directions and other vessels under sail using the down-Channel fair wind, or reaching across the Straits.

"By dam! It's busy indeed," the Old Man muttered. He was standing by the binnacle watching the bearing of the Foreland. When it came abeam he straightened up and said, "Port y'r hellum."

"Port y'r hellum, sir." I put the wheel down and the ship's head swung to starboard.

"Ease y'r hellum."

"Ease y'r hellum, sir." I put the wheel up a few spokes and the ship's head was checked, moving but slowly.

"Steadeee! Keep her on sou'west half west," said the Captain, at the same time taking his whistle from his pocket to give a shrill call.

"Sou'west half west, sir," I repeated. A moment later, the Mate came along.

"Lee braces, Mr. Fowler. An' when ye're finished give her the fore an' main royals, if you please."

"Aye, aye, sir," Mr. Fowler replied. He was turning away when the Captain added, "Ye can muster the hands at eight bells and send the starboard watch below."

The Mate walked smartly forward, blowing his whistle and hailing, "Lee fore brace." But his order was almost drowned by a confused shouting at the break of the fo'c's'le, and a milling about, a stamping of feet, a sharp grunting howl followed by a heavy thud.

A black figure came tearing around the after end of the forward deck-house, to end up in full collision against the Mate, who promptly grabbed him by the throat, while the hands came running aft to surround them.

"By the name of all that's holy!" exclaimed Mr. Fowler. "What the hell goes on here!" By this time the Bos'n had a firm hold of a small, ragged boy who was shivering with cold and whimpering while he stood, bare-headed, with the tears smearing his dirty face. He was clutching a loaf of bread and a lump of meat. A dozen voices explained how they had caught him in the fo'c's'le at the food lockers, how he had run out of the starboard door, had butted Able Seaman Brown fair in the middle of his belly and escaped.

"Well, I'm damned!" ejaculated Mr. Fowler. "A stowaway! After all these days! Alright, Bos, lock him up in your paint locker." He paused, looking at the small woebegone boy, and thought better of it. "No," he continued, "put him by the fire in the galley, he looks as though he could do with it, poor little devil." Then, to the boy, "And mind you stay there or next time we catch you, it's over the side you'll go . . . so you will."

The yards were trimmed, fore and main royals set and Mate and Second Mate mustered their watches on the quarter-deck. A little in front of the men stood the Bos'n with the stowaway.

"What's your name, boy? And what d'ye mean by stowing away in my ship?" the Captain shouted from the poop. "Where's y'r home? Where d'ye come from?"

"Richard Beale, sir," the boy replied, and that was all he could get out. He choked with tears and buried his face in his arms, amongst the ropes of the mizzenmast. He sobbed with such abandon that the stony mood of the Captain seemed to be touched and even Able Seaman Brown muttered, "Pore little barstard."

"Alright," the Captain said, "we'll see what he has to say in the forenoon. And, by God, I'll put the young scoundrel ashore if I have to dump him on the beach."

The starboard watch went below, taking young Beale with them. With one hand he still held on to the meat and bread, with the other he knuckled the tears from his eyes; but as he shuffled his way past Banbury he gave him a quick, furtive grin and a slow, knowing wink. For Richard Beale to break down and blubber before a crowd of men was completely out of character. But he was starving and weak with hunger, and shivering with cold; and for seven days had been living in constant dread of being discovered and put ashore.

Daylight brought a cold, grey morning, the wind still north and veering eastwards. The tide had been favourable until high water and, off Dungeness, foresail and mainsail were set because we were clear of the shipping which crowded the Straits of Dover. When we of the port watch went below at eight o'clock the ship was going through the water at about six knots, perhaps $4\frac{1}{2}$ to 5 knots over the ground for the current had turned against us with the first of the ebb. We had been on deck since midnight, the hard sea-chests on which we sat in the half-deck seem very comfortable and we ate our breakfast—Morris, Le Patourel and I—and supped the steaming coffee with relish. The Second Mate was on the poop, the Old Man was resting on his settee in the chart-house, the watch on deck was "standing by", Isdale was at the wheel and Banbury, my old watch-mate for three years in the *Main*, sat in his oilskins talking with us. It was then that he told us why the stowaway had given him the wink and the grin.

When we turned out for our dinner at seven bells, 11.30, we were off the *Royal Sovereign* light-ship. Visibility was poor. It was dirty weather with driving rain but a fair wind was chasing us down-Channel and the Old Man gave no sign of wanting to waste it by hauling up for the coast to land the stowaway at Newhaven or Shoreham. That would be the last chance because it would be dark by the end of the afternoon watch and to land him anywhere else, further down the coast would cost twenty-four hours or more. By midnight we were past St. Catherine's light, Isle of Wight, and at eight o'clock in the morning on November 30th Portland Bill was astern, over our starboard quarter. We were heading south-west for the open Atlantic. We had taken our departure and the stowaway was entered on the Articles as a member of the crew at a wage of five shillings per month.

Young Beale was born in Launceston, Tasmania, and, for some mischief which we never could worm out of him, at the age of fourteen he had been placed on board the famous old passenger clipper *Sobraon* which at that time was anchored in Sydney Harbour as a reformatory ship. After three years he was released and went, or was sent, to Newcastle, N.S.W., to join the *Thistlebank* a big four-masted barque. In her, he made the voyage across the Pacific to the west coast of South America and then round the Horn to Antwerp. The voyage had lasted thirteen months so that, even if his wage was not more than ten shillings a month, his "pay-day" would be four or five pounds and for young Beale that was a lot of money, certainly more than he had ever had at one time before.

From Antwerp, the British Board of Trade shipped him to London and somehow, with his few pounds, plus a few odd jobs and a certain amount of artful strategy he had managed to live for four months. He was a little chap with a mop of brown, curly hair, and a plump, fresh face with blue eyes which could assume an expression of worldliness far exceeding his eighteen years, or become so round and innocent that he looked like a lost child. So long as the warm summer weather lasted, life in London was easy; there were all kinds of ways of earning a few shillings. But when winter came and it was wet, foggy, cold and grey, and all his money was gone, it was no longer such a fine lark. It was just plain "crook", as he put it.

So back to the East End, to the docks, to find some ship that would take him home again. It was not easy, there were not so many ships loading for Australia and there were plenty of youngsters wanting to go in them as boys or ordinary seamen; even his certificate of discharge from the *Thistlebank* did not do the trick.

However, in the Shipping Office, where the crews were engaged, he was able to find out which ships were on the point of sailing and that is how he picked on the *Arno*.

He had come aboard at the same time as the crew, carrying his own bundle. On his shoulder he had a big sea-bag which he had taken from one of the sailors who was so drunk that he did not resist and was no doubt delighted to see it walking over the gangway by itself. In the fo'c's'le with all the confusion of fifteen men milling around, many of them rather drunk, picking their bunks and settling their gear with a good deal of argument, good-natured and otherwise, Beale was not noticed. When all hands were called to unmoor and warp the ship out of the lock into the river he stowed himself away down in the forepeak below the fo'c's'le, just over the chain locker. He had not been worried by the anchoring at Gravesend because he knew that the ship was still in the river, but it was a terrifying shock when, for a second time, his hiding-place vibrated and roared with the noise of the cable rushing out when the ship, instead of bowling down-Channel, anchored in the Downs.

Grabbing his bundle, he climbed the iron ladder and gently raised the forepeak hatch. The fo'c's'le was deserted and dark except for a lantern that hung abaft the windlass where it shed a small pool of light on the carpenter who stood at the break. The carpenter was so engrossed, easing the break as the ship took the chain, and occasionally staring up through the skylight and listening for the Mate's orders, that Beale—covered by the noise of the windlass—was able to crawl over the hatch coaming and creep stealthily out of the fo'c's'le. Again on deck in the darkness, mixed up with the sailors, he was safe from detection. Looking for a better hiding-place, he managed to find his way into the coolie galley. As a galley, this was now idle for no coolies would be carried on this voyage. Some old sails lay there, ready for the sailmaker to repair when we should be away from the land. Just inside the starboard door there was a coal-bin, now empty.

Cautiously feeling his way about, Beale discovered these. He put his bundle in the coal-bin, crawled inside a fold in the pile of old sails and went to sleep. In the morning, daylight came through large port holes on each side of the doors; compared with the forepeak, where he could not tell night from day, he was in spacious luxury. And here he stayed, hiding in the coal-bin by day and sleeping on the sails at night. In the dark, when the coast was clear, he occasionally raided the ship's galley for a mug of water and, as long as his small supply of food lasted, he kept his spirits up. But the days passed and the ship remained at anchor. His food was gone; he was miserably cold all the time and ravenously hungry. Once, he managed to steal a batch of fresh-baked bread from the galley—for which we apprentices were blamed—and when at last he heard the hands on deck getting the ship under way, he took the desperate step of raiding the fo'c's'le and was caught.

We had taken our departure and were steering south-west for the open Atlantic; yet, for some hours more, we were off the coast. The weeping northeast wind held throughout the day and, with every sail set that would draw, we made the best use of it. Captain German was anxious to be clear of the Channel before it shifted to the west, as it was quite likely to do. Towards the end of the afternoon watch, coming on dusk, we ran through a fleet of trawlers making for Brixham with their sheets well eased out; their brown sails, their decks and everything about them, including the oilskins of their crews, glistened in the rain. It was an uncomfortable ten minutes for us as they crossed our bows or ran under our stern but, for them, it was a normal part of their daily lives and those who passed close enough waved and gave us a cheery hail.

50

At sunset, Start Point was abeam some nine miles off to starboard. And, when I went to the wheel at eight o'clock, the yellow flash of the Eddystone, more than twenty miles away, was touching the low clouds every half-minute and about the same distance over the starboard quarter the loom of Start Point could also still be seen in the sky. There was very little traffic; only a few steamers and it was still too soon to meet homeward-bound sailing-vessels heading for Falmouth; they would have to beat for it, anyway, with that north-easter. Mr. Fowler came to stand by the wheel, with his back to the binnacle, and remained there, silently watching the faint glow from the lights until they were gone. That was our last sight of England. The next land would be Australia.

Three days later we were truly clear of the land for, as we headed south-south-west, passing Ushant some fifty miles off, the wind had suddenly shifted to the south-east. The man at the wheel instinctively put his helm up to avoid being caught by the lee. Mr. Fowler called the watch to the braces and, at the same moment, Captain German came out of the chart-house.

"We'll make a fair wind of it, Mr. Fowler. Damn' lucky we are it didn't go sou'west. We'll be getting away from the land before it does, as it will indeed." Then to the man at the wheel, "Steady her on west-nor'west." Then to the Mate, "Alright, Mister; lee braces, smart as you please."

"Aye, aye, sir," replied Mr. Fowler. He slacked away to windward and we hauled the yards forward a couple of points. The wind was abaft the beam, strong and steady, the best point of sailing for any square-rigged ship, every sail getting its full weight, and we had every sail set except the main skysail. The ship was deeply laden but she lay over to it until the water came rushing through the scupper-holes and wash-ports. It swirled about our knees as we stood by the rail, coiling up the ropes. Big seas beat against the weather side and slopped aboard over the weather bulwarks. A hard shower of hail drummed noisily on our oilskins and then swept away to leeward. We were wet and our hands were numbed with the cold but we were content as we stood on the slanting deck, looking at our ship going along so handsomely, doing better than nine knots.

The afternoon watch was nearly over and through the murk and scud the grey of the western horizon was faintly tinged with the colour of sunset. Sammy Bullock was amazed by it all. So far, he had only seen the ship running before the wind, on an even keel, and when she put her rail down he slid into the scuppers, landing on his backside, up to his neck in water. He got to his feet and stood there in his new yellow oilskins. He gazed aloft at the motionless, swollen sails. Then he looked over the side where the sea dashing past was so close that by stretching out an arm he could have touched it. The expression of delighted surprise on his face was comical; he could only grin and chuckle.

"Damn'" lucky we were. Had the wind gone to the south-west we would have been faced with the choice of beating back and forth between Ushant and the Scilly Isles or running back, perhaps to Falmouth, to lie at anchor wind-bound again. As it was, we stood out clear of the Bay of Biscay and, when it did come on to blow from the south-west, two days later, Finisterre was a good 250 miles to leeward. We had plenty of sea room and it was as well for it blew a whole gale.

With all hands on deck we shortened down smartly, clewing up the royals, fore and mizzen topgallants, mainsail and cro'jack; and, when we had the sails fast and the yards braced up on the port tack, the *Arno* was taking the weather comfortably, heading north-west. It was the first test of our new crew and everything had gone as smoothly as though they had been months in the ship. After all, all square-rigged ships rove their running gear through the same fairleads and, no matter how dark the night, any sailor knew exactly where he could put his hand on the rope he wanted, just as surely as when up aloft he would stand on the rat-lines of the rigging, swing out his leg and step on to the footrope that he could not see.

After twenty-four hours we wore ship; and, for two days, we stood down to the south-east, plugging along as close to the wind as the ship would sail. It was a typical December gale. The wind screamed in the rigging and the crests of the seas gleamed white through grey curtains of rain as they smashed aboard, filling the decks waist-deep, as the ship laboured and thrust her way through them. She laboured and thrust, meeting the seas broad on her bow with a smack that made her quiver and sent up fountains of spray as high as the main yard, fifty feet above the deck; she would have been more comfortable without the main topgallantsail and the fore and mizzen upper topsails. She climbed over the high swells and slammed down into the trough. That was Captain German's way; his boyhood in small, wooden barques had left him with the belief that a large, steel ship, with her steel masts and stout, wire rigging, could be driven when the weather was such that many another man would have hove her to. Indeed, as soon as there was any sign of the weather easing, but when it was still blowing hard, he gave her more canvas.

That was at seven bells. We had just turned out and Paddy and Morris brought our breakfast into the half-deck. The galley was in the starboard side of the forward house—the weather side. Heavy spray and sometimes whole seas landed on its door and it was something of an adventure to get there, dodge inside and out again, and carry the food to its destination without losing it or having it swamped with salt water. Streaming with water, breathless with laughter and with their exertions, they put the kid of porridge and the hook-pots of coffee down on a sea-chest and sat there, holding on to them. When Morris had recovered his breath he exclaimed, "That bloody South Welsh-man on the poop is crazy. He's given her the fore and mizzen to'gal'nts'ls and now, goddamit, they're setting the mains'l."

"Listen to the smart North Welshman!" I answered. "Young Portmadoc, not been to sea a dog-watch, telling old Swansea how to sail his ship!"

The wind, as strong as ever, had hauled to the west and they were indeed setting the big mainsail. The starboard watch had boarded the tack, had taken the sheet to the main-deck capstan and were heaving it well aft. With the additional canvas, the ship lay over so far that, when she rolled, the seas came aboard over the lee rail to pile up on the quarter-deck against the break of the poop. The Second Mate was having a hard time down in the scuppers, sliding the hitch of the rope-stopper along the sheet as it was hove in. The water was over the top of his sea-boots, sometimes up to his waist. At last, it was enough and he yelled, "'Vast heaving! Belay main sheet."

Hardly was the sheet fast to the bitts on the rail than everyone was startled by a loud pounding coming from Mr. Fowler's cabin which was at the port side of the break of the poop, facing forward. The water on the lee side of the quarter-deck was so deep and was rushing against his door with such force that he could not open it. And neither could the starboard watch, until they rove a line through the ring of the door handle so that they could lay back on it and pull the door open. Then the water poured inside and filled the cabin as Mr. Fowler emerged wet, and purple in the face. His expression as he looked up to the poop, where the Captain stood, told more plainly than any language he could have used just what he thought of it all but, before he could say any-thing, the Captain got in first.

"You'd better get the carpenter along, Mr. Fowler, and ship your weather-boards. We're going to need them if we're going to make a passage." He paused, smiling, and then added in his own quaint language, "And now stand by the chronometer, please, and I'll get an 'ob of the orb'." He was happy; it seemed to be his kind of weather. To windward, the clouds sailed swiftly through a clear sky and down to leeward the sun shone brightly on the spark-ling wave-crests for the first time since we had left the Downs and the horizon was a hard, blue line. It was an observation of the orb under ideal conditions.

I went to the wheel at eight bells, well wrapped up and wearing oilskins and sea-boots for, although the coast of Spain was somewhere down to leeward, it was still very cold standing for two hours on the wheel-grating with no shelter. The ship lay her course so comfortably that the watch went to the weather braces, checked the yards in a point and got them off the backstays. She was all the better for it and steered more sweetly than any yacht; 21 feet 4 inches of her hull was below the water-line and the ship and cargo weighing some 4,000 tons were being driven through the water at a good eight knots. Driving southwards, the *Arno* buried her lee bow in a welter of dazzling foam that broke into myriads of snowy morsels which gleamed in the sun and threw their light up into our faces and into the belly of our sails. We set the royals and, when the frequent hard squalls came out of the wind-clouds, we stood by halliards but only rarely lowered away.

Then it moderated. We lost the heavy westerly swell and, in about Latitude 34° North, we got our north-east trades. We were ten days out from Portland Bill and, including our beat to the northward, had sailed some 1,450 miles, at an average speed of six knots. The decks were dry. We unshipped the weather-boards from the door-sills and opened wide the doors. The sun shone brightly and the tops of the deck-houses were festooned with drying clothing and bedding. When we washed decks, Captain German padded about the poop in bare feet and, in the forenoon, after he had taken his morning sight, his "ob of the orb", he sat in a deck-chair as well content as the rest of us that, for the time being anyway, we had done with hard weather.

He had brought six small Stilton cheeses aboard which the old sailmaker had stitched up in a skin of duck canvas. The canvas had then been covered with white paint, having first been dampened with water so that the paint could not get through to the cheese. I had had the job of doing this while Captain German stood by to see that it was properly done. Then we hung the cheeses from the awning spar, over the saloon skylight, to dry. They were sealed, watertight and airtight, and would be in prime condition when he disposed of them in Australia. Sometimes, as he sat there smoking his pipe, when I was at the wheel, he would talk to me, about anything that came into his head. I think that he was just wanting to talk for talking's sake because like most shipmasters, he was lonely.

"Those young men who came from the *Ems* make a lot of noise in the dog-watch," he said one day.

"Well, sir, we all like to sing, sometimes."

"Singing you call it," he exclaimed, "shouting and banging on your water-tank with marlin spikes. One of these days you'll burst it, then, by dam, ye'll pay for a new one. It's those two devils Morris and Mantell . . . mostly Morris, the damn' rascal."

He was not really complaining. So long as we stuck to our quarters we were free to do what we liked in the second dog-watch, from 6.00 to 8.00 p.m. That was the recognised time for merry-making; no one was sleeping and, for the

54

only time during the twenty-four hours, both watches could enjoy some leisure together. The fo'c's'le hands yarned and smoked, played cribbage, sang and sometimes danced—waltzing with each other to the music of an accordion. Our half-deck was in the port side of the after house, what on coolie passages was the women's hospital. It had a door at each end—one leading on to the quarter-deck, the other at the forward end opening on to the main deck. In the second dog-watch we were frequently joined by two or three from the fo'c's'le who were so young that they were more at ease with us than with the old shellbacks forward.

There was, of course, Sam Bullock, and a young Cockney of twenty-two named Perry who had just come out of the Navy, where he had been a signal-man. He was also making his first deep-water voyage in a sailing-ship but, because of his naval service and his training in the "Brigs", he had been signed on as able seaman. And there was the stowaway. Beale was not much as a singer but he had one song which must have earned him many coppers outside the London pubs. It was a real tear-jerker, about *pore leetle bybie Jack, yer muvver weel not come back*. His solo performance was a masterpiece, with his cap on the deck at his bare feet and his blue eyes raised aloft when he sang the concluding words *till Gawd sends Hees ayngels right dayun from above for Dadeee and bybie Jack*! Mostly, he was content to sit there and listen and smoke our tobacco and at quieter moments he taught us several different ways of playing poker.

However, six of us, plus Bullock and Perry, could and did make a lot of noise although, out of respect for the quarter-deck, the after door of the half-deck was kept closed at such times.

We were a carefree crowd and we got on well together. Banbury and I, in our watches below, were working hard at our books studying navigation and Morris and Le Patourel were just as keen. Every day, after taking his sights, Mr. Fowler would give me a slip of paper with the elements, the sun's altitude and the chronometer time of the morning sight, courses and distances sailed since the previous noon and the midday meridian altitude. "Here you are, me son," he would say, "ob of the orb! See what you can do with it."

And each day we would figure the ship's position which I put on a chart I had brought for the purpose and entered into my own log of the voyage. These were good trade-wind days, working on deck or up aloft in the warm sunshine with a fresh breeze and the ship rolling along before it through an ocean of deepest blue, with no thought of hard weather past and still to come. Only Morris seemed to have the knack of getting into trouble. He was the real ebullient Celt—tall, handsome and quick-witted. He would boil and effer-vesce when interested or excited and would do or say whatever came into his head and damn the consequences, never even thinking of them. He came from what he called Welsh Wales; he spoke Welsh and sometimes sang beautiful Welsh songs. As a result, when he was at the wheel, the Captain would occasionally speak Welsh with, or at, him. Probably the latter, because the effect was always the same. When he was relieved, Morris would come down from the poop scowling and muttering, "Damn' hoontoo." The word "hwntw" being a North Welsh expression of contempt for the South Welshman.

On Christmas Day, twenty-six days out, we were 2,750 miles from Portland, making good passage and Captain German's Christmas mood was the more mellow. At lime-juice time, when all hands mustered on the quarter-deck, the Captain and Officers were also there and the Steward with a large pitcher of rum. Pannikins were drained with a good deal of lip-smacking and very hearty cries of "Merry Christmas, Captain!" Then they went forward to a dinner of fresh pork and plum duff.

We were dressed for the brief meal period in our monkey-jackets with collars and ties, for the Captain had kindly arranged that, after he and the two Mates had finished, we were to eat our Christmas dinner in the saloon. A pretty table was set for us, decorated with little streamers of coloured paper and, in the centre, a decanter of port wine. The old steward, wearing a white jacket, waited on us with all the aplomb of bygone years when he had served the passengers aboard the clipper ship *Sobraon* in her heyday. There was soup, roast pork, plum pudding, almonds and raisins and the wine—a feast of abundance and happiness which warmed our hearts and heads. We toasted the folks at home and drank a glass in thanks to the Captain.

But, unfortunately, the irresponsible Morris sat next to the sideboard and on it, just next to his elbow, was an unopened bottle of brandy. Before any one could anticipate his impulse and stop him, he seized the bottle, slid the back of his knife smartly along its neck, and knocked the top off. He poured the brandy into our wine glasses and shouted, "Merry Christmas Captain bach!" as he drank his down. The rest of us sat stupified and shocked, but only for an instant. Captain German had been watching through the skylight which was immediately above the table and he was properly furious. He came into the saloon, blazing with anger.

"Get out! Get out of my saloon!"

And we did. We tumbled over each other in our haste to get away from his wrath, most of us with an acute sense of disgrace and just as full of rage as the Old Man. As soon as we got into the half-deck we jumped on Morris and brought him down to the deck where we sat astride of him, boxing his ears and cursing him for a goddamned, ungrateful, bad-mannered swab who had caused us all to be tarred with the same dirty brush.

Morris, his fire of the moment extinguished by the mauling and the realisation of what he had done, did not resist but said that he was sorry.

"Sorry, God damn it!" said Banbury, "Go up on the poop and say that to the Old Man."

But Morris did not think much of that, for the moment.

We changed back into our dungarees and those of us who were below turned in until four o'clock, to wake up feeling very ashamed and with the bleak knowledge that not having had our dinner in the half-deck we had not been able to save any part of it for supper. Supper would be tea and hard-tack. That was a problem which we discussed back and forth, with much indignant reviling of Morris, until the extraordinary proposal was made that I should put it to the Old Man!

"Go on, Long'un," said Paddy who could always inject a little humour into the most trying situation, "Isdale and Banbury are both older than you but you are much bigger."

I have a very clear recollection of all that day and particularly of that evening. We had seen nothing of the Cape Verde Islands but they were there, some 150 miles to windward, astern, and some of their colour and calm seemed to extend to us. The sea was very blue and slight, the trade wind was fading and, in the closing day, the ship was bathed in a warm, rosy-yellow light. I trod gingerly on to the poop and went to the open door of the chart-house where the Captain sat smoking his pipe and writing. He looked up, frowning.

"Sir," I said, "I've come to apologise for our behaviour at dinner time. We are greatly ashamed and very sorry."

"Apologise!" he exclaimed scornfully. "Young gentlemen! How would your father like it if he invited me to his house and I behaved like that? He'd never ask me again. And that's the last time any of you will eat in my house, my saloon!"

"Yes, sir, I know. It was all done so quickly that we didn't realise it. Perhaps the port wine was too much for us."

"Port wine rubbish! It was that damn' scoundrel Morris. I saw it . . . and heard it."

"I'll send him up, sir, but we're all to blame."

"I don't want to see him." He gave a couple of furious puffs at his pipe, while I remained standing outside his door. "Well," he said, "that's all, isn't it?"

"Yes, sir," I replied and then very diffidently went on, "We don't have anything left from our dinner to eat for our supper."

He was aghast. "Well I'm damned!" he ejaculated. "You'll eat hard-tack, then, and I hope you enjoy it."

There were no carols that dog-watch, nor any other kind of singing. We were too deeply chagrined. We got our tea from the galley and were settling down in silence for a meagre supper when the old steward came across the quarter-deck, carrying a tray with a napkin draped over it. He came to the door, head in the air, with an expression of extreme reserve on his face. He whipped off the napkin to reveal six small loaves of bread and a plate on which reposed a large tinned tongue.

"For the young gentlemen!" he said with a sniff of disdain. "And please don't break the dish and let me have it back—clean—when you've done."

It was our turn to be struck with amazement. And humility. Captain German had heaped coals of fire on our heads very effectively.

5 *A Happy New Year*

The following week we unbent and sent down the stout sails that had brought us from the Downs and replaced them with old, fine-weather canvas. Our turbulent Christmas had fallen on a Friday; on the Saturday, in the forenoon, we of the port watch shifted all the jibs, staysails and spanker and, on Monday, both watches were kept on deck in the afternoon. That day, when the starboard watch "turned to" after their coffee, at 5.00 a.m., instead of the usual washing down of decks they shifted the royals and topgallantsails. We continued with the topsails during the forenoon until seven bells, 11.20. Then we went below and joined the starboard watch for dinner; and, at noon, both watches came on deck to shift foresail, mainsail and cro'jack.

It was a good system, for the foresail and mainsail each spread nearly 3,000 square feet of canvas and when rolled up on deck they were so heavy and bulky that it was as much as all hands could do to haul them to and from the sail-locker. It was Mr. Fowler's idea and he and the Second Mate ranged about among their men with words of encouragement and banter and the men fell in with their urgent mood. They understood that it was important to get the sails down and stowed in the sail-locker while they were thoroughly dry, before the rain squalls of the doldrums. The ship was in about Latitude 10° North and they also knew that they could look for quiet watches on deck at night, and a snooze curled up on the main hatch if they felt like it and had no look-out or trick at the wheel.

Only old Hans Hanssen seemed inclined to demur until the Mate caught his eye and said, "Come on, Hanssen, old son, put your back into it! Ye know damn' well that if ye were in a German ship ye'd never be getting an afternoon below. They'd put you down in the chain-locker with a chipping hammer and a pot of red lead if they couldn't find work for ye on deck."

By the end of the watch we were finished. All the fine-weather "rags" were aloft, old sails, bleached white and soft with their years of use but sound enough for the weather we should meet over the next few thousand miles while we wandered through the doldrums and into the south-east trades.

On New Year's Eve there was just enough wind to fill our sails and the *Arno* was ghosting along at about two knots. A young moon was sinking behind the clouds which lay massed on the horizon. Elsewhere, the sky sparkled with stars which here and there cast twinkling reflections among the patches of phosphorescence that flickered in the sea. At midnight, sixteen bells—eight for the old year and eight for the new—chimed from the poop and were answered by the deep note of the big bell on the fo'c's'le head as all hands came aft to the quarter-deck to muster and to wish Captain and Officers a Happy New Year, hopefully carrying their pannikins.

There was no marching around the decks singing *The bells are ringing the Old Year out* as there had been in the *Main*. The men had not been long enough in the ship to form a "fou-fou" band. Everybody, crew and officers, seemed to be too middle-aged for such youthful pranks and the Captain, apparently, did not feel justified in lighting the ship up with blue flares. After all, he was a Welshman and, with his memories of the Dundee *Glens*, it was natural that he did not have the Scotsman's enthusiasm for hogmanay.

But the steward was there with his pitcher and a bottle—spirits for the men and port wine for the apprentices and boys. There were cries of "Happy New Year, Captain!", to which one man added heartily, "Amicus humani generis," before he passed the back of his hand across his lips. It was ecclesiastically intoned and was heard by everybody.

"What's that!" cried the Old Man. "What did that man say?"

A little man stepped forward, somewhat sheepishly, touched his forelock and said, "Latin, sir, means 'friend of the human race'. I was just saying thank you, sir."

Captain German considered this for a moment, then smiled and said, "Thank you. Happy New Year, men. Alright Mr. Fowler, relieve the wheel and look-out."

All kinds of people found their way into the fo'c's'le of a sailing-ship. In the *Main* there had been a derelict schoolmaster who would recite Homer's *Odyssey* in Greek, or passages from Shakespeare, as he stood his look-out on the fo'c's'le head. And here was Able Seaman D'Arcy spouting Latin.

It was the last thing you would have expected of him because in speech and appearance he was typical of thousands living in St. Pancras, which was his home, or in any of the other boroughs of London. He was of medium size, sturdily built, with a good-humoured, open face, hair the colour of a coconut-fibre doormat, and just as thick and springy. His parents, who kept a green-grocer's shop, were devout Roman Catholics and, from the day of his birth, had decided that he should be a priest. All his schooling was bent in this direction until, when still only a youngster, he was sent to a seminary in Italy. He went through his noviciate and finally attained the goal so dear to his parents' hearts and became a monk in a monastery, vowed to celibacy and religious exercises.

When he told me this a few days later, as we squatted in the scuppers, washing the paint of the bulwarks, I could not help laughing. I did not mean it unkindly but anyone who looked less like a dedicated monk would have been hard to find. He crinkled his short nose in a grin, sharing my amusement, but a monk he had been, with a shaven pate, for eleven frugal and chaste years. Chaste, however, only up to a point. Close by was a nunnery and, whether or not it was true, as he insisted, that they would not leave him alone, it seems that somebody had climbed the wall once too often.

After the north-east trades had left us, we dawdled through the doldrums—the area of light variable winds, calms and sudden squalls, that extends some three hundred miles on each side of the equator. The ship ran, lingered or loitered at the whim of the heavens in a manner of which the following occasion is typical.

A squall was seen building up on the lee quarter. There the ocean was the colour of ink, and the horizon was hidden by a dense black pall of rain. This was no cat's-paw. We swung the heavy yards around just in time as the deluge poured on us with a roar like a cloud-burst. *First the rain, then the wind, all your sheets and halliards mind*, runs the old sailor's couplet. With the rain bouncing knee-high from the decks, we stood by royal and topgallant halliards while the wind whistled and shrieked through the rigging. The first impact of the blast put the ship over until the sea came through the scupper-holes and wash-ports of the bulwarks, then she lifted her lee-rail and moved ahead.

On the poop the Old Man was bare-headed and bare-foot, wearing white shirt and duck trousers which clung sodden to his long limbs like a loose skin. But, instead of "Lower away your royals", the order came to set foresail and mainsail and the *Arno* fairly leapt through the smooth sea until the squall blew itself out, which it did within the hour, leaving the ship idle again, under a blazing sun, waiting for the next zephyr.

Leaving the ship idle, but not the crew. For the watch on deck, these days were busy intervals of sunshine and rain, with buckets of caustic soda, sand and canvas, and sand and holystones; washing the paint of life-boats, tops of deck-houses and bulwarks; scrubbing the teak deck-houses and all the other teak in the ship, down to the bare wood; and, at last, we got down on our knees with our "prayer books", scouring the decks with holystones and sand until they were white. We were getting all ready for the dry weather of the south-east trade winds when we would be just as busy with pots of paint, linseed oil and buckets of Stockholm tar. We dropped everything to run to the braces and

61

trim yards, tacks and sheets, so that the sails should get every breath of a breeze, no matter from which point of the compass it came.

Because of this persistence and in spite of the frustrating calms, we averaged about forty miles a day through the doldrums, crossed the Line when we were thirty-six days out from Portland Bill and six days later picked up the south-east trade wind.

It had come after a squall so menacing that the end of the world might have been at hand. A wall of black cloud advanced and covered the sky until, at noon, it was so dark that the lightning that split the heavens flashed with blinding white brilliance. Thunder growled and rumbled in the distance and rolled and cracked deafeningly over our heads, around our ears. We ran all jibs and stay-sails down, hauled up the clews of foresail, mainsail and cro'jack and squared the yards, for little wave-crests flecked the indigo blue of the ocean, whipped up by a small, cold breeze which came from dead ahead and took the ship flat aback. As she gathered stern-way we manned the port fore braces, laying the fore yards abox, and the gentle breeze pushed the ship's head to starboard, faded away and then left us becalmed again.

Then the heavens opened in a downpour so dense that we might have been in a thick fog. The water poured down poop and fo'c's'le ladders and from the tops of deck-houses. It lay inches deep on deck, and spouted through the scup-per-holes splashing noisily over the side; the little sea was beaten flat.

When it eased off and we could see again, we found that we were not alone. The ship had drifted into the middle of a large school of whales. They were all around us, some so close that we could have touched them with a boat-hook. They had not been heard because their blowing was covered by the noise of the rain. At first, we thought they were sleeping, then some raised their enormous heads and others rolled over, exposing their white bellies as if they were enjoy-ing the stinging rain and relishing the fresh water. A mile or so to port, to the eastward, was another ship, heading north, the first vessel seen since we had left the Channel. She had come along with the breeze that had taken us aback and there she lay, her rusty hull deep in the water, her sails, blue in the shadow of the clouds, sodden as ours, hanging lifeless. There was not enough air stirring to exchange flag signals but we hoisted our ensign and she ran up the tricolour of France.

Then the wind came out of the east; it swept the heavens clear of the heavy rain clouds and, when we had time to look for them while we coiled the ropes up, off the deck, we saw the school of whales away in the distance, heading into the eye of the wind, and the French ship far astern, scarcely to be seen through the rain which hung about her.

As we got further south, the wind freshened, and for seven days we averaged about two hundred miles per day, heading south-by-west. It was wonderful sailing, steering "full and by", the yards off the backstays, the weather leach of the mizzen royal just giving an occasional wind-tremble, the ship going along at eight to ten knots, thrusting her way over a sea of deepest blue, through wave-crests which gleamed in the sunlight, crumpled under her bows and spattered us with sparkling spray.

By the time we reached Latitude 25° South, all our work on deck had been done. Deck-houses and bulwarks shone with their fresh coats of varnish and paint, the pine decks had taken up the tar which had been so generously applied, and we had shifted sail again. All hands had been busy in their watches below greasing sea-boots and overhauling oilskins, getting ready for the weather of higher latitudes. And, a few days later, we got our first taste of it.

It came in a night of utter darkness, in the middle watch, midnight to 4.00 a.m., when we were on deck. The wind had eased and there was lightning in the sky ahead, so cro'jack and mainsail were hauled up in anticipation of a shift of wind. When I went on the poop at 1.00 a.m., to make two bells and trim the lamp in the binnacle, I could hear Captain German and the Mate talking as they stood by the lee rail. I was putting the lamp into its socket when a sharp shower of ice-cold rain hit us. With the first drops, the Old Man said, "Main and cro'jack braces, Mr. Fowler." No sooner had we got to the braces than the wind whipped around from the south-east to south-south-west, taking us by the lee. Fortunately, the ship still had good way on her and so answered her helm smartly and swung to port while we were hauling the main and mizzen yards round—which we did without difficulty because they were blanketted by the fore.

On the foremast, however, the sails were getting the full weight of the wind, they were flat aback. We were having a hard time and, in spite of the Mate's urgent, "Haul, bullies, haul!" and the cries of the fore-hand, "Hee-boho-bust-her," we could not get an inch on the braces. Then the Old Man ran her off, and the wind came out on the beam. The sails on the foremast started to flap and flog about and we got the yards around. But the weather leach of the big foresail had wrapped itself around the stunsail boom-iron which was under-neath the yard-arm and, when the wind got hold of the sail, it filled with a vicious jerk and tore itself free. But, in doing so, it ripped a hole in the canvas—a split twelve feet long, right down to the reef-band.

"Belay all!" hailed Mr. Fowler. "Clew garnets and bunt-lines. Cheerily, lads! Up with her and reef her before we lose the goddam sail."

We got the foresail hauled up to the yard and then went aloft to reef it. It was quick thinking on Mr. Fowler's part. Had he delayed, the sail would have been torn to rags.

63

I was the first on the yard and laid out to windward; I sat astride the yard-arm reeving off the reef earring, laying back and hauling the reef cringle close while the men on the footrope lighted the sail toward me. When it was enough, I gave a hail and made the earring fast while they hauled taut to leeward. Then I left my perch, fifty feet above the water, with nothing behind my back but the South American continent, about eight hundred miles away, and came in, on to the footrope to join the others tying the reef points.

Down from aloft, we hove the tack down and then trimmed the sheet. The sail set well but it looked odd and the old Norwegian "John Smith", who confessed to sixty years on the Articles but who was probably much older, said with a chuckle, "First time I ben goin' along wit' t'ree royals an' a reef' fores'l."

At 4.00 a.m. we went below, glad to get out of our wet clothing and into our bunks for a short three and a half hours.

We came on deck again at eight o'clock to find that the starboard watch had unbent the sail and lowered it down on deck. With both watches we got it out of the way, into the coolie galley, carried the new sail forward and, before two bells, 9.00 a.m., had it set. It was blowing hard. But we had a crew of experienced sailors; everyone knew just what to do and when to do it and, at seven bells, lime-juice time, they had their reward, it was "splice the main brace" and a welcome tot of rum in addition.

6 Running Our "Easting Down"

At the close of day on January 21st we were in Latitude 37° South, fifty-three
days out from Portland, the ship still heading south-east, tearing along under
all the sail that she could bear. Only the cro'jack was furled; Captain German
had hung on to it in spite of Mr. Fowler's many hints until even he was persuaded that she went better without it, carried less weather helm and, in the
squalls, did not gripe so strongly to windward. He was a driver and, in spite of
the light airs of the doldrums, we had averaged seven knots since crossing the
Line.

Down to leeward, a mass of cloud was caught on the heights of the lonely
island of Tristan da Cunha. With Mr. Fowler, my watchmates—Le Patourel
and Morris—and the Bos'n, I stood by the lee rail, looking at it until it was
hidden by the darkness. It was the first sign of land we had seen since leaving
the Channel.

"Well, Bos," said Mr. Fowler, "you're giving it a wide berth this passage."

"Yes, sir," replied the Bos'n. "I never want to see that place again, for all
that they were so kind to us."

When the Bos'n signed Articles for the voyage in the *Arno* he had given his
name as Richard Whitehead, forty-six years old, born in Manchester. But in
those days it was possible for a seaman to use any name he fancied if, for some
reason, he did not wish to use his own. Whatever the Bos'n's real name may
have been, there is no doubt that he had been an able seaman in James Nourse's
ship *Allanshaw* when she went ashore on Tristan da Cunha. The story he told
us about it during the anchor watches when we lay in the Downs was correct
in all its details in spite of the fifteen years which had passed since it happened.
The only Manchester man aboard the *Allanshaw* when she was wrecked was
listed as Thomas Mannion and he was the same age as Richard Whitehead.

The 1890s were unlucky years for James Nourse. The fleet then numbered
nineteen fine sailing-ships and in the first six years of that decade seven of them
met with serious trouble, five being lost.

In July 1890, my old ship the *Main* when dropping down the Hughli River
to Garden Reach, in charge of a pilot but with no tug, collided with and sank

65

a fully-loaded steamer which was lying at anchor. She herself was damaged and had to be docked for repairs.

One month later, the *Volga*, only three years old, was wrecked in the Torres Straits while on the return passage from Fiji to Calcutta.

In March 1893, the *Allanshaw* was lost and, in December of the same year, the second *Volga*, only two years old, was wrecked at Port Castries, St. Lucia.

In April 1895, the *Arno* was abandoned in the Atlantic and, six months later, the *Avoca*, with a cargo of jute, was destroyed by fire in the Indian Ocean.

Finally, in November 1896, the barque *Grecian* was swept by a hurricane on to the island of Montserrat, the sole survivor of her crew being her Third Mate Thomas Keogh who, nine years later, was Third Mate with us in the *Main*.

Going to sea in sailing-ships was a hard life but it had the compensations of excitement for its monotony and of adventure for its dangers. And, to the young in heart, these were the currency of romance.

In a different sense, alert shipowners were adventurous also and, by the end of 1896, James Nourse had built five new ships to replace those lost.

Seven days after passing Tristan da Cunha we were five hundred miles south of Cape Agulhas, the southernmost point of Africa. In that week we had covered some 1,620 miles at an average of about 230 miles per day, or just short of ten knots. We had come down to Latitude 43° South and were in the zone of Latitude 38° to 60° South—a broad stream of wind about 1,400 miles wide. The only land mass to encroach on it is the tip of the South American continent; so, with nothing to affect it excepting occasional local changes of temperature and atmospheric pressure, for most of the time the wind blows steadily from the western sector of the compass, anywhere from north-west to south-west.

In the "roaring forties" as these latitudes are called, the wind is strong and fresh, pushing a long procession of great seas before it. Sailing-vessels bound for India and Australia made full use of it to run their "easting down", to run the thousands of miles that they had to go to the eastward.

It was fine summer weather down there and, although there was enough wind to drive our deeply laden ship through the water at about eight knots, we had no hard squalls or gales and it was not really cold, except on those occasions when the wind hauled to the southward and it seemed as though we could almost smell the antarctic ice. And that was as well because the combers constantly curled aboard over the bulwarks, filling the decks with a mass of water which swilled about from side to side and rushed fore and aft as the ship rolled and pitched heavily before the following seas.

Turning out before midnight for the middle watch was a sleepy, reluctant struggle to get from under warm blankets, to get dressed standing on our sea-chests because the deck was inches deep with the water which, in spite of all the caulking, forced its way through the door jambs and over the weather-boards which were fitted there; then to thrust feet into damp sea-boots, get into cold oilskins and scramble out on to the quarter-deck for the muster and four hours on deck.

This voyage in the *Arno* was for me the fifth time of crossing the meridian of Cape Agulhas and the third time of running the easting down; these waters and the weather of the Southern Ocean had become almost familiar. I enjoyed the day watches on deck most when working aloft where I could see the whole circle of the horizon. The thought of the vast distances of ocean which surrounded us never lost its fascination nor did the endless succession of long, high seas coming up from over the horizon, miles astern, racing past us as though to hurry us on our way, with the albatrosses soaring with motionless wings over their crests.

We were very much on our own. Steamers never go down so far south and only once did we sight another sailing-vessel. A cloud of black smoke rose from her main deck and, at first, we thought she was on fire. Then we saw that her fore topgallant yard was down, she had masthead hoops for look-outs in her fore cross-trees and we recognised her for a Yankee whaling ship. The smoke came from her try-works. It was rather humbling to think of her men putting off in their boats, hunting whales in those seas.

At noon on February 24th, according to our figuring of Mr. Fowler's sights, Cape Borda on Kangaroo Island was only forty miles away and Adelaide only 150 miles off. In the half-deck we were all agog at the thought of seing Australia and having a run ashore, and the same holiday spirit pervaded the entire ship's company. It had been a fine passage all the way from the Channel, with no really hard weather. The last blow had been on the previous day when the south-west wind had suddenly turned bitterly cold and we had been pelted by heavy showers of hail.

At sunset, Cape Borda was abeam about eight miles off. At that distance there was not much to be seen but the flashing light was all that we really cared about; that and the fair breeze and the smooth water as we passed into the lee of Kangaroo Island. I went to the wheel at eight o'clock and relieved the fat, jolly, Able Seaman Brown. Before handing over to me he muttered, with a low chuckle, "Semaphore termorrer, me son. Get rid of the powder the next day an' go alongside Saturday mornin'. An' oh! Won't I sink a couple o' pints uv beer." As I took hold of the wheel he beamed at me and said, "East by north, an' keep her goin', son."

"East by north," I repeated. The wind was fresh; it came over the land carrying the scent of soil, trees and the bush—strong and sweet after the heat of a summer's day; very sweet after our three months at sea.

In the forenoon of the next day we approached our anchorage off the Semaphore. We ran before the wind and the water gurgled at our bows, rippled and splashed along our sides. The Bos'n was laid up and I was acting in his place, working the crowd, with Mr. Fowler, on the fo'c's'le head. Banbury and Isdale were on the poop putting up hoists of signals giving our name and port of registry, the port we had come from, and the yellow quarantine flag. The pilot-jack flew at the foremast head with a red burgee to say that we carried explosives in our cargo. In the brilliant sunshine the gaily-coloured flags floated merrily in the breeze. There was the rattle of the sheaves in the blocks as halliards and sheets were let fly, and the intoxicating smell of the land was in our nostrils. It was wonderful! Even the cook's tabby cat had climbed up on top of the galley skylight where he stood with arched back, excitedly sniffing the breeze.

At noon the anchor was down in four fathoms of water and we ran up the rigging and out along the footropes of the yards to make the sails fast with a snug harbour stow. It was Thursday, February 25th. We had sailed the 13,300 odd miles from Portland Bill in eighty-seven days. A good passage.

By 1.30 p.m. the port health authorities had been and gone, and a small tug towed us into the Adelaide River. Some five miles upstream we anchored again. A red-painted covered lighter, resembling a floating barn, was moored there; and, when we had let go the tug, she brought it alongside. We had come about eight miles from the anchorage to the Powder Ground and, by the time we had made the lighter fast and the tug had left us, the afternoon was done.

We stood looking at the shore which, in that part of the river, in those days of 1909, looked dreary, uninhabited and uninviting. The river was only about two hundred yards wide and the tongue of land we had come around and which separated us from the sea—the Lefevre Peninsula—was only a short mile across; it was a waste of mangroves, shea-oaks and scrub. The opposite bank, to port, appeared to consist of swamp and grassland.

The roof of the powder lighter was flush with the top of our bulwarks and Morris had the idea that we should go for a swim. It had been a hot day. So we stripped where we stood—there was not much to take off, just a singlet and dungaree trousers—got on to the roof of the lighter and dived into the river. It was wonderfully refreshing. We were making for the beach, about fifty yards away, when I heard gurgles, grunts and the thrashing of water behind me. I turned, and there was Paddy. He was purple in the face, struggling frantically to keep his head above the surface. He could not swim a stroke but still he had jumped in with the rest of us.

Treading water, I grabbed his elbow and wrist and immediately he had the sense to remain quiet, taking in great draughts of air. When he had recovered his breath he grinned and said, "Let's get to the beach, Long'un." I hailed Morris and, with Paddy between us, a hand on each of our shoulders, we got him to shallow water. There he learned to swim, and that well enough so that with all of us around him he swam back to the lighter unaided.

Charles Le Patourel was a brave little sailor. In the 1914–18 war, a few years later, he was a Lieutenant, Royal Naval Reserve, and was awarded the Distinguished Service Cross.

By noon next day, Friday, having left our twenty tons of gunpowder in the lighter, we were three miles further up the river, warping the ship alongside the wharf at the foot of what looked like the main street with, as A. B. Brown pointed out, a couple of good-looking pubs within a stone's throw. It was the lunch-hour and the wharf, which gave right on to the street, was well peopled with curious bystanders watching the latest arrival from England. There was nothing novel in this. The people of Port Adelaide saw plenty of sailing-ships; two or three lay at other wharves close by and our *Arno* was the tenth to arrive in the last six weeks. They were interested. We, of course, knew that this was because they had an eye for a fine-looking clipper.

Mr. Fowler realised this. They were his audience. It was a warm, sunny morning and he stood on the fo'c's'le head in his blue trousers and gleaming white shirt, with his shiny peaked cap cocked jauntily over one eye as he encouraged us at the capstan with all the good old-fashioned sailorly cries that he could think of.

"Oh-oo-oo! My hearties! Oh-oo-oo! Bust her! Cheerily now, my lads! Heave a pawl, just one pawl! 'Vast heaving. Belay that. Now your breast lines and backspring . . . handy with that heaving line. Lay back and haul, merrily, my bullies . . ."

His rich musical voice echoed from the buildings across the street. The crowd loved it, so did he, and so did we!

That afternoon the hatches were opened and a gang of stevedores were soon in the 'tween-decks, slinging the cases of cargo which the dockside crane lifted out and swung ashore. They were a good-natured lot of rascals. For a shilling, one of them filled my bunk with lovely fresh fruit. But rascals they were. One of us was on duty down below all the time they were working there to see that they did not pilfer the cargo. We may have been something of a deterrent but not much. They could open a case, empty a bottle of beer and have it back in place with the case all nailed up, in the twinkling of an eye. They were artists with their cotton hooks. If accused, they fixed you with a liquid gaze of injured innocence, their words of denial floating on beer-laden breath. We hated the job.

There was no work on Saturday afternoon or Sunday. On the Saturday, we took the train from Port Adelaide Station to Adelaide City which we found to be charming and most friendly. We were six hungry young sailors so, before going to a music hall, we made for a restaurant. ALUN MORRIS was painted in gold letters on the signboard. It looked rather more expensive than we could manage on our few shillings.

"I don't know, Morris boy," I said. "He's one of your countrymen. More than likely he'll throw us out."

"The hell he will!" said Morris. "Not if we behave ourselves and don't go pinching the knives and forks. Or broaching any bottles of spirits that may be standing about," Banbury chimed in.

It was clean inside, with white tablecloths and white curtains at the window. We were the first customers. We stood, hesitant, wondering if we could afford it when, from behind a screen which evidently hid the kitchen door, a small plump woman appeared. She had black hair and rosy cheeks and spoke with the unmistakable cadence of North Wales.

"Good evening boys. Sit you down and I'll bring you something to eat. You'll be from one of those sailing-ships in the port. You'll be hungry, indeed to goodness!"

To this Morris replied in fluent Welsh. She beamed with pleasure and we, not understanding, could nevertheless hear much repetition of "Morris Portmadoc" and "Morris Dolgarrog". The upshot of it was that we were welcome and not to worry. We ate a hearty meal of mutton chops and fried potatoes with cups of strong black tea followed by treacle tarts while the good lady sat with us, continuously talking in Welsh with Morris, marvelling at our appetites. And our bill must have been less than half of what it cost her. She was a good soul who shrieked with delight when little Paddy, standing on tiptoe, threw his arms around her and planted a kiss on each of her cheeks.

Then we went to the music hall, the *Tivoli*, where the stars were Frank and Jen Latona and "Baby" Watson. The first two were famous all over the world in those days and "Baby" Watson was famous in Australia. She was an accomplished little artist who looked to be about five years old, with a head of close curls, dressed in lace and ribbons like a doll. She captured our hearts and really made our eyes moist when she sang Richard Beale's song about *Poor little baby Jack*. The lump in our throats was so big that we could not join in, much as we wanted to do so.

On the Sunday we went for a picnic. If we had known what we were in for on that day and in the following week we would probably have stayed quietly on

70

board. The *Arno* had no smart Captain's gig but two quarter-boats, normal-sized life-boats, were in their chocks under davits. Our plan was to take one down river and into the Gulf of St. Vincent for some sailing and a swim.

"The port quarter-boat?" said Mr. Fowler when I went to ask his permission. "An' what on earth would ye be doing with it? . . . Going out in the Gulf! Didn't ye have plenty sailing already? Isn't eighty-seven days enough?" He was smiling, hesitating while he turned it over in his mind. "Alright, away ye go. Ye'll be less likely to run into trouble out at sea than ye would be if ye went ashore . . . an' with no money in your pockets!" Then he gripped my shoulder and said, rather more earnestly, "Alright my son, away ye go. But watch the tide and mind ye don't get 'to-hell-an-gone' to loo'ard. If ye do, ye'll never get back unless we send a tug for ye. And if that happens ye'll be in plenty of trouble."

We provisioned the boat with a breaker of fresh water, bottles of cold coffee, and bread and cold meat from our previous day's dinner, and pushed happily away from the ship's side. The same southerly wind that had brought the *Arno* up to the Semaphore was still blowing so we stepped the mast, set the lugsail and had a grand run down the river. A strong flood tide was against us but the breeze was so fresh that we were off Pelican Point at the entrance of the river in less than two hours.

Clear of the land, the breeze was very fresh but we hauled the sheet aft, brought the tack down to its cleat on the weather bow and, with the wind abeam, raced across the sand flats which were just about covered. We were sailing with our lee gun'ale awash, all sitting up to windward. In the shallows, the steep seas slammed against our weather bilge and flung fountains of spray high as the masthead until we were wet to the skin and the water streamed from our heads and poured from the belly of the lugsail. It was grand fun. The sun shone bright and warm and we sang one of our favourite ditties:

> *"Shore, sailor, shore, sailor, pull for the shore*
> *Pull like a sonofabitch but don't break the oar*
> *Safe in the life-boat, sailor, clinging to sin no more,*
> *Leave that dreary sinking wreck and pull for the shore."*

In deeper water it was quieter. We sailed about five miles into the gulf but the tide was sweeping us to the northward, to leeward, and the wind showed signs of easing, so we went about and stood in towards the land. After a beat of some six miles, we brought up alongside the jetty in Largs Bay where we spent the afternoon. We sat on the hot timbers of the pier and ate our lunch, surrounded by an admiring group of small boys and girls. We frolicked with

71

the children in the water, took them for a short sail and landed them on the jetty again. Then we got under way to return to the ship while the children stood waving and shouting good-bye, many of the boys watching us with envy and the firm determination that they, too, would be sailors one day.

It was slack water and the breeze still held so we were able to run the five miles back to the river. However, when we rounded Pelican Point what had been a fair wind was now dead against us. We tried beating but the river was so narrow that on such short tacks, what with having to ease the halliard and dip the lug around the mast when we went about, we made very little progress against the ebb tide which was running against us at a rate of about three knots. There was no help for it. We dowsed the sail, lowered the yard, got the oars out and had a hard pull of five miles back to the ship.

We were very tired but we came alongside, singing our life-boat song, to find the Mate and Second Mate looking out for us. They helped us to hoist our boat and swing it in, on to its chocks. We were tired and very hungry and we ate our supper in silence quite convinced that we had had a wonderful day.

Three days later, the last of our Adelaide cargo went over the rail, 616 tons in all, and after the hands had had their dinner a tug was made fast alongside and all mooring-lines hauled aboard except a backspring—the heavy hawser that we had put out through the hawse-pipe, aft. On the wharf it led forward, around a bollard, then back through the hawse-pipe to be made fast at the bitts on the quarter-deck. Astern of us, the end of her jibboom a few feet clear of our taffrail, the British barque *Carmoney* had moored the previous day; ahead, we were just as close to a large French barque, the *Bonchamps*.

There was not much room for manoeuvring but the tug, her engines moving astern, pivoted the *Arno* on the backspring and canted her bows clear of the Frenchman. We cast off the backspring, hauled it aboard and the tug turned us and towed us down stream, back to our anchorage off the Semaphore.

The wind was still southerly and several other vessels were already there, waiting for a shift that would enable us all to get away. We found ourselves in the outside berth which proved to be a mixed blessing. It would give us a good offing when the wind did change; we would be able to get under way without running foul of the other ships, or into shoal water, but it was a good three miles distant from the jetties at Largs Bay or the Semaphore.

When satisfied that the ship was "brought-up" and lying quietly to her anchor, the pilot and Captain German went ashore in the tug. As soon as they were away, we rigged the hoses and spent a busy couple of hours scrubbing the decks fore and aft, while the cook dumped the galley refuse that had accumulated while we were at the wharf.

We went around the pin-rails to make sure that all running gear was clear. By the time the decks were dry, we had the ship ready for sea again.

There were no anchor watches for us apprentices that night because we had to bring the Old Man aboard. He had left orders with Mr. Fowler that he wanted us at the Semaphore jetty at ten o'clock, so we swung the boat out, lowered it to the water and pushed off an hour beforehand. The wind had dropped to a calm and we got there with time to spare. Banbury, Isdale and I took it in turns to be coxswain of the boat and this night I was in charge. I went to the shore end of the jetty to wait for the Captain while the others each found a soft plank and coiled down for a snooze. We had all been up since dawn.

At last a rickety old victoria-type hackney-carriage came slowly to a halt and the Old Man got out. As his feet touched the ground, he let out a hail.

"*Arno* ahoy!"

"Aye aye, sir," I replied and ran to his side.

He was standing in the dim light of the carriage-lamp, a bony finger stirring a small pile of loose coins in his palm. He was humming softly to himself, smiling, and swaying gently on his long legs. There was a slight argument about the fare but, in the end, the cabby gave in and the Old Man turned to me.

"Lay hold of that sack, de Mierre boy, before this man goes away with it. Present from Cap'n Pugh. My old shipmate Pugh . . . a nice feed for all hands."

It was a gunny sack and, with a bit of an effort, I slung it over my shoulder. It held a dozen big fat rabbits and weighed all of fifty pounds. It seemed three times that much by the time I had stamped the 600-yard length of the jetty. The stamping was to warn the others of our approach, so that when we got to the steps they would be sitting on the thwarts with oars tossed, and would have a lighted globe-lamp in the sternsheets and the cushion on the quarter-bench, all ready for the Old Man.

We passed through the inshore tier of ships as, one after the other, they struck eight bells—midnight. The man on watch in the *Grasmere*, a handsome little Norwegian barque, leaned over the taffrail and hailed a "good night" as we pulled under her stern. By the time we had put the Captain and his rabbits aboard and, with the help of the hands on anchor watch, hoisted our boat clear of the water and frapped the falls to the davits so that she would hang quiet against the rolling of the ship, it was past one o'clock and we went thankfully to our bunks. It had been a long day and we would be turned out again at 5.30 a.m.

In the morning when we came on deck there was not a breath of wind. The ship was drenched with dew. It lay in fat globules on deck-planks and tarpaulins, hung in crystal drops from the rat-lines and dripped in small showers from aloft. Instead of the usual wash–down we dried the decks and rails with swabs; then we went aloft and loosed all the sails, leaving them hanging in their gear to air and dry. A hot sun was mounting in the cloudless sky and, when we pulled the Captain ashore in the forenoon, it poured on our backs, and the sea was like a blazing mirror.

Banbury, who was coxswain for the day, brought us alongside the jetty with a wide sheer, man-o'-war style, putting on a bit of a show for the benefit of the other boats' crews who were waiting there.

"In bow," he hailed. And little Le Patourel tossed and stowed his oar, seized his boat-hook and stood with it upright in the bow.

"Way enough," was Banbury's next command as he put the tiller over. We tossed oars and stowed them, blades forward, as the boat came gently alongside the steps to be held stationary by Paddy with his boat-hook.

The Old Man was pleased. He even looked it and he smiled when he said, "Alright, boys. Come here for me at five o'clock."

When we got back on board it was dinner-time and after our six-mile pull we were ready for it. The Old Man had been as good as his word. There was considerable commotion around the galley door. The young cook, happy at having something to work with that would enable him to show his skill, was whistling cheerfully as he stirred the stew that simmered in a large cauldron. His cat, replete with rabbits' offal, was curled up on a pile of skins that lay on the bench opposite the stove. I stood with the other "peggies" from the fo'c's'le; all holding our kids, we waited impatiently for our "whack" which at last the cook dished out.

"There ye are, me lads," he said. "An' it's the first time ye'll be tastin' a real rabbit stew. There's onions in it, and 'taters, 'n carrots and turmuts. An' ye know what else?" His eyebrows went up, almost disappearing under his cap, and his face broke into a wide grin. "A couple o' pounds of nice fat salt pork that I pinched from the harness-cask when the old steward wasn't lookin', all chopped up in small pieces; when ye eat it ye'll think it's Christmas again."

"Fair enough, Cookie," said Able Seaman Brown. "Smells fine," he added as the steam from his kid floated up about his nose. "What ye goin' to do wit' them pelts? Ye can't sell 'em here. The place is lousy with rabbit skins."

"Ye can have 'em!" exclaimed the cook. "An' good riddance."

"What do you want with them, Brownie?" I asked.

"Want with them! Why, I'll clean 'em with ashes and a bit of alum, and stretch them to dry. Then I'll pound the hell out 'uv them till they're as soft as a baby's bottom. An' I'll line me monkey-peajacket with 'em to keep me warm when I'm at the wheel, homeward-bound round the Horn."

Clutching his pelts and the kid of stew, Brown went forward and I returned to the half-deck where we all agreed that no sailor had ever before eaten salt junk and rabbit that tasted so much like turkey.

All hands spent the afternoon aloft, re-stowing the sails. Over to the eastward it was so clear that from the mizzen royal yard I could see the dome of the Town Hall in Adelaide, a good eight miles away. Across the gulf, to the westward, there was a haze along the horizon. The land on that side was about thirty miles off, too distant to be visible. But, as we looked around before going down on deck, Banbury said, "Maybe that haze is dust, kicked up by a breeze. Come on. It's time to be away to pick up the Old Man."

We pulled easily ashore, two of us wiping around, getting all shipshape and the cushions turned dry-side uppermost, ready for the Old Man. He came along the jetty shortly after we got there and was accompanied by a little old man whose wrinkled brown face was almost covered by a curly white beard. He wore a panama hat and a white suit. What made the greatest impression on us was that, in spite of this tropical rig-out, he was wearing a shiny brown leather glove on one hand. He was the perfect image of the old time shipmaster. We knew that this must be the old shipmate, "Cap'n Pugh", and we thought that he had come down to see Captain German off.

But no. With all possible courtesy, Captain German gave him pride of place coming down the steps, then jumped smartly into the boat to stand there to receive his senior, his guest. It was indeed Captain Pugh. He stood smiling while he looked us over, then said to Banbury, "Good evening, cox'un," and to the rest of us, "Good evening, boys." After which he stepped neatly and nimbly aboard.

It was a lovely evening. The sun was down to the horizon, shining like a great red ball through the haze that we had noticed, suffusing it with an apricot-coloured glow that spread high in the heavens. It touched the little old man, too, threw warm lights on his white hat and suit and made his face shine like a piece of polished mahogany. Whatever he was doing ashore in Adelaide, this excursion to our ship was very much to his liking; he fairly beamed with pleasure as he sat in the sternsheets, his gloved hand resting on the gunnel, chatting with Captain German. He looked right and left, watching our rowing, listened to the liquid sound of the "plop" as the blades of our oars bit the water, and craned his head to look up at the spars of the other sailing vessels as we passed them close by.

Approaching the *Arno*, Banbury gave the order, "Oars starboard, hold water port." Then, putting his tiller over and with some signs of astonishment on his face, he hailed, "Way enough." We were also a little startled but we got our oars tossed and stowed and held the boat stationary by the jack-ladder.

It was Captain Pugh who had shaken us. With his right hand we had seen him spin his gloved left hand around until it came away from his sleeve. He put the hand in his pocket and took out a shiny metal hook which he screwed in its place. Then he gave us a grin and ran up the rope ladder with the agility of a youngster.

It was about ten o'clock when Mr. Fowler came to the half-deck door to turn us out. Half an hour later, by the time we got the boat under the ladder, we took Captain Pugh aboard and pushed off. He lit his pipe as soon as we were away from the ship and sat contentedly smoking while we pulled the three miles to the jetty, making fifteen miles for the day. As well as old man Pugh we had taken a gunny-sack into the boat, containing, of course, the land-bound sailor's delicacy—a couple of pieces of salt beef and salt pork—and, in addition, three of Captain German's Stilton cheeses. I took the sack on my shoulder to carry it to the end of the jetty where a hackney-carriage was waiting. The old chap thanked me kindly, then reached out to shake hands and, as I watched him disappear in a cloud of dust, I found to my delight that he had given me ten shillings.

"Ten bob!" cried Morris when I got back to the boat. "Let's go and have a beer before we push off. We've earned it, indeed whatever."

"Let's have two beers," said Paddy. "Ten bob, that's one shilling and eight pence each; enough for three beers!"

We drank our beer at the pub close by while we smoked our pipes. Then, all aglow, got back to the boat.

"Crikey!" said Banbury. "There's a breeze. Come on, or there'll be hell to pay when we get alongside."

A fresh breeze was blowing from the north-west. In the bobble that it kicked up in the shallow water, the boat was doing herself no good, bumping against the timbers of the jetty. We quickly got aboard, pushed off, stepped the mast, hoisted the lug-sail and went clipping along at double the speed we could have made under oars. We were worried and so stationed Paddy in the bow with the globe-lamp to make sure that they could see us coming. When we were close enough we could see that aboard the *Arno* the topsails had been loosed, and the crowd was walking round the capstan on the fo'c's'le head, heaving short, singing the lugubrious chanty *Fire down below*.

Banbury brought us smartly under the davits while we unstepped the mast and stowed the sail. We grabbed the blocks of the falls, hooked on and yelled, "Hoist away." As soon as there was a strain on the falls three of us scrambled up the ladder, leaving three to fend the boat off the ship's side as it was hoisted.

The Captain was pacing impatiently athwartships at the break of the poop. The moment our feet touched the deck he called, "Alright, Mr. Fowler.

We'll cast to port. Head sheets to starboard. Break out your anchor and sheet home your topsails. And send de Mierre to the wheel."

I was lucky. We were all very tired. The others had to run up aloft to loose topgallants and royals. I could stand leaning against the wheel-box, just obeying orders at the helm.

The ship was riding to the wind, heading west-north-west, and when the anchor left the ground the head sails—fore topmast staysail and inner jib—canted her head to port. The lower topsails were sheeted home and she gathered sternway, moving in a curve that would bring the wind out on the starboard side.

"Midships y'r hellum."

I repeated the order, kept my helm amidships while the hands forward trimmed the head sheets as the swinging of the ship brought the wind out on the starboard bow.

"Hard a'starboard," murmured the Old Man when the topsails filled.

"Hard a'starboard, sir." I gave her the helm and as she gathered headway, the ship swung more rapidly to port, her bows crossing a path of bright moon-lit water against which masts, rigging and all the cordage of the running gear stood out sharp and black as did two conical buoys, fine on our port bow. These carried bright-green flashing lights, marking the position of a wreck. The Captain watched their bearing closely until they were on the other bow and we had passed well clear to windward of them.

"Steady her on sou'-sou'-west."

"Sou'-sou'-west, sir." Then I struck five bells. It was 2.30 a.m. Both watches were setting every stitch of canvas possible—topgallants, royals, main skysail, foresail, mainsail, cro'jack and all the staysails on main and mizzen. The Old Man was making for the Backstairs Passage between Kangaroo Island and the mainland. That would cut two hundred miles from the distance to Melbourne. He was making the most of the fair wind, to get down to the strait before it shifted to the south-west or, worse still, to the south. This was the season of highest frequency for the "Southerly Buster", a sort of Australian *pampero*. They sometimes happened after a dry, hot spell such as we had had and they came without warning. With a cloudless sky, the wind might drop suddenly and then come with an icy blast out of the south and be blowing a howling gale in a matter of minutes.

That was the gist of the talk between Captain German and Mr. Fowler as they stood by the binnacle. But the wind was steady and fresh, the *Arno* heeled as steadily to port, going quietly through the smooth water at a good ten knots and steering very sweetly. Sheets, tacks and braces were so perfectly trimmed that every part of the vast area of canvas—more than twenty thousand square feet of it—received its proper share of the thrust of the breeze in perfect balance. The ship seemed to steer herself, once I had her steadied on her course.

The Old Man puffed at his blackened clay pipe as he looked around and then aloft at the sails of the mizzen. In the moonlight they were the colour of bleached grey clam shells but they were very beautiful against their background of starlit sky.

"Not carrying any weather helm, de Mierre boy?"

"No, sir, neither any lee helm. She's just going along by herself, sir."

"Aye. Well, keep her that way." He turned to Mr. Fowler and said, "I'll away below. Let me know if there's any change. Good night."

"Aye aye, sir. An' good-night to ye."

At 4.00 a.m. I made eight bells. The look-out on the fo'c's'le head chimed a reply and with his hail, "All's well," I could hear the tramping of both watches coming aft to muster on the quarter-deck.

There were some new names and some of the old ones were missing. Five men had been left in Adelaide. The Bos'n had been discharged and four A.B.s, including Flynn the chantyman and Connor the New Englander, had deserted. Why they did so is anybody's guess. They were all men in their late forties or early fifties, no longer so young as to be thirsting for adventure. Whatever wages were due them were left behind and they went ashore with empty pockets which, at first glance, seems stupid.

But they had been in the ship only three months; their pay was £3 per month, total £9. They had received one month's pay in advance when they signed Articles in London and very probably had bought as much from the slop-chest in the way of tobacco, boots, dungarees, etc., as the Captain would sell them against the amount due to them after the advance had been worked off.

So we can be sure that they had left very little behind and the few shillings that this may have been was a cheap price to pay for a passage to Australia. Australia offered much for the seasoned sailor. There were many shore jobs that he could do, at good wages and with an eight-hour day; or he could run round the coast in other sailing-ships, at £5 the run from port to port, taking the place of other deserters. And, if and when he felt like it, he could ship homeward again at Australian wages of £4 10s per month—half as much again as he had signed on for in London. Maybe they were not so stupid.

After two days of moderate, favourable winds, on March 7th, we picked up the light on Cape Otway at four bells in the first watch, 10.00 p.m. and, with the wind free on the port side, stood up towards Port Phillip Heads, some sixty-three miles to the north-east. Shortly before dawn we were nearing the Pilot Ground so we shortened down. Hardly were we down from aloft when the man on look-out struck one bell; he had sighted the lights of the pilot vessel, over to the eastward. We burned a blue flare and she promptly responded by altering down towards us. The Pilot climbed over our rail just as the sun came up from behind the land to the north-east.

"Good morning, Pilot."

"'Morning, Cap'n. You can give her the to'gal'nts'ls and royals, please."

When the Pilot came aboard we were less than five miles from Port Phillip which is a completely land-locked gulf. It is about thirty-four miles wide from east to west and extends thirty-one miles to its northern extremity at Port Melbourne in Hobson's Bay. The entrance to this gulf is between two head-lands—Point Lonsdale and Point Nepean. The distance between is just over $1\frac{1}{2}$ miles but the passage between the shallows that extend from them is about half that width. For a sailing-ship, with favourable winds, this is wide enough for comfortable navigation but in relation to the large expanse of water in the gulf on one side and to the vastness of the ocean on the other, it is extremely narrow. The tides pour through the entrance at a speed of from five to eight knots like a mill-race, known to sailors as the "Rip".

It must have been close to high water for, with the fresh breeze and a strong current under her stern, within half an hour of leaving the pilot-cutter the *Arno* was approaching the "Rip" and the Pilot asked for the mainsail to be set. The wind took hold of the great sail and it ballooned, billowed and cracked over our heads, but all hands were on deck to handle it. With the port watch I was down in the lee scuppers hauling the sheet aft at the same time as the starboard watch were heaving down the tack.

It was a moment that is still vivid in my memory. It was so unusual for the ship to be sailed so boldly, piling on the canvas, so close to the land. When the main sheet was fast to its bollard we stood, fascinated, by the lee rail. For those thrilling minutes it was within a foot of the creaming water that flew astern. In the tumult of the tide race the sea boiled around us. Rocks, wet and shining with weed, flashed by so close that we could have pitched our caps on to them. Melbourne only thirty miles away! We should be up there by noon. Such was our excited talk while the wind sang merrily in the rigging and in the brilliant sunlight the *Arno* fairly leapt through the water.

But once clear of the gut, and of the shallows that crowd the gulf for the first ten miles, the wind backed to the northward and we had a hard beat of it, the whole day long. The sun was down when at last we got up to Hobson's Bay. As we approached our anchorage, we moved quickly about the decks. The Mate and Second Mate let the halliards run on all three masts—royals, top-gallants, upper topsails, staysails and jibs and the lower topsail sheets. The air was full of a cheerful noise.

79

There was the throaty chuckling of the patent sheaves of the big halliard blocks, the rattle of jib and staysail hanks, clattering down the stays, like the jingles of a host of tambourines. And through it all came the hearty song of the sailors, in rollicking tones that wandered up and down the scale with their "he-bo-ho-yaho-ho-ho-ho-ho", as we hauled on the ropes, hand over hand. They were happy that the anchor would soon be down, that they had reached the port of final unloading with its promise of fresh food, foaming beer and friendly females, and a whole night of undisturbed rest when they went to their bunks. The few days in Adelaide had served only to whet their appetites.

The wind went down with the sun. The ship lay to her anchor, motionless. After a long day, hauling on sheets, tacks and braces, beating up the bay, and all the sail handling, even the toughest was glad to get his head down when a last pipe had been smoked after supper. That is, unless, like me, he had an anchor watch to keep.

Mine was the lucky draw—the first two hours, 8.00 to 10.00 p.m.—and then seven hours below. The street-lights ashore seemed closer than the short mile and a half that they were distant from us. Across the bay the leading lights for Williamstown and Melbourne winked and flashed. Near by were the riding lights of two other sailing-vessels, dripping their warm, yellow reflections on the placid water. Otherwise, they were not even dark shapes; the glimmer of the oil-lamps in their fo'c's'les and cabins was too feeble to be visible. Only the occasional sound of their bells, marking the passage of the hours, broke the stillness of the night.

In the morning we rigged the hoses to wash down. All the brass-work was polished and finished off with powdered whiting so that it sparkled in the sun. Mr. Fowler went about the decks, his eyes everywhere, making sure that all should be ship-shape for port. The yards were trimmed dead square to a hair's breadth and some of us were sent aloft to shake out and furl again those sails that he found lacking in perfection for a harbour stow.

Up aloft, when the job was done, there was time to look around and at the other ships. Astern lay a big four-masted barque with stump topgallant masts. The other vessel was a couple of hundred yards away to port. She was a very graceful four-masted barque with double topgallants and royals, deep-laden with wheat. A tug had given her a line and, as we watched, she broke out her anchor and passed close by on her way down to the "Rip" to start her homeward passage. We could easily read her name; it was *Wendur*.

"What a beauty!" exclaimed Bullock who was with me on the fore topgallant yard. "There goes my next ship," he said. Bullock had taken to the life of a sailing-ship like a duck to water and his face was alight as he watched her go.

For me, no sailing-vessel was so beautiful as a lofty, three-masted, full-rigged ship but the *Wendur* was indeed good-looking and she was also a smart ship. Once she had crossed the Pacific from Newcastle, New South Wales, to Valparaiso in twenty-nine days, or just about half the usual passage time; it was a distance of 6,330 miles over which she averaged about 218 miles a day. Such extraordinary passages, however, were most frequently due to a lucky succession of favourable conditions; wind and weather were more the governing factors than exceptional seamanship. On this voyage she had left London a month before we did and had taken ninety-one days from the Channel to Adelaide, compared with our *Arno*'s eighty-seven days.

During the forenoon a steam-launch from the Agents came out from Port Melbourne with the news that we would not go alongside until the following morning. So we spent the day getting all the ropes off the decks. We hung them in long coils over the rat-lines and stopped them neatly to the shrouds. Then the cargo pendants were rigged over the main hatch. In the morning, steam would be raised on the donkey-boiler and we should be ready for discharging as soon as we got alongside.

Another visitor of that forenoon was a boat from the "bald-headed" barque, with four apprentices at the oars and the beetle-browed Captain in the stern-sheets. This was Captain Mullen coming aboard to look around and have a yarn with our Old Man. He was coming to look at his old ship, for it was he who had been given command of the *Arno* following her abandonment four-teen years before.

The barque, his present command, was the *Pinmore*, a vessel destined for an adventurous but sad end. In March 1917, she was destroyed by a German commerce raider commanded by the so-called "sea-devil" von Luckner whose victims were practically all defenceless sailing-vessels. That meeting was an unhappy coincidence because von Luckner is said to have sailed in the *Pinmore*'s fo'c's'le as a seaman in 1902.

The following day we towed up the Yarra River and made fast alongside the wharf between two other vessels, a three-masted barque, the *Loch Etive*, and the four-masted barque, *Province*. The *Loch Etive* was then over thirty years old but in the past she had once made a passage to Melbourne in seventy days. On this voyage she had sailed from the Clyde five weeks before we left the Channel and gone out to Adelaide in ninety-one days. She is also worthy of notice because Joseph Conrad served aboard her as Third Mate in his youth.

On March 19th, all cargo discharged and with 850 tons of dirt and rubble ballast in the hold, we towed back to Hobson's Bay and anchored about two miles out from the Railway Pier of Port Melbourne, in company of several other ships already there, waiting for orders. The ten days at the wharf had passed like a flash and were wonderfully pleasant. As in Adelaide, there had been the same disagreeable periods in the hold trying to frustrate light-fingered stevedores. Otherwise, we kept our *Arno* looking smart; we stood on the quay, scrubbing and scaling away the rust and crust of salt, and painting the ship's side.

The Seamen's Mission at the foot of Flinders Street was not far away and we spent several happy evenings there with the apprentices and sailors of the other ships in port. The fun was organised by a group of young men and ladies who were so completely at home with the sailors that these soon shed their shyness and, egged on by their shipmates, got up on the platform to sing their song or give whatever entertainment they were famous for in their own ships.

Our effort was to make fools of ourselves in a charade which was so involved that nobody could guess the word we were supposed to be acting until in the last scene our clown, Paddy, with his face blackened with burnt cork, crawled about on all fours, sniffing very loudly. Then everyone yelled "Black tracker!" and Paddy brought the house down by walking off on his hands. That and a Welsh song, in a deep baritone voice, by Morris who was still dressed as the farmer's wife of the charade, made us the hit of the evening.

On that occasion we met Rob Anderson. He had served his time in the ships of the Loch Line and had just passed for Second Mate. He was bubbling over with happiness and spontaneous fun. He took us to his home where we met his pretty sisters and his father, Captain Anderson, who was Manager of the stevedoring company which was handling our ship. It was a most fortunate meeting. Once the old man had looked us over, we were made very welcome. For Morris, Mantell and me, the house in Albert Park became a home during our stay in Melbourne and, less than a year later, my friendship with Rob Anderson was of very great help to me.

We lay in Hobson's Bay for ten weeks before we received orders.

Our crew of working hands on deck had been reduced to seven A.B.s, one ordinary seaman, Bullock, and six apprentices. Five seamen had been left in Adelaide and two in Melbourne. Beale, with a "pay-day" of one shilling, had gone back to Tasmania. The other ordinary seaman, a youth named Cousins, had also been discharged. He had previously been a golf caddy at Epsom, where our Owners played. Whatever illusions he may have had of the romance of the sea perished very quickly. During the voyage he had been continually miserable.

For us apprentices there was plenty of boat work and sometimes it was a challenge; one that we enjoyed. In the late months of Australian autumn the weather was frequently boisterous with strong winds and, in the shallow waters of Hobson's Bay, rough seas. The *Arno* and all the other ships lying there were empty except for their ballast which lay on the floor of their holds. With that weight as low as it could be placed and all the heavy top-hamper of lofty steel masts and yards, in anything of a blow, or in any kind of a swell, we all rolled heavily and crazily, the ships often rolling in opposite directions and looking rather ridiculous.

But ridiculous or not, in those conditions, to put the boat in the water and get safely away from the ship could be a hazardous exercise, as we found on one breezy morning.

Among the able seamen was one Jos Hedderson. When he joined the ship he had given his age as forty-six but, if that were true, he was prematurely old. He had grizzled mutton-chop whiskers and unfailingly wore a deerstalker cap, with a peak before and behind, ear-flaps always turned up and their ribbons tied in a little bow on top of the crown. He looked very quaint but he was a disagreeable, pig-headed man, a regular old whale of a sea-lawyer. Nothing in the ship, nobody in the ship—himself excepted—was any good. He refused duty and, all efforts to bring him to reason having failed, he had to be taken ashore and put in jail.

A gale of wind from the north had been blowing all night and it was still fresh in the morning when we swung the port boat out. When the boat was level with the rail, Mantell and I jumped in and stood—he in the stern and I in the bow—to fend off from the ship's side as it was lowered. Paddy and the Second Mate were standing on the topgallant rail lowering away when, all of a sudden, the ship rolled heavily to starboard. In trying to preserve his balance, Paddy let the forward fall "take charge". The rope flew off the belaying pin on the davit, out of his hands, and my end of the boat dropped. I was pitched out, luckily clear of the ship's side, took a header into the water and sank several feet.

To save the boat—now hanging almost vertically from the after davit—from being swept astern by wind and tide, the Second Mate immediately let the after fall go with a run. The heavy boat crashed down to the water and I took the full force of its splash in my face the moment I got to the surface. Instinctively, I seized hold of the gunnel and climbed into the boat where I found Mantell collapsed in the sternsheets, one hand clutching the other, evidently in great pain. When my end of the boat had dropped, to save himself he had made a wild grab at the after fall, just at the moment when the Second Mate let it go. His hand had been taken into the block and one of his fingers was mashed to pulp.

We got Mantell aboard for first aid. I put on dry clothing and at last we got away from the ship with our four passengers—Mantell going to hospital, Hedderson going to jail and the Captain and Mr. Fowler going along to make sure that he did so.

We were pulling against a strong head wind and a nasty short sea. It soon became evident that we were being driven astern faster than we could pull ahead, and being swept out into the gulf.

"Pull, boys, pull!" cried the Old Man. "Lay into it!" He got to his feet. "Come, Mr. Fowler. We'll have to help them." He left the tiller and sat with me, double-banking, pulling stroke.

Mr. Fowler took off his bowler hat and carefully stowed it in safety in one of the lockers of the sternsheets. Then he went to the second thwart to add his weight to Isdale's oar. Our position was hardly improved. Although we pulled with all our strength we made no headway. We still drifted astern. Poor Mantell was almost fainting with pain and our only consolation was that old Hedderson, perched up in the bow, was getting well soused with spray.

It seemed hopeless to go on bucking wind and sea, losing ground all the time. We could have hoisted the lug-sail but with a dead head-wind it would have meant a beat of several hours and about twelve miles to cover the five miles straight-line distance to the pier.

The Old Man decided to make for the shore, about two miles away to the eastward. It offered no shelter but we would find shallower water where we could anchor until the wind eased. So Captain German went back to the tiller and, hardly had he taken his seat, than our luck changed. Away inshore he sighted a small tug heading up towards Port Melbourne. Without loss of time, we burned a blue flare. The tug immediately altered course down to us, we gave her our painter, stowed oars with some thankfulness and, in less than an hour, were alongside the pier.

And then, of course, the wind dropped and the sun shone merrily overall as our passengers walked along the pier and we pulled back to the ship.

At four o'clock we were back at the pier again, our boat all dry and ship-shape, waiting for the Mate and the Old Man. The first to appear was Mr. Fowler. Weaving jauntily in short tacks he came down the pier, steering a rather erratic course, several sheets in the wind but still under command. At the head of the steps one of the timber piles of the pier, a mooring bollard, rose to a height of about four feet. Here Mr. Fowler brought up.

He draped an arm nonchalantly over the bollard and stood there with his bowler hat cocked over one eye. A massive gold watch-chain of a type very popular with shipmasters, fashioned like the anchor-cable of a ship, hung across the paunchy waistcoat of his neat blue suit. He beamed at us very happily, his face red as the rising sun, but he would not come aboard.

84

Then Captain German came along the pier followed by a nondescript young man who carried two large rabbits. Morris took the rabbits and passed them down into the boat while the Captain was paying the young man for his services. Whatever he received, the young man was far from satisfied. He looked at the coppers in his hand, then at the Old Man and poured out a flood of such foul language that it was new even to us. We were shocked both at the language and the disrespect and Morris' instant reaction was to swipe him across the face with the bony back of his hand. Just as promptly, the young man—who was much the heavier of the two—aimed a hefty blow on Morris' face and then took to his heels. Morris, the blood streaming from his nose and wild with rage, went after him and got so close that he was able to make a flying tackle. Down they both crashed with a hollow thud that echoed and boomed under all the timbers the length of the pier.

Morris jumped up and hauled the young man to his feet, shouting, "Get up you foul-mouthed swine. Come on; put your hands up while I knock the bloody head off you." The young man had no alternative but, although he got in a couple of smart raps to Morris' face, he was no match for him. Not only had Morris played rugby for his school but he had also been something of a boxer. In a matter of minutes he delivered a succession of hearty punches to the young man's head and finished up by catching him a smack on the jaw which sent him flying backwards to land with a mighty splash in the sea.

We ran down the pier and watched for him to break surface. It was not deep. He could stand with his head above water and make his way to the beach even if he could not swim. Being assured of this, we ran back to the boat. As we took our places at the oars, Captain German spoke rapidly in Welsh to Morris who made no reply, blushed and hung his head, but seemed pleased. We never did learn what was said but I am sure that the score for one bottle of brandy was wiped off the slate that afternoon.

"Come, Mr. Fowler, come aboard."

Mr. Fowler had remained supporting his bollard through all the strife, quite unperturbed; if anything, he smiled more broadly in approval when Morris knocked the beachcomber overboard. To the Captain's hail he responded with a dignified, "Aye aye, sir," and came down into the boat where, no doubt to emphasize his soberness, instead of sitting firmly down he perched his fat backside on the gunnel with his feet on the quarter-bench.

"Come inboard, Mr. Fowler. Sit down properly or ye'll be over the side."

"Thank ye, sir. I'm fine," replied Mr. Fowler.

We had pushed off from the pier and sat with our oars tossed, awaiting the word of command.

"Give way all. Pull, boys, pull," came the order. We pulled one powerful united stroke and Mr. Fowler tipped over backwards into the sea. Fortunately, he had kept his grasp on the gunnel and, with his legs pointing to the sky, by great exertion he was just able to raise his purple face above water. His bowler hat, floating on its crown, bobbed about close to his head and the whole incident struck us as being so comical that we were convulsed with laughter and had great difficulty in pulling him aboard. He was no mean weight. When at last, after hauling on arms and legs, we had him safely in the sternsheets we sat down and roared with laughter. We laughed so heartily that in spite of his discomfiture Mr. Fowler joined in; probably, the laughter plus his ducking put him on a more even keel.

The hands were sweeping down for the night when we got alongside. A row of grinning faces lined the rail. Morris had a handsome black eye and the water was still dripping from Mr. Fowler's clothes. He climbed the jack-ladder under perfect control and, with his hat square over his brows, walked across the quarter-deck to his cabin, very composed, as though to come aboard in that condition were quite normal.

When we were not handling our boat we joined the men down in the lower hold where, during all the time that the ship lay at anchor, they were employed chipping and scaling the rust off the inside of the hull-plating, the frames and the iron stringers. We worked by the light of candles wedged into pieces of hoop-iron which had been bent in such a way that they could be clipped on to the frames. It was a necessary but disagreeable job. All day long the empty ship echoed to the monotonous pounding of chipping-hammers and it was a vast relief when at last they were put aside and in blessed silence we covered the bare metal with a coating of boiled linseed oil. When that was dry and well set it had the consistency of an adhesive plastic film and made an excellent base for the red oxide paint that we put on top of it.

Able Seaman Brown was the only one of us who did not seem to mind the racket of the chipping-hammers, the dust and the flying flakes of rust that stuck in your hair, stuck to your skin, got down inside your clothing and stuck to your belly, and kept you squinting to protect your eyes. Brown hummed or whistled to himself while he worked. Nothing could sour his good humour.

At "smoke-ho" time, mid-morning or mid-afternoon, when we paused for a fifteen-minute spell, Brown would settle himself on the dirt ballast, in a hollow that fitted his curves. Then he would get his pipe going, haul a newspaper from under his dungaree jumper and puff and read with all the peace and composure of a West-End clubman.

But, one morning, what he read made him take his pipe from his mouth and shout with laughter. It was an account of two young women who, when walking on the beach, had been assaulted by a sailor from one of the ships in port. What had amused Brown was that while the sailor attacked the one the other belaboured him with her umbrella but with little deterrent effect because she in turn was hove down by the sailor who treated her with equal ardour.

This, of course, started much ribald talk and joking among the men which filled me with youthful fury. "What's so bloody funny about it?" I said. "Think of the poor young women. That swine should be castrated and then hung."

Brown roared with delight. "He was hung alright. Castrated! I think he should get the Victoria Cross or, anyhow, the Distinguished Service Order. He earned both of them."

So the days passed. We were feeding well, working reasonably from six o'clock in the morning until 5.30 in the evening and, when not ashore, getting a lot of sleep. For some part of every day we apprentices were in our boat, pulling the two miles to the pier and back. It was a very healthy life.

Many sailing-ships came through the anchorage, bound in or outward, or to take up a berth close by, waiting for orders. Among the latter were two three-masted barques, the *Loch Ryan* and my old friend the *Quilpue* that I had first seen four years before when roaming the Liverpool Docks and with whom we had been in company in the Atlantic when homeward-bound after our three-year voyage in the *Main*.

The *Loch Ryan* stays in my memory because her four apprentices—tough young Scots—included one who had already served an apprenticeship in marine engineering. Now in his third year in the half-deck he was the happiest example of the rollicking, windjamming sailor that I ever met.

Then there were two full-rigged ships that held our special attention. One was the *Cromdale* which had been built in 1891, one year after I was born, two years before the *Arno*. She was one of the last of the wool-clippers, beautiful and lofty. But now the steamers had taken the wool and she had taken her place, along with the rest of us, carrying whatever freight she could get. She had brought lumber from Norway, with a passage of 114 days.

The other ship was not so good-looking; she lacked the painted ports and white masts and yards of the *Cromdale*. Her exterior was just workmanlike and economical, her hull painted the same colour as her masts and yards—a sort of pale yellow-ochre, so-called mast-colour. But she had made a smart passage of seventy-three days from Hamburg. For a deeply laden ship that was very good. We watched her in silence as she towed by, her crew with arms folded, on her rails, looking at us just as attentively. She was sharply silhouetted against the evening sky. The water gurgled merrily under her forefoot, so close was she, and tinkled along her side-plating. Before she passed in front of it, the low sun coloured the face of her white figurehead, and under her counter I read: *Melpomene*, Hamburg—little thinking that I would ever see her again.

In the last week of May we got our orders for Newcastle, New South Wales. Our good times in Melbourne were coming to an end. Morris, Mantell and I had been especially fortunate because most of our weekends had been spent at Captain Anderson's house. Mantell had lived there for some days after he came out of hospital. The girls were as beautiful as they were charming, to one he had lost his very susceptible heart and the prospect of sailing was, for him, very sad.

Then, to our complete astonishment and joy, Captain German sent for me to tell me that he had agreed with Captain Anderson that his two daughters and their friend, Eileen Manning, should come aboard and have tea with the three of us.

They came on the Friday afternoon, bringing baskets of cakes and dainties. We, spick and span in our monkey-jackets, received them at the gangway. Captain German was there, too. He was going ashore in the launch, and he greeted the girls with a heartiness that was a little embarrassing.

"Welcome aboard my ship, young ladies. I'll not be back before five o'clock. Until then please make yourselves at home in the saloon. And see that these young men behave themselves in there." Then came the embarrassing part. After pausing and blushing, with a puzzled expression on his face, he added. "We'll be away at daylight. They'll not be ashore again. You can use my cabin for your 'hugging, mugging and kissing'!"

And blushing more deeply than ever—even as deeply as we—he went over the gangway.

Captain German was very much the simple sailor. His last remark was only his solution of the awkward problem of how to let the young ladies know that if they wished to use his bathroom and W.C.—the only ones in the ship—they were welcome to do so.

It was all very kind of him, much more than we three deserved after our conduct at Christmas, and more than any of us sought in terms of "hugging, mugging and kissing". Actually, we were all a little overcome by our responsibilities as hosts in the Captain's "house". It was a very sedate and very happy party.

But at last they had to go. And poor Mantell, waving at the vanishing launch, could not see them for his tears.

7 Newcastle, New South Wales

By noon of the following day the *Arno* was at sea. We had towed from Hobson's Bay in a flat calm and there was very little wind outside. However, it was from the north-west—a fair wind—and, in her ballast trim, drawing only sixteen feet of water, with every stitch of canvas set, the ship went quietly along at about five knots.

At noon on Sunday we were off Wilson's Promontory where we hoisted our numbers—the string of flags giving our name and port of registry—and on Friday, June 4th, at daylight, in company with three other ships, we were outside the entrance of Newcastle harbour. It was a slow and uneventful passage of six hundred miles from Melbourne which we had covered in six days. With a tug ahead and the Pilot aboard, we passed between the breakwaters and into the harbour where we made fast to the dolphins alongside one of the ballast jetties in Stockton.

Newcastle, New South Wales, lies at the mouth of the Hunter River which flows down from the north until it meets the point of land where the city is built. It then turns north-east for the short run of three-quarters of a mile to the breakwaters and out to sea. The eastern bank of the river is the peninsula of Stockton which in 1909 contained only a few streets of houses and pubs at its southern end. From these, less than a mile away to the north—where the half-dozen ballast jetties are located—was a narrow neck of sandhills between river and sea.

Across the river, on its western bank, is Carrington with its mile and a half length of loading berths, its railway tracks bearing long trains of coal-hoppers which the cranes would lift from the trucks and swing over the hatches for tipping into the holds of the vessels moored there. That was known as the "Dyke" and, like the ballast jetties, every loading berth was occupied. The port was full of sailing-ships and it really was a forest of spars, masts, yards and the jibs of the cranes that rose above the clouds of coal-dust. Never before had we seen so many sailing-vessels crowded so close together. There were thirty-two of them, all told, sixteen British, nine Norwegian—most of them former British ships—three Germans, two French and two Russian-Finns.

The British ships were the *King Edward, Cambrian Princess, Pharos, Comlie-*

At sea, with skysail and royals furled, the *Arno* looked like this, her sister-ship the *Forth*

bank, *Sardhana, Olivebank, Naiad, Caradoc, Pinmore, Arno, Cromdale, Owee-nee, Isle of Arran, Melville Island, Lyderhorn,* and the *Clan Macpherson.*

The others were: from Norway, the *Dalston, Western Monarch, Illawarra, Ingomar, Canterbury, Hiawatha, Mabella* (ex *Anaurus*), *Lysglymt* and *Majorka* (ex *Clan Mackenzie*); from Germany, the *Reinbek* (ex *Lord Roseberry*), *Ellerbek* and *Goldbek* (ex *Miltonburn*); from France, the *Hoche* and the *Brenn*; and the Russian-Finns were the *Glenbank* and the *Favell.*

In the dog-watches at sea, most of the sailor's yarning was about the ships he had sailed in and the men that he had sailed with. So, for him, Newcastle was an exciting place; a grand place. Practically all the ships were already known to him by experience, by reputation or by name. And, with so many ships in port, at night the little town was crowded with sailors, one could almost say infested with them; and, inevitably, old shipmates met and rejoiced at their meeting and drank freely and with jollity.

In a more restrained manner, this was also true of the sixty or seventy apprentices who roamed the streets. More restrained, because we had neither the money nor the taste for so much beer and we usually ended up, still very sober, at the Seamen's Mission to meet the apprentices from the other ships and make a lot of noise with our swapping of tall yarns and our boisterous laughter.

Each group generally stayed together under the watchful eyes of the senior apprentices, in a sort of one-for-all-and-all-for-one spirit, to make sure that the first voyagers behaved themselves and that no one got to windward of them. There were four of Andrew Weir's ships in port and their combined number of some twenty young men, all wearing the same house-flag in their cap-badges, put them in a dominant position.

But they were a happy lot. In these rather dreary times of a completely mechanised Merchant Marine, when there is so much debate on what additional creature comforts and financial inducement must be held out in order to attract young men to a life at sea, I have often thought of them. Of creature comforts they had none at all. Of money only the return of the premium paid by their parents as an earnest of their good behaviour, dribbled out to them in careful accord with the rate of efflux of their indentures.

But in their long voyages they came to know the unselfish comradeship which gave the sailing-ship apprentice some compensation for the very hard life that he shared with his shipmates. Of course, none of them bothered their heads with such thoughts. They were just jolly young sailors, happy to be with their own kind, joking and chaffing about their respective ships and the people in them. And it was amusing to see the eagerness with which the youngest took part in the sailor-talk. Young Stringer of the *Isle of Arran*, a first voyager, the peak of his cap cocked over one eye, puffing a big pipe, talked with Banbury and me almost with awe because we were within a few weeks of finishing the four years that he had just started.

Then back to our ships, some to the Dyke and we to the ferry across to Stockton, to walk the few streets past the pubs where the crews of the German ships, which lay astern and ahead of the *Arno*, were singing a rousing sailor's song. We left the road and took the path which led to our jetty, trudging ankle-deep in the soft sand until we saw something that brought us to a halt. On the crest of the dune, close ahead, a black shape against the moonlit sky, was a small sturdy figure. He stood with his legs apart and arms outstretched, his head thrown back, addressing who knows what phantoms of his befuddled brain.

"I'm D'Arcy!" he shouted. "That's my name, Dominic D'Arcy. *Homo sum.*

I'm a bloody man. I don't care a shoot for any Virgin. I don't care a shoot for Je-ee-sus." His voice rose to a scream and sank like an expiring rocket, so that the name Jesus came out like a moan. Then he collapsed, as though his final blasphemy had felled him.

He lay with his face in the sand, inert as a dead man. So we opened the neck of his shirt, picked him up and carried him down to the ship and into the fo'c's'le, where we pushed him into his bunk.

In that period of waiting for our loading berth we spent the days on stages hung over the side, scaling and painting the hull. The morning following our encounter I took my place on the stage, next to D'Arcy who looked as fresh as a daisy.

"Morning, D'Arcy," I said. "How did you sleep?"

D'Arcy grinned. "Slept like a dead man, I did. But I woke up with a mouth like the bottom of a parrot-cage . . . sand and all. Bunk full of sand too. Damned if I know how I got there. None of the blokes in the fo'c's'le know anything about it. Was it you half-deck people?"

Then I told him. How we had found him spouting Latin and how he had cursed and blasphemed, so terribly that a bolt from heaven had struck him down.

As he listened, the changing expression of his face passed from silly "broth-of-a-boy" satisfaction to horror. "Oh no!" he said; clutching the amulet—the religious medal that hung inside his shirt—he crossed himself, muttering rapidly. And for many days thereafter he was a very sober member of the crew.

On another night, walking along Hunter Street on our way to the ferry, we came across two of our seamen standing one on each side of a lamp-post, relieving themselves of some of the beer that they had been drinking with so much jollity but so little discretion. Roaring with laughter they were, each standing directly in the other's line of fire, like a couple of dirty urchins. Then the police came along and Frank Brown, forty-one, and Michael Shawn, fifty-two, spent the night in jail. Next morning they were sentenced to a fine of twenty shillings, or seven days' imprisonment for improper behaviour.

The following week we moved over to the Dyke and made fast at the coal wharf, between the *Oweenee* and the *Cromdale*, with a whole fleet of fine ships stretching away in both directions; and here we nearly lost our cat, Slushy—the "Cook's Mate", as we called him.

Stockton had not appealed to him at all if one excepts the abandon with which he flung the sand about after the call of nature had been met. He did prefer that to the cold, wet, iron scuppers. But he made no attempt to go aboard any of the other ships lying there. They were Germans and Russian-Finn and perhaps presented problems of language or diet or, what is more likely, perhaps they had no sailor-cats aboard.

At the Dyke in Carrington it was different. There were endless British ships awaiting his inspection. He stalked down the brow—the broad gangplank that spanned the few feet over the pontoon which held the ship off the wharf—and literally swaggered along the quay.

"Look at him, Jack Desborough," I said to the cook. "That cat's up to some mischief. He is probably going to get drunk, or something, and end up in jail. Look what happened to Brownie and Mike Shawn for peeing against a lamppost."

The cook grinned as he watched the cat disappear. "He'll be alright. He's not all that fond of beer. It'll be 'something', I expect. And they'll not run him in for that. Not in this town! He'll be back."

But the days passed without any sign of the moggy. The cook had gone the length of the wharves calling him by name and was really worried that he might have been shanghaied aboard some outward-bounder. They were sailing every day. It looked hopeless.

When we took up our loading berth I was made night-watchman. "You're big enough and fat enough to look after us all while we're asleep. And if there's anything comes along that ye can't handle there's meself'll come and help ye." So said Mr. Fowler; and I was delighted. The nights were usually amusing, sometimes exciting and there was a cosy fire in the galley to sit in front of once all hands were aboard. During the day I slept soundly in the forenoon, in spite of the noise of the coal being dumped into the hold. I went ashore every afternoon, very often ending up at the Mission for a cup of tea, a pipe and a yarn with the Chaplain. He was a very fine young parson named Ives. He seemed to love his work among seafaring men and was equal to any situation that might arise whether of fists or fellowship. Fists, of course, were only used in the bouts of boxing that he arranged, any other occasion of fisticuffs would be enthusiastically taken care of by a dozen or more volunteers to "throw the swine out".

One or two other apprentices who were acting as night-watchmen of their ships would also be in Mr. Ives' study and I often met there a boy named West from Shaw Savill's barque *Pharos* and sometimes a young American who was an ordinary seaman aboard a Welsh barque, the *Caradoc* of Aberystwyth. It was through meeting him that I recovered our cat. Walking back to our ships we came to the *Caradoc* which lay three berths ahead of the *Arno*. She was a neat little vessel that I had often admired when passing by and I was glad to go aboard and have a look around.

And a really trim little barque she was. Most of the crew, forward and aft, were related and there was as much Welsh spoken as English. Even the American boy had a few phrases. There was a snug fo'c's'le just forward of the galley, in a house on deck abaft the foremast and, aft, her handsome poop extended forward of the mizzenmast. It had two thwartship ladders at the ship's side, port and starboard. It was when going up one of these that I heard our cat. Under the ladders were a couple of lockers and, from one of these, I heard a loud and desperate yowling.

"What have you got in there?" I asked.

"Couple of cats," replied the young American. "The she-cat belongs to the ship. The one that's making all the noise is a tom that she called aboard. Sounds like he's through with her. We put 'em in there to get 'em out of the way till we get to sea. We sail in the morning."

As soon as I called, "Where's Slushy," the tom-cat went frantic, so we opened the door. The she-cat was fast asleep and did not stir but the tom, our Slushy, made a spring on to my shoulder and I carried him ashore with his claws firmly embedded in my jacket.

Saturday nights were the busy nights. There was not much time to sit quietly in the galley. From about eleven o'clock until the early hours of the morning, groups of sailors—most of them very drunk—would come staggering along the quay and many a time it was necessary to repel boarders, by banter and persuasion, and direct them to their own ships. All the ships were obliged by law to spread nets under their gangways. They were called shea-oak nets, after the name of the local beer, their purpose being to catch the sailor should he fall from the gangway and so save him from breaking his head on the pontoon or falling into the water to drown.

I kept a wooden belaying-pin lying handy on the topgallant-rail, not with the expectation of attacking anyone but as a defence should some quarrelsome drink-crazed interloper draw his knife. There were such, especially among the Russian and Swedish Finns. One had always heard that Swedes and Finns could do anything—that is, make anything—with a bit of timber and their sheath-knife, but it came as a surprise to learn, one Saturday night, that they are just as ready with the knife in a fight.

It was shortly before midnight. Three Scandinavians stumbled slowly past the *Arno*, stopping every few paces, to shout in their wavering, sing-song language. They were shouting very loudly, each apparently insisting that his story was the one that should be heard. They were thus in the condition when excessive good spirits can, in a flash, become violent.

They were a Finn from the barque *Lyderhorn* and two Swedes belonging to the *Cromdale*. At the foot of the *Cromdale*'s gangway they stopped to have a final shout at each other before parting. They made enough noise to wake all hands aboard both of our ships. So the watchman of the *Cromdale*, also a Swede, went on to the wharf to stop it and to send the Finn on his way.

That was the spark which made fun explode into fury. The Finn flew at the watchman with fists and feet. There was the sickening hollow thud of vicious body blows; the cracking smack when bony fists struck face, jaws, head; the horrible squealing retch when swiftly aimed kick dug into testicles or groin.

It was murderous, frenzied fighting. A chill silence fell when knives were drawn and suddenly there came a wild scream from the Finn as he fell—dead.

Several from the *Cromdale* ran down her gangway and Mr. Fowler, who had come aboard a few minutes earlier, came out of his cabin and over to me where I stood, horror-struck, by our gangway. It had all happened in only a few minutes.

They carried the dead man aboard, leaving the wharf quiet again except for a couple of hands, who with buckets and brooms, swilled away the pool of blood.

"The crazy sons of bitches," said Mr. Fowler. "At first I thought they'd got you. Don't you go pulling any knives, me son. Have a capstan-bar handy." He gave a fat chuckle and returned to his cabin, leaving me with my feet on the ground again, which was no doubt the purpose of his remarks.

Our own crew was a model of good behaviour. There were only eight of them in the fo'c's'le—the young ones: Bullock (eighteen), Perry (twenty-two), and D'Arcy (thirty-two); and five old shellbacks of whom Brown, at forty-one, was the youngest and the Norwegian, John Smith, at sixty-one, the eldest.

After the episode of the lamp-post, Brown and Shawn had evidently persuaded the other three that they could all get more comfortably tipsy on board.

Instead of rolling along long after midnight, they would come down the wharf about nine o'clock pleasantly oiled but well under control. Between them they carried a couple of gunny-sacks heavy with food and bottles of beer and sometimes they stamped along to the tune of a capstan chanty that Brown had made popular with us all. It was about a ship manned by fishes instead of sailors—one of the few chanties that bears repeating.

Long before they hove in sight I would hear fragments of the chorus but they were quiet as they came over the gangway, led by Brown with a clowning, tiptoe tread, a hand to his mouth, pretending panic, when his sack of bottles rattled and clinked too loudly. But his fat figure shook with his chuckles when he lowered the sack gently to the deck and then hauled out two bottles for me.

A little later, when I went forward on my rounds, I looked into the fo'c's'le as I walked past and saw that they had made the hurricane-lamp fast to the break of the windlass. It hung a few inches above the deck and about it were ranged the bottles of beer. On one of the now empty sacks, spread like a table-cloth, were the provisions they had brought from the shore: fresh butter, bread, a cold leg of mutton and a pile of raw onions.

Old Hans Hanssen was on his knees carving the meat and the other four sat on the deck with legs outstretched, leaning against sea-chests or stanchions. Each clutched his bottle and, with cheeks bulging with food, they were hard put to it to avoid choking, what with their happy laughter at the glorious sight of all that beer and their attempts to sing as well. The lamp-light shone through the bottles, it cast a warm glow over the bleak, comfortless fo'c's'le and on their weather-beaten faces.

As I went aft again I could hear that they had had a drink and a swallow and were at the chanty again, shouting the chorus. "Smith", Norwegian (sixty-one), Hanssen, German (fifty-three), Palberg, Swedish (forty-nine), Shawn, Canadian (fifty-two) and Brown, English (forty-one). Truly, old sailors. Both in experience and, for the hard life of a sailing-ship, also in years. But it was the only kind of life they knew. They were inured to it, seasoned. And, in a gale of wind, on a black, dirty night, Smith and Hanssen would climb up aloft and swing from the weather rigging on to the foot-rope of the main topgallant-yard just as confidently as any youngster, if a trifle more deliberately.

Five old sailors, not conscious of their five different nationalities but only that they are of a kind, were singing the chanty:

> "*Up jumped the eel with his slippery tail*
> *Shouting 'All hands wash decks and I'll wipe the rail!'*
> *Blow ye stormy weather*
> *We'll all pull together,*
> *Blow you stormy weather blow, blow, blow,*
> *Blow you stormy weather bl-o-o-o-ow!*"

In the morning, Sunday morning, I hoisted ensign and house-flag and then went to call Mr. Fowler. He had been carrying a fair load when he came aboard the night before. He had walked up the gangway with steady careful steps, returned my salute by politely raising his bowler hat, and stalked solemnly across the quarter-deck to his cabin. He took a lot of waking. I rapped on his bunk-board with the haft of my sheath-knife, getting no response. Only when I rattled the blade against his water-bottle did he give a final snore and grunt and open an eye.

"Gone seven bells, Mr. Fowler. Time to turn out."

"Och, to hell with it. Leave me be, now, will ye!" His eyes closed again.

"Could you not manage a bottle of cold beer, sir?"

"Eh! What! . . . What's that ye said?"

He raised himself on one elbow and by the time I had taken a tumbler from his bottle-rack and filled it he was sitting up. He drank thirstily. When the bottle was empty he gave a raucous sigh of satisfaction and a belch that would have gladdened the heart of any Arab sheik.

"That was fine and cold. Thank ye, son."

"Present from Able Seaman Brown, sir. Had it in a bucket of water all night." I was leaving his cabin when Mr. Fowler stopped me. "Did the Cap'n come aboard?"

"No, sir. He won't be back before tomorrow forenoon. He's spending the weekend with friends, on a farm or what they call a sheep station."

"Ay, so he is. I remember now." He looked at me thoughtfully, then went on. "Do ye mind what day of the month it is?"

"Sunday, 20th of June, sir."

"So it is. An' nine days from today ye'll be out of your time. Or had ye forgotten that?"

I grinned. How forget the date one had been living with for four years. Not with any longing for release; like old Brown, I too was inured to the life, but more as something to accomplish, a period of training and trials that must be gone through, must be completed before one could be accepted as an able-bodied seaman or, what for me was of greater importance, before I would be eligible to sit for the examination that would make me an officer, a qualified Second Mate . . . if I passed. No, I had not forgotten.

"Ye'll be out of your time before we're ready to sail . . . so ye will. An' did the Old Man not tell ye that he's wanting to sign you on as Third Mate at A.B.'s wages . . . to come to the west coast and home in the ship?"

"No, sir. He didn't say anything to me."

"Well, he will. An' what'll ye do?" He paused, staring at me as I smiled with pleasure at the thoughts that were racing through my head. A cabin to myself . . . eat in the saloon . . . off a tablecloth . . . £4.10s a month . . . a "pay-day" of £30 or £40 when we got home. All that money for eight or nine months when for four years I had received nothing . . . and for a large part of that time was not worth more.

Mr. Fowler must have read my thoughts from my face for he delivered himself as follows.

"As Third Mate ye'll still be in my watch, and I'll be glad to have ye. But don't be a goddamned fool, boy. Don't do it. Stay around in sailing-ships and then . . . before ye can get command . . . and when you're too bloody old to go in steam . . . there won't be any sailing-ships left . . . under the British flag.

They'll all have gone to the Norwegians and the Finns. An' then what'll ye do?

"Sure. You're happy in sail. So was I when I was your age. And I tried steam—bloody awful Liverpool-Welsh tramps. And when I got the chance to go Mate in sail again I near wept, I was so happy. But I'd be better off today if I'd stayed in steam. . . . It's too late to change now.

"No, me lad, don't you do it. You go up to Sydney and get a ship home and ye'll be away to sea again with a Second Mate's ticket in your pocket before we've finished discharging in Valparaiso."

For me that was a completely new idea. As the weeks passed and we had remained at anchor in Hobson's Bay, it seemed probable that my indentures would be completed before we could get away from Newcastle. But never for a moment had it occurred to me to do other than stay in the ship until she got home. It was what I wanted to do. But the more I thought about Mr. Fowler's advice the more right it seemed. There would be about £5, return of premium, due me, and that should be enough to keep me until I got a ship.

So when, during the course of the week, Captain German asked me if I would like to stay in the ship as Third Mate, I thanked him for his kindness and said that I would like it very much, but I thought it better that I should leave with Banbury and Isdale and get home as soon as possible to go up for my ticket.

"Is that what you really mean to do? You'll not have any idea of staying out here, on the coast, or just messing about . . . like a beachcomber?"

"No, sir. I'll get home just as soon as I can."

"Well, I'm sorry, boy. But you're right."

By the end of the week the *Arno* was full of coal up to her hatch coamings, 2,745 tons of it, and at daylight on Monday, June 28th, a tug came alongside and took us out to the Farewell Buoy where we moored. Banbury, Isdale and I went ashore with the Old Man to the Shipping Office to sign off. Here, also, nine able seamen were to be signed on the Articles. The residue of our premium was paid to us, in my case £5, and Captain German gave us a hearty hand-shake with our indentures and wished us good-bye and good luck.

We went back on board immediately afterwards because Mr. Fowler had invited us to a farewell dinner with him and the Second Mate, Mr. Raad. And for the last time we sat at table in the *Arno*'s saloon. It was a very kind gesture and Captain German must also have had some part in it, for there was a bottle of wine. Mr. Fowler filled our glasses and he and Mr. Raad wished us success.

"You are all able seamen now, boys, able to hand, reef and steer . . . all three of you fine sailors and I wish you all the luck in the world," said Mr. Fowler.

98

Then came our good-byes in the half-deck and, at last, the moment to climb over the bulwarks and down the jack-ladder into the boat. Fat old Brown, Perry, Bullock, Morris and Le Patourel gave us three hearty cheers and Mantell joined in very wistfully at the thought that we might touch at Melbourne on our way home. "And, if you do, you know who to give my love to." That was his good-bye.

We waved as long as we could see them and then made our way to the Sailors' Home where we felt very lost and uprooted.

The *Arno* and the four-masted barque *Comliebank* were to sail the following afternoon and that morning, after breakfast, we sat talking about it, trying to make plans, where to watch them go, how to get lunch and how to spend the time before the steamer left for Sydney that night. We must see them sail. Captain German and the Captain of the *Comliebank* had had so many arguments about the sailing qualities of their ships that they had finally boasted themselves into betting a champagne dinner in Valparaiso to be paid for by the one who arrived there last.

On the Newcastle waterfront it was expected that the *Comliebank* would win but we were quite sure that she would not. Our coolie ships were built for speed; she was just another fat, heavy carrier. She was only eight feet longer than the *Arno*, had three feet more beam, was about two feet deeper in the water and was carrying about seven hundred tons more cargo.

"She's no bloody clipper," said Banbury. "Old Man German will sail rings around her."

"Who's no bloody clipper?" The voice came from the Reverend Mr. Ives, Chaplain of the Mission. He was standing in the doorway with a broad smile on his handsome young face.

"I'm sorry, sir," said Banbury, blushing. "We were talking about the *Arno* and the *Comliebank* and where to go to watch them sail."

"Well," replied Mr. Ives, "I think I've got the answer to that. I came along to see if you'd like to come for a picnic up on the headland. You'd have a grand view from there."

So, shortly after mid-day, we set out with our baskets of food and climbed up on top of the headland. At that time it was still a very pleasant place, a grassy cliff-top with trees and scrub and, although it was Australian mid-winter, the sun shone brightly. Below us, we could see Nobby's Head and the break-waters thrusting out into the wide Pacific. We built a fire of brush-wood on which Mr. Ives boiled a "billy" for a brew of tea and we sat eating our sandwiches, keeping an eye on the *Arno*'s mastheads that we could see over the contour of the hill.

At last they started to move as the tug brought her around, into the channel. Then she was in full view, towing out between the breakwaters. Already we could see the hands running up the rigging to loose sail and we imagined that we could recognise those loosing topgallants and royals. There was a fresh off-shore breeze and as soon as she was clear of the breakwaters she sheeted home her topsails. The tug took her line aboard and went alongside for the Pilot and very soon afterwards she was under full sail.

We were so engrossed that we had no eyes for the *Comliebank* which came along half an hour later. Isdale sat, tailor-fashion, on the grass talking to Mr. Ives, apparently unmoved. Banbury and I stood at the edge of the cliff, not speaking, watching while royal and skysail yards were hoisted. Then, feeling the breeze, the *Arno*, our ship, became smaller and smaller until, at last, was hull-down and her sails were only a faint blue shadow on the horizon.

Never before had I felt so heartsick, so alone; and Banbury put his face in his hands and wept.

We had only been eight months in the ship. They had been happy months but there had been nothing about them to account for the depth of our feelings.

It was something else.

Before we joined the *Arno* we had been in the ship *Main* on a voyage that lasted three years and took us to New York. It was mid-winter, the ground was covered with snow, the harbour was full of ice and we six apprentices spent two weeks shovelling in the hold, discharging the mud and rubble ballast. When that was done we were sent below again to bale out and dry the bilges which were full of stinking water that had drained out of the ballast.

We were disgusted and rebellious. We could not refuse but we complained —so loudly that the Mate, Mr. Bate, could hear—that, rather than sailors, we were being treated like "bloody navvies and sewer-rats".

Mr. Bate had burst out laughing and then said, "Sure, you're all sick of it. But, believe me, you'll look back on these days as the happiest time of your life."

Now we knew that he was right. For four years we had lived the closely interdependent life of a sailing-ship; hard but sheltered. We had "belonged" to the ship, had been part of a family dwelling under the same roof—the ship. And now she had gone, taking all that with her and leaving us behind.

The happiest time of our lives had come to an end.

8 Sydney, New South Wales

After watching the *Arno* sail, Banbury, Isdale and I took the night steamer to Sydney. The fare was four shillings each, second class, and in Sydney at the Sailors' Home we paid thirty-six shillings for two weeks' board and lodging. The remaining couple of pounds in our pockets seemed a lot of money. The sun shone brightly, even though the end of June was mid-winter, and the days passed pleasantly.

But they passed very quickly and it proved difficult to find a steamer that needed a few young seamen and that was also going home. There were several sailing-ships that would have signed us on, including the *Cutty Sark*—the *Ferreira* as she then was. She lay out in the harbour and we went on board with the Chaplain of the Seamen's Mission to have a look at her. Her decks were littered with piles of sand ballast which stevedores were shovelling down the hatches into the holds but the Mate, who was supervising, gave us a warm welcome. In honour of the Chaplain's visit he gave us glasses of sweet Madeira wine and he also offered to sign the three of us on.

But we had not left our *Arno* to go wandering about the seas in another sailing-ship. We wanted to get back to Britain. How foolish we were! We were so young that we had all the time in the world but we never even paused to think that we were missing the opportunity to serve as able seamen in the most famous of all sailing-ships.

After two weeks of tramping the docks and haunting the Shipping Office, our money was nearly gone. Isdale gave it up and, while he still had enough to pay his passage, went back to Newcastle. Then our luck changed. Banbury signed on as A.B. in the White Star liner *Runic*, going home via the Cape, and I found the Orient liner *Ormuz* in dry-dock. She was twenty-three years old and had been built in a period when naval architects were still influenced by sailing-ship design. Her masts and funnels had a swift-looking rake.

I walked around the edge of the dock, wondering how I could approach someone in authority, when I almost collided with a slender, brown-faced officer who came out of the ground, as it seemed, at the head of a flight of stone steps. The cuffs of his trousers were tucked into sea-boots but the three

The Orient Line *Ormuz*

chevrons of gold braid on each shoulder told me that he was the man I was looking for, the Chief Officer.

Before he could get away, I brought my heels together and saluted.

"Yes, my lad. What is it?"

I quickly explained the position and asked if he had need of an able seaman. While I spoke, his gaze alternated between me and the men he had left ranging the anchor cables in the bottom of the dock. When I had finished he replied.

"Yes, there is a berth for an able seaman but, I'm sorry, I must promote one of my own ordinary seamen."

"If you're willing, I'll take you as a supernumerary, at one shilling the month, and you can berth aft and mess with the quartermasters."

This I accepted gratefully. I spent my last few shillings on my uniform, a blue jersey with ORIENT LINE across the chest in red letters, and a round sailor's cap with an *Ormuz* ribbon on it.

After my four hard-working, hungry years in sailing-ships, the passage home to London was like a pleasure cruise.

My duties were very light. Entering and leaving port, I was stationed on the bridge so that I could see what went on there and, at sea, after the crew had finished washing down in the morning, I spent the forenoon with a swab and a bucket of fresh water wiping the salt off the white enamel of the deck-houses of the promenade deck. The rest of the day was my own and I passed the time either talking with the third-class passengers whose deck space was just forward of the quartermasters' mess, or at my textbooks studying navigation.

Having been invited to do so, I sometimes took my problems to the Chief Officer, or the Second Officer, Mr. Brewster, both of whom willingly gave me their help. Indeed, all four bridge officers were very cordial and, in spite of their comfort and magnificence, needed little prompting to start them talking with some nostalgia of their own sailing-ship days. Even the Commander, Percy Layton, returned my salute with a smile, and used my name if he had occasion to call me.

Comfort and magnificence! That is how it seemed to me. I frequently found myself thinking of good old Mr. Fowler, a fine Irish gentleman, up to his waist in water, driving the *Arno* across the Pacific with her belly full of coal, and I wondered why he stuck it. I had come to realise that "steam" was not all dirty, hungry tramps. These men never soiled their hands; they wore smart uniform, played cricket and other deck sports with the passengers—that is, with the first-class passengers—danced with them and dined with them. And what must *their* food be when, in the quartermasters' mess, our meals surpassed the best that any sailing-ship could produce for her Captain even on Christmas Day.

Captain German ate his champagne dinner at the other man's expense, for the *Comliebank* arrived in Valparaiso one day after the *Arno*. And, a week before the *Arno* left Iquique, homeward-bound, I passed for Second Mate in Liverpool. Mr. Fowler had been right.

There had been a few happy weeks with my family and then a few more at Nautical School, to brush up and be prepared for the examination room and the kind of treatment I might expect from the examiner, Captain Keating. He was a fiery little Irishman who struck terror into the hearts of many young candidates. "I'm here to find out what you know," he would shout, "not what you don't know."

The navigation paper gave me no trouble.

Using models, I had to put a sailing-ship through all normal situations such as getting her under way from a crowded roadstead, tacking, wearing, taking in sail and heaving to in heavy weather. I also had to describe how I would send down yards and topgallant masts. This carried me back to my experience in the ship *Main* and I almost forgot the examination room and Captain Keating until he stopped me by saying, "Alright, Second Mate. That will do." I was lucky.

The Merchant Service Guild existed to protect the interests of certificated officers should they be involved in any professional trouble. I joined the Guild and when I had paid my subscription they surprised me by telling me that the Nelson Line was wanting a Second Mate for the *Highland Scot*.

It did not take long for me to decide. The Nelson Line had a fleet of steamers trading to South America. It sounded very good. I was elated that with a brand-new certificate in my pocket and no experience of steamers, I should be offered a Second Mate's berth in such a company. It was a bit too good. I should have known better.

The Marine Superintendent was a short man with a black jowl and deep-sunken eyes. He read my references slowly, handed them back and said, "Alright, she's in the South-West India Docks in London, all ready to sail. There's a pound for your train fare."

I thanked him and asked, "Where is she bound for, sir?"

"Bound for? Why, she's coming round to the Mersey."

"To load, sir?"

He opened his mouth to speak, then closed it again as though to suggest that my question was rather silly and needed no reply.

I boarded the *Highland Scot* in the dark of a winter's evening on the last day of November. It was about a year since I had sailed in the *Arno* from the same dock. When I saw the black, lifeless shape of the steamer it was with some misgiving; she resembled so closely the rusty-looking old crock that had been tied up in the same corner twelve months earlier. I climbed aboard up a steep wooden ladder and jumped down on to the after well-deck where the noise of my arrival caused the first sign of life. The door of the galley at the after end of the port alleyway was slowly opened and an old man carrying a hurricane-lantern came to meet me. He raised the lantern to have a good look at me and then lowered it again, before uttering a word.

"Good evenin', sir. You'll be the new Second Officer, ah suppose. Ah'm the steward. They told me you was comin', so I've got yer bed made up and I'll give ye a hand wi' yer dunnage."

We entered the black tunnel of the alleyway, struggling with my heavy sea-chest, until at the forward end the old man stopped and opened the door of my cabin.

"Half a mo', sir. I'll just make a light."

I expected a blaze of electric light but, instead, the steward produced matches and lit an oil-lamp that hung in gimbals against the bulkhead. He noticed my astonishment and explained, "No steam ont' donkey-boiler, no dynamo runnin'. Mebbe we'll have light termorrer and mebbe some heat." While he put the matches back in his pocket he looked at my sea-chest and then, after a diffident little cough, he said, "That's a lot of gear you've brought with you, sir, if you don't mind my saying so."

"Well," I replied, "it's no more than I'll be needing. What with white suits and all that. It'll be midsummer when we get down to Buenos Aires and that place can be as hot as Calcutta, so they say."

"Buenos Aires!" he exclaimed. "This packet'll never go down there again. She's for the knacker's yard if I know anything about it. You can see for yerself in the mornin'." He paused, wagging his old head, and then said, "But ye'll be ready for a bite of supper. Nice dish o' ham and eggs, nice pot of hot tea?"

The ship was as cold as an ice-box and I was hungry. Twenty minutes later I sat in the fusty-smelling saloon and thoroughly enjoyed the meal. I was very young—my nineteenth birthday was only three months past—and although the steward's remarks were a bit of a shock I was not worried. I lit my pipe and paced the lower bridge until the cold drove me below, and to bed.

In the morning, before breakfast, I went up to the bridge and chart-house which did indeed suggest that the old ship was bound for the breakers. There were no compasses in the binnacles, the chart-house was bare of charts, tide tables and sailing directions—that is, Admiralty Pilot books for the British coast. There were no sounding tubes should we have to cast the lead and no distress signals or blue flares. As Second Officer all these were my responsibility. When the Captain came aboard in the forenoon I met him at the gangway with my list of missing items.

Captain Brown was a genial man in his early forties. He was not disturbed. "That's alright, Mister. Hughes' have got the compasses, safely stowed away. You'd better go up there and tell them that they've got to deliver them today without fail, so that they can be shipped and ready for swinging when we get down river tomorrow. They can bring the charts and other gear at the same time." He looked at my list again and then continued, "We'll not be needing any sounding tubes, nor any distress signals, I hope, but we'd better have some. Did you find the patent log and log-line?"

"Yes, sir. They are alright," I replied, and I went on my way to Hughes', the nautical instrument people in Fenchurch Street.

As I walked away from the ship I saw her by daylight for the first time and the sight was not encouraging. She showed every sign of neglect. Her sides were covered with rust and she was so light that the upper half of her propeller was above water. A vessel of 3,060 gross tons, she was 320 feet long. Her designed speed when she came from the builders was ten knots and at her launching some fair lady had christened her *Spindrift*—a nice, romantic, sea-doggy name, better fitted to her element than her present condition. She was twenty-one years old and she looked every year of her age.

I wondered what her speed would be with only half of the propeller biting the water and what she would be like if we met any kind of dirty weather. It would not be a good idea to go to sea in a sailing-ship in ballast—drawing so little water—having left the half of your sails ashore. But I knew very little about steamers and concluded that whether deep-loaded or flying light, in ballast, they were perhaps expected to do what was wanted of them regardless of the weather.

When I got back on board in the afternoon it was to find the cabin next to mine occupied by a little man with a white moustache and "mutton-chop" whiskers. This was the Chief Officer, Mr. Ellis, who had grown old in his seafaring but for some reason or other had never been given command. He and I were the only watch-keeping officers and it would be a case of four hours on the bridge and four hours below, off duty, until we arrived in Liverpool. There was a cook in the galley; and, in the engine-room and stoke-hold, singing and the rattling of shovels showed that preparations were being made to raise steam. There was already steam on "t' donkey-boiler". The electric light could now be switched on and the radiator in my cabin was so hot that I shut it off.

While there was still some daylight I went aft to the poop to look at the mooring lines, to see how they led to the bollards on the wharf and where they were made fast on board. This would be my station—with four seamen—when we moved away in the morning, some time before dawn. On the bridge I found everything in order. Steering and standard compasses were shipped in their binnacles and the charts which would take us down to the North Foreland and into the Channel were there, all handy whenever we should need them.

Next morning, I was awakened by the rattling of my door, the noise of its curtain being ripped aside and the glare of the electric light that the steward switched on before he placed a large mug of tea on the table near my bunk.

"Nice cup o' tea," he said by way of greeting. "It's five o'clock, sir, an' pretty soon we'll be heavin' short and ye'll have to nip aloft and loose the main 'torps'l'." He grinned to show that he had got my measure, and so did I. His little joke and the hot, very sweet tea brought me to life. Half an hour later I was on the bridge, moving the handle of the engine telegraph through its various positions and checking that the response from the engine-room was correct. The small wooden steering-wheel was in the open, outside the chart-house and I put it slowly over to starboard and to port which caused the steering engine in the wheelhouse on the lower bridge to clatter *chugity-chug* and the chains and iron rods to clank along the waterways and grind over the rusty iron fairleads and sheaves, all the way aft to the quadrant at the rudder-head.

I was so absorbed by what I was doing, and by the racket that the steering gear was making, that I gave a startled movement that nearly dislocated my neck when the steam whistle burst into a sudden wheezy roar over my head. It was the Captain who had pulled the whistle lanyard. He was there with the Pilot.

"Helm and engines all correct, sir," I promptly reported to cover my confusion.

"Steam on the whistle, too, Mister. Isn't there?" he replied with a smile. "Alright. We'll go to stations. Single up aft, please. Let go everything but your backspring." Then he hailed Mr. Ellis on the fo'c's'le-head.

"Get your head-ropes and backspring aboard as soon as the tug's fast for'ard. Hold on to your breastline. And send a hand to the wheel, please."

"Aye aye, sir. Tug's fast," hailed Mr. Ellis in reply.

The tug pulled our bows away from the wharf, we got our lines aboard and moved through the lock into the river. We were not going far. It was a quiet and lonely departure. There was no crowd waving from the dock-head. The only sign of life was the small stream of horse-drawn carts, lorries, bicycles and heavy-shod workers crossing the swing-bridge when it closed behind us.

With still an hour to go before sunrise it was very dark, and bitterly cold. Under my feet the deck trembled to the throb of the propeller with its *splash-splash-splash-splash* as the blades beat the water. It was only going at slow speed. There was an ebb-tide carrying us over the ground and, in spite of the early hour and the sparsely lit buildings ashore looking so dead, the river was full of life. Craft of all sizes moved in all directions, shouts and vivid language, the hooting of tugs and the growl of our own whistle filled the air until we had worked our way past Woolwich and Erith and into the Long Reach that took us to the place below Gravesend where we swung compasses and changed Pilots and where I ate an enormous breakfast.

We were away again an hour before noon and at noon I went on the bridge to keep my first watch as an officer. The Captain and Pilot were up there also, so it was no real test. That was to come later.

It was the second day of December, 1909. The wind blew in freezing squalls out of the north-east, sighing and moaning and whipping up the muddy water so that small sprays, carried high by the freakish "williwaws", spattered on the canvas dodger, and the marshes on either side of the river looked inexpressibly dreary and grey.

We passed a very forlorn-looking Southend shortly after four bells and, as the Captain lowered his binoculars, he turned to the Pilot.

"Funny old weather, Pilot, isn't it? The glass going down as though it were going to blow like hell from the south'ard."

"Well," replied the Pilot, "if that's what you expect I don't think you'll be disappointed or surprised. They were talking about foul weather at the Pilot Station and saying that before the day's out we'll get it hard out of the sou'west. That's what they say." He filled an old briar with black-looking shag and produced a cloud of smoke that made my eyes water as it crossed my nose. "And I think they're right," he went on. "I wish we could do a couple more knots so that I could be sure of getting home to my Missus before the wind starts howling down her chimney and she becomes quite certain that my body—all complete with cork lifebelt—will be washed up on the beach, right outside her front door in St. Margaret's Bay."

Captain Brown chuckled. He lit a cigarette while the Pilot went to the compass and checked the bearings of his channel buoys, after which he came back to his subject.

"You know, Cap'n, I think you'd be wise to drop the hook in the Downs and see what tomorrow brings. This old hooker is as light as a balloon on the water and she can't make better than eight knots in slack water, in a calm. God knows what she'll be like if you do have a sou'wester and a flood-tide against you." He paused to mark the effect of his words, then, seeing no result, went on, "And they can't be in a hurry to have her up in the Mersey. She's bound for the breakers, isn't she?"

Captain Brown remained silent for a few moments, evidently considering the Pilot's remarks. He walked to the lee wing of the bridge, flicked the butt of his cigarette over the side and came back amidships.

"Well, Pilot, I'll tell you what we'll do. We should be off Deal by about six o'clock. If it looks all that bad, we'll anchor. If it doesn't, I'll go on. But it will be about midnight before we get down off Dungeness. And if it does blow up and I have to give it a wide berth, we'd have trouble getting you away. So whether we anchor in the Downs or not, we'll put you ashore in Deal.

"And then," he added with a smile, "you'll be with your Missus for supper in any case."

Off Deal we steamed slowly inshore and the right kind of blast from our whistle—given by the Pilot—brought a boat alongside for him so smartly that there was no need to anchor. The wind had gone to the west and a fair number of vessels lay in the Downs, but there was nothing particularly threatening about the weather.

At eight o'clock I relieved Mr. Ellis. When my eyes were used to the darkness, and I had identified in my mind the lights that flashed and revolved on all sides, he gave me the course. "She's yours," he said and, without another word, he went below. I walked the width of the bridge expecting to find the

Captain in one of the wings. But no. I was alone. "She's mine," I muttered to myself and I was not so sure that I liked it very much. The wind was blowing fresh, with frequent squalls of rain and sleet and the night was as black as the inside of a sea-boot. In my anxiety at my sudden responsibility I saw lights of other vessels everywhere. Green lights to port, red lights to starboard, as though all the ships in the Channel were crossing my bows. And me heading into them at full speed.

Then, just as I had decided to alter course to avoid them, down came a dense squall of rain, shutting everything from view, and I stood by the helmsman, fists clenched in my pockets, waiting for a crash. Then the squall was away astern and the other ships—I had not imagined them—were astern too. A few cracks appeared in the clouds and for a moment a couple of bright stars twinkled at me. I took a deep breath of relief and, more composed, had another look around. The South Foreland light was eight miles astern. Abeam, about five miles away, Folkestone was putting its glare on the low clouds. On my port bow was the red flash of the light-vessel on the Varne Shoal.

I felt more at ease. "Hell," I said to myself, "I've been acting Bos'n of a sailing-ship. I can be Second Mate of any bloody steamer."

A few minutes later the Captain came out of the chart-house. I was surprised to see that under his greatcoat he was wearing pyjamas. I was still more surprised when he spoke. He took a quick look around and a glance at the compass. "Well, Mister," he said, "it's not so bad. She's going along alright. This course'll take us down to the Royal Sovereign and if you find that you're going to pass Dungeness less than four miles off you can haul her off a point." After a short pause he added, "Well, I'll go and get some sleep. If you're in any doubt and need any help don't forget that two heads are better than one. Good night, Mister."

"Good night, sir."

With mixed feelings I watched him close his door. Encouraged by his confidence, I was not quite so confident myself—just a little scared. "Good enough for any bloody steamer"—I wondered. I was not quite so sure.

But my first night-watch in charge of a steamer was so exciting that I soon lost all sense of indecision and apprehension. I forgot everything but my interest in the bearings of the Varne and Dungeness lights and the lights of the vessels going the other way. All going the other way. Only once did I have to act in a hurry. A bright-green side-light suddenly appeared under my port bow— a sailing-vessel. "Hard a'starboard," I said to the helmsman. "Hard a'star-board," he repeated quietly. We swung to port and I walked quickly to the starboard wing of the bridge where I was just able to make out the shape of a small topsail schooner, running into the land for shelter.

Running for shelter, for it was blowing hard. The flood tide was against us and in the first hour of my watch, whatever distance the old engines did, we covered only five miles over the ground. As we approached Dungeness, we lost the protection of the land and felt the full force of the gale. The wind, out of the south-west, howled with a wavering scream and drove before it a sea that in the shallow water rose in ridges of high racing combers. They slammed noisily against our starboard bow in rapid succession and sent streams of spray flying across the fo'c's'le-head. We started to pitch heavily. Our bows rose steeply, then came down with a resounding, hollow boom. The engines roared as the stern was thrown high and the propeller raced uselessly in the free air until it was muffled by the engineer at the throttle or by the stern coming down and burying it deep in the water again.

Wind, tide and sea were more than the engines could cope with. We were not even holding our own and the man at the wheel was having a hard time keeping the ship on her course. "Haul her off!" We were being blown off, for suddenly the ship swung to port, the wind was abeam and the light on Dungeness was flashing over our stern.

"Hard a'port," I ordered.

"Helm is hard a'port," the helmsman replied. "She won't answer, sir."

With wind and sea abeam the old ship picked up her skirts and did her eight knots, heading for the coast of France, answering her helm for a couple of points until the wind caught her bows and blew her back into the trough, rolling violently and being carried bodily up-Channel.

I went to the engine-room telegraph and, so that there should be no mistake about it, rang from "Full Ahead" to "Full Astern" and then to "Ahead Dead Slow". I was walking to the chart-house when the Captain appeared.

"What's the trouble, Mister?"

"Blowing so hard she won't stand up to it, sir. She's fallen off and we can't get her back on her course."

"How's your helm?"

"Helm's hard a'port, sir. Engines dead slow."

"Alright," he replied. "Full ahead on your port helm. Give an extra ring and maybe they'll give her a bit extra steam, if they've got it."

I rang the telegraph to "Full Astern" and then to "Full Ahead" where I left it. The reply from below was equally vigorous and the engines went ahead with all the power they had. The *Highland Scot* swung to starboard until her bow met wind and sea. The sea threw her over into a heavy roll to port and the wind put her back in the trough.

The Old Man watched her quietly for a few moments, holding on to the binnacle, while he made up his mind. Then came his next order.

"Hard a'starboard."

"Hard a'starboard," repeated the helmsman as he put his wheel over.

"If the old girl won't face it, she can run for it, Mister. We'll go back to the Downs."

The old girl made a brave start, she turned away to port, but when her stern came up into the wind and sea it was blown and thrust back and again she lay in the trough.

"Well I'm damned!" exclaimed Captain Brown. "Stop her. Helm amidships. Full astern." And then, against all discretion, putting a dangerous strain on the rudder, the next order was, "Give her twenty degrees of port helm."

But it was no use. The ship gathered sternway but once more her stern was pushed back and she lay broadside to wind and sea. It was as the Pilot had said. The ship was as light as a balloon and her propeller and rudder were not deep enough in the water to be effective in that kind of weather.

"Stop her. Helm amidships."

I wondered what the next order would be. The wind had gone to the south-south-west, now blowing a whole gale, a forty- to sixty-mile-per-hour wind, with shrieking gusts of even greater force and frequent heavy squalls of rain. We could not keep her going astern and back under the lee of Dungeness because all the coast between Dungeness and the South Foreland was open to wind and sea—a dead lee shore. We lay athwart the Channel, heading east-south-east. About fourteen miles away, the light on Cape Gris Nez flashed through the murk and less than two miles to leeward, on our port bow, was the light-vessel marking the southern end of the Varne Shoal. It would do no good to go ahead. The French coast was also unprotected and there would be a fair chance of running foul of the Varne light.

In that part of the Dover Strait the stream of the flood at half-tide normally runs at about two to three knots; but, with a howling gale behind it, it was probably flowing north-eastwards at twice that rate. In addition, a wind blowing at a speed of sixty miles per hour is said to deliver a thrust of about fifteen pounds per square foot and our high, exposed side gave it some thousands of square feet to work on. Wind and tide together were carrying and blowing us over the ground at a speed which at times may have been as much as eight knots. With engines stopped, broadside to wind and sea, the ship was being swept swiftly up-Channel.

For the moment, it seemed that there was nothing to be done but watch and wonder what to do. We rolled so widely that we almost dipped the rails under and so violently that, in my innocence of steamers, I half expected the boilers to come adrift from their beds and go crashing through the ship's side. For an instant I thought it had actually happened when the wooden covers of the starboard lifeboats were ripped off by the wind to go flying through the air, smashing themselves to splinters against the funnel and the stokehold ventilators with the devil's own pandemonium.

Nothing to be done. A surprising situation it seemed to me. That a large steamer could meet such conditions and have no power that she could use anywhere but in that one place under her stern, where it could not do any good. I thought of all I had gone through in sailing-ships, which were supposed to be obsolete. How they could show their canvas, in greater or lesser area, to suit any wind that blew. And, what is more important, set it where it would do most good—forward, amidships or aft—so that no alert seaman could get his ship into the position that we were in.

When she was launched, the ship had been classified as a steel screw schooner; perhaps at that time she had been furnished with a fore and aft foresail, a mainsail, staysails and jibs. But, if so, these had been left ashore as unnecessary years before; the only sign that they might once have been carried was the spread of shrouds and backstays of the foremast and main mast.

Watching and wondering what to do. We swept past the Varne light-vessel so close that we could see it rearing and plunging at its mooring, its lantern gleaming blood-red through the rain and flying spindrift. A few minutes later we got the backlash, the backwash from the shoal, when the seas flung themselves aloft in a mad maelstrom and smashed against our bows.

"Poor devils," exclaimed the Captain, looking at the light-vessel which was soon far to windward. "But," he went on, "they'll be alright so long as their moorings hold." Then, "No other ships about, Mister, but we'd better put up two red lights."

So I left the bridge and, with one of the hands, went to the lamp-locker under the fo'c's'le-head. We found the two red globe-lamps—the lights to be shown by a vessel not in need of assistance but not under command—filled them with oil and carried them to the bridge where they were lit and hoisted on the signal halliards.

Shortly afterwards, we picked up the double flash of the light-vessel moored at the southern end of the Goodwin Sands. It was on our port beam, dead to leeward, about nine miles off. At the time, we were being driven across the northern end of the Varne Shoal where there was enough water; but in the shallows the seas broke around us with a furious noise. The engines were put full speed astern and the propeller beat up a foam that streamed past the bridge. The whole ship rattled and shook but the force of the gale and the speed of the racing tide had increased so greatly that we made no sternway. The bearing of the South Goodwin light did not change.

"Stop her."

We stood holding on to the bridge rails against the wild motion of the ship. Over the stern, some seven miles away, were the lights of Dover, too far off and too unattainable to offer any comfort. Overhead, the two red lights swung to leeward in the wind. I looked at them with an odd and uncomfortable feeling of helplessness—and swallowed hard. I was put on my mental feet again by the voice of the Captain. His quiet tone drove away my momentary sense of confusion.

"Well, Mister, it looks as if we were going to end up on the Goodwins. And if we do, there won't be any Christmas dinner for us this year."

Then, he actually gave a happy smile and, seeing my amazement, explained, "I was just thinking about the Pilot and his Missus. Damn' good job we put him ashore in Deal. Oh well," he continued after a brief silence, "I don't suppose it'll do any good if we have to use it, but you'd better get a distress signal all ready. And you'd better turn the Mate out and tell him what's going on . . . and to call all those who are below."

I went down to the wheel-house on the lower bridge and opened the new box of rocket bombs—small canisters about six inches long and two inches in diameter. I put one in a side-pocket of my jacket, placed the detonator and lanyard very carefully in the breast-pocket and went outside. Holding on to the rail, I fought my way against the wind until I reached the ship's side. There, bolted to the deck, was the socket—a bronze tube, much like a miniature howitzer, pointing upwards and outwards. I removed the wooden cap, made sure that the inside was free of water and inserted the rocket. Next, I put the detonator into the hole in the centre of the rocket, hooked one end of the firing lanyard to the small wire loop of the detonator and hitched the other end to the rail. All was ready. It only needed a smart jerk on the lanyard and the rocket would go soaring aloft to burst with a loud explosion and a shower of bright-green stars. I did the same on the other side and then went below.

Mr. Ellis was curled up on the 'thwartship settee of his cabin, firmly wedged there against the rolling of the ship. Except for his sea-boots, which were slithering about the deck, he was fully dressed and sound asleep. As I entered the cabin he gave a snort, opened one eye, and then listened while I told him that we were driving down towards the Goodwin Sands, and gave him the Captain's message to call those who were below. He swung his feet slowly to the deck, passed a wrinkled old hand through his white hair and reached for his sea-boots.

"The Goodwins, eh? Then we'll be bound for Davy Jones's locker." He thrust a foot into one of his boots and held the other for a moment between his knees while he thought about it. Then, stifling a yawn, he growled, "To hell with Davy Jones. I don't care a damn for him. Alright. I'll turn 'em out."

It was probably the difference in our ages. I cared a great deal about Davy Jones and his locker. While Mr. Ellis was pulling on his other sea-boot I went into my cabin and took my sea-boots off, also my long oilskin coat. If it came to swimming I would be better without them. Then I put on a pair of low shoes and returned to the bridge.

In the black darkness of the night the light on the South Goodwin was very bright. It was still five miles away but it seemed terribly close and there was now another light, flashing every ten seconds, about two points to the eastward, broad on our port bow. Captain Brown stood by the compass, looking at them.

"Well, Mister, that's the East Goodwin and it looks as though we'll be going between them and I don't know a thing that we can do. Can't bring her up with the anchor . . . water's too deep and the chain wouldn't last five seconds against this wind and sea." For a moment his sang-froid left him. "What a bloody mess! . . . And the hell of it is that if we lose her on the Goodwins they'll probably be delighted. They'll get more out of the underwriters than any ship-breaker would pay them for her old bones . . . And we won't be there for any inquiry."

Then he turned to me and his next remark took me aback.

"You're just fresh from sail. What would you do if you were in a sailing-ship?"

A sailing-ship! All kinds of thoughts raced through my head in the minute or so before I replied. If I were in the Channel in that kind of weather I'd have the ship under lower topsails and fore topmast staysail, running for shelter. She would be clipping along at such a speed that she would answer the smallest touch of her helm. But if she were in our position, with the Goodwin Sands close under her lee and the wind abeam, I'd let the mizzen topsail sheets fly, put my helm up, and away she would go before the wind and around the Foreland to the shelter of the Downs. But we could not do any of that.

Then I had the idea.

I had been in a deeply laden sailing-ship in heavy weather, with all sails furled, comfortably hove to, her weather bow held up to wind and sea by a small weather cloth spread in the mizzen rigging. If a few square yards of canvas would do that for a deep sailing-ship they should do even more for a steamer, as light as we were.

"Sir. I'd like to go down into the forepeak with a couple of hands and see if we can find a tarpaulin. If we do, we'll roll it up on the deck in the fo'c's'le, cut some holes in the leading edge and reeve short lengths of line through them. We'll stop the roll up with rope-yarns, bring it out on deck and carry it as high as we can get in the fore rigging. Then we'll make the edge fast to the shrouds with the pieces of line, cut the rope-yarn stops and unroll the tarpaulin outside the rigging as we come down. When we are on deck again I'll blow my whistle. Then, sir, if you go full ahead with your helm a'starboard it should push her head around."

"Alright. Away you go. Try it."

In the fo'c's'le the hands—all old shellbacks—were calmly puffing at their pipes, as little concerned about Davy Jones as Mr. Ellis. But they got to their feet while I explained what we had to do and were very alert when I told them that as far as I could see we had less than half an hour to do it in. Two of them lifted off the hatch, another lit a hurricane-lamp and the four of us got down the iron ladder into the unfamiliar fore-peak.

We floundered around in the dim light, falling over drums of paint, coils of rope and wire, blocks and tackles and other gear but we found everything we wanted and hauled a large tarpaulin up into the fo'c's'le. There, we stretched it out, rolled it up and made all ready for our climb in the rigging. It was a sheet of heavy tarred canvas about eighteen feet wide and twenty-two feet long—as long as three tall men and as big around as one of them.

We dragged it out on deck, abreast of number one hatch where, on our knees, we held it against the coaming, ourselves hanging on to the ring-bolts there while the ship rolled so far over to leeward that the lights on the Goodwins flashed at us, as it seemed, from half way up in the heavens.

"Roll, you old bitch, roll," the old man next to me growled through his whiskers. "That's the only bloody thing she can do," said another as she came up again and flung herself violently over to windward.

"Let go!" I yelled.

The tarpaulin rolled madly across the deck, to fetch up with a smack against the bulwarks and was followed by the four of us who made the same swift passage on our backsides. Watching our chance, so that the rolling should help us, we lifted the tarpaulin on to the rail, hauled it into position between rail and shrouds and then got up there ourselves, right in the eye of the wind that screamed in our ears and forced the breath back down throat and nostrils if one faced it.

The moment she began her roll to leeward, we picked up the tarpaulin, held it to our breasts and started on our way aloft. We were helped by the ship rolling away from us—which reduced the steepness of our climb—and by the power of the gale pushing against our backsides. Then we hung on, pressed against the shrouds by a wind force that was increased by the momentum of the swing back to windward.

Another roll to leeward, another scramble up the rat-lines and we were high enough. We made the leading edge fast to the shrouds, cut the spun-yarn stops and unrolled the tarpaulin as we came down. The wind held it firmly in place but, to make sure, we secured the bottom edge to the rigging screws.

Then I blew a long, shrill blast with my whistle and we stood by the rail watching our canvas, waiting to see what would happen. It was a tense, exciting moment. The light-vessel was so close that one of the men snatched the cap from his head and shouted, "We're going to hit her." Then the deck started to tremble under our feet; the engines were going full speed ahead. The ship swung away from the wind and kept on swinging until the wind was astern and the tarpaulin that we had put up there with so much trouble was whipped from its lashings to go floating through the air as though it were a mere rag.

A tense, exciting moment

We cleared the light-vessel but passed it so close that, by the light of its lantern, reflected on the water, we could read the big white letters SOUTH GOODWIN on its side.

I left the men leaning against the rail, talking about it, and walked aft on my way to the bridge. When I got to the top of the ladder that led from the well-deck, I bumped in the darkness into a small group of men who were wearing lifebelts and standing by the boats. One of them stepped out and took me by the elbow. It was the old steward. He was still wearing his white coat and cloth cap, sodden with rain.

"Didn't I say that ye'd be nippin' aloft to loose a 'torps'l'?"

"So you did, steward. But we lost the bloody thing."

He chuckled. "Shan't be needin' it any more." He gave his lifebelt a smack. "Shan't be needin' this either, sir."

On the bridge I found Mr. Ellis looking at the lightship which was fast dropping astern. Captain Brown was standing by the compass conning his ship. The lights of the houses in St. Margaret's Bay were twinkling occasionally between the rain squalls. Five miles ahead was the shelter of the Downs.

"May I lower the two red lights, sir?"

"Eh! By God! Yes, lower them. Thank you, Mister."

In the Downs, when day broke, we found ourselves in company with a large fleet of stormbound vessels.

We were lucky to be there. While we were drifting off Dungeness and the Varne Shoal, at the mercy of wind and sea, many other vessels were in more serious trouble. Off Folkestone a small sailing fisherman was lost with her crew of six men. Not far away, off Beachy Head and just west of Dover, two steamers were driven ashore, fortunately with no loss of life.

In the Bristol Channel, the steamer *Thistlemor* was outward bound from Cardiff to Capetown and astern of her the S.S. *Arndale* was on her way to Montevideo. Both ships steamed into a hurricane of terrific force, heavy seas swept their decks. On board the *Thistlemor* everything movable, including large, iron cowl-ventilators, was washed over the side and, finally, the tremendous weight of water crashing aboard stove in her hatches, flooded her holds (already containing some four thousand tons of coal) and she sank like a stone, off the Devon coast.

Her Captain and eighteen of the crew were drowned; in such furious weather it is remarkable that any were saved. The *Arndale*, herself badly damaged by the seas, picked up nine men and took them back to Barry where she also landed her own Second Mate whose legs were broken.

Brave, even foolhardy, were the steamer sailors of those days. Your ship was loaded, you had a crew and good engines. What excuse could there be for remaining in port and missing a tide? "The weather! Ah, hell! Here, take my umbrella." That would be the Marine Superintendent speaking, perhaps the owner. So they went to sea regardless of the weather. That is what they were supposed to do. It was their job.

The Isle of Man steamer *Ellan Vannin* left Ramsey after midnight and was swamped a few hours later, on the bar at the entrance to the Mersey River, with the loss of all on board—ten crew and twelve passengers.

We were lucky to be there, quietly at anchor in the Downs, in the lee of the South Foreland, while wild clouds raced over our heads and in the Channel, only three miles away, we could see the fury of the seas on the Goodwin Sands.

After two days the worst of it was past. On the third day we got away, bound west again. We did not have far to go, only about 560 miles to Liverpool, but the wind was still fresh and still ahead. It was three days later when we anchored in the Mersey, on Sunday evening, December 8th. It was pleasant to hear the comfortable sound of church bells and to see all the lights of the shore and the ferries crossing the river so constantly. It had been a very tiring passage.

Next morning the Marine Superintendent came aboard. The Captain was standing by the ladder to receive him and I was also there with a couple of the men to make sure that the rope ladder was placed in the best position and that the tug's lines were well secured. Captain Brown got a curt nod in response to his salute—mine was ignored—and together they went into the saloon, with the stoop-shouldered, bandy-legged Superintendent uncouthly leading the way. He had not said a word of greeting to Captain Brown and his black jowl wore the same dour, dispeptic air as when I first saw him.

I watched them disappear into the alleyway and fell to pacing the well-deck wondering what they would have in store for me. If, as now seemed certain, the *Highland Scot* was going to be broken up, would there be a berth for me in one of the other ships, perhaps one of the new ones, recently built. I had discussed this with Captain Brown who thought it a possibility and said that he would add his recommendation.

Then I was sent for. In the saloon I found them sitting at the table, with the chart and the open log-book before them. Captain Brown introduced me as if I had never met the Superintendent before and went on to describe how the ship had been saved from the Goodwin Sands by the tarpaulin in the fore rigging.

"Yes, yes," the Super replied. "I know that from your log-book. It's all there. The ship was saved and the tarpaulin was lost." He fell into a gloomy silence, as though he were not quite sure which was the greater misfortune.

Then I spoke up. "Excuse me, sir. I hear that this ship is not going to load. She's to be sold for breaking up. Would you please tell me what my orders are now?"

For some moments he did not speak. He seemed to be very uncomfortable. But it was not on my account. He put a hand to his mouth to muffle a loud belch and then he replied, "We've nothing else for you just now." He pushed five golden sovereigns over to me.

"Thank you, sir. Will the tug be alongside long enough for me to get my gear aboard?"

"Aye. She'll take you whenever you're ready."

118

I pocketed the money and got to my feet. Captain Brown, who looked unhappy, also stood up, his hand outstretched.

"Good-bye, Mister."

"Good-bye, sir."

The old steward and the three men who had handled the tarpaulin with me were at the ladder to say good-bye. Each gripped my hand till it hurt.

In the tug, on the way to the landing-stage, I stood looking astern at the old crock. She was stemming the outgoing tide with which she had a picturesque affinity. The yellow river water was in a harmony of colour with her rusty flanks and the swift-running ebb in accord with her age and the approaching, ignominious end to her life.

My first steamer. My first berth as an officer—Second Officer!

I should have known better.

9 *S.S.* Sierra Blanca

At the Merchant Service Guild they were disappointed that the berth in the *Highland Scot* had ended so soon, but my visit was most timely.

"You've heard of Thompson, Anderson, of course? No! They own the *Sierras*, you know."

I knew the *Sierras* as a fleet of sailing-ships but I also knew that they had all been sold.

"Well, now they have two steamers and are looking for a Third Mate for one of them, the *Sierra Blanca*.

I went to see them and met an elderly gentleman who sat before a confusion of papers in a small, dark office. This was Mr. Anderson, one of the owners. He was most cordial. So I had served my time in Nourse's coolie ships. Yes, of course, he knew them well. Fine ships, very fine ships. And my face being so burned, he supposed that I had just returned from the east.

"No, sir. It must be the wind." And I told him how I had spent the last eight days in the *Highland Scot*.

"Well, well, well. It's been a terrible week." Then he spoke about the *Sierra Blanca*. As Third Mate my pay would be £5 per month, but as the ship was going around to the Tyne to load, I would not be required to join for another ten days or so. He would let me know. His face lit up when he read my home address. He had spent the happiest of times as a young man, walking and cycling in that part of Cheshire. Lovely country, lovely country.

I ran down the bare wooden stairs, into the street, completely under his spell. What a charming gentleman! His ships must be wonderful.

It was very late when I got home. All were in bed except my father and my young brother. They had been sitting by the fire with their books and the room was very cosy with the kind light of its oil-lamps and the heavy velvet curtains.

"Ho, ho, my boy! Glasses, Max. A cigar, my boy?"

So my father and I sat with tumblers of warm sherry while I told them of my adventure in the *Highland Scot* and young Max, his chin cupped in his hand, never took his shining, eager eyes from my face. Then I went to bed and slept for seventeen hours without stirring.

The *Sierra Blanca* lay at Commissioners Staithes, Percymain. A staith is an elevated wharf for shipping coal. The word derives from the Icelandic *stöth*, a landing-place; but to the Geordies of Tyneside the staithes were known as the "spoots". When I went on board, from the top of the staith, tons of coal poured down the spoots into the holds with a roaring, rattling noise and clouds of dust.

Bound for Junin and Pisagua on the west coast of South America, in northern Chile, we sailed on December 23rd down the North Sea and through the Channel, both smooth and grey as a sheet of pewter. In those narrow waters with their busy coastal traffic I was not allowed to stand my normal watch alone. Instead, I went on duty with the Mate, which meant that until the ship was clear of the English Channel we were on two watches, four hours on the bridge and four below.

This was then common practice. The idea of three watch-keeping officers each doing four hours of duty and having, in theory, nothing to do for eight hours was hard for the owners of tramp ships, and even for their Masters, to digest. After all, their ships had got along very well for years with only two mates. The result was that, in spite of his Second Mate's ticket, the Third Mate was often treated like a kind of probationer who could be allowed to keep a watch after the ship was clear of the land but only when the Captain was available, that is, during the hours before noon and midnight.

For a young man just fresh from sailing-ships, it was a good system. Steamers were different. This was not the semi-derelict *Highland Scot*. The *Sierra Blanca* was only four years old and very much alive. Her Master, Captain Richard Compton, had served his apprenticeship in the company's sailing-ships but had later been navigating officer in the passenger-steamers of the Bibby Line. From the moment we dropped the Tyne Pilot, our tramp steamer with her coal cargo was navigated with all the care of an Atlantic liner. While we were on the coast, frequent bearings of lighthouses and lightships were taken, to check the distance run and the course made good and the distance off the land.

On Christmas Day we were clear of the English Channel. The weather was fine and the horizon clear of shipping. I relieved the Second Mate on the bridge while he went to his Christmas dinner with the Captain and Mrs. Compton, the Chief Engineer and the Mate. I ate mine afterwards by myself and thought of the past four Christmasses in my sailing-ships, of the fun in the half-deck with my fellow apprentices, the Mate, his mandoline and the carol-singing and of the kindliness of the Captains in having us in the saloon for our meal. That spirit was missing. We carried three apprentices and I would have been glad of their company but they were not invited to eat in the saloon.

Still, it was a festive day. I slept throughout my watch below, ate my lonely supper at five o'clock and went on the bridge to relieve the Mate so that he could join the others from 5.30 p.m. to 6.30 p.m. At one bell, 7.45 p.m., I went to the chart-house on the lower bridge, had a look at the chart, read and signed the Captain's night-order book and then kept my first watch. It was a beautiful, cold, starlit night and without incident until I handed over to the Second Mate at midnight.

A festive day. I should have said, unusual. That was the only afternoon watch below and the only quiet second dog-watch I was to enjoy for some months.

I do not think that the *Sierra Blanca* was typical of such ships. The Captain appeared to take no interest at all in the work going on about the decks. This was natural, because a steamer, only 375 feet long, with bare, steel decks, a few wooden derricks with their gear and a couple of metal life-boats, was not difficult to keep clean and shipshape. One head was quite enough, particularly when it was on the shoulders of a Mate like ours. He was also unusual. He was about forty years old and had been in command of the full-rigged ship *Sierra Lucena*. When she was sold and he had to go as Mate of a tramp steamer it must have been a bitter disappointment but, if so, he did not show it. Perhaps his anodyne was work. The care and maintenance of such a steamer may have been simple but for him it was never finished.

Once the coal-dust had been washed from every nook and cranny, the few seamen and the apprentices were kept busy from dawn to dark until the *Sierra Blanca* was as trim about her decks as a homeward-bound sailing-ship. Any illusions I may have cherished about the duties and dignity of an officer were quickly shattered by a working day that ended only when I came off the bridge at midnight.

The day after Christmas was the pattern of all the thirty odd days until we entered the Straits of Magellan. Called at 7.00 a.m., I got into a tub of cold salt water, then ate breakfast and relieved the Mate on the bridge at 7.45 a.m. so that he would have time to bath and shave before he ate breakfast. Before going below, he pointed to a wooden bucket of fresh water and to a small sailmaker's bench.

"When you've taken your sight, Mister, you might give the bright-work up here a good wipe with fresh water to get the salt off it. Then there's the flags to overhaul. Most of them need some repair and you'll find all the bunting you want in that bag."

That was something of a shock. I was not to pace proudly back and forth, cocking an eye occasionally at the compass as I passed the wheel-house. But

S.S. *Sierra Blanca*

there was nothing to be done about it. I was a very small minority of one and could not begin a voyage that would last several months by refusing to obey orders. However nonchalantly given, they were orders. And, anyhow, I was new to the ways of steamers.

To put it as briefly as possible a "sight"—an observation of the sun or any other heavenly body—means measuring height, altitude above the horizon, with the sextant as an angle at the point of the observer. Using this altitude, calculations are made which give the time at ship. The ship's chronometer always shows the time at Greenwich and the difference between the time at ship and the Greenwich time tells you how far you are east or west of Greenwich—gives you your longitude. So it is necessary to take the chronometer time at the very second when the altitude is observed, something which, in sailing-ships, the Captain and the Mate did for each other.

In the *Sierra Blanca*, the Mate explained, we took our own chronometer time and he told me how I could count the seconds by repeating to myself, in the rhythm of a grandfather's clock, the words "and one, and two", and so forth, between taking the altitude and going to the chronometer. Deducting from the chronometer reading the total of the seconds counted gave the Greenwich time of the observation.

So I got out my sextant, took my sight, my chronometer time and a compass bearing of the sun. In half an hour I had worked out the ship's position and checked the error of the compass. Then I put sextant and books aside, abandoned navigation and came down to earth.

It was a nice bridge. The rails were covered by a varnished teak-wood bulwark; the wheel-house, amidships, was also of teak. This was the brightwork. It had been well cared for and, every morning, as on this first morning, I swabbed every inch of it with fresh water and wiped it dry—"got the salt off it". Then I turned to needle and thread and scraps of bunting, sitting on the bench repairing the code flags. When, after some days, they were done, old canvas covers for mooring-wire reels and covers for cowl-ventilators appeared and, with palm and needle, twine and beeswax, I cut and ripped, patched or made new covers, sewing as I had been taught by the old sailmaker in the ship *Main*.

At one bell, 11.45 a.m., I got my sextant out again and was joined by the Captain, Mate and Second Mate, all with their sextants to get the sun's altitude for the calculation of the latitude at noon. Then I turned the watch over to the Second Mate.

At 12.30 p.m. I was back on the bridge to relieve the Second Mate while he went to dinner. At one o'clock it was my turn to eat; by the time I had finished, an hour and a half of my watch below had gone. That, as it proved, was not at all important. The important thing was that I should not take too long over my dinner. According to Mr. Vooght, the Mate, there was so much to be done and he had so few hands to do it that he would like me to give him some help with the work on deck.

There was to be no afternoon watch below. Instead, my sailmaker's bench was taken on to the fore deck where I spent the afternoon sewing canvas. To help me I had one able seaman and, between the two of us, we made new tarpaulins—two for each of the four hatches—of tough, green-coloured, watertight canvas. That occupied many days and when they were finished I sewed tight-fitting canvas covering on the handrails of the ladders to the bridge, the well-decks and lower bridge.

At 5.00 p.m. I relieved the Mate on the bridge. By the time I had finished my supper it was six o'clock. I went to my cabin and sat for the first quiet moment for almost twelve hours, smoking a pipe. It was the second dog-watch, the time for fun and singing, jolly talk and chaff with one's shipmates. But the only company I had was my own and it was enough. I was content just to sit and read until it was time to go on the bridge.

When I went up there I found the Captain talking with the Mate who very curtly gave me the course and went below. We were in the middle of the Bay of Biscay but except for the December cold we might have been in the tropics. The sky was brilliant with stars. The only breeze was of our own making as we steamed our ten knots through the smooth sea. It was very beautiful. I took a deep breath of the keen air. Then the Captain spoke.

"I didn't see you up here with your sextant in the dog-watch, Mister."

"The dog-watch . . . sextant, sir?"

"Yes. For star sights. Twilight is the best time. The stars are bright and you get a good horizon."

"But, sir . . . " And I went on to say that I had only just passed for Second Mate. At that time the examination included latitude by Pole Star but no other stellar navigation. I did not know any stars, nor how to work them out.

"Well, you'll have to learn, Mister. Stars are better than the sun and you can always find them where they'll be of use to you. Stars to the north and south for latitude—by ex-meridian, of course—and east and west for longitude. I want all my officers on the bridge for star sights in the dog-watch. And I want a star azimuth to be taken in every night watch."

I took another deep breath. He noticed my dismay and relaxed a little. He came down to my level long enough to point out a sequence of bright stars and the shape of nearby constellations that made them easy to identify. He also explained the method by which I could calculate the star's true bearing— its azimuth—to check the deviation of the compass. As for latitude and longitude, he supposed that I had brought textbooks with me and, anyhow, the Second Mate or the Mate would give me help if I was in trouble.

When he had gone below I took bearings of every star that I had learned that was suitable for the purpose. From my calculations I found that each gave me the same error of the compass, the same deviation. It was a good exercise. I felt better and was confident that with some study and a little help I would be able to work out latitudes and longitudes.

But it was not so simple. I had difficulty in getting a clear understanding from my textbooks and I got no help. The Second Mate had no time. He was always in a hurry to get done with his own figuring so that he could go to his bunk for a brief three hours before turning out at midnight. When I went to the Mate with my questions, all the hours of help that I gave him on deck counted not at all. His eyebrows went up in an exaggerated expression of surprise while he exclaimed, "You don't know that!" I went to him for help only once.

The consequence was that I took observations of stars which I could not identify with any certainty, went to my cabin and worked up a position that was rarely correct and just managed to get it done before going on watch.

After four happy years in sailing-ships I was often as heartsore as a homesick first-voyager. I had never before met that kind of cold aloofness. But the bridge for the last four hours of a long day brought some comfort. The clouds moving slowly across the calm face of a large, pale moon, made my troubles seem small and transient.

We made the eastern entrance of the Straits of Magellan when we were thirty-two days out from the Tyne. A heavy swell rolled up from the south-east and it was a sudden and pleasant contrast when we steamed round the point into smooth water. Although it was summer down there the skies were heavy with cloud; frequent hard squalls of rain and sleet whistled across the dreary plains of the Tierra del Fuego, the southern side of the straits. But later the scenery became so grand that cold and wet were forgotten. In the narrows, close at hand, walls of rock rose from the still, grey water, sometimes holding in their clefts glaciers whose upper surfaces were white with snow until they ended abruptly in a cliff of ancient ice that fell into the strait like a motionless cascade of jade.

Where there were low hills, they were covered with lush-looking pasture; and in the distance snow-covered peaks stood out against the sombre sky. Cleaving this stark grandeur, the strait wound its way like a silver path for more than three hundred miles to the Pacific Ocean.

At sunset we anchored off Punta Arenas to pass the hours of darkness. Heavy rain was falling and in the dusk the little collection of wooden buildings looked very lonely and forlorn. We hove up at daybreak and at sunset we passed out of the straits and headed north.

Ten days later we arrived off Junin, our first port of discharge. It was only an open roadstead, the town little more than a hamlet, nestling between the sea and the high, brown cliff that skirts the coast of Chile.

The sun had not yet come up over the land when a whaler pulled smartly alongside, bringing the port officials and the Pilot. We had no sickness aboard so pratique was immediately granted and the Pilot took us slowly to a berth inshore where we anchored.

Junin is one of the northernmost ports of Chile, not very far south from the Peruvian border. If you went due east, overland, you would come to the Brazilian coast and the Atlantic Ocean, somewhat to the north of Rio de Janeiro. So it is well in the tropics and in that part of the country where rain is practically unknown.

Regardless of whatever the south-east trades were doing out in the wide Pacific Ocean, we had steamed up the coast well in the lee of the high land. The day before our arrival had been spent rigging the derricks and rolling the tarpaulins off our four hatches. So, as soon as the ship was brought up, lying securely to her anchors, the agent gave a sharp blast on our whistle. A small tug, which had been standing by, brought the lighters alongside with the gangs of chattering Chileno stevedores with their shovels and other gear. They were a tatterdemalion crowd but they seemed very happy, boiling over with typical Latin vivacity. During all the weeks that we were discharging our coal cargo, the ring of their shovels, their jokes, snatches of song, noisy argument and loud laughter rose above the ceaseless rattle of our steam winches. I liked it; after the cold unfriendliness and loneliness of the past seven weeks it was refreshing. One of the busiest of all was a skinny, undersized urchin who might have been twelve years old; hanging from the piece of string that kept his ragged trousers up were several hanks of bagging-twine and a couple of tin mugs. At frequent intervals he would come running bare-foot on the hot steel decks, lean his tousled head over the hatch coaming and yell in a high falsetto voice to the men working below, "*Quien quiere agua? Quien quiere hilo?*"—"Who wants water? Who wants twine?" If the answer was water, he lowered a bucket with one of his tin mugs; if twine, he dropped one of his hanks. The coal was not being hoisted out of the hold in iron tubs or grab-buckets to be dumped loose into the lighters; it was being put into gunny sacks which were sewn up and put into rope slings, ten bags at a time, in convenient form for handling at the jetty and transporting by the cog-wheel railway that climbed up the face of the high cliffs to the tableland where it would continue its journey to the silver-, copper- and lead-mines where it was to be used. Thus we were spared the clouds of coal-dust which would have risen if the cargo were being discharged in bulk. But it was a slow business and even working at all four hatches we could only discharge about three hundred tons per day.

At each hatch a tally-clerk from the shore was checked by one of the ship's company also keeping count of the number of slings of coal-bags which were swung over the side and lowered into the lighter. I did this at number two hatch where my tally-clerk companion was a middle-aged, gentle-mannered little man. He wore a rather ragged large straw hat, pink collarless shirt, old linen jacket and faded blue jean trousers; elbows, knees, and seat had many neat patches but his clothes were fresh and clean at the beginning of each day. No matter how stifling the heat that rose from the steel decks under the mid-day sun he remained as clean as his tally-book with its orderly rows of strokes, vertical and oblique, and as neat as the many cigarettes that he rolled so nimbly. This he did with amazing swiftness while the empty slings were being returned to the hold. It was in these intervals, too, that he taught me many Spanish words and phrases. At five o'clock work in the hold finished for the day. The stevedores dropped their shovels and made for the iron ladders to climb up on deck, urging each other on with noisy, ribald joking. For their journey ashore we had lowered one of the big steel life-boats. I was in charge of this with a crew consisting of the three apprentices—Hopkins, Chubb and Simpson —and a young ordinary seaman. For such a large boat, that was not a very robust crew, particularly as we were very deeply laden by the time all the stevedores had managed to squeeze a place for themselves. However, they were a decent crowd and it was not long before each of my crew had a couple of

Apprentice H. J. Chubb

men helping him, pulling and pushing, with lusty shouts of, "*A tierra, a tierra!*" Back alongside the *Sierra Blanca*, we hooked on the boat falls, then scrambled up on deck, up the rope ladder, to haul the falls hand tight, leaving the boat to lie alongside against stout rope fenders. The sea was smooth and she would come to no harm. Then I went to my number two hatch and made sure that the lighter ropes were well clear of the water so that no one could use them as a means of getting aboard during the night or, what might be more

At 4.30 a.m. next morning the night-watchman brought me a cup of tea and then went off to call my boat's crew. A quick shave and a tub of cold salt water brought me fully to life. I took my place in the stern sheets of the life-boat with a couple of ship's biscuits in my pocket. I was ravenously hungry and it seemed that the others were the same, for I noticed that each of them was crunching and munching as we made our easy way to the jetty. That cold tub, I think, merits further comment. For the Captain and the Officers of the *Sierra Blanca* it was a kind of fetish; there is nothing noteworthy about a cold tub taken in the tropics but we had begun the first day out from Newcastle-upon-Tyne, a few days before Christmas, and continued all the five months that I was in the ship, even during our passages through the Straits of Magellan where the water cannot have been far above the temperature of ice.

For me, life in the *Sierra Blanca* was hard, dull and certainly unromantic but it had its moments of soul-restoring compensation. Those morning trips in the life-boat were very beautiful. We left the ship a half an hour before sunrise when the dawn was a pale rosy flush in the sky above the black silhouette of the high cliffs. Overhead and in the west, the stars were bright. Every dip of the oars stirred up gleaming globules of phosphorescence, our gentle bow-wave broke into myriads of scintillating sparks and our wake swirled and twisted, writhing in the sea like a path of luminous pale-green vapour. Apart from the noise of our own progress, the only sounds came from the waking sea-birds with their muffled cries and from the breath-blowing and gasping of the seals when they broke surface. The return journey was equally pleasant. At the jetty we had nosed our way in among the boats of the local fishermen who were landing their catch. We embarked our stevedores who took their seats very quietly, all of them carrying the small bundles or baskets which contained their breakfast and midday meal of garlic-flavoured cold fried sardines, highly-spiced sausages, raw onions, bread and wine. They helped willingly at the oars and we were back alongside the ship again before six o'clock, ready for another day's shovelling and tallying.

Including two Sundays and a Feast Day when no work was done, two weeks passed before the last slings of the coal that we had brought for Junin were lowered into the lighter. On the Sundays each watch of sailors and firemen had been given a "liberty day" but, apart from some crude spirit and rather raw wine, the respectable little town had not much to offer them and all came aboard again very quiet and reasonably sober. There was nothing for us either; the streets were unpaved, and the flat tableland at the top of the cliff which we

The four-masted barque *Galgate*, which was similar to the *Engelhorn* in which Brother Max sailed ascended by the cog-wheel railway was no better. It was a desert marked by a few huts at the terminus of the railway that led to the mines and a primitive sports-ground covered with sand and jagged flints where purple-faced and sweating sailors and apprentices from the *Galgate* were playing a difficult but friendly game of soccer against a local side of nimble, wiry Chilenos.

The heat was intense for in that part of Chile at that time of the year—the first part of February—at noon the sun is within a few degrees of being immediately overhead. For us it was even too hot to stand watching; we had no ball to kick about and neither did we have the prospect of drinking some of the beer which lay cooling under a pile of wet sacking, in the shade, and which would really constitute the winning goal for the footballers of both sides. We wandered a few hundred yards up the railroad track until there was nothing between us and the point at which it vanished among the high, ochre-coloured ranges of the Andes that skirted the narrow plateau. Sandy removed his cap, passed a handkerchief over his perspiring face then flung out an arm in a dramatic gesture.

"Will ye look at yon bloody wilderness of mountains. And never a blade of grass nor a drop of water. But over there are the rich mines of Potosi. And think of yon Spaniards with their steel caps and breastplates climbing about among them under the burning sun. I'd sooner have the stokehold. Let's awa' oot of this, doon to the beach."

In the town we found a restaurant which was fly-blown but gave us a very savoury meal of stewed fish and shellfish, corn bread and a glass of wine. Then we went back to the ship. There was nothing more to do on shore, and there was nothing to do aboard. As there were still many hours left of our "liberty day", we took the jolly-boat and fishing-lines, pulled over to some rocks which lay not far from the beach and dropped the anchor. All this part of the coast teems with fish which accounts for the activities of the colonies of seals and the flocks of pelicans, cormorants, gannets, terns and many other kinds of sea-birds. I sat in the stern sheets staring into the depths of the clear water, looking for fish, when suddenly there was an imperative tug at my line, an equally sharp jerk by me and I hauled a fine, fat rock-cod aboard. We were doing well; fishing was good and Sandy was chuckling with glee.

"To Hell with thon dry hash, we'll hae fried fish and chips tae our supper."

It was very still. There was no air and the sun down at sea level seemed to burn even more fiercely than it had up on top of the cliff. But we did not mind that. Beads of sweat ran down my face and dripped off the end of my chin but the fishing was exciting. The jolly-boat occasionally rose to the swell, tugged at her anchor, and brought her bow down again on the water with a refreshing splash. It was much better than sitting, stifling in one's cabin on board the ship, with nothing to do. That was the way of my thinking until I realised that something had happened up in the bow. There were no more merry little tunes and no noise of Sandy hauling fish aboard. Instead there was a most miserable retching and groaning, for poor Sandy, who could stand hours of the heat in the oil-smelling engine-room and the stink of bilge water in the most furious weather without turning a hair and without a quiver in his stomach, was miserably seasick. His cap lay among the fish in the bottom of the boat. His listless hands and unhappy head hung over the gunnel while, with a violent and urgent squeal, he got rid of the last remnant of that very tasty but rather oily lunch. He sat up again, put the wet cap back on his head and looked at me with a sheepish smile.

"Och aye, here's the braw fisherman frae the Isle o' Skye, feeding the fishes instead o' catching them."

"Ho, ho, the rueing of it," I gave him in return. At that, he gave a really hearty burst of laughter, so that I thought that he was completely recovered and said, "Shall we go ahead with the fishing, Sandy?"

"Nay, nay," he replied. "Didn 'a I tell you I'd rather have the stokehold. Let's get aboard again or I won't have any appetite for these fellows when they come along at suppertime.

With the last of our Junin cargo aboard them, the lighters were by no means full, so they also carried stevedores and tally-clerks ashore and, of course, young Pepe—the twine and water boy. At my, "*Adios*, Pepe," his little monkey face lit up and he replied, "*Adios Piloto*." Then, wrinkling his brows until he found the words, he added, "Suppose I no see you no more . . . Hullo!"

Shortly before midnight, we hove up the anchor and headed south at half speed for the passage to Pisagua, about thirty-five miles away. Before dawn, two anchors were down and we had run wires out to a buoy astern so that the ship would lie steady, without swinging, should a fresh breeze spring up from the north. The roadstead was more exposed to northerly winds than had been the case in Junin. When we took the stevedores ashore that evening in the big steel life-boat, we found that some provision had been made for this at the jetty This was the usual structure of a deck supported by stout wooden piles driven into the bed of the sea, the spaces between them being deliberately left open so that in bad weather the seas and the swell could pass through, under the jetty, without wrecking it. But, in addition, at the place where the steps ran down to water level, a gibbet-like spar projected from the deck above the stairs, and extended four or five feet beyond the line of the jetty. Its similarity to a gallows was heightened by the knotted ropes that hung from it.

During the week that we lay at Pisagua we found this very useful. On several occasions, when I took the boat to the jetty, the rise and fall of the swell was so great that it would have been dangerous to lay her alongside. The only thing to do was to hold the boat clear of the jetty—Hopkins in the stern and Chubb in the bow each fending her off with the loom of his oar—while the stevedores, watching their chances, seized the rope, leapt clear of the steps and swung one by one into the boat. It was quite exciting, particularly in the dark of the early morning, but my boat's crew were young enough to get a lot of fun out of it.

Here, I had further thoughts of getting out of the *Sierra Blanca*. When the last of the coal was out, we were to go to load saltpetre—nitrate of soda—at Iquique and Antofagasta, for some port on the continent of Europe. That meant, of course, that we would be home again within about three months. But I hated the prospect of the daily humiliating and baffling struggle with stellar navigation and, short of breaking the Articles, I was prepared to do almost anything to avoid it. There were two or three sailing-ships in the anchorage and moored just ahead of us was a three-masted, full-rigged ship that reminded me of the *Arno*. *Saxon* was her name and, when I first spoke with her Second Mate, I thought I was going to be successful. She was laboriously discharging her coal cargo with her own crew, which was the usual practice of sailing-ships, and he was a bit fed up with life after many days of work in the heat and clouds of coal-dust. He was a young man, about my own age, and I thought he looked at me with some envy although, in truth, there was nothing in my appearance or dress to inspire this. We did not wear uniform in the *Sierra Blanca*; we did not even wear collars and ties. Our garb consisted of the usual rough serge trousers and a thing called a patrol jacket—a single-breasted garment, also of blue serge, which buttoned right up to the neck where a stand-up collar could be fastened with hooks and eyes. We had no brass buttons and the only attempt at something like uniform was the badge on my peaked cap that apprentice Chubb had kindly given to me. But the young man was quite happy in his ship and I could well understand his reasons for not wishing to leave her. As it turned out, I did much better by staying where I was, not that I had any choice in the matter.

Two weeks later I was given the balm that would not by any means sweeten my relationship with the Mate, but enabled me to hold my head up and taught me that professional pride meant more than being rather better than a good able seaman.

We came into Antofagasta late one afternoon. After the Pilot and Captain had left the bridge and I had time to look around, I saw, lying about a quarter of a mile away, a steamer called the *Lime Branch*. I was filled with excitement because I knew that Rob Anderson, whose family had been so very hospitable to us in Melbourne, was her Third Officer. After supper I went on the bridge and with the powerful electric torch that we used for this purpose, I called her up. She was such a blaze of electric lights shining from the portholes of all her cabins that I was afraid I would not be able to pick out her lamp when she signalled in reply, or that there would be no one on deck to see my torch. But there was no doubt about it, her reply flashed out from her fore mast-head and was so bright that it must have had a visibility of ten miles.

So I made my signal, "De Mierre Third Officer to Anderson Third Officer, come aboard for a yarn." His reply, "You come over here." My, "Sorry have no boat in water." His, "Coming right away."

When his boat clattered alongside, Chubb who was now night-watchman, ran to the rail where the rope ladder was made fast and peering into the darkness hailed in his boyish voice, "*Que quiere hombre?*" At this there was a guffaw of laughter from the Captain and the Mate who were standing on the lower bridge and who, no doubt, had been watching the exchange of signals. There was no reply from the boat but presently, in the light of Chubb's hurricane-lamp, Rob's merry face appeared over the rail. In a moment, he jumped to the deck and we grasped hands with many greetings and chuckles of pleasure.

We went to my cabin where, in the dim light of the oil-lamp, we sat on the settee exchanging all the news of our doings during the year since we had last seen each other in Melbourne. Then I told him of my life in the *Sierra Blanca*, with its working day from seven in the morning until midnight, when we were at sea, and all the trouble I was having in trying to "shoot" stars. Rob listened so intently that he let his pipe go out, his expression passing from sympathy to amazement. Then he got to his feet.

"Well, I'm damned! The bloody swine! He's got you doing that just because you are fresh from sail." He paused a moment and then went on, "Let's go aboard the *Lime Branch*; Bill, our Second Mate was navigator of Western Ocean mail-boats running to Montreal and I'll lay a month's wages that he could sail rings around these chaps, with sun, moon or stars. He will teach all you need to know in half an hour."

When I went to the Mate to ask permission, he said, "Oh, so he's the Third Officer of the *Lime Branch* is he? He's wearing so many brass buttons and gold stripes that I thought he was the Captain of the Port. All right."

On board the *Lime Branch*, the dining saloon was also used as a wardroom. It was brightly lit and all deck officers and engineer officers who were not on duty were sitting there, smoking and yarning. A couple of them were playing cribbage but when Rob brought me in they all jumped to their feet to make me welcome. "Bill" was a big, round man with a red, jolly face. He listened carefully while Rob explained my difficulties, then laid a great hand on my shoulder.

"Well, well, son," he boomed. "You come with me and we'll fix them."

We went to his cabin and for two hours Bill coached me so well that star sights for latitude by ex-meridian and for longitude, and ex-meridian of the sun became simple. He gave me a copy of Johnson's Ex-meridian Tables and a planisphere from which I could see the position of all the bright stars in the heavens. He also read me a little lecture and explained that, as Third Officer, my duty while on the bridge was to keep a watch and do the necessary navigation and not to spend my time up there sewing canvas or wiping bright-work. And, he went on with some emphasis, my afternoon watch below was a period in which I was supposed to rest so that I would be alert and efficient when I went on the bridge from eight o'clock until midnight.

I was more than grateful and when I returned to my cabin I was so full of comfort and confidence that I was asleep the moment my head touched the pillows.

We left Antofagasta in the middle of March which, down there, was close to the time of the autumnal equinox and we experienced the usual wild weather of that season as we made our way south towards the Straits of Magellan. With nearly six thousand tons of nitrate lying rocklike in her holds, the ship was deep in the water and heavy seas smashed over her bows while clouds of spray swept across the main deck and over the bridge. During these days there was very little work being done about the decks by the crew. And I was left to enjoy the luxury of my afternoon watch below undisturbed. But the routine of the second dog-watch—the period from six till eight in the evenings—was maintained. The wind blew fresh, strong or at gale force from anywhere in the sector of the compass that lies between south-south-west and west-north-west and, although it was bitterly cold when it was southerly, there were always stars to be seen, appearing briefly between the masses of ragged clouds that raced across the sky. It was these conditions that previously would have had me rising in mental agony and apprehension. How to find the star that you had chosen as being suitable for observation if no other groups of stars or constellations were visible to lead you to it, to identify it for you, and such stars as were to be seen gave a quick tantalising twinkle and were then covered by cloud?

Now, thanks to Rob Anderson and the genial Bill, I was calm and self-possessed. Not only was I sure that the results of my observations would be correct but I went on the bridge having calculated in advance the point in the heavens where the stars would be found—that is, how high they would be above the horizon and how they would bear by compass. Then all I had to do was to put the star's estimated altitude on my sextant, watch for a break in the clouds, and level my sextant at the point on the horizon below the known position of the star. All of a sudden, there it would appear, gleaming either a shade above or below the horizon, like a bright light on another vessel. Then it was gone but in that instant when it was to be seen a small adjustment of the sextant had put it directly on the horizon and I had the correct altitude; I had my sight. It was thrilling. On the passage out, I had welcomed with feelings of relief any thick, dirty weather with a dense cloud-packed sky or even fog. Now, I found star work exciting and quickly realised its value. Stars were scattered all over the heavens—north, south, east and west—and all at the same time so that one had endless possibilities for observation.

That first night when I took my correct results to the Captain his eyebrows went up in surprise but he gave me a warm smile and said, "That's better. In fact it's perfect. I suppose the Mate or Second Mate gave you some help." The Mate who was leaning over the chart-table comparing his results with the Captain's mumbled, "Not me, sir." Then he turned to me and said, "I suppose Mr. Foote gave you a hand."

"No, sir," I replied. "The Captain of the Port in Antofagasta came to my assistance." My answer seemed to startle the Captain but, leaving the Mate to explain, I left them and went to my cabin, glowing with contentment, to smoke a quiet pipe before going on the bridge to keep my watch.

10 *Montevideo, Dunkirk and Antwerp*

Two weeks after leaving Antofagasta, we were anchored off Montevideo where we had called for orders—that is, for instructions regarding the port at which the cargo was to be discharged. We lay there during all the daylight hours of one day while the Captain and Mrs. Compton went ashore to visit the agent and, no doubt, to have a look at the town. During this time, the Second Mate and I shared the duty on the bridge of keeping anchor watch while the Mate, with all hands of his small crew of seamen and apprentices, taking advantage of the fact that the ship was lying in sheltered water, steady and on an even keel, washed and painted our two masts and the funnel.

At first, when I went up on the bridge to take over from the Second Mate, I could see no sign of him. Then I found his backside, kneeling legs and feet, sticking through the door of the wheel-house. Inside, he had a wooden bucket containing sand and water and I realised that he had spent his anchor watch holystoning the teakwood gratings that covered the deck in there.

"Well, well," I said joking. "I thought you did all the holystoning you were ever likely to do when you were an apprentice in that hungry Aberdeen barque *Invercauld*."

He rinsed the sand from his fingers and got to his feet but he did not seem to see any humour in my remark. "I suppose that in Jimmy Nourse's ships you never did any holystoning. You had a crowd of Indian coolies to do it for you."

"No," I replied, "it wasn't at all like that. We did everything in Jimmy Nourse's ships that is done in any self-respecting windjammer. The only difference was that we did it very much better. I was an expert with a holystone but I'll be damned if I ever thought that I'd be expected to handle one myself once I passed for Second Mate and went to sea as an officer."

The Second Mate went below and I climbed on top of the wheel-house to the standard compass to check the bearings, after which I took a couple of turns back and forth across the bridge while I made up my mind what to do. In spite of all the wisdom of Bill's advice, I could hardly loll about the bridge while the ship was lying quietly at anchor and every other man-jack of the crew was hard at work under the constant gaze of the Mate who himself had his bare arms up to the elbows in a tub of yellow paint.

The only thing to do was to buckle to with good grace, which I did, at the same time resolving that that would be the end of it. After that day, I was determined that I would try to lead the life of an officer. So, first to the wheel-house to swab up the mess of water and sand left by the Second Mate's efforts, to raise the gratings on their edges, and then leave both doors and windows wide open so that the place would dry. The rest of the time I spent down on my hands and knees, holystoning the grating which covered the deck in each wing of the bridge. At the close of the afternoon, by the time I had put my gear away and put all the gratings back in place, bridge and wheel-house were spick and span and shipshape. It had been a fine, hot day and the warm land breeze had done its work. The crew had also finished and gone below. In the golden light of early evening, the freshly-painted masts and funnel glistened and made our ship look very smart.

Supper that day was one of the few occasions when we all sat down for a meal at the same time. The Captain was particularly cheerful and was very pleased and complimentary about the work that the Mate had managed to get done. He was very talkative and gave a lively account of everything they had done ashore; how, at the agent's office, the only orders he had found were that we should pass within signalling distance of St. Vincent, Cape Verde, and how he had met the Captain of the large four-masted barque that we could see lying off the port. She was a Nova Scotiaman, the *Howard D. Troop*, and she needed a Second Mate. My visits to the *Galgate* and the *Saxon* must have been noticed for the Captain looked at me with a smile and said, "Would you like to go, Mr. de Mierre?"

In reply, I asked, "Would you allow me to go, sir?"

"Not now, I wouldn't," the Captain replied. "I wouldn't be getting his Second Mate to take your place. Would I?" he ended with a grin.

This, of course, raised a round of general laughter in which I joined with all sincerity.

My life during the twenty-four days that passed from the time we left Monte-video until that sweet Spring morning when Ushant was sighted, was in com-plete contrast with the miserable, out-of-my-element existence of the outward passage. I was still as lonely; in fact, rather more so. Our duties were so ar-ranged that I did all the relieving of the bridge at meal-times. Thus, I went on watch at 7.45 a.m. so that the Mate could clean himself up before sitting down with the Captain, Mrs. Compton and the Second Mate. I, of course, had eaten beforehand. At noon, I was relieved by the Second Mate who had the watch until 4.00 p.m. But, as soon as the cabin bell voiced its jangling clatter, I took over again so that he could join the others at dinner. I ate mine when they had finished. It was the same at supper-time when I relieved the Mate. So, while we were at sea, I ate all my meals alone, with nobody to talk to. And now, there was no conversation when I relieved the Mate in the mornings and evenings; we merely repeated to each other the course being steered and then he went below. It was the same with the Second Mate when he relieved me at noon and midnight. I was in Coventry.

We left Montevideo at the beginning of my watch so, after the Captain had gone below, I remained on the bridge until midnight. When I relieved the Mate in the morning, the usual bucket of fresh water and swab of cotton waste were waiting for me in front of the wheel-house. For the moment I ignored them and got busy with my sextant but, at eight o'clock when apprentice Hopkins came away from the wheel and reported the course to me, before he could leave the bridge I assumed the exaggerated "lah-de-dah" accent of Third Officer Groome of R.M.S. *Ormuz* and, giving him a slow wink, said, "Oh, Hopkins, please remove this beastly bucket before I fall over it and break my neck."

"Yes, sir," replied Hopkins who grinned with delight as he picked up the bucket and went below.

I passed a very agreeable morning watch, pacing the bridge, watching the steering and enjoying the morning air and brilliant sunshine. As the sun climbed in the heavens, warming the land that lay just over the horizon, a fresh breeze streamed in from the south-east. It whipped the sea to sparkling life and brushed a merry song across my ears. I had taken a latitude sight of the sun, ex-meridian, and worked up the noon position some time before the Captain, Mate and Second Mate came up with their sextants. When we got the sun's altitude at noon all I had to do was to check that my calculations were right, making any small correction, if necessary, and I had finished.

That afternoon I spent my watch below, asleep in my cabin, and I had no word with the Mate until I went up to relieve him on the bridge at eight o'clock. He was about my height—two inches short of six feet. But I was not yet twenty while he must have been about forty years old. He was very greatly my senior in years, rank and service at sea, with all that that connotes. I had not yet completed five years at sea; my Second Mate's ticket was only six months old; he had been at sea about twenty-five years and had been Master of sailing-ships as large as those in which I had served my apprenticeship. So he was terrifyingly my senior.

I walked over to the weather wing of the bridge where he was standing and said, "Alright, sir." His reply was to turn slowly and stare at me, his eyebrows raised in an expression of deep grievance while he passed his hand along the varnished teak-wood rail of the bulwark.

"It's *not alright*," he said. "You didn't clean off the brightwork this morning. I suppose you forgot it."

"No, sir," I replied. "I've decided that I did enough of that kind of thing when I was in the half-deck."

To this he made no answer but continued, "And you did not turn out this afternoon to give us a hand on deck."

"I'm sorry, sir," I replied, "But after we left Antofagasta and the weather was too bad for any work to be done on deck and I rested in my afternoon watch below, I found I was able to keep a better watch when I came on the bridge at night."

"You mean you're not going to turn out in the afternoons to help me with the work on deck?"

"Yes, sir, that's what I mean."

For some moments he made no movement but stood there, hands thrust deep into his trousers pockets, head lowered, while he gazed at me as though baffled, or searching for words to express his feelings. Then he repeated the course being steered and turned to leave the bridge. But, before going below, he fired his parting shot.

"More assistance from the 'Captain of the Port' I suppose."

So I was in Coventry. The Mate was not speaking to me which I could well understand and possibly the Second Mate remained aloof so that there should be no mistake whose side he was on.

The *Sierra Blanca* was steaming her unspectacular ten knots through one of the pleasantest parts of the world's oceans. With every mile, the weather became warmer. However, during the hottest part of the day there was a refreshing breeze blowing up from the eastward over thousands of miles of ocean and, at night, after the sun had gone down, light airs came off the land carrying the indescribably sweet scent of fruitful, tropical earth. The sea subsided to mirror-calmness and the sky was brilliant with stars. I enjoyed my duties and enjoyed them the more because I knew that I was doing them well. It was not pleasant to be treated so coldly by my "shipmates" but I got used to it and the compensation was that my self-confidence was firmly restored.

There was no change in the Captain's behaviour towards me and it was during these days that his pretty Irish wife spoke to me. I remember this because it was the only time that she did so.

Some fifteen days out from Montevideo we were off St. Vincent, Cape Verde, with hoists of flags flying, asking for our orders, but the only reply was that we should proceed to the Channel and report when off Lloyds signal station, Dover.

In all these days since leaving Montevideo, and for the remainder of the home-ward passage, the Mate drove the Bos'n and his little crew with the energy of a man much younger. And he followed the well-tried practice of sailing-vessels which was intended to keep the ships in sound condition for thirty or forty years. But it all took a long time and, when we entered the Channel, although life-boats, rails, deck-houses and cowl-ventilators gleamed like those of a ship on her maiden voyage, the decks had not been touched.

We were thirty-eight days out from Antofagasta when we had Ushant abeam and it was at eight o'clock in the evening, the time of my going on watch. This was in the last week of April. The sun had set but the whole western half of the sky glowed in the lovely, soft colours of northern twilight. There was no wind but the gentle breeze of our own making and Captain and Mrs. Compton stood in the starboard wing of the bridge looking at the light as it dropped astern. Visibility was excellent and such outward-bound ships as we saw were too far away to bother us. It was a quiet watch and when the Second Mate relieved me at midnight I went to my cabin and turned in with a warm feeling of content-ment, glad that the voyage was nearly over.

Four hours later I was again on the bridge for we were in the English Channel. As on the outward passage, I was considered too inexperienced to be left in sole charge of the ship. I went on watch with the Mate. It was a perfect Spring morning. After a look into the wheel-house to make a mental note of the course we were steering, I went and stood in the wing of the bridge where a moment later I was joined by the Mate who astonished me by giving me a cheery greeting.

"Good Morning, Mister," he said and, before I could reply, he went on, "Wonderful morning, isn't it. And I think it's going to be a fine warm day." He paused while he took a close look through the binoculars, sweeping the horizon from port to starboard. When he had replaced the glasses in the teak-wood box that hung from the rail, he continued, "Well, there's nothing in sight except those fishing-smacks inshore, and they're becalmed. Keep a good look out, Mister, and I'll go below and get a bath and shave while I've the chance."

As I say, I was astonished. I thought about it while I paced the bridge and could only come to the conclusion that this sudden cordiality was an outburst of the "homeward-bound" spirit—"Channel fever" as we called it in sailing-ships. After all, it was a full four months since we had sailed from Newcastle and in only a day or two his wife would be coming on board to join him. Satisfied that I had the answer, I watched the sunrise and the growing day, so busy with my thoughts that I did not notice the passage of time until the ordin-ary seaman of the watch brought me a cup of coffee and a buttered ship's biscuit. It was 4.45 a.m., now broad daylight. Almost at the same moment, the Mate reappeared. When I had finished and placed the mug and plate on top of the flag-locker in the wheelhouse, he came over to me.

"Well, Mister, there's not much sense in both of us being up here, twiddling our thumbs, so to speak. There's lots to do today. I'll stay on the bridge and look after the ship while you take the three apprentices and the ordinary seaman and give her a good wash-down. Start on the fo'c's'le-head and see that the young beggars give a good scrubbing around the windlass, under the steam pipes and around the winches. By the time you get amidships the fore deck will be dry and the hands can start painting when they turn to at six o'clock."

So this was the explanation, the "homeward-bound" spirit. We set to with a will. The youngsters scrubbed vigorously; they too had Channel fever. The powerful jet of water from the nozzle of my hose washed all the dirt away over the side. The sun was warm and the iron decks dried quickly. As soon as they came on deck the Bos'n and his men were able to start painting while we continued aft with our scrubbing. We managed to finish the job, right as far as the flagstaff at the stern, before the end of the watch.

After breakfast I went to my cabin and lit my pipe. I was sitting reading when the senior apprentice, Hopkins, appeared at my door.

"Sir," he said with a grin, "The Chief Officer sends his compliments and wants to know if you like red paint."

"Please give my compliments to the Chief Officer, Hopkins, and tell that I do like red paint and if that is what he is using on deck I think he could not have made a better choice."

Hopkins quite properly repeated my answer verbatim so I was not at all surprised when, a few moments later, the Mate came to my cabin, purple in the face and practically bursting with indignation. He was so excited that he was almost incoherent but the substance of it was had I really given such an impudent message to Hopkins?

I got to my feet. "Well, sir, he brought me your very polite question and I think I sent back a polite reply. Did you really mean that you wanted me to come on deck and give you a hand?"

"You know bloody well I do."

He was right; I had known. But—and I think his realisation of this added to his fury—I was not willing that, when my time was my own, he should send a messenger for me, or expect me to come to heel at a blast from his whistle. However, this was now clear so I spent the forenoon (my watch below) with a bucket of quick-drying red paint and a long-handled striker—an implement much like a hoe, the metal blade being replaced by a brush. And I must admit that I enjoyed it. A safe five miles away on the starboard beam was the lighthouse marking the Casquets—the dangerous rocky outposts of the Channel Islands. The sun shining from a cloudless sky was hot but our speed stirred up a merry little breeze and it was exciting to be in the sandy-green waters of the English Channel again.

At noon we were back on the bridge, the weather more like midsummer and the now completely painted forward portion of the ship looking as bright as a new toy—red decks, light green watertight canvas covers on the hatches, white rails, yellow masts and derricks, white cowl-ventilators with freshly painted scarlet mouths and, finally, the yellow funnel with its black top. It was Mrs. Compton's childish delight at everything she could see from the bridge that gave me the idea that our workaday ship looked like a toy. When they had gone below the Mate approached and tried another gambit.

"Well, Mister, it's our watch on deck but if you want to get some rest you can go below." Then he paused, screwed up his face into what was meant to be a whimsical smile and continued, "Of course, if you don't, there are a hundred and one things you could do."

"Such as . . . ?" I asked.

"Well, the Bos'n and his gang are still working around number three hatch. There's still the after well-deck and the poop to get done. They're slowing down and if you went and gave them a hand maybe you could stir 'em up."

They may have been slowing down but when I joined them I thought they were doing very well for men who had already had five hours of it. With the age-old spirit of the half-deck the apprentices had formed themselves into a little gang of their own and, even though the splashes of paint on their clothing, Chubb's red nose and the great red hand imprinted on the seat of Simpson's trousers suggested that there had been some skylarking, they were easily holding their own with the men. At eight bells, four o'clock, we were so nearly finished that I stayed until the job was done which left barely time enough to get cleaned up and have my supper before going on the bridge at six o'clock.

By eight o'clock we had Dungeness abeam. Two hours later we were approaching Dover at reduced speed, on "stations"; the Mate on the fo'c's'le-head with the carpenter, standing by the windlass in case we had to anchor; the Second Mate, whose watch it was, at the engine-room telegraph; and myself working the signal lamp, asking for orders. Fortunately, the tide was now against us and with the engines going "dead slow" the ship was just able to stem the current, remaining practically stationary, while we waited for the reply to the signal that I was repeating very slowly, over and over again: "*Sierra Blanca* from Antofagasta for orders." At last, after about twenty minutes, which seemed very much longer, we got the instruction to discharge our nitrate cargo at Dunkirk and Antwerp.

144

This news seemed to please the Captain, as though it was what he expected, for he already had his mind made up about what he was going to do.

He stuck his head over the canvas "dodger"—the weather-cloth above the bridge rail—and hailed the Mate. "Away there, Mister."

"Ay ay," replied the Mate.

"It's Dunkirk. I'll go round the Foreland and anchor in the Downs till daylight."

Then we were moving ahead again, the windlass coughing and spluttering after its long rest as the starboard anchor was hove out of the hawse-pipe and held just above water-level, ready for letting go. By 11.30 p.m. the anchor was down, the ship lying quietly in a snug berth not far from the end of the pier at Deal. At midnight I was on the bridge again to keep anchor watch until four o'clock.

It was a mild April night with a sweetly scented breeze coming off the land, but as I bent over the compass muttering to myself the names of the lights, I shivered as though an icy gale were blowing down my neck and I could hear the clangour of topsail sheets, lifts and all the other cordage of a sailing-ship beating against the masts. For the moment I was back aboard the *Arno*. She had lain in the same position and I could almost hear the gruff kindliness of Mr. Fowler's voice murmuring, "That's right, son, Gulf Stream and South Goodwin."

I was very tired. When the watch ended twenty-four hours would have passed since I got out of my bunk and I had spent practically the whole time on my feet. Once more I shivered, shook myself, then leaned against the binnacle and thought of the advice Mr. Fowler had given me on that bright Sunday morning in June ten months ago. Many times during the last four months I had regretted having taken it. For my taste, life in a tramp steamer was not at all attractive and I might just as well do another couple of years in a sailing-ship, as Second Mate, leading the kind of life I had become used to. Then I would have my sea time in—that is, the stipulated period of service in charge of a watch—and could sit for examination as Mate and Master and perhaps even Extra Master. And that would be time enough to go back into steamers, in some good liner company such as the Orient or the P & O or perhaps even the Cunard Line.

At four o'clock we were under way again for it was broad daylight and Dunkirk was only forty miles away. Now I had a watch below that nobody was likely to rob me of. I went to my cabin and fell into a deep sleep as soon as I stretched, fully dressed, on the settee. When I came on deck again it was to find that we were picking up the Pilot who took us into harbour.

Dunkirk was a pleasant little town in 1910. It had not yet been battered about physically or morally by the armies of two long and terrible wars and, like most European seaports, there was a quality of resilience in its morality that enabled it to withstand, perhaps accommodate would be the better word, the exigencies of the constantly changing seafaring population, and to help them to spend their money, without loss of either dignity or the air of provincial respectability.

We were seeing it at its best, in beautiful Spring weather. All the piers and quays were well paved and very clean. From all four hatches the slings of bags of nitrate were swung out of the ship and landed on the quay to remain there until waggons came along to haul them away. It was a slow process but there was nothing to be done. We had to accept the situation with good grace.

As a matter of fact, a subdued air of domesticity hung about the ship for Mrs. Mate and their small boy had arrived and were living aboard, and the Chief Engineer's wife had also joined her husband. There were other changes too: the Second Mate had gone to England to sit for his examination as Mate and the apprentices had gone home. So I was left pretty much to myself, going around to see the hatches were open in the mornings and that the stevedores had everything that they wanted, giving occasional attention to the mooring-lines and having them slackened off as necessary as the ship rose in the water; and, at the end of the day, making sure that nobody had run off with any of our beautiful manilla rope slings, and that all hatches were properly covered for the night.

It was not an arduous day and there was never any night work. The Mate and his family did their shore-going during the daylight hours so in the evenings I roamed the narrow little streets of the old town, usually accompanied by Sandy Bothwell. We sampled the beer at all the bars within a convenient radius but found it warm and insipid. No amount of the brine pickles which were put before you to increase your thirst made it taste any better.

Then, one night, our luck changed. We had decided to go back aboard the ship but when we turned into the broad street which flanked the waterfront we found ourselves midway between a crowd of yelling men who were hurling stones, taunts and curses and a troop of cuirassiers that was galloping down the street towards us. Instinctively we dived into the nearest doorway, managing to get inside just as the steel shutter was rolled down. For a moment, in the darkness, we wondered where we were and what was going on. Then lights were switched on and we found that we were in a comfortable room with red, plush-covered seats running along the wall, tables and chairs and quite a handsome bar.

This was the café *New Golden Star*. The only other occupants were the fat, jolly couple who owned the place, Monsieur and Madame Leclerq, their pretty daughter Blanche, a most efficient barmaid from Lancashire and a well-dressed middle-aged French gentleman who stood at the bar.

Outside, the din of stones hitting the metal shutters, the noise of the horses' hooves, the rattle of harness and accoutrements, shouts of soldiers and workers was such that no conversation was possible until their action had drifted some distance up the street. Then the old couple rose from their seats and came to greet us with arms upraised and many exclamations of welcome and thankfulness that we had found shelter with them.

"*Mon Dieu! C'est terrible cette grève,*" cried the old lady while her husband patted her plump shoulders murmuring words of comfort and calm. It was evident that the trouble which had been brewing in the docks had boiled over and all the stevedores had gone on strike.

Sandy had taken the old lady's outstretched hand and, as he led her back to the table, he was saying, "That's alright, Mother, that's alright. They'll never keep that up very long. It'll soon be over." His merry, smiling face was enough to restore confidence in any circumstances. Then, looking over his shoulder towards the bar, he went on, "Yon's a fine sight o' bottles ye have there and a wee drappie o' whisky or brandy is all we need to calm our fears." He looked around with a grin and added, "We'll be honoured if ye'll join us and we'll drink to yon liberty, equality and brotherhood that's going on up the street, and *Vive la France* and God save the King, even though he's no a Stuart."

We all sat down around the table while the Lancashire girl, who was probably the only one of them who had understood Sandy's little speech, brought the drinks. Then, on the insistence of Monsieur Leclerq, she joined us. The two young women and I drank "stoot"—stout—the others drank whisky and brandy. Then the Frenchman got to his feet to propose a toast.

"*C'est vrai* . . . 'ee no Stoo . . . art . . . 'ee ees dead." For a moment he was so affected that his English quite left him and he continued, "*Oui, c'est vrai. Le Roi Edouard Sept est mort. La France a perdu un ami.*" He raised his glass and, when we were on our feet, said with great solemnity, "*A la mémoire d'Edouard Sept, roi d'Angleterre, ami de France.*" As we all sat down again he concluded by repeating, "'ee was a gude fren'."

This was a shock to us. The ship had no wireless and we had not known that the King was seriously ill. But so it was, and this day, the sixth of May he had died. For the moment we were all cast down, everyone making whatever appropriate remark he or she could think of. Sandy turned his glass slowly around, staring into the liquor while he muttered his favourite: "Ho, ho, the rueing of it."

"Is that the best your Bobbie Bur-r-rns can do?" I said. "I'd rather chant 'Can honour's voice provoke the silent dust?'"

" 'Or flattery," continued Sandy, "soothe the dull, cold ear of death.' Aye, yon Thomas Gray must ha' come frae north o' the Tweed and he's right. The King is dead. Long live the King. Long live good King George."

This took us out of the politely solemn but rather awkward posture that our little company had assumed and each raised his or her glass to drink that toast, and the several others that followed, with enthusiasm. As the evening wore on it was natural that other toasts should be thought necessary, including, of course, several to each other; and so, by about eleven o'clock, we had all become old friends. The petite Blanche—she may have been anything between seventeen and twenty-two years old—had become very drowsy after her third "stoot" and with her little hands clasped around Sandy's arm she rested her head against his shoulder, trying desperately to keep awake. The old couple beamed amiably on us all. The Lancashire girl, making tantalising use of her eyes, was trying to carry on a conversation in French with the French gentleman while Sandy and I were discussing that most interesting topic, namely, what would be our next ship.

Then everybody fell silent and in the same instant realised that the streets were quiet. With a sudden determination, as though he had just come out of a dream, the French gentleman got to his feet and said, "Now I go 'ome to my wife and kids." We took an affectionate farewell of the old couple and the two young women, became terribly involved in the exchange of courtesies with the French gentleman and at last made our way back to the ship through docks that were as still as Gray's country churchyard.

The strike did not last long. After a few days we left for the short run to Antwerp. As soon as the ship was moored we were invaded by noisy gangs of Flemish-speaking stevedores.

The ship became a cheerful bedlam with the busy rattle of winches and the shouts of the men working in the holds, sometimes coarse laughter and shrieks of feminine mirth for in each hold two or three women were employed stitching up bags that were burst or torn. I had never before seen the sexes mixed in manual labour aboard ship, except, of course, in India where the traditional superiority of the male ensured propriety; so I was very interested and only sorry that I could not understand the jokes that raised such hilarity.

Perhaps it was just as well. One day a young woman came along on her way to work in number three hold. She was very poorly dressed in thick woollen stockings and heavy boots, a dirty, rather ragged skirt and over her head a shawl that was pinned at her breast. But she was beautiful. Golden hair peeped from under the shawl and the face that it framed was a perfect oval with the complexion and colouring that must have inspired the medieval artists of these

148

parts—delicate features, eyes of vivid blue, round and innocent looking as a child's. She had rosy cheeks and white teeth flashed between the red lips of her little mouth and, as though this were not enough, when she approached me, her smile of greeting produced the most delightful dimples in her cheeks.

I was entranced. I was very young, with no kind of experience with women. My only thought was that a face of such sweetness and beauty would be a perfect model for a madonna. So I spoke to her, asking if she spoke English.

She chuckled gaily. "Yes, I spik English." Then, making the most unmistakably lewd motions with her hands, "Tonight, you and me. Very good."

Whatever the expression on my face, she grinned in the manner of one who has got the best of the joke, then swung her leg over the hatch coaming, expertly located the topmost rung with her clumsy boot and started on her way down the vertical iron ladder into the lower hold. But when she was half way down, a young, curly-headed stevedore ran up the other side of the ladder, thrust his hand up her clothes and brought her to a halt.

The young woman threw back her head and in a voice that must have been audible over the whole ship she yelled, "Let go my . . . Let go my . . ." The word she used was from the coarse, unrestrained English of the fo'c's'le and all the men and the other women in the hold shouted with laughter in which she joined with equal gusto.

A merry set of rascals. Pieter Breughel did not have to invent the frolicsome Flemings that he loved to depict four hundred years earlier and the intervening centuries had not changed them.

The evenings were very quiet. The merry stevedores had gone ashore, the winches were silent and I found that I was expected to stay aboard and look after the ship. The engineers were responsible only for the engine-room and the winches; the Captain, of course, came and went as he wished and the only other deck officers were the Mate and myself. Every evening for the first four days, as soon as supper was over, the Mate would come to my door to tell me that he was going ashore. Then he and his wife and little boy would go down the gangway and walk up the quay and into the town.

At first I did not mind because the docks were crowded with sailing-ships, steamers and large barges. These last were especially interesting. Their living accommodation at the stern housed skipper, wife and often several children, and was always shiningly clean. Frequently, little gardens were cultivated in boxes on the cabin roof. So long as I did not go too far from the ship I could wander about the wharves and have a good look at the craft which lay alongside. Then, tired out, I would return to the ship, and make a final check of the mooring-lines before turning in.

But, as the end of the week approached, I decided that I had to see the town. The cargo was going out quickly and there was every likelihood that by the middle of the following week we would be away. So, after supper, I changed, went along to the Mate's cabin, tapped on his door and told him that I was going ashore. He came out into the alleyway, dressed in his shore-going clothes and said, "We can't both go ashore. Somebody has to stay by the ship."

"No, sir," I replied, "but I've been aboard four nights and now I think it's my turn."

We went down the gangway in a rather ridiculous little procession and, on the quay, the Mate said again, "I thought I told you that I was going ashore. And that we can't both go."

"Yes, sir, you did. But I've kept the ship these last four nights and tonight I'm going to have a look at the town . . . and get a decent meal . . . for a change."

I walked up the quay followed by the Mate and his family whose pace slowed down as I increased my distance from them and when I got to the gate and looked around, they had turned back and were going aboard again.

It was not a pleasant thing to have done but I did not bother my head about the Mate's chagrin. I was too full of a fierce indignation at his utter lack of any consideration for me in spite of the fact that I had worked an unbroken twenty-four hours, helping him to get the ship ready for port before arriving at Dunkirk. In his mind, he was still the Master of a windjammer and I a senior apprentice. So I left the docks and made my way towards the town muttering to myself, "To hell with him. A few days more and I'll be leaving the ship . . . and if I never see him again, that will be wonderful."

Where to go and what to do was no problem. I was not the reckless, wife-in-every-port type heading eagerly for strong drink and weak women. I wanted to walk about the streets and see the cathedral and the other sights of the city; this I did until darkness fell. By that time the pugnacious mood had worn off, my feet were sore from the cobblestones and I was very hungry. Fortunately for me, Antwerp was having some sort of May fair on one of the wide boulevards and it drew me by its noise and the loom of its flares.

For several hundred yards the boulevard was lined with booths, alfresco restaurants, small merry-go-rounds for the children and tents for the usual side-shows as well as one large one containing an exhibition of the most horrific waxworks. It was very gay and crowded with people young and old. Chickens, ducks and sausages were grilling, boiling and frying. Cauldrons of stew simmered and gave off the most appetising aroma. There were all kinds of cooked meats. Fat, jolly women presided over glowing braziers, wielding curiously shaped pans and waffle irons, producing delicious-looking doughnuts and waffles that were evidently in great demand.

150

It was difficult to find a place until a good-natured Belgian family—Pa, Ma, their pretty daughter and her young man—kindly made room for me at their table. On their recommendation, aided by my halting French and their halting English, I made a wonderful meal of young chicken and sausages followed by several waffles which one ate two at a time, with a layer of thick, sweet cream between them, like a sandwich. They were as light as sea foam and so tooth-some that it was difficult to know when one had eaten enough. The cream squirted out over our faces, hung in gobbets from Pa's moustache and resulted in such an exchange of personal remarks and merriment that by the end of the meal we were quite at ease with each other and had become good friends.

At the breakfast-table next morning the air was electric. The only one who did not notice this was the little boy. He was about five years old and had probably been very happy to climb aboard again the previous evening because there were all kinds of games he could play, whereas to trudge after his parents, or to sit watching them eat and drink must have been for him a dull and weari-some way of passing the time. He knelt on the settee eating a rich mixture of thick, sweet, condensed milk and porridge and piped a happy, falsetto "Good Morning" when I came in and took my seat.

His parents sat in grim silence but the effect of the tension on Captain Compton was to make him more than usually talkative for that time of day. He told a succession of Irish stories that brought peals of laughter from his wife—as though she had not heard them many times before—and from me. However, nothing could thaw the frozen faces of Mr. and Mrs. Mate; a sideways glance to the head of the table and a half smile was as far as they would go until, at last, the Captain produced that one about the two Irish women talking over the fence while they hung out their washing. It was then quite a new story but it was also a little broad for the breakfast-table.

"One of the women pointed to a shirt that was hanging on her neighbour's line and said, tauntingly, 'An' what's wrong wit' your husband, Mrs. Rooney? Did ye not see that big brown stain on the tail of his shirt. Or is that the best ye could do wid it?' 'You're a liar. It's rust!' screamed Mrs. Rooney."

Mr. and Mrs. Mate could not resist. They laughed as heartily as the rest of us and the little boy crinkled up his nose and joined in as though he completely understood the joke and startled us all by shouting "Jesus Christ!" as though to say, "That was a good one."

His parents were shocked and so was Mrs. Compton but I noticed that her eyes twinkled over the napkin that she had instinctively placed before her mouth. I found the sudden change in Mr. and Mrs. Mate—from the lofty air of injured dignity to unexpected and quite acute embarrassment—very comical and I had difficulty in restraining my mirth. After the first few seconds of purple-faced containment the Captain gave up the effort and roared with laughter.

At the end of the following week the ship was empty. By eight o'clock on the morning of Friday, May 20th, we had dropped the Antwerp Pilot and were heading for the Bristol Channel where the ship was to load another cargo of coal for the west coast of South America. Before midnight we were clear of the Straits of Dover. Late in the afternoon of the following day a sturdy cutter bore down to us and we picked up our Pilot. We rounded the Lizard at midnight and before supper on Sunday evening were tied up alongside the quay in our loading berth at Barry.

Next morning, before breakfast, I went on the bridge to get my nautical almanac and the notebooks that I had left in the wheel-house. With all its varnished teak and polished brass, teakwood gratings and coconut matting, it was a nice bridge but I noticed that already a film of coal-dust was settling down. The brass binnacle cover in the wheel-house had lost its polish and was showing tarnish where the sweaty hands of the helmsman had grasped it when he covered the compass before leaving the wheel.

There was a pot of grease and a lump of cotton waste on the deck, between the flag lockers; instinctively, I picked it up and laid a coating of grease over the brass binnacle. I put the grease tin on the locker, next to my books, and then brought in the teakwood gratings which I stood on their edges against the after bulkhead. Next, I rolled up the matting that extended the full width of the bridge, and brought that inside.

Coming out of the wheel-house, clutching the tin of grease, I met the Mate who came up the ladder on the port side. Before giving himself time to see what had been going on, he blurted out, "Where are you going with that grease? I was just going to ask you to be so kind and polite as to put a coating of grease on all the brass-work up here."

"Yes, sir," I replied. "That is exactly what I am doing." He looked at me with an air of disbelief then noticed the absence of gratings and coconut runner. He went into the wheel-house and while I was putting grease on the engine-room telegraph I saw through the windows that he was touching the binnacle to make sure that I had spoken the truth. Then, rather red in the face with discomfiture at his too hasty sarcasm, he left the bridge.

It was all I could do to stop myself from calling after him, sarcastic in my turn, "If you like, sir, I'll run up aloft and grease the mizzen royalmast before I leave the ship." But I thought better of it. That would have been impudent and quite unbefitting an officer, even one with greasy hands.

11   *S.S.* Sutlej

My efforts to go back in sail ended when I received a letter from James Nourse Ltd. The *Arno* had arrived in Middlesbrough three months before and was laid up, waiting to be sold, but I was offered a berth as Third Officer in the *Sutlej*, the latest of their four steamers. Three weeks after leaving the *Sierra Blanca* I was back in Barry looking for my new ship.

I found her in the dry dock. Before going there she had filled her bunkers and her Indian seamen were squatting about her upper-works, washing off the coal-dust.

The *Sutlej* was a bonny-looking vessel. On each side there were four lifeboats under davits on the boat deck. And all the deckhouses for the accommodation of Captain and officers, chart-house and wheel-house were of varnished teak. She had a yellow funnel with a black top. Below the black top a ring of long, red triangles encircled the funnel. This was intended to represent a crown and derived from her service in the transport of Indian emigrants for the Crown Agent for the Colonies.

At the main masthead was the white flag with the blue St. Andrew's cross and the red diamond in its centre that I had sailed under for the four years of my apprenticeship. I had the feeling that I was coming home again.

Before I had finished paying off the cab, a Tindal or Bos'n's Mate came with four lascars to get my baggage. I followed them up to my cabin on the starboard side of the boat deck. There, a young man greeted me with a smile and, speaking rapidly in Hindustani, explained that he was the officers' servant, that his name was Yusuf and that he would do the unpacking. My Hindustani was limited and rather rusty but I managed to tell him that I would do it myself. I wanted to settle in properly. It was a nice cabin and likely to be my home for a long time. Yusuf's face showed his disappointment. After I had searched my mind and found the word for "Thank you" he cheered up but all the time that I was stowing my things away in drawers, lockers and wardrobe and filling the rack with my sea-stock of reading matter, he squatted on his heels outside the door making a mental note of where everything went.

There was no need to change out of my shore-going clothes which consisted of a double-breasted blue jacket and trousers to match. This was the dress favoured by the majority of officers in the Merchant Service. The buttons of the jacket were detachable and could be quickly changed from black to brass; the suit could be worn with equal propriety afloat or ashore. All I had to do was to put on my uniform cap and I would be in harmony with my surroundings.

According to Yusuf, the Captain, Chief Engineer and Chief Officer were

The author, 1911, S.S. *Sutlej*

walking about under the bottom of the ship, so I sat on the settee and had a good look about me. The cabin was about seven feet square. The settee was against the after bulkhead. The forward bulkhead, between bunk and door, was occupied by a table and a wash-stand with a teak cover the same height as the table. There was a large port hole on each side of the door. It was bright and airy and high enough above the water-line to remain dry unless we should find ourselves deep-loaded in a gale of wind.

154

I put my pipe down and went out on deck just as the Captain and Chief Officer came up. Their greeting was cordial but had that slight reserve which is usual when sailors who are going to be shipmates meet for the first time. The wise junior does not volunteer any information about himself; he answers questions briefly. Any attempt to impress would be fatuous. Not only would it be resented but the passing of the first few days at sea will show what kind of shipmate you are going to be.

Four years before, Captain Brown had been Mate of the ship *Lena*. When she was sold he went as Chief Officer of the steamer *Ganges*. Now he was to make his first voyage in command. Mr. Potter had been Mate of the ship *Avon* and had already made one voyage in the *Sutlej*. With my service in the ships *Main* and *Arno* there were four of the company's ships to talk about, so the ice was soon broken.

"Well," said Captain Brown, looking at me with a smile, "you'll be needing some gold stripes for your sleeves and a couple of shoulder straps for your whites. If you haven't got them already you'd better go ashore and see the tailor." He turned to Mr. Potter, "You heard what the Chief said? They'll not be finished with that stern gland before the end of the day. We'll not get out of here before tomorrow noon. I'll away ashore."

"Aye aye, sir," replied Mr. Potter. He watched the Old Man disappear and then went to the spare cabin that was next to mine, where a grey-haired lady sat in a wicker chair, darning socks. She was the typical sailor's wife of those days when voyages were very long and as much as three years might pass before they saw their husbands again. Their lives were very lonely except for the rare occasions when, if their husband was senior enough, they were permitted to be with him on board his ship while she was in a home port. Such things as annual leave, or any leave at all, with pay, were then practically non-existent in the Merchant Service.

I, too, made for the shore, to look for the tailor, cherishing visions of gold braid and myself looking as smart as Rob Anderson had done in Antofagasta.

The following day, a Friday, we left the dry dock and made fast alongside a wharf where two or three lorries were waiting for us. They were loaded with marine stores.

Mr. Potter nothing loth, I took it upon myself to check and sign the carter's lists and watch the Serang and his men stow everything away. I spent the rest of the time examining my new ship, my mood exhilarated by the occasional glint of that gold stripe on my sleeve. It was really quite insignificant, only a quarter of an inch broad instead of the usual half inch, but it was the first such thing that I had ever worn and it warmed my heart.

The *Sutlej* was 350 feet long, that is, about one hundred feet longer than the average length of the company's sailing-ships and, like them, she had been designed for the coolie trade. All the decks were of wood.

The carpenter was a Norwegian who had been for years in the company's sailing-ships, the last being the *Erne*, where the donkeyman had been his shipmate. Yellow hair, sprinkled with grey, fell from under the peak of the carpenter's cap and wide, blue eyes shone in his open, honest face. The donkeyman was an arresting figure, about six feet tall and broad-shouldered. He was a West Indian of mixed ancestry; some African and probably some English blood ran in his veins. His name was Tudor Cunningham. Perhaps, two and a quarter centuries earlier, a Tudor Cunningham had left his farm in the Welsh marches to fight for the Duke of Monmouth in his rebellion against King James II, only to end up in slavery, tilling an alien soil with the Negro slaves on some island in the West Indies.

Our Second Officer, new to the ship and also new to the company, arrived on the Saturday, accompanied by an elder brother. His name was Grey and he was a short, plump man with fat, red cheeks, a brown moustache and a roguish, liquid eye. He must have been in his late thirties and, as I learned during the months that we were shipmates, he had already served as an officer in a dozen steamers of almost as many different companies. He was evidently a rolling stone and one could not help feeling that his brother had come down with him from the north of England to make quite sure that he joined his ship. From Manchester to Barry, via Cardiff, is a long journey.

We sailed in the early evening on Monday, June 20th. By the time we had swung compasses in Barry Roads and the adjuster and Pilot had gone, the sun was sinking below the horizon, leaving behind it a golden after-glow that made the smooth sea before us shine like the inside of a pearl-shell and lit up the windows of the cottages that dotted the fields behind Breaksea Point, a short two miles away. I had spent a couple of hours walking in those country lanes the previous afternoon. The atmosphere was now so clear that I could see the hamlet where I had had tea. That had been a very deliberate feast of thickly-buttered, fresh-baked scones, strawberries still warm from the sun and a bowl of rich cream. I knew that it would be several years before I would have the chance to eat another like it.

Captain Brown stood in the starboard wing of the bridge and when the Pilot's boat was clear of the ship he gave his orders; to me at the engine-room telegraph, "Full ahead."; to the quartermaster at the wheel, "*Dow tora.*" It meant "port a little" for the ship's head started swinging slowly to starboard.

Less than four weeks before I had been in the same spot, inward bound in the *Sierra Blanca* and now I was bound outward again to Torrevieja, on the coast of Spain, where we would load a cargo of salt for Calcutta. That would be our terminal, or home port, for the next three years or more. I liked the prospect because I liked the ship. No one was going to ask me to swab the salt off the bright-work, or to put a smear of grease on the brass-work in the *Sutlej*. And the trade would be interesting; running out of Calcutta, through the Torres Straits to the Fiji Islands or round the Cape of Good Hope to the West Indies, practically all the time in "flying-fish" weather. That was the manner of my thinking as I began my first night watch of the voyage.

About three hundred miles east of Gibraltar, Torrevieja lies roughly midway between Cartagena and Alicante. We were off the port in the middle of Sunday afternoon, after a quiet passage of six days. We had arrived at a time when the little town was deep in the embrace of its siesta. Captain Brown had already been there several times, in the *Ganges*; with engines moving "dead slow" he took the ship to a berth about three quarters of a mile from the beach and anchored.

Three hours later, in the cool of the evening, the Port Authorities and agent came aboard and our arrival was made official. We were now in Spain; the agreeable aroma that they brought with them—a combination of eau-de-Cologne, Havana tobacco, a whisper of garlic and a more audible note of human being—confirmed this.

They may have been slow in coming to life on a Sunday afternoon, but before seven o'clock the next morning lighters full of salt were alongside at all four hatches with gangs of stevedores. We were ready for them. On the passage from Barry the crew had spent much of their time lining the holds with bamboo matting. Derricks were up and we had steam on the winches. Very soon the large iron tubs that the lighters had brought with them were being filled, hoisted and swung inboard to be tipped down the open hatches. It was a good, clean cargo and simple to load. The salt had been produced from sea water, evaporated by the heat of the sun in the salt-pans that covered many acres of the land behind the beach. It was very heavy and would soon settle down into an almost solid mass. We used no shifting-boards but Grey and I went below at frequent intervals to make sure that it was properly trimmed throughout the breadth of the holds. This was, perhaps, an unnecessary precaution, because the trimmers knew their job at least as well as we did; but ours was the responsibility.

It was a pleasant anchorage, well sheltered from the prevailing winds and, of course, in the last week of June the weather was perfect, with long days of hot sunshine. This meant that the Serang, with his mates and twenty-five seamen could really get to work on the never-ending task of cleaning the ship.

As part of this process we put the life-boats in the water and took the opportunity to exercise the crew, both seamen and firemen, at the oars and in stepping the mast and using the sail. It was Captain Brown's idea and provided a welcome change for firemen and engine-room officers who very soon were challenging the sailors to race against them.

It took eight days to load the six thousand tons that put the ship down to her marks. We left Torrevieja in the cool, sweet air of dawn on July 6th. Four weeks later we lay, with engines stopped, off the Eastern Channel light-vessel, at the head of the Bay of Bengal, waiting for the Pilot. The south-west monsoon was blowing fresh and in the shallow water, meeting the ebb tide, it raised a nasty, short, high sea. Most of the time we could only see the Pilot's whaler when, for a moment, it balanced on the breaking crests of the mud-yellow seas. Then it would disappear as it pitched steeply down into the hollow of the trough until, at last, they worked their way into the relatively smooth water under our lee.

Then we steamed through the Saugor Roads into the Hughli River and by the late afternoon were ninety miles from the sea, moored bow and stern, between four buoys at Princeps Ghat. I had thoroughly enjoyed the day. In the ship *Main* I had towed up and down the river twice in the course of my three years' voyage in her, so I was in familiar waters. At that time I had been a rather grubby, but carefree apprentice. Now I was on the bridge of a twelve-knot steamer, wearing a smart white uniform and paying as much attention to the pilotage and to the Quartermaster at the wheel as though to get the ship safely around the sandbanks and through the narrow channels that swept close to the shore were my responsibility. But I still found time to look for those things that had made such an impression on me when I had first seen them four years before. The broad river, all aglitter with sunshine, alive with country craft of great variety, some with high deck cargoes of bales of straw or coconut fibre. They spread large, tattered, patchwork sails and went bowling up river before a fair breeze and flood tide, with their crews asleep on top of the cargo, in the shadow of the sail. Others, not so fortunate, struggled to cross the stream, their almost naked men toiling and sweating at the oars under the blazing sun.

I heard again the constant, plaintive keening of the kites as they hung motionless in the air, their heads ranging from side to side in their search for offal borne on the flood. Sometimes the dense foliage of banyan, peepul, mango trees and coconut palms that lined the banks parted to reveal villages of colour-washed houses—white, pale blue, red and saffron—and crumbling temples, with ghoul-like, evil-looking vultures sitting on the roofs. The beaches were thronged with women, washing clothes, up to their waists in the water, people bathing and children frolicking in the surf that was stirred up by our passing.

At Hastings the river pilot was relieved by the Harbour Master, the "mud-pilot", as he was called, who took us to our berth. There waiting for us was Esau, the dinghy-wallah, with his gaily painted dinghy. The bulkhead of its little cabin was covered with small boards, each bearing in brass letters the name of one of the company's sailing-ships. The Esaus, father and son, had been the dinghy-wallahs ever since Captain James Nourse made his first voyage in the Indian emigrant trade, the "coolie trade", fifty years earlier.

But no one wanted to go ashore. It had been a long, hot, busy day and after dinner it was pleasant to sit, yarn and smoke on the boat deck and to look at the distant lights of the city, twinkling across the *maidan*—the beautiful, large common that bordered the river for almost two miles and extended an even greater distance away from the river.

Next morning, for a couple of hours, the ship was like a bedlam. Dinghies, with yelling dinghy-wallahs quarrelling for custom, crowded around the accommodation ladder. The crew of sailors and firemen, now dressed in clean white dhoties, many clutching a precious umbrella and at the same time juggling with bundles and boxes, were going ashore. An equally noisy assembly of gharry-wallahs waited for them at the landing-stage, their appetites, or, rather, their tongues, whetted for the delights of an argument, many arguments —how much to the Shipping Office, then to Howrah railway station for the long journey to their homes somewhere in northern India?

Serangs, Tindals, sailors and firemen, they were all Moslems and all came from the same neighbourhood. The Serangs were pretty much like paternal chieftains. They chose their men and their word was law and, on board the ship, orders or reprimands were given only through the Serang. Only he was responsible for his men and if he was a good man you had a good crew—one that was like a united family and that came back with you voyage after voyage. It was an excellent system.

The Serang and a handful of his men remained by the ship. Hardly had the last dinghy, loaded with grinning, chattering sailors, left the gangway, than crowds of cargo workers, men and women, came on board and went down the open hatches into the 'tween-decks. Large steel lighters had made fast abreast the doors that had been opened in the ship's side and soon the men were shovelling the salt into shallow baskets which were placed on the heads of the women who passed by in an endless chain. As they walked by the scales that had been placed at the side doors, the baskets were emptied into a sack which, when it reached the required weight, was spilled down a chute into the lighters.

It was a pleasant way to be working cargo. Instead of the rattle of steam winches, the only noise was the soft padding of the women's bare feet and their monotonous chanting of the same three or four notes, over and over again.

Calcutta was then a beautiful city. It was not yet overpopulated. The streets were kept clean and at night the pavements were not yet infested by poor people, sleeping there because they had no other home. The motor-car, with its unseemly haste, had not yet arrived. There was an air of general prosperity. In the evenings, the Strand Road which ran along the river bank was full of fine carriages with uniformed coachmen and grooms, bearing wealthy Europeans, Indians and Parsees and their families, and of ticca-gharries, hired by humbler folk of the same races, all enjoying the breeze that came upstream, after the heat of the day.

On the river, steamers arrived or sailed at every high water, mooring or unmooring at slack tide, arriving with the last of the flood and going down to the sea on the first of the ebb. All the berths between Hastings and the Howrah Bridge were occupied by steamers except for a handful of native-owned sailing-vessels that lay tucked away in a quiet berth, just above the bridge where they would remain until the south-west monsoon, blowing up the Bay of Bengal, had spent its force. I had first seen them four years before when, in the ship *Main*, we had towed up river to go into dry-dock in Howrah.

There were six of us apprentices in the *Main*, all making our first voyage, and in spite of the rude shock of hard reality with its continuous physical work, little sleep and scanty food, we still cherished the romantic, boyish dreams that had called us to the sea. So sailing-vessels were of the greatest interest for us and while our ship was in dock we walked across the bridge one evening to have a closer look at them.

We found a collection of the quaintest vessels we had ever seen. There were large dhows with high poops and slanting quarter-decks, with quarter-galleries and carved, decorated sterns—a legacy, no doubt, from the early Spanish and Portuguese navigators. These had come up from the Andaman Islands, the Maldives or even from far-off Zanzibar. There were small wooden brigs and barques, with square stern windows, lanyard rigging, hemp shrouds and single topsails. Some of these were old opium clippers, ending their days under native ownership, frequently owned by their Moslem master, trading around the coasts of India, Burma and Indochina and in the Java Seas. We

High poop and decorated stern

went on board several and everywhere we were most kindly received and from one we had some difficulty in getting away again.

She was a full-rigged ship of only 900 tons, named *Allum Ghier*. She had no accommodation ladder but there were wooden steps on the ship's side, flanked by manropes. We entered on her quarter-deck through a door in her bulwarks.

Country craft! We had expected things to be neglected and awry—"parish-rigged". But we might have been boarding a man-o'-war of a hundred years earlier. Her decks were white, all running gear neatly coiled up; and her boats still wore the black paint and white bottoms of former days. Awnings were stretched taut to ridge ropes over the quarter-deck and poop, varnished teakwood deck-houses and polished brass sparkled in the light of the setting sun. There was the satisfying, ship-shape smell of freshly tarred lanyards and the scent of the sugar cargo that she had brought up from Mauritius.

There was no one to be seen and we were daunted by such spick-and-span orderliness. We felt like intruders and were turning to get down to the dinghy again when a row of heads bobbed up on the poop. Then, as one man, her crew led by their Captain got to their feet. They had been at their evening prayers.

As we watched them, the bearded Captain came to us, a gentle smile on his face, his hands (palms pressed together) placed against his chest in greeting. We had learned some few words of Hindustani and now one of our number, Browne, took off his cap and said, "*Salaam alaikum*, Captain sahib"—"Peace be unto thee, Captain, sir."

The old gentleman beamed with delight, saying in reply, "*Alaikum salaam.*" Then, in soft-spoken, sing-song English, he went on, "But please do not go. I am very happy to give you welcome in my ship. Yes. I see you think she is beautiful. Come, we will see everything."

And so he took us around. We walked forward to the fo'c's'le head where we wanted to see how they had run in and housed the jibboom. We looked inside the forward deckhouse where the crew, seated on clean straw mats, were already being served their evening meal by two small, solemn-faced boys who ladled out on to the brass and pewter platters heaps of rice and savoury-smelling curry. Then we were taken aft, into her saloon which was suffused with the golden light of sunset coming in through her stern windows. Here the original mahogany panelling spoke of its kind treatment, and under the skylight flourishing green plants hung next to the ornamental brass lantern.

We were filled with wonderment at all the signs of peace and order that surrounded us. Here were no bullying Second Mates, no dirty, ragged, hungry apprentices. No odd mixture of Liverpool-Irish, Germans and Scandinavians brawled in her fo'c's'le. All over the little ship there was an air of family unity,

162

of quiet competence. The Captain must have sensed these feelings in us for, with a chuckle, he said, "My ship she is. Seventeen years, now, I have her. My Mate is my brother; Serang is my wife's brother. My two sons, sailors in fo'c's'le. All men in fo'c's'le relations—nephews, brothers, cousins—and the two small chokras that you have seen are my grandsons."

Then we went up on the poop where he gave us dishes of halwa—a kind of nougat, very sweet and toothsome—and small cups of strong, black coffee. He invited us to stay and share his evening meal but this we recognised as a final courtesy, and we got up to go. It was falling dark. So, with many smiles and salaams and expressions of thanks, we took our leave.

Five weeks were to pass before the *Sutlej* got to sea again. It was just about the hottest time of the year because the monsoon had already been blowing for four months. There was much less air stirring, and the heavy downpours of rain bringing their momentary relief, so frequent during the early part of the monsoon season, were now only occasional showers that made the heat more oppressive.

After the salt cargo was discharged we took the ship to the Kidderpore Docks to fill our bunkers. The coal was carried on the heads of women in the usual small baskets and dumped down the bunker hatches, raising its own cloud of fine dust to add to that stirred up by the shovelling at our berth and all the other coaling berths on the wharf. We were compelled to keep doors, port holes and ventilators firmly shut. It was like a brief period in purgatory and the only escape, when not on duty, was to go to the nearby Fairweather House—a sort of hostel for ships' officers—where one could enjoy cool drinks, sitting under a large fan, and where for a moderate charge one could stifle on a cot, under a mosquito net, in relatively clean air.

There was another alternative but I do not know that any of us took advantage of it. We tied up at the coal wharf quite early in the morning and it was still dark when we passed through the locks. But there must have been a "scout" stationed there, charged with the task of reading the ship's name, for not long after we were fast alongside our berth several of us received billets-doux written on pink, scented notepaper. They were delivered by a respectable-looking, uniformed house-boy but had been written by a damsel whose enterprise was superior to her virtue.

The message I received was brief but very cordial, it ran somewhat as follows: "Dear Mr. Third Officer, So hot and dirty in the docks. My bungalow on Hastings Road so cool and so clean. Fairweather House such a beastly bore, man. Come and have a jolly time, wine and song, with pretty young Widow."

It was a relief to get back to our mooring in the river where the ebb and flow of the tides brought some movement of the steamy air and where the seamen who had remained with us splashed around with hoses and swabs removing the grime of the coal dock with the enthusiasm that I had first seen when I joined the ship in Barry.

Chips had four Chinese carpenters from the shore to help him. They were good, quiet workers. Chips was used to them, had learned their language of Pidgin English spiced with Hindustani and within the week the sleeping platform was completed on both sides and a partition had been built amidships to separate the single men and boys from the married couples and their children and from the single women.

This partition was the only concession to modesty and it was a rather imperfect one. Up to 850 coolies would be sleeping down there and on the long voyage through the tropics of the Indian Ocean and the South Atlantic it was important that nothing should impede the ventilation. So the partition consisted simply of a large-meshed wire screen, like chicken wire, and was the only separation between the sexes. At night, all slept in long rows on the shelf and on the deck beneath it, with no further provision for privacy being possible on either side of the screen. This open 'tween-deck, in the absence of cabins, was in some measure a protection for the buxom young women because no adventurous swain could get among them without immediately being spotted, even if he got past the Sirdar on watch at the top of the hatch ladder.

But when we left Calcutta forty days would pass before we arrived at Demerara and for forty nights the young women would be sleeping, or trying to sleep, while lying cheek by jowl with, or within earshot of, the tender intimacies of the married couples. It was a situation not at all conducive to chastity and it is certain that many of them would gladly have dispensed with all such protection and even with the wire screen itself. Indeed, its mesh was sometimes found to be so greatly enlarged and distorted as to suggest that some were in touch with young men who had been able to penetrate their defences.

This service of carrying Indian workers overseas, then known as the "coolie trade", came into being when slavery was abolished in the British colonies in about 1840. In the West Indies the freed African slaves either took to the bush or demanded wages higher than the planters were willing to pay; so some other source of labourers able to work in tropical climates had to be found. After unsuccessful trials with Chinese and Malays, arrangements were made between the Crown Agent for the Colonies and the Government of India for the recruiting of Indians, which proved very successful. This is not surprising when one considers the terms and conditions that were offered.

The emigrant was given a five-year indenture that entitled him to free quarters, free food, clothes and medical attention with pay of one shilling per day and, of course, free passage to the colony and back to India after the indenture had been completed if he did not choose to stay in the colony. An important stipulation of this agreement was that forty of each hundred emigrants should be women and thus it was possible for men to take their families with them and for single men and women to find mates to share the new life.

Captain James Nourse, the founder of the company, carried his first coolies in a small wooden ship, the *Tasmania*, in 1858. Over the next fifty years, during which his fleet had once reached the total of twenty iron and steel sailing-ships—fast clippers that combined safety with their speed—about 300,000 coolies must have been taken to the West Indies and the Fiji Islands, and at least half as many brought back to India again. It is a remarkable fact that there is no record of any of them being lost through the perils of the sea.

Now the beautiful sailing-ships had been replaced by steamers.

These were busy days for everybody. Just as soon as the preparation of the lower hold had been completed and it had been well lined with bamboo matting, lighters and country boats dropped down stream skilfully working their way to us with oars and their rags of sail and using the tide until they could get their lines aboard and make fast alongside. Now, in addition to keeping the dynamo and the pumps for circulating the water in the sanitary system going, Tudor Cunningham's donkey-boiler was supplying steam to the winches and frequently, during the day, he would walk around to watch them at work, pausing at each hatch with a smile of satisfaction on his handsome, brown face while he listened to the smooth rumbling of their gears, the click and cluck of their pistons when the heavy slings of rice were lifted out of the lighters, swung inboard over the hatches and lowered down below.

The Second Officer and I spent our days in the holds supervising the stevedores in the stowage of the plump, clean bags, and watching their marks to make sure that the cargoes for the different ports—Demerara, Barbados and Trinidad—were properly separated so that they would be discharged at the correct destination. The Engineer Officers were as fully occupied as engineers always seem to be when the ship is in port. They are a little like housewives, their work never done. No matter for how brief a period, once their vessel is at anchor or made fast to a wharf, something terribly important has to be done and the Captain, trying to look as though he understood it, listens to the Chief Engineer's tale of woe about a steam-chest, or "yon bearing getting hot". And now, of course, with the ship immovably moored, and sailing-day a good two weeks away, they had a glorious opportunity for a real "Spring cleaning". The engine-room skylights were opened wide and from them came the rattle of chain-pulley lifting-gear, the clanking of metal and a babel of Hindustani mixed with Clydeside and South Wales English.

Any shore-going was reserved for the weekend. We could not afford to go more often and, after working from early morning throughout the heat of the day, our river mooring was probably as cool as any place in Calcutta, once the sun had gone down. And a glass of well-iced, fresh lime juice, while perhaps not so good for the stomach, was a better remedy for heat than many bottles of beer. So, in the evenings, the Second Officer and I sat in canvas chairs on the boat deck. He was most interested to learn from me what it was like to be at sea for four or five months in a sailing-ship crowded with coolies, and I listened to his stories of being caught in pack ice in a tramp steamer in the Bay of Fundy or of hauling logs through the surf on the west coast of Africa as well as a few bawdy yarns of Shanghai and Nagasaki. But I was also listening to the drowsy creaking of the timbers of the country craft that were made fast alongside, and to the snoring and muttering of their coconut-fibre lines as they strained to the flow of the tide.

The crews of these country boats lived as family units, a bald-headed old patriarch in command, the rest of them in descending age down to the tremendously earnest small boys who went about the cluttered, loose-planked deck as if the problem of care and maintenance of the craft lay entirely on their puny, brown shoulders. For all their childish appearance, the whole of the housekeeping seemed to depend on these capable little fellows. Throughout the day, while the rest were manhandling the heavy bags of rice, the youngsters were busy in and out of the wickerwork, mat-covered cabin or crouched on their haunches on the after deck, drawing buckets of muddy river water in which they washed the clothes of the others, pounding the ragged, grey dhoties on the deck as though they were indestructible but, in some inexplicable way, bringing them to snowy whiteness by the time they spread them over the cabin roof to bleach in the hot sun.

They were the cooks, too, and whenever time permitted they worked with curry-stone and roller, grinding chillies, turmeric, garlic and spice seeds, winnowing and washing the rice, preparing strange-looking fish or fat, grey prawns. Their little clay stove glowed in the dusk. The smell of burning embers and the appetising scent of the simmering curry and hot, fresh-baked chapatties drifted up to me.

In spite of their appearance of ragged squalor there was a definite sense of orderliness governing the lives of these country-boat crews. Once the sweat and toil of the day was over, before any thought of rest or food, each man shed his soiled loincloth and poured water over himself or, hanging on to a line, wallowed in the flowing stream over the side. Then, clad in clean dhoties they

166

sat down for their one big meal of the day and, when this was finished, the hookah was kindled and its comfortable bubbling could be faintly heard, punctuating their conversation, as it was passed from one to the other.

When the last of the cargo had been stowed we took aboard all the things necessary to care for 850 Indian men, women and children; to feed, clothe, comfort and amuse them on a voyage that would last about six weeks. The items of food, in addition to the staples, rice and dhal, included every kind of spice that could be required to flavour a curry. And, on the poop, where the vegetables were kept in well-ventilated racks and lockers, were pens containing enough sheep to give them at least two good meals of fresh meat during the voyage.

It is certain that most of the coolies, whose humble existence had probably known a diet consisting only of pulses and chilli peppers, sometimes rice and dhal and very rarely such things as meat and potatoes, would find the meals and other luxuries placed before them sumptuous, once they had overcome their seasickness and become accustomed to their unusual surroundings.

While all these stores were being shipped, the Surgeon was busy with the two Indian dispensers, stocking the dispensary and equipping the hospitals with bedding and all the pots and pans usually found in such places.

At last we were finished, everything was in its proper place and the ship ready for inspection. Then the "Burra Sahibs" came aboard, officials of the Government of India, the Crown Agent of the Colonies, and a Medical Superintendent. They looked at everything including the whole ship's company and went ashore well satisfied with everything they had seen and also with the refreshments that terminated their visit.

That night we left Princeps Ghat and moved two miles down river to Garden Reach to moor alongside the jetty a short quarter of a mile from the coolie depot. The coolies had been recruited in various parts of Northern and Central India and brought by train, over great distances, to Calcutta to wait until their numbers were completed.

Thus, for days and even weeks they had been housed, fed and clothed, leading a life of happy idleness—a most unusual experience after spending their lives toiling in the fields from dawn to dark. Now that part of the adventure was over. The day had arrived when they were to leave, to go to a country the whereabouts of which were quite unknown and who could tell if all they had been told about it were true. The only thing they were sure of was that they were to travel far, far over an ocean that none of them had ever seen and most of them never heard of.

Many would sleep but fitfully that night, tormented with worry about what they had done, weeping silently as they thought of the homes they had left. These were mere hovels, but they had been born there and all the friends and family they had ever known had lived in that dusty little village. It would not be surprising if a few were to panic and try to run away at the last moment.

So, as soon as the ship was fast alongside the jetty, I was sent ashore with a party of twenty lascars to bring the coolies to the ship, to make sure that none escaped. It was a thing that I was to do many times during the next three years but on this first occasion I found the setting so romantic that it has remained firmly fixed in my memory.

It was four o'clock in the morning, there was still an hour before the first signs of dawn would appear in a sky that was brilliant with stars and lit by a large orange-red moon which was sinking behind the trees across the river. In the compound, they were waiting for us. The superintendent and his fierce-looking but rather benevolent Sikh watchmen had our coolies sitting on the ground, pretty much in the order that they would live in aboard ship. As soon as they saw us, all started to shout at once and the air was filled with their commands.

"*Jaldi. Jaldi. Uth! Uth! Uth! Jehaz log ki-sath aggi chalna. Ek-dam. Jaldi. Jaldi!*"—"Quickly. Quickly. Get up! Up! Up! Go along with the ship people. At once. Quickly. Quickly!"

Followed by their cries, we came out of the compound on to the thick, powdery dust of the road—a close-packed procession of figures clad in white saris and dhoties, flanked by my sailors in their uniform of blue jean smocks with red sashes around the waist. We marched down an avenue of trees whose foliage met over our heads making a black darkness that intensified, by contrast, the glittering surface of the river and the shafts of moonlight that struck our company through the trees.

Each clung to his bundle; wives with children held close to husbands and fathers and their bare feet sometimes stumbled in the dust as they stared intently ahead for their first glimpse of the ship that soon came into sight. At Calcutta there is a rise and fall in the level of the Hughli River of seventeen feet at Spring tides. Now, at low water, the *Sutlej* lay with her main deck flush with the jetty. She was a blaze of light, with large electric clusters shining at the gangways. Soon the coolies were walking aboard and being guided down into the 'tween-decks.

At first it was a scene of noisy confusion, of wailing mothers and yelling children, as the hundreds of bewildered coolies milled around down there, but the Purser, Surgeon, compounders and a half dozen headmen, or Sirdars, soon brought about some order. Several hours would pass before the tide would serve for sailing, which was all to the good as it gave time for the people to settle down and for the cooks, chosen from among their number, to prepare their first meal.

We sailed shortly after midday. It was September 15th. Six weeks had been spent in Calcutta and it was good now to be making for the sea, with a strong ebb-tide hurrying us on our way. At sunset we stopped off the Eastern Channel light-vessel to land our Pilot. A big, glassy swell rolled up from the south, meeting our port bow so that it was flung high in the same moment as the ship fell violently over to starboard. There was little or no wind and there were no breaking seas, but the Pilot had as much difficulty in getting away as he had had in boarding us on that blustery day of our arrival. It was a case of dropping his baggage into the whaler and then making a jump for it.

It was a poor start for our coolies, as the cries and squeals and odours that came up the open hatches testified. But they had eaten two ample meals, in still water, since they had come on board so they had something to work on! It might have been worse. At midnight we were in good deep water, seventy miles from the shallows of the pilot-ground. The sea was smooth and when I made my rounds, after coming off the bridge, wind-chutes and cowl-ventilators were pouring a sweet breeze through the 'tween-decks. There, all was very quiet; the only noise was that of people sleeping the deep, deep sleep of exhaustion.

When the Pilot left us that evening we were at the beginning of a track that stretched away around the southern tip of Africa and then up to Demerara, British Guiana, more than ten thousand miles away, where we should arrive in about forty days after leaving the Hughli River. For sixteen days we would be steaming down the Bay of Bengal and through the wide South Indian Ocean before we arrived at Durban where we were to fill our bunkers. After leaving Durban we would follow the South African coast for three days, with ports of refuge and, if needed, assistance close at hand until we rounded the Cape. Then came the long stretch of three weeks and more than five thousand miles across the South Atlantic Ocean to the West Indies.

Our *Sutlej* was a good ship, "well found" as the saying goes, but she was no bigger than the average steamer of three thousand tons. She was about the same size as the *Sierra Blanca* but we were putting to sea with more than nine hundred people aboard. We had no wireless and our eight life-boats would hold about four hundred and forty people, if we had to use them and if we could get them all away from the ship. Today such a voyage would be regarded as a foolhardy adventure that international maritime regulations would not permit. In 1910 it was different. Only very few ships were equipped with wireless and it was unusual for passenger ships to carry enough life-boats to accommodate the total passengers and crew. After all, for centuries sailing-ships and steamers had sailed over great distances, crowded with emigrants or troops, and the occasional major disaster was accepted as pertaining to the "perils of the sea".

The year before, in thick fog, on a cold, black January morning the White Star liner *Republic* was in collision with the Italian liner *Florida* out in the Atlantic Ocean, somewhere near the Nantucket light-vessel. Of the two ships only the White Star liner had wireless and she promptly sent out distress signals which were picked up by an American shore station and re-broadcast to all ships in the vicinity. The *Republic* was so badly holed that it was realised that she could not stay afloat for long. The Italian's bows were stove in but she was in no danger of sinking. The sea was smooth so the *Republic*'s passengers were put on board the *Florida*. Thirteen hours after picking up the distress signals the *Baltic*, another White Star liner, arrived on the scene. The passengers of both ships and some of the *Republic*'s crew, 1,650 souls in all, were transferred to the *Baltic* which took them to New York.

The *Florida* was able to make New York under her own steam and attempts were made to tow the *Republic* back to harbour but she sank thirty-nine hours after being in collision. Her Captain had been quick to recognise the plight of his ship, his officers and crew were efficient, the sea was smooth and there was no loss of life.

But this was the first time that distress signals had been sent out by wireless telegraphy and the newspapers of the day wrote of it with such dramatic fervour that their readers were left with the impression that everybody was saved because the wireless operator of the *Republic* had heroically stuck to his post.

Then, when it ceased to be interesting or news-worthy, the incident was forgotten. In all the excitement over the wonders of wireless the question of adequate life-boat accommodation for passengers and crew had received no attention. That was to come a little later.

So, however venturesome our voyaging in the *Sutlej* may have been, it was certainly not foolhardy for those days. Ours were fine-weather voyages, in latitudes where there was no ice, where fog was rare and where the only dangers would be the normal ones of fire, stranding, extremes of weather—such as cyclones—or collision. We were so infrequently near the tracks of other vessels that the risk of collision was slight.

We had the seas to ourselves, or so it seemed. Sometimes on our way down

In the scented breeze of Ceylon

A Coconada brig

the Bay of Bengal we would cross the path of the mail-steamer on her way from Madras to Rangoon or Singapore. And sometimes the sweet-smelling breeze that came over the island of Ceylon drove before it ancient-looking sailing-vessels of Cochin or Coconada—little brigs or barquentines, bound for the Andamans or Burma. But these were exceptions. On most passages we sighted no other vessel from the time of dropping the Hughli Pilot until rounding the Cape of Good Hope and then neither smoke nor sail across all the thousands of miles of the South Atlantic until we arrived in the West Indies. One paced the bridge and kept a look-out for other vessels, but perhaps rather casually. In the kind of waters we were in, where could they be coming from and where could they be going to?

So on the fine, clear nights, keeping the middle watch when I was Second Officer, I did not hesitate to post the stand-by quartermaster in the wing of the bridge to keep a look-out while I got my sextant and "shot" stars. These were occasions that both the bearded Moslem quartermaster and I greatly enjoyed; he feeling very important with a pair of binoculars slung round his neck, and I, having removed my shoes, clutching a bull's-eye lantern to my chest, tiptoeing down to the lower bridge to read the chronometer time in the chart-room where the Captain was sleeping. I would do this four times, "shooting" stars to the north and south for latitude and the east and west for longitude, ending up with a very accurate position when I had worked them out at the collapsible table in the wing of the bridge.

But there was one night that I shall never forget.

We were in the Indian Ocean, a few hundred miles south of the equator. The heavens were heavy with stars but it was so dark that there was no meeting of sea and sky. Where the horizon should have been seen, even faintly, was only an infinite blackness. The sea was as smooth as glass and from it, here and there, the brighter stars were reflected in steady brilliance. Our bow-wave, with its phosphorescence, spread on either side like the head of a luminous arrow.

I was wide awake. It had just gone four bells. The quartermaster going off duty had given me the course and I stood for a few minutes by the compass while his relief got the feel of the helm. Then I moved away and in the same instant almost froze with shock. Close on my starboard bow a brilliant white light started flashing and in the same moment I saw the faint glimmer of a red side-light and fore-masthead light . . . just coming into view.

DOT . . DOT . . DASH! DOT . . DOT . . DASH! The single letter emergency signal "U", meaning, shouting, "YOU ARE STANDING INTO DANGER! YOU ARE STANDING INTO DANGER!"

Thank God that I immediately gave the right order, "*Dow chakkar!*"— "Hard a'port!" and that I gave it calmly. Although I stood with tingling scalp, gripping the rail, as we swung to starboard and passed under the ship's stern so closely that the foul black smoke from her funnel was acrid in our nostrils.

Where could they be coming from? Where could they be going to?

When I had the ship back on her course again we spoke to each other with our Morse lamps. She was the British steamer *Trelawny* from London, going to Fremantle and other Australian ports. Then she vanished in the darkness and I spent the rest of the watch suspecting approaching ships in every reflected star and with a sharpened awareness of my responsibility for the safety of the people sleeping so peacefully in our crowded 'tween-decks.

It was exciting to see again the fringe of palm trees thrusting above the horizon and then, a little later, the slender white column of the light-house that marks the entrance of the Demerara River. Exciting, because this had been the first landfall of my first voyage and I tasted again some of the pleasure of that day five years before.

The same noisy, old tug, with its chattering, laughing crew, came alongside, bringing the same courtly mannered old Pilot. In the ship *Main* we had stuck in the mud on the bar and had had to wait for high water.

"Nip tide. De moon in apogee," the Pilot had explained. It was the first time I had ever heard the word and now I waited, hopefully expectant, for him to repeat it. It was past high water and the *Sutlej*, her engines going at full speed, was ploughing a furrow in the soft sea-bed with everything in the ship rattling with the vibration. But he remained silent and watchful until we scraped our way into deep water and then anchored us just a little way past the lighthouse.

Next morning, after a meal that they were too excited or too despondent to enjoy, our coolies left us. The river steamer was alongside and they walked across the broad gangway to board her, carrying their humble belongings and struggling with the children. They were reluctant children, many of them yowling lustily in the temporary despair of their heartbreak. Some had to be carried aboard the steamer clinging to the necks of good old "Chips" and his shipmate Tudor Cunningham. Even several of the young men were in tears and also many of the young women. And these were not the frail-looking, small-boned, little Indian ladies that we see in western cities. They were robust, broad-shouldered, lively country girls whose pranks and hoydenish romping on the fore-deck had been so amusing, and sometimes embarrassing, to my hours on the bridge in the forenoon watches, accompanied as it was, by mischievous languishing glances in my direction and graceful little gestures of invitation.

It was all a joke, a game, in those long weeks of idleness when all they had to do was tell stories, sing and dance. They had been wonderful weeks of smooth sailing with bright sunshine, fresh south-east trade winds and the silken smooth swells of the doldrums where the flights of glittering flying fish delighted them and where the frequent squalls of heavy rain had thrown them into a fervour of happy clothes washing. They had been wonderful weeks but now they were ended and even the most forward and frolicsome among the girls gave me a shy, sad smile as I watched them leave the ship.

Unless one had a craving for warm beer or the more powerful local rum, there was nothing to tempt one ashore. And, after the long, hot day about the decks,

A calm

after going up and down hatch ladders and after six continuous weeks of watch-keeping, it was good to stay aboard for a long night's sleep.

On one night, however, we made an exception. The two compounders who had assisted the Surgeon in looking after the medical needs of our passengers, were Indian Christians, both of them having been born and educated in the colony. They were keen, jovial, young men and we were invited to spend a jolly evening at the house of the younger of the two. His mother, grandmother and sister—a pretty young woman of about eighteen—received us most kindly. Our party consisted of the Chief Officer, the Purser and myself and we did indeed spend a jolly evening in a drawing-room that, with its frilly lace curtains, satin cushions, pink and blue ribbon, plush-framed photographs of relatives and an upright piano, draped with a handsome shawl of Benares brocade and surmounted by an alabaster model of the Taj Mahal, must have been the counterpart of many such drawing-rooms in England. The only difference was that all the windows were wide open, the furniture was of wickerwork and we sat in the mellow light of oil-lamps.

The mother and grandmother wore saris and smiled happily as we stood about the piano which the young lady played most capably, while her brother sang nostalgic songs about a London that he had never seen, one of which longed for ". . . a night in the West, in the Dear Old Town". Then Mr. Potter and I sang *Sailor's Alphabet* with its rousing chorus:

"So merry, so merry, so merry are we,
No mortal on Earth like a sailor can be,
So merry, so merry, as we sail along,
Give a sailor his grog and he'll never go wrong."

Simple words and a simple tune and very soon the nimble, brown fingers were banging it out as though it were an old favourite and even the mother and grandmother joined in. Then followed tea and delicious, home-made cakes and Indian sweetmeats; and, finally, leave-taking when our two young friends, carrying lanterns, escorted us down the dusty lane to the jetty.

We sailed in the evening of the fourth day. Thirty-six hours after leaving the river, we arrived with the sunrise at Bridgetown, Barbados. The anchorage was crowded with shipping of all sorts, alive with steam launches, boats under oars and the beautiful schooners coming in from the sea, bowling along, reeving their way expertly through the anchored vessels, carrying sail until the last moment and then gliding into the careenage to come gently to rest in their berths.

But lighters and stevedores were waiting for us and as soon as the anchor was down we took their lines and had them fast alongside. In no time, the holds were crowded with noisy, cheerful Barbadians, winches rattled ceaselessly throughout the day. Burly boss stevedores stood on deck, by the hatch coamings, waving hands to direct the men who drove the winches, shouting at the men who toiled in the hold, to encourage and amuse them, all kinds of witticisms, many of them crude, most of them personal: "Come on, shake it up! Jes' because I'se burned kinder dark from stannin' here in de sun don't t'ink I'se de same as you black loafers down dere. Jes' yo' get movin' or I'll come down and give you all a kick in de ass dat'll make you all fart like a jackass."

The effect of this was to make the men laugh like jackasses. They shouted their mirth, mixed with their own ribaldries, but they worked well. At sundown, we were at sea again, bound for Trinidad.

We did not have far to go and early next morning we passed through the Boca del Mono (the monkey's mouth), a picturesque name for the narrower entrance to the Gulf of Paria. Before breakfast we were at anchor with a dirty little Bristol Channel collier fast on our starboard side and cargo lighters, bumboats and washerwomen's boats to port. The following day, at midnight, we were away again. The last of the cargo had been discharged, the genial young women had brought back the laundry and we had taken aboard enough good Welsh coal to get us to Demerara and Calcutta.

We were back in Georgetown after an absence of only five days. One day was spent topping up our fresh-water tanks, taking vegetables and livestock aboard and embarking a new Surgeon and Indian compounders. The following day the river steamer came alongside with our "return coolies", and the short interval of quiet was ended. The 'tween-decks were again crowded and the hospitals, male and female, were fully occupied.

Our passengers were a fair cross-section of the thousands of Indian workers then in British Guiana. Some, having completed their five-year indenture, were going home again with their savings. Others who had spent many years in the colony, working for their own account, were going back relatively wealthy, their wives hung about with necklaces of silver and gold coins. A few had been failures, had not saved during the years when they were fed, clad and housed by the planters and were going home as paupers.

A fair cross-section of any society, up to this point. But then, there were the lepers. These poor people were not sent back to India by every return sailing but only, as now, when there were sufficient of them released from the leper colony to warrant reserving space for them, isolated from the others. These were not as yet crippled by the dreadful disease and when I had to go among them, as I was making my rounds at midnight, I always found them to be cheerful and, if not sleeping, chatting happily together. Apart from the more visible pitiable evidence of missing toes or wasted, shortened fingers, they seemed to be very normal people and their brave demeanour in the face of their dreadful plight soon quelled any fears or feelings of horror or revulsion. They were not in pain and their attitude was rather that of people who realised that the worst that could happen to them had happened, so there was nothing left to worry about.

After a passage of forty-two days we were back in Calcutta a week before Christmas. We had had six weeks of continuous fine weather and, although the south-east trade winds had been fresh in the South Atlantic and in the Indian Ocean, not even a breath of spray came over the rails, for our holds were empty. We were a happy ship. For me it was a wonderful contrast to the moribund air of the *Highland Scot* and the bleak absence of companionship and cheese-paring gloom of the *Sierra Blanca*.

We used to spend the dog-watches smoking and yarning in the Purser's cabin. The Purser, James Comyn, was always unfailingly cheerful and was known to all his friends as "Sunny Jim". He was about forty years old, and had been many years at sea.

Jim's cabin had the usual ship's furniture but there were also a couple of wicker chairs, several brightly-coloured, needleworked cushions and other feminine touches quite definitely the work of Mrs. Comyn. I never met the lady but I came to know her very well from her husband's frequent affectionate talk about her and the almost life-size, three-quarter length photograph that was firmly secured to the bulkhead. The pose had been arranged to show off "woman's glory", her hair, to the best advantage. She was half turned away, her head poised so that the handsome profile was emphasized and the mass of curly hair that almost covered the width of her back, rippled down to the bottom edge of the picture.

There was also a gramophone with a large, fluted, tin horn that was decorated in red lacquer and gold in the Chinese manner. By present standards its tone was nothing to rave about but our hearts were warmed and our smoking pipes made sweeter by Jim's romantic tunes, such as Elgar's *Salut d'Amour*, *Songe d'Automne*, *Caprice Viennoise*, and many others. They filled my head with dreams and, when I left the cabin to walk along the dark deck on my way to the bridge for my watch, the gentle seething of our bow wave and the starlit sheen of the heaving ocean seemed to be part of the melodies.

The Second Officer, Grey, was a pleasant shipmate who was never late in relieving me at midnight. His only fault, at that hour, when I was longing to get my rounds over and climb into my bunk, was his noisily cheerful greeting and his insistence that I wait to hear some smutty joke or another verse of an interminable ditty about the squire's son who got into the dormitory of the ladies' boarding-school. This may, indeed, have been a tavern song of the early eighteenth century, its lilt had the flavour of that period—like its words. He was the typical rollicking sailor of the story-book, whose sense of fun must often have led him into mischief and aroused impulses which just had to be followed in order to complete the frolic.

There was, for example, the lifebuoy that hung on a skid outside each wing of the bridge. Attached to it by a short lanyard was a canister which hung by a loop that was part of the plug in the centre of its top. It contained the chemicals for producing acetylene gas. In case of need, a sharp jerk on a toggle that hung from the awning spar released the lifebuoy which, in its fall, tore the canister away from its plug. On striking the water it emitted a bright flare to serve as a guide to the person in distress and to the boat that would come to pick him up.

"You know," said Grey, "this thing just fascinates me. And there's one in each wing of the bridge. Just inviting me to twitch the old toggle and see what happens, and my fingers itch to do so."

We both chuckled at the absurdity of the idea and I left the bridge to go my rounds of the 'tween-decks. When I came up on the main deck again, aft, by number four hatch, I got the strong unmistakable stink of acetylene. I ran to the rail just in time to see the flare and the lifebuoy dancing in the sea as we passed them by. Grey had found the temptation too strong to resist. I went back to the bridge where he stood amidships, chewing a biscuit and drinking cocoa.

"You silly swab," I exclaimed, "you've released the lifebuoy! Now what'll you do if some crazy coolie takes it into his head to jump over the side!"

"What lifebuoy? I never touched the bloody thing."

He followed me to the lee wing of the bridge where I saw the toggle hanging on its wire, half a fathom below the awning spar.

"Well, I'm damned!" said Grey. "I wonder how that happened." As he spoke he gently pulled the wire raising the toggle to its normal position.

"Well," I replied, "you've got four hours to think about it . . . and how you're going to explain it to the Old Man in the morning. And, in the meantime, for your own peace of mind, you'd better have the stand-by quartermaster ship another buoy and flare in its place."

That Christmas Day was merry, as long as it lasted. At midday we gathered on the lower bridge at the Captain's invitation, to drink a glass of sherry with him.

Then we went down to the saloon for our Christmas dinner—seven of us: the Captain, the Chief Engineer, the three bridge officers, the Purser and the Surgeon, Dr. Stuart-Oliver, who had made the passage from Demerara with us and was spending a few days in the wonderful climate of Calcutta before returning to Britain.

It was a delicious and abundant meal: fat, curried prawns and rice, an enormous turkey, plum pudding, mince pies and almonds and raisins. We drank champagne—a present from the Surgeon. It was so good that it overcame the reserve that officers of the Merchant Service usually had in the presence of their Captain and left some of its sparkle under our tongues.

The Surgeon was an accomplished man of gentle breeding. He quite skilfully drew the Captain out and others of us, too, so that conversation was general and, indeed, at one point hilarious.

Himself a Scot, the Surgeon told the story of the Scotsman and the Englishman who were on a walking tour in Fifeshire when they came to a signpost bearing the legend: *5 miles to Auchtermuchty and those who cannot read ask the blacksmith*. The Englishman shouted with laughter but the Scot could see nothing funny about it and for the next several minutes trudged along in silence.

All of a sudden he stopped. "Man! I see the joke the noo. The blacksmith might be oot."

That was then a new story and we laughed heartily. That is, all except Captain Brown. His home was in Fifeshire. He startled us and raised further laughter when, looking sincerely puzzled, he asked, "Well, what was the joke?"

In the evening all except Grey went ashore. I also had an invitation but, rather than leave him to eat his Christmas supper alone, I decided to remain aboard. Giving him a rupee for himself, I sent Esau, the dinghy-wallah, to the beach for a half dozen bottles of beer and we sat in the cool breeze on the boat deck, smoking and yarning. Grey was in high spirits and, after we had each drunk a large bottle of beer, we were very talkative. Then I realised that the only other noise in the ship came from the carpenter's and donkeyman's cabins, under the fo'c's'le head, and it occurred to me that they were the only ones on board, beside ourselves, to whom Christmas meant anything.

So we took the other four bottles for'ard and had no great difficulty in getting them to overcome their bashfulness and share them with us. It was a happy evening after all and when I went to my bunk I was soon asleep. During the night I was awakened by a noise in Grey's cabin, by drawers being opened and shut and the slamming of his door. Then all was quiet and I concluded that he had gone ashore. I was surprised because since the day he came aboard in Barry he never had gone ashore, neither during the weeks in Calcutta before we sailed nor in the West Indies. But I thought no more about it. He was a grown man well able to look after himself.

When Yussuf brought me a cup of tea in the morning he was worried. He had not been able to wake the Second Officer and while he spoke I could hear a loud snoring coming through the bulkhead. I went round to Grey's cabin and found him fully dressed, curled up on the settee, on his side, and purple in the face. A tumbler and a couple of empty whisky bottles lay on the deck. Shaking achieved nothing and I saw that he was unconscious and that what I had taken for snoring was stertorous breathing. Now thoroughly alarmed, I told the Chief Officer who called the Captain, and Grey was carried ashore and taken to hospital.

I went about my work that morning, keeping an eye on the stowage, but I was sick with anxiety and when the Purser and Chief Officer got back with the news that Grey was dead I was shocked. It was what I had feared. All the morning I had been telling myself that his refusal to go ashore was his way of protecting himself against his weakness and that my, so well-intentioned, bottles of beer had destroyed his defences. It was my fault that he was dead. If I had gone ashore and left him on board, alone, he would still be alive.

By noon, I could stand it no longer. I went to tell Captain Brown of my part in the tragedy, how I had sent ashore for the beer and aroused Grey's craving for drink. Captain Brown was sitting in his cabin with the Chief Officer and the Purser, all looking very thoughtful.

"The two of ye drank six bottles of beer," he said. "That would do ye no harm."

"Well, no sir. We drank two bottles and Chips and Tudor Cunningham helped us to drink the other four."

"Och aye," sighed Captain Brown. He looked down at a small table, near by, on which I noticed a bulky envelope, addressed in red ink, and a half-empty bottle of laudanum. Then he turned to me again, saying "There's no need to fash yourself, Mister. It was none of your doing."

12   *Promotion and Disaster*

A week later I was promoted to Second Officer. Grey's cabin had been given a thorough Spring-cleaning and I settled in, well content with my good fortune, and not at all inclined to dwell on the distressing events of the morning following Christmas Day. That cabin was to be my home for more than two years.

Again we sailed for the West Indies, to Demerara, Trinidad and Surinam, with "green" coolies out and "return" coolies back. A new Third Officer was to be sent from England, to join us in Calcutta. In the meantime, Captain Brown had managed to find a man to serve in that capacity for the voyage. In the ports of India and the Far East, worthwhile, qualified ship's officers are not usually to be found unattached and looking for a ship. If they are, it is a foregone conclusion that there is something in their history that accounts for their condition.

Our man was no exception. He was about forty years old, perhaps more, had gone to sea years before I was born and did not even have a Second Mate's ticket. Cecil Robb was tall and very spare. He had a leathery, lined face with wide-set, grey eyes, a snub nose and a large mouth with lips that parted easily in laughter, to reveal strong, white teeth. All the many wrinkles lay in amiable directions and the merry face was capped by close, red curls of almost negroid crispness. He was scrupulously clean. There was no sign of dissoluteness or loose living. He was not with us very long before one knew that he had not got ahead because he was having too good a time enjoying life as it came along.

That voyage the gramophone was played only occasionally. We spent the dog-watches listening to Robb's stories. They continued from night to night and would have made a fascinating book. He had served his apprenticeship in the Aberdeen clippers, carrying passengers and emigrants to Australia and racing back to London with wool. But, when he failed to pass for Second Mate, he signed on in another full-rigged ship bound round the Horn for Seattle where he accepted a "have one on me" from a friendly stranger in a bar and woke up in the fo'c's'le of a small wooden barquentine that was beating its way off the land against a stiff gale from the south-west. He had been shanghaied.

The barquentine was going to hunt seals, mostly poaching. As a ship she was a vile contrast to those in which he had been brought up but she was very sturdy as she had to be, nosing her way about, in the Bering Sea, where they landed on the ice-floes to slaughter their defenceless victims.

Back in Seattle, Robb left the ship with a good "pay day" and made for the Great Lakes for the summer. In the winter he joined the Chicago fire brigade and then went down east, to New Bedford, Massachusetts, and signed on in a barque to go after whales in the South Atlantic. After that he joined the United States Navy, as a bluejacket, for the brief period of their war with Spain. When that was over he went as bos'n in a ship bound from New York to Calcutta where he was paid off.

He liked his first glimpse of India, wanted to see more of it and did not hesitate when he was offered a job as guard on the railways. It was an easy life, luxurious when compared with the rigours of a sailing-ship's fo'c's'le, and for the next few years he travelled the length and breadth of the country. Then, one day when he was sitting under a punka in Spence's Hotel, Calcutta, enjoying a cool drink, someone slapped him on the back so heartily that he nearly lost the end of his nose on the rim of his glass.

Robb jumped to his feet and stood wiping the wasted whisky that had splashed his linen jacket, muttering a few gentle curses, to find himself staring at one who had not only been a friend of school days in Dundee, but had also been senior apprentice when they were serving their time in the Aberdeen clippers. Now he was Master of an Indian-owned steamer, trading on the coast and to Burma, the Straits Settlements and Java. Of course, such a meeting was fittingly celebrated. Robb's train left without him. He went back to sea again, this time as Third Officer of his friend's steamer.

The idea was that he should brush up on his navigation and pass for Second Mate but that was never fulfilled. They were always in and out of port, the atmosphere was not conducive to study and Robb was too popular, perhaps too indolent. He had found a new and easy way of life. Once started, he never had trouble in getting a berth as Third Officer on the coast, in country-owned ships. And so he continued, going to sea when he felt like it and stopping ashore as long as his money lasted. With us he would make two long sea passages, each of six weeks, and with very little opportunity of going ashore in the West Indies.

"Three months the round voyage!" His eyes gleamed, he rubbed his hands together. "This is my chance. When we get back I'll go up again and that stuck-up Port Commissioner will give me a Second Mate's ticket." He turned to me with a grin. "You'll help me, won't you?"

Yes, I would help him. And that right gladly. That was the sort of response that Cecil Robb always called forth; and, anyhow, I would be "going up" myself. So all that voyage I studied during my afternoon watch on the bridge and for the last three hours of my watch below in the forenoon. While Robb did not work quite so hard, I kept him at it, with my textbooks and letting him use my sextant.

It had been many years since he had taken the trouble to concentrate but he had the excellent memory of most sailors and long before we rounded the Cape of Good Hope, on our return to Calcutta, he was equal to the navigation and all the theoretical questions of the examination. In fact, he was not the same person who had joined us three months before. He sparkled with good health and high spirits. He almost crushed the bones of my hand at leave-taking.

"Good-bye. Ye don't know how thankful I am t'ye for your help. And don't you worry. I'm going to put my papers in this very afternoon. And when I've got my ticket ye'll come ashore and have dinner with me at the Bristol. Nay, the Bristol be damned. We'll go tae the Great Eastern."

He had been paid off that morning. His pockets were full of money. He was truly sincere in his expressions of thanks and good intentions but the dust of the city was in his nostrils. His jinn, sliding free of its bottle, had him by the arm. I never saw him again.

The "stuck-up" Port Commissioner, Commander Goldsmith, Royal Indian Marine, proved to be a quiet-spoken man who took his job seriously. My examination in navigation was the same as I would have faced in Liverpool or London. But, for that part of it dealing with seamanship, he was assisted by Captain Legg, Master of the Brocklebank liner *Malakand*. So I was kept very busy; while I was answering the question of one, the other would be waiting to pop his question at me. Captain Legg appeared to enjoy the opportunity of putting himself back aboard a sailing-ship while putting me through my paces. The ship I was supposed to be in was constantly in trouble. In dense fog we met an iceberg and lost our jibboom and fore topgallant mast. Then he had me on a lee shore with no room to wear ship and the wind so light that it was certain that the ship would miss stays. It was the classic case of those days and was solved by "club-hauling". The usual preparations for "going about" were made but, in addition, the end of a warp—a stout rope—was put out through the hawse-pipe on the lee side of the quarter-deck and taken forward, outside everything, to a point abreast the foremast where it was made fast to a kedge anchor that was hung from the rail. The other end of the warp was taken to a capstan on the main deck.

Then, when the helm was put hard down and the ship came up head to wind, the kedge was dropped and at the same moment men ran round the capstan, heaving the ship's stern up to the kedge anchor. At that point the ship was on the new tack, heading away from the land. The warp was cut with an axe, a kedge anchor was lost but the ship was saved.

The ship was saved and I had forgotten all about steamers which was what the old boy wanted for he barked with a suddenness that made me jump.

"You're on the bridge. A dark night. You see a bright, white light three points on your starboard bow. What do you do?"

"Take a bearing," I replied.

"Correct," he said, slapping the table. "Most young men I put that question to start talking about stern lights and guessing what it might be when what you want to know is whether or not your courses are converging."

They both smiled and shook me by the hand and the "stuck-up" Port Commissioner gave me my Mate's certificate.

The *Malakand* had brought out our new Third Officer. A week later we sailed, this time for Madras and Suva, Fiji. During the three years that I was aboard the *Sutlej*, we made eight round voyages out of Calcutta—five to the West Indies and three to the Fiji Islands. On all the West Indies voyages we took coolies to Demerara, Surinam or Trinidad but on three occasions, there being no returning coolies for us, we carried cargoes of rice and gunnies to Barbados, Martinique, Guadeloupe, Havana and other Cuban ports and then went across the Atlantic in ballast to Torrevieja for a cargo of salt for Calcutta.

These were exacting voyages. The Chief Officer was an easy man but a lazy one. He left everything to me. Once the loading commenced and the lighters and country-boats were made fast in tiers three deep, abreast our hatches, it demanded my attention all day long and frequently throughout the night.

I still have a vivid mental picture of the little cubby-hole of an office. Its narrow door opened on the main deck; its inside, steel bulkhead was part of the engine-room casing, I can still see myself sitting in there with the sweat dripping off my chin, surrounded by lightermen, some squatting on the deck, others filling the doorway, all reeking of betel-nut and perspiration. All patiently waiting for me to give them receipts for the bags or bales that they had delivered to the ship. I enjoyed it. It gave me a satisfying sense of my own importance.

But it was good to get to sea again, even with the decks crowded for the long, calm passage with sorrowful, bemused coolies. Six weeks of watch-keeping; forty-two days of orderly routine to compensate for the intense heat and long hours of work at the moorings in the Hughli River and to prepare for the days to come—for in the West Indies we would be just as busy.

After landing our coolies, we timed our arrival at the various ports for day-break, never going alongside a wharf, always anchoring in the roadstead and, most frequently, we were at sea again before the end of the day, bound for the next port of discharge.

And so two or three weeks passed, working cargo by day and keeping sea-watches on the bridge by night. Only rarely did we remain at anchor for a complete night's rest and there was no chance to go ashore unless we arrived on a Sunday or a public holiday.

This happened when we came to Guadeloupe and I was delighted. I wanted to walk within touch of grass, flowers and trees, and perhaps find the place where, five years before when I was there in the ship *Main*, I had seen such unusual dancing.

We had had one "liberty day", one day when we were allowed to go ashore to tramp the dust and cobblestones of Point-a-Pitre. That is all there seemed to be. All roads very soon led into the hills and walking was work—hot work in blue monkey-jackets. Each mile of greenery looked like every other. We had come to this conclusion as we sat in the shade on the roots of a big tree, mopping our brows and idly watching a group of young Negroes who were seated close by.

They were three couples and presently one of the men started to whistle. It was like the call of a bird—two, clear minor notes in descending scale, then a pause. The same notes were constantly repeated, while in the intervals the whistler moved his head in a time beat of his own devising.

The other men and three women sprang to their feet and commenced to dance to the silent beat and the strange music of but two notes. They were not joined in dance. Each stood separately, knees close together, elbows pressed to sides. They did not move from the spot on which they stood but bare flutter-ing feet, swaying hips and trembling shoulders seemed to bring to reality a whole orchestration of unheard music, of beating tomtoms and squealing pipes, beyond the vibration of the two haunting notes. Those two minor notes were repeated with the insistence of dripping water, with the compulsion of hypnosis. The dancers rolled their eyes, grunted and whinnied in ecstasy. The perspiration streamed down their faces. Then the whistling stopped and they flung themselves to the ground, shrieking with happy laughter.

It was 1906. We had seen and heard our first "jazz", years before the word was invented.

I found the tree but this time sat and smoked my pipe in silence.

The Fiji voyages were a welcome change from the long monotonous round to the West Indies and back. The very name Fiji and the ports Suva, Levuka and Lautoka had a romantic and exciting South Sea Island flavour. Everything was different. The cargo, for the greater part, consisted of an immense variety

186

of goods, implements and luxuries that had been brought out from England for trans-shipment and was destined to find its way to who knows what remote island in the South Pacific, to be traded at the general store for copra, to serve on the plantations or to give comfort and pleasure to some lonely planter.

Even our passengers were different, for usually we went to Madras to embark Tamils and only on one occasion did we have, in addition, a number of emigrants from northern and central India, from Calcutta. In such confined quarters they did not mix well. Facially they were strikingly different. The Tamils were of pure Dravidian stock, descendants of the original inhabitants of southern India, a highly intelligent, sturdy people with many handsome men and beautiful women. Their skins are very dark, some quite black and their language is as different from Urdu or Hindustani as Welsh is from Spanish. That was the only voyage on which we had trouble. There were quarrels between jealous women, supported by husbands, in languages that neither understood. So speech descended to gesture, insulting gesture of such obscenity that on one occasion a young Tamil caught a Kashmiri by the throat and would have strangled him had they not been separated.

From Madras we steered south of the island of Java, into the Arafura Sea and the Torres Straits where, after a run of twenty days, we stopped off Thursday Island to pick up the Pilot who would take us down between the Barrier Reef and the mainland of Australia for a distance of five hundred miles and leave us off Cairns, in Queensland. We then passed through a break in the reef, the Grafton Passage, and continued eastwards.

The waterway inside this part of the Barrier Reef bristles with rocks, sands and small islands. The channels frequently change direction and the pilotage was especially difficult because there were no lighted buoys or beacons marking the dangers. So, as long as we had the Pilot aboard, the Chief Officer and I kept alternating watches—four hours on the bridge and four hours below, the Third Officer doing duty with Mr. Potter.

On our first Fiji voyage we arrived at Thursday Island at noon which meant that I had the watch until 4.00 p.m. and again from 8.00 p.m. until midnight. My only night-watch below was from midnight to 4.00 a.m. This, of course, was no hardship but, as I have said, Mr. Potter was an easy-going and lazy man, and he had never made the effort to learn anything about the stars. His watch-mate, the Third Officer, had just passed for Second Mate and knew as little about stars as I did when I joined the *Sierra Blanca*.

Every time the Pilot altered course he naturally wanted to know the compass error on the new heading so that he could be sure that he was making the correct course. When this happened at night, in my watch below, I was called and had to run up on the bridge and climb on top of the wheel-house, in my pyjamas, there to stand for a moment, rubbing my eyes, while I found a suitable star. Then I would take its compass bearing, run down to the chart-house and work out the azimuth or true bearing and so find the error. This did not take more than ten or fifteen minutes but, as I was sometimes turned out two or three times, when I was called to go on the bridge at 4.00 a.m., my watch below had given me very little rest. When I was relieved, four hours later, I tumbled into my bunk after a hasty breakfast.

On that first Barrier Reef passage there were two such nights. We dropped our Pilot at about seven o'clock in the morning of the second day and headed out into the wide Pacific Ocean. The Third Officer resumed his normal watch and, before going to breakfast, I went into the chart-room to wind the chronometers. The chart-room was also the Captain's sea-cabin but luckily for me he was down below, taking a bath.

It was lucky for me because when I raised the lid of the felt-lined well in which our three chronometers were housed I could not suppress an exclamation of alarm. The indicators on their dials showed that they had been running for fifty hours! The previous morning I had been so anxious to get into my bunk that I had forgotten to wind them.

I had been guilty of a very serious lapse. When out of sight of land we could only be sure of the distance that we had travelled eastwards if we were sure of the accuracy of our chronometers. At sea they were wound up at the same time each morning so each day the same portion of their main spring was being used and each day they were running under the same mechanical tension. Now, my carelessness had allowed them to run for an extra twenty-six hours, unwinding a portion of the main spring that had not been so released for years.

What would this do to the daily gain or loss? I was a very worried young man.

When taking observations for longitude, of sun or stars, our calculations would give us the time at ship. The difference between this and the time shown by our chronometer would give us our longitude, tell us how far we were east of the meridian of Greenwich. If my carelessness had caused an unknown error in our chronometers of one minute we might be fifteen miles ahead or astern of the observed position. And five days after dropping the Pilot we would be steaming through the New Hebrides Islands. Would we have fine weather when we came up with them? Or would we, and they, be shrouded in heavy tropical rain, dense as the thickest fog? Would it be daylight or dark? Should I not tell Captain Brown? Warn him! The very thought made me shudder and I passed the days in an anxiety that was like a sickness and that was only dispelled when, at dawn on the fifth day, we found the island of Santa Maria resting on a placid ocean, just when we expected to see it.

At that time, Suva was a modest little town, having one small jetty running out into the lagoon. The islands depended on the coconut palms for copra and on the plantations of sugar cane and bananas. It was there that our coolies would serve out their indenture, cultivating and harvesting and working at the sugar mills in just the same way that their fellows were doing in the West Indies.

The Fijian was not interested in such unceasing, regimented work. His own village life and the labour of its women were normally enough. He only exerted himself and accepted work at the behest of his tribal chief or if he needed the money for something that he particularly wanted. These were the men who were brought on board to discharge the cargo—brawny giants with enormous heads of springy hair, some of them having it bleached with lime so that its normal black was turned to the red of coconut fibre. Their faces were heavy-featured, and sombre in repose. But they were mirth-loving and very often some muttered bubbling of vowels—which is how their language sounded—caused peals of hearty, unrestrained laughter.

They worked well under the supervision of a young New Zealander and, after four days, we went around to Levuka where for one day we lay alongside a wharf landing cargo, and then continued to Lautoka, both places being only a few hours' steaming from Suva.

So far this visit to the South Sea Islands had been disappointing. The wild-looking, tree-clad mountains which were everywhere in the background were generally covered by heavy blue rain-clouds and, at sea level, hard squalls of rain were frequent. In Suva, when evening came, it was dark and lifeless and there was nowhere to go. Levuka consisted of one main street, now very muddy, flanked by dense groves of coconut palms, a few wooden buildings and one general store.

But Lautoka was different. Even the climate was more agreeable. We entered early in the morning and made fast alongside a small, wooden jetty. The arrival of such a large ship seemed to be an event, for all day long the wharf was crowded with laughing, chattering natives—those handling the cargo that was landed and many more who lent their efforts as a mere gesture of comradeship and good will. However, towards the end of the day it became evident that the ship was not the only attraction. A group of men came along, some bearing on their shoulders a great hollow log, while others carried on their heads large wooden bowls that were placed on the ground, and filled with kava.

All this was in preparation for a singing and dancing, a *meke-meke*, in honour of their Chief who was to travel with us back to Suva. He arrived shortly before sunset—a tall, well-built man who smiled happily as he walked about among his people. They greeted him with loud cries of welcome, some of the young men leaping high off the ground, arms raised aloft, while they let off a piercing, yodelling yell, just as they had done on our decks in Suva, on sighting some swift-sailing catamaran riding the surf outside the reef, a good two miles away.

The Chief's acknowledgment of the loyalty that was expressed so noisily was as charming as that of any descendant of an ancient dynasty. The few words he spoke before taking his seat on the pile of mats that had been placed for the members of his family were received in respectful silence and smiling approval.

This gathering took place on a small grassy clearing that lay to the left of the road that ended at the jetty. To the right, were clumps of plantains, papaw, bushes of bougainvillea, jasmine, hibiscus and feathery bamboo; and, a short distance beyond, visible through the foliage, was the sea. As soon as the Chief was seated all the others squatted where they stood, except for a group of about twenty men who sat in rows in front of the *lalli*, the hollow log. Buxom young women, clad in brightly-coloured kilts of native cloth, were busy about several small mounds of earth from which broad leaves of plantain protruded; others went around, ladling kava into the cups of coconut shell or calabash which everyone had brought with him; and the singing and dancing commenced.

The music was provided by men beating the *lalli* with short, heavy clubs. It must have been divided by a partition into two cavities of different length, for it gave two deep, mellow tones that were beaten out with a rhythm that was taken up by the men seated before it, in a song of solemn beauty. Deep-chested *basso profundo* voices sang a trio of notes that was continually varied, and followed by the others, up and down the scale, in many skilful changes between harmony and counterpoint. The music had an organ-like quality that was not disturbed when the singers started to dance.

They remained seated and their dancing consisted of slow movements of their arms in a pattern of perfect precision. Heads were moved in unison, muscles and fists were flexed and released in a way that caused the surfaces of the naked, brown bodies to ripple, almost to shimmer, in concord with the dance.

The dignity of the whole performance suggested that it was some kind of obeisance to the Chief. When it ended, there were loud cries of his name. "Jonni Munrye Wee Wee," they chanted with their applause and all faces were turned towards him as though eager to see his pleasure. Anthem or not, it was the overture. The talk and laughter became general. The earth and leaves were lifted from the mounds and the meats and yams that had been baking in them were distributed; the kava circulated and the *lalli*, with many variations in time, beat out livelier melodies in which everyone joined.

The golden light of evening turned from dusk to darkness. Lamps and torches were lit and the merriment continued until at last it was time for us to sail. Slowly we moved past the end of the jetty where the people were now chanting a strain of such sadness that it could only have been a song of farewell. We passed the cluster of trees that separated the road from the sea; the air was sweet with the scent from the flowering shrubs. To starboard, the foliage on a small, rocky islet was so tall and so dense and so close that, from the poop, we seemed to be looking at the lights on the receding jetty as though up a dark waterway.

Now the singing was very faint. Sometimes it was interrupted by the piercing yell, always followed by the concerted cry, "Sa ... MOH ... theh!" I lingered, held by the beauty of the moment: the barely audible singing and that long-drawn-out Samothe—God be with you. Beside me, the Chief stood holding the rail. For as long as his voice would carry he had replied to the cries from the shore. At last nothing could be heard. Even the land had disappeared in the darkness. He took the garland of flowers that had been hung about his neck and gently let it fall into the turbulence of our wake.

On our third voyage to Fiji, we arrived off Thursday Island at the close of day on April 16th. Its rugged, hilly shape stood out, sharply black, in the fading light. Lamps were being lit and, one by one, little yellow lights appeared in the houses along the waterfront and on board the pearling schooners in the anchorage. There was no wind. The splash of waste water pouring from our sides, the occasional squeal of a pump in the engine-room and the rattle of shovels in the stoke-hold served only to heighten the quiet of the moment.

We had had our fill of dirty weather. When the Pilot left us at the mouth of the Hughli River the wind was light, from the north-east, and for the first twenty-four hours there was nothing to suggest that we might experience anything unusual. However, by sunset of the second day the wind was blowing hard from the east and the sharply falling barometer told us that we were heading for trouble. The sky, all the way from east to south-south-west, was a dense mass of swirling, black clouds. In the south-west, where the sun had gone down, the heavens blazed for a few moments with a copper-coloured afterglow that burnished the sea and the ship, as though they were reflecting the flames of a furnace.

When I relieved the Third Officer at midnight, I found Captain Brown smoking a cheroot, up to windward, behind the weather-cloth. The Old Man called me over. This is the substance of what he said: the wind had settled in the south-east, the barometer was still falling and we were in the path of a cyclone.

"But I think it's still a long way off and that it may move away, north and eastward. So we'll continue on our course, Mister, and hope to get across into finer weather, before the centre catches up with us. I don't think I'd avoid it by running away to the eastward. We've got three hundred coolies below and five hundred and fifty more of them will be kicking their heels, waiting for us, in Madras." He walked amidships, took a good look around and then continued, "She's doing her twelve knots and not making any fuss about it. Call me if there's any change for the worse. Good night."

It was indeed blowing a whole gale with a big swell rolling up from the east-south-east, topped by high seas that frequently slammed noisily against the weather side, sending clouds of spray across the decks. But, as the Old Man had said, the *Sutlej* went along well. There was no cargo in the 'tween-decks and she was not deep in the water. She was buoyant and in good trim to stand up to almost any kind of weather.

For the rest of the watch there was nothing to do but mind the weather and stare into the black darkness that was only relieved by the occasional vivid flashes of lightning and by the glow of the main-masthead light weaving its wide arc to the wild rolling of the ship. I was glad when the Chief Officer came to relieve me at four o'clock. The wind was blowing at hurricane force but we were not taking any water on deck. I made my rounds of the 'tween-decks where I found most of the coolies fast asleep, exhausted by fear or seasickness, and then went thankfully to my bunk. I had been sleeping for about two hours when I was awakened by the deep bellow of the steam whistle and by the roar of a great sea pounding against the side of my cabin where it also deposited, with a loud thud, the forward lifeboat that it had torn from its lashings.

I jumped out of my bunk and, almost as soon as my feet touched the deck, I felt the ship swinging to starboard, bringing wind and sea on the port quarter. I heard the shouts of the Serang and his men as they hauled the boat clear of the door and secured it again in its chocks. On the bridge, they were blowing the whistle because it was raining so heavily that visibility was reduced to only a few yards. They had also reduced speed.

Now there was no doubt about it. We had a cyclone to deal with. The wind blew with incredible fury, with gusts that must have been at more than eighty miles per hour and the air was so thick with flying spume and rain that, from the bridge, the fo'c's'le head could not be seen. Then, with ominous suddenness, the rain stopped, the wind dropped and overhead there was a clear patch of deepest blue in the sky.

We were at the calm centre of the storm, in a windless, almost airless arena, surrounded at all points of the compass by that evil-looking wall of solid, black cloud. The confusion of the sea was appalling, the spinning cyclone was driving it into the centre, from all directions, so that it rose in roughly pyramidal masses and fell in swirling whirlpools of foam. It was without trend or direction. There was no point of the compass where the ship's head could lay comfortably and she was thrown about from side to side and from bow to stern, with fearful violence. One steep mountain of water, rising to starboard, pushed us over so far that another one, coming up on the port side, smashed in a few of the portholes in the 'tween-decks.

The poor coolies down there had been in agonies of terror and these few port holes had been left with the protecting steel dead-lights raised so that at least they could see a little daylight. Now they screamed in panic as the deluge of water came in upon them. They were making a rush for the ladders when Chips and I and a half dozen lascars met them and drove them back and away aft, clear of the mess. The dead-lights were soon secured over the broken portholes and the lascars bailed out the water.

Up on deck again, we were greeted by an amazing sight. Winged creatures of every kind were alighting on all parts of the ship. There were crows, magpies, hawks, green parrots, small white cranes, many brightly-coloured birds —large and small—and even butterflies and insects. All settled where they first came down, sitting with drooping wings, evidently in the last stages of exhaustion. Poor things! They were doomed. When we had traversed the centre, the wind would blow with hellish violence and sweep them away.

But their presence brought some comfort. We were less than eighty miles from the Indian coast and it meant that the cyclone had already passed over the land and was now travelling eastward, into the Bay of Bengal. By noon, the wind was upon us again, a fury out of the north-west. Again, great crested seas came roaring down. But they were regular and we were able to get back on our course with the comfortable knowledge that we were heading for better weather. At eight o'clock the following morning, we were fast alongside the wharf in Madras and that same afternoon we sailed again, bound for Suva, with our full complement of emigrants. We had had the worst of the weather but it was not a fine passage. The winds were strong and the seas rough in the Bay of Bengal and off the coast of Java, with much rain. Most of the time the coolies had been miserably seasick. We were glad of the prospect of sheltered water inside the Barrier Reef and the smooth, short passage from Cairns to Suva.

Then we got our Pilot who brought news so shocking that the toll of death and grief filled our minds for days.

The year was 1912. Only four days before, the White Star liner *Titanic* had sunk in the Atlantic with terrible loss of life. The great ship of 46,000 tons was being driven through the water at high speed when she struck an iceberg. It happened shortly before midnight and two and a half hours later she sank, carrying her luxury and splendour and hundreds of lives to the bottom of the ocean.

Like the *Republic*, she was equipped with wireless but her signals of distress were made in vain because no other vessel near enough to give immediate help heard them. A short ten miles away, lying in the pack-ice with engines stopped, was the steamer *Californian*. She, too, had wireless but she had only one operator and he had gone below and was asleep in his bunk.

On this occasion there was no "miracle" of wireless to blazon in the newspapers. Instead, there was a tale of horror, of the terrifying ordeal of the 2,206 passengers and crew, among them 544 women and children, waiting through hours of tortured anguish, with the certain knowledge that if no other ship came to their assistance, half of them would perish. The *Titanic* had lifeboats sufficient for only 1,178 people and the sea was thick with drifting ice.

When, at last, they could wait no longer, what dreadful scenes there must have been; of tragedy, of men who watched their wives and children being placed in the boats; and of heroism, of women who preferred to remain and die with their husbands. At 2.20 a.m., the ship went down and 1,503 men, women and children were drowned.

Two hours later the Cunard liner *Carpathia* arrived on the scene and rescued the survivors: 315 men, 336 women and 52 children—703, all told.

We were a quiet, sad group at the dinner table that evening, each thinking of the disaster in his own way. The Chief Engineer was particularly affected. The fate of those in the engine-room and stokehold had been terrible. But when the coffee was placed before us he heaved a deep sigh, then produced a fat Burma cheroot and, with a timid smile, looked at the Old Man.

"D'ye mind if I smoke, sir?"

"You know damn well I do," replied Captain Brown. "I'll allow no one to smoke in my saloon . . . except, perhaps, the Owner . . . or a Customs Officer now and again."

The Chief laughed. He knew what the Captain's reaction would be. It was an old trick but it had worked, for now we were all smiling and were not even cast down when, with a lightly philosophical air, the Chief voiced the thought that had really been going around in his mind.

"I know comparisons are odious, sir, but our boats and people on board are in about the same proportions as those aboard the *Titanic*."

"Aye, so they are," replied the Old Man. "And that's the way they've been in these ships for fifty years or more." Then, with a kind smile for the Chief, he added, "At least, we don't have any ice to bother us and if you'll see that your crowd keep the engines running as sweetly as they do, we'll do our best to keep her afloat."

Ten days later we were in Suva and, after a further ten days, left for the return passage to Calcutta with our full complement of coolies and all the beds in the male and female hospitals occupied. By the middle of the afternoon we were well clear of the west coast of the island and I took cross-bearings of two prominent, conical hills, in order to fix a good position as a point of departure.

Then, I walked to windward, to the starboard wing of the bridge, and stood there, sniffing the breeze. The ship was empty of cargo and rolled quite heavily in the moderate swell. I was puzzled because, while at the standard compass, on top of the wheel-house, I had felt a hot blast of sulphurous fumes when the ship rolled to windward. Then, with a shock, I had the explanation. When the ship rolled to leeward, to port, bringing above the surface part of the side that had been under water, there was a hissing and a cloud of steam until the wind-ward roll put it down again. In the hold were six hundred tons of coal, taken aboard in Calcutta as an additional supply for our bunkers, separated from the part of the hold reserved for cargo by a temporary wooden bulkhead. The coal had evidently ignited by spontaneous combustion and was now blazing so fiercely that the ship's side plating was red-hot. The hot fumes I had noticed were being sucked out of the cowl-ventilator as the ship rolled to windward and, of course, being forced back when she rolled in the opposite direction. This efficient ventilation was now a perfect set of bellows that had brought to violent life a fire which must have been smouldering for many days.

When I told him, Captain Brown swung his bare feet to the deck and sat upright on his settee, looking at me doubtfully.

"You say the ship's afire? I didna hear you blow the whistle for fire stations."

"No, sir. I said that the coal in No. 2 hold is on fire."

As he heard my report all sleepiness left the Old Man.

"Alright," he said. "I'll go up on the bridge. You call the Chief Officer and the Purser and tell them to get the coolies off the decks and down below; and get them aft, out of the forward 'tween-decks. And then get the Serang and his *khalasis* to settle this fire of yours." He was smiling as he concluded this string of instructions.

"Aye aye, sir." And away I went.

The coolies did not understand what it was all about but they gave us no trouble. The forward part of the ship was soon isolated. Having trimmed the ventilators so that they became ineffective, we rolled back the tarpaulins in the 'tween-decks and lifted a couple of hatches with the idea of taking hoses down there. But the heat was so intense and the gas so noxious that this was out of the

195

question. We replaced tarpaulins and hatches because it seemed that the best way to fight this fire would be to unship the ventilator cowls on the main deck and pump water down their shafts from three or four hoses. When this had been done we went to the bridge to report.

"Well, sir," said Mr. Potter, "we're putting a lot of water down there but the shafts are so far from the ship's side that I don't think we're reaching the seat of the fire. Short of getting the hatches off and going down there with our hoses, and that would be difficult with all these coolies aboard, I don't think we'll get the better of it."

So it was decided to return to Suva, about nine hours' steaming away, hoping that the fire could be kept under control until we arrived there. There were only about eight miles to go before coming up with the coast again and, from that point on, we would be close under the land in case of sudden emergency.

It was about 4.30 p.m., and for the next hour there was no change. All seemed to be going well until, all of a sudden, a thick column of black smoke and a stream of glowing sparks rose into the air out of the ventilator-shaft and we knew that the fire had burned its way to the surface of the coal, that the wooden bulkhead was alight and so probably was the underside of the pine planks of the 'tween-decks. At the same moment, the Serang came to the bridge to report that this was indeed the case. The pitch in the seams was melting, the oakum caulking burning and tongues of flame darting up through the deck.

Now that the blaze was free, unconfined by the bulk of the coal, the ventilator shafts were acting as chimneys and there was no alternative. We had to plug and seal them, open the hatches and get down to the fire with our hoses before it was too late.

But what about the coolies? They were weeping and wailing. The 'tween-decks were full of smoke. Many of the coolies were coughing uncontrollably. The Purser, the Surgeon and his staff were having difficulty in preventing panic. Captain Brown lost no time in making up his mind. There was only one thing to do. To ensure their safety and the safety of the ship, we had to land them on the beach as soon as possible. On that coast, it would not be easy because, for a great part of its length, right close to the low coral cliffs and reefs, the water was too deep for anchoring and there were not many beaches free of rocks and reefs.

Captain Brown pored over the chart until, at last, he pointed to a spot that had twenty-five fathoms of water and a sandy bottom for a distance of about eight hundred yards. It was right abeam of us, and would be a tricky bit of navigation for one whose whole seafaring life was devoted to avoiding such places—unless you had a Pilot aboard.

"Alright," he said. "Hard a'starboard. Half speed." Then he leaned over the fore side of the bridge and hailed Mr. Potter who was down in No. 2 hold. "Stand by your windlass, Mr. Potter. We'll be anchoring in twenty-five fathoms. We'll use the port anchor and you'd better put the fifteen-fathom shackle in the water before you let go."

"Aye aye, sir," replied Mr. Potter who had been climbing out of the hold while the Captain was speaking and now he and the carpenter ran forward to the windlass.

"Ease your hellum. Steady as you go. Slow."

"Slow," I repeated as I moved the engine-room telegraph. The beach looked uncomfortably close. A Quartermaster was in the chains, heaving the lead, getting no bottom. Suddenly he sang out, "T'is bahm, sahib. Thirty fathoms, sir." This was immediately followed by twenty-five fathoms. The engines were put "full astern" and, the moment the ship had lost her headway, they were stopped and the anchor let go.

As soon as the ship was lying securely to her anchor, the stokers relieved the sailors in the hold and all boats were swung out, ready for lowering. The sun was just setting and within half an hour it would be dark. Quickly and very calmly, Captain Brown gave his orders. The sick were to be landed first, then the women and children and, finally, the men. The land was only about four hundred yards away but no sign of civilization could be seen. For a distance of about two hundred yards, before getting to the beach, the boats would have to cross an outcrop of coral. The state of the tide was such that this should be possible, but we had to be sure that all the sailors wore boots to protect their feet when beaching the boats.

About a mile and a half to the eastward there was a narrow gap in the reef, leading into a shallow bay and a small village. The Third Officer, Mr. Farrow, was to leave immediately with the "sea-boat", while there was still enough daylight to find the passage. He would find a police station, or general store, with a telephone. He was to speak with the Harbour Master in Suva, tell him what had happened, that all the coolies were on the beach without shelter and ask him to send the river steamer, the one that had brought them aboard, as soon as possible, to take them back to Suva. We would return there as soon as the fire was extinguished.

The job of landing the sick was horrible. The poor things were terrified when they were lifted, or coaxed, from their beds and placed in the two boats that had been lowered until the gunnels were level with the rail. The rapid descent, the jolt and splash when the boats hit the water caused them to cry out in alarm. The sea was smooth because the breeze was off the land but, before we had made our way clear of the ship, black clouds darkened the sky overhead and, out of them, the wind came in hard squalls with a deluge of rain that beat on the sea with a hissing noise, like a vast escape of steam, and soaked everyone to the skin.

About seventy-five yards from the beach, the boats grounded. We dropped over the side, relieving them of that much weight, and were able to push them some distance further before they stuck again. Then, the only thing to do was to take the sick in our arms or on our backs and carry them ashore. Underfoot, the coral was rough and uneven. Knee-deep, we splashed and staggered through the water, in constant danger of falling on our faces and inevitably shaking and jarring our charges who, in their pain and terror, wound their bony arms in a strangle-hold about our necks. Most of them were wasted by disease, their bodies covered with bandaged, suppurating sores. Many had high fevers and, in their cold misery, suffered uncontrollable attacks of shivering and ague, for the rain had settled into a steady downpour. Some of them, through dysentery, incontinence or fright had fouled the sodden blankets in which they were wrapped. It was a relief to put them down on the sand, by the trees that lined the beach and then go back for those who were healthy and clean.

From the shore, things looked serious in the sullen, rain-grey dusk. The *Sutlej* had a list to starboard. In the glare of the cargo-lights, the swirling cloud of smoke that rose from the hold glowed fitfully as though reflecting the fire below. The remaining five boats were in the water and were rapidly being filled with women and children who got into them from the accommodation ladders that had been lowered on each side of the ship. It was an unusual and frightening adventure, particularly when the time came to get from the ladder into the boat; with the cries of encouragement and the help from the Serang and boats' crews, the women were handed to their places and their children were lifted bodily from the ladder and put down beside them. With the example of the first few, the remainder embarked with more confidence and, before I got alongside again, the whole flotilla was on its way to the beach.

The Surgeon returned to the ship with me. He was worried about his in-valids, lying on the open beach, in the rain. We did not know how long it would be before the river steamer came for them, or if she would come at all. Something had to be done for their protection and comfort. As the landing was going so smoothly the Old Man agreed that my boat should be loaded with some dry blankets, soup extract and condensed milk, two forty-gallon deck-shees of fresh water, kindling, a few lanterns and a number of tarpaulins and canvas screens, and a couple of cooks. The boat was well filled but it was a light cargo that was landed without trouble and my boat's crew went about the task of rigging the tents with an alacrity which showed that they were getting as much youthful enjoyment out of this part of the adventure as I was. Here was something to write home about; here was a tale that would gain much in the telling in the bazzars of Ferozepore in faraway Punjab. To make more room in the boats all their gear, except oars, had been left on the boat-deck and we had brought a number of the masts with us. These were thrust obliquely into the sand and the awnings and tarpaulins were set up between them and the spidery roots of the mangroves. Lamps were lit, fires built and soon the cooks were warming pans of soup and milk, while we went back to the ship, there to resume our part in the task of landing the remaining coolies.

It was about 9.30 p.m. before the last of them was on the beach and I was able to go aboard, get a bite to eat and learn what was happening. Farrow had landed at the small village where a planter, a retired sailor, had made the telephone call for him. The river steamer would be sent as soon as possible. The fire was still blazing fiercely and Mr. Potter and the stokers were standing on the floor of the hold, up to their knees in water, while they directed their hoses at it and at the under-side of the 'tween-deck. Their position was dangerous because it was no longer possible to get out by using the iron ladder that was immediately in front of the wooden bulkhead, so rope pilot-ladders had

A beach on Viti Levu, Fiji Islands

been hung over the forward end of the hatch. The men were blinded by smoke and steam and, their faces black with smoke, had wet cloths tied over mouth and nostrils.

Six hundred tons of burning coal is an evil thing but, like most evil, it brought about its own destruction. The bulkhead collapsed and the whole mass spilled down with a rush that caused the water to surge forward with a force that washed Mr. Potter and his helpers to the other end of the hold. In this they were lucky because they were carried clear of the flaming fragments that came hurtling down.

From the deck it looked like a glimpse of hell. There was nothing to be seen but smoke and a vast cloud of stinking, sulphurous steam, rising high into the air. Then Mr. Potter and his men appeared, climbing up into the 'tween-deck, there to pick up their hoses and pour streams of water on that part of the coal which had not been submerged. There was not very much of it and it lay spread out and exposed. By one o'clock in the morning it was all over, the fire was out.

The Old Man called us to his cabin on the lower bridge, to "splice the main brace", and we stood there sipping neat, red rum from Barbados and saying, "Thank you," and "Good health, sir."

"No ice to bother us, sir," the Chief added.

"No, Chief," replied the Old Man. "No ice. Just a wee bit fire in yon coal of yours."

"Aye," breathed the Chief, with a sigh of satisfaction as he swallowed his drink. "Just a wee bit fire and a nice wee beach, right handy."

The shallow-draught river steamer *Rewa* arrived at daybreak. As it was high water and she was a stern-wheeler, the castaways were able to walk aboard, over her bow, by way of her broad gangplank. We followed several hours later, after the ship had been put back on an even keel. Back in Suva, one day was spent discharging the burned out ashes and clinkers into lighters and in undergoing survey. The following day, we made our effective departure, after a delay of only three days.

The return to Calcutta was uneventful but for me it was full of interest and excitement. After dropping the Pilot at Thursday Island, we headed for Timor and into the Java Sea. These were waters full of names that had delighted my imagination before I went to sea: the Moluccas, Celebes, Bali, Lombok, Macassar, Malacca. And we were bound for the small island of Pulo Laut that lay close to the south-east coast of Borneo. There we replaced some of the coal we had lost in the fire; just enough to get the ship to Calcutta, for it was dirty-looking brown lignite.

Ghosting along in the Java Sea

The coal came down in iron buckets, along an overhead wire, and was dumped into the hold from a gantry. All the work of tipping and trimming was done by little, brown-faced Dyaks who wore hats like inverted saucers and who looked like animated mushrooms. In the evening, we walked up to the mine, about a mile away through dense jungle. We had been invited by the manager and his staff, three lonely Dutchmen, for whom any strange foreign face and the possibility of a variety in conversation was an occasion for a celebration.

They lived in simple thatched bungalows and all the domestic side of their existence seemed to be in the capable hands of lissom, young Malay women. These moved very silently on their bare feet as they waited at the table, placing

Off Singapore

dishes of rice and a variety of curries and chutneys before us. They had the prettiness of youth and were clad in brightly-coloured sarongs, with silk kerchiefs tied over their heads, level with their brows. We were so accustomed to the Indian idea of male house-servants that we could not conceal some expression of surprise when, as soon as we arrived and were seated in comfortable wicker armchairs, the girls appeared with trays of drinks, although no one was rude enough to make any pointed remark.

Our host noticed this and explained that the local men would not work as houseboys which left them the choice between Chinamen or local women.

"We like the women," he said. "They're good girls. They keep everything clean, including themselves. The old woman in the kitchen looks after them and they look after us and do it very well."

He spoke with an avuncular air but, when we were at table, I thought I noticed very friendly glances accompanying the murmured Malay when dishes were being offered. As the Manager said, it was an arrangement that was good for them all and the old crone, who kept peeping around the kitchen door to mark our appreciation of her cooking, looked as though she were the kind of person who would make quite sure that things stayed that way.

The meal was as varied as it was abundant, the beer was cold and the conversation interesting. The Manager loved the natural life of the surrounding forest, and the broad veranda was hung with beautiful orchids and other flowering plants that he had collected. There, also, lived two monkeys—a gibbon and a pretty capuchin—and an Indian myna. This bird had startled us by producing a low, protracted, suffocating, bronchial cough followed by a shout, in pure Clydeside, "Will ye no be quiet. I'll wring yer bluidy neck, ye noisy bastard." He had been left behind by the Second Engineer of a tramp steamer, who was glad to be rid of him.

It was a delightful evening, a most refreshing change from the daily, rather monotonous round aboard ship.

On June 8th, one month after leaving Suva, we were back in the Hughli River. Having landed the coolies at Garden Reach, we went straight into the Kidderpore Docks for a purgatorial week of dry-docking and bunkering. While I stood on the poop, supervising the mooring of my end of the ship, Yussuf came running aft with my letters from home. The first that I opened was from my young brother Max. It was written from Newcastle, New South Wales, on board the barque *Engelhorn*. It was his first voyage and the letter was full of the fine passage they had made to Adelaide, the thrill of racing to the eastward down in the roaring forties and of the good times ashore. Like the rest of us, he ignored the hardship and seemed content that he had chosen a life at sea. I was not surprised. I remembered all too well the eager young face as he listened to my tales of the sea. He had not chosen the sea, it had chosen him. And when that happens, there is nothing to be done. But I put the letter in my pocket with a feeling of sadness and a sense of foreboding.

That was a Saturday evening and perhaps I should describe a sultry hour or two with "jollee young widow" in Hastings Road. But it just would not be true. The work of coaling would not start until the Monday morning, so I took a first-class ticca-gharry with a pair of spanking horses and drove at a fine gallop, with whip cracking the air, while the driver shouted terms of endearment to his horses and continually stamped a foot on the loud silver-toned gong to clear the way. We drove the length of the river bank, along Strand Road and over the bridge to Howrah where I would dine and remain for the week-end with a kind family whose house—a gracious relic of pre-mutiny India, at least one hundred years old—was always a home to me when I could go so far from the ship. It stood in the middle of a large garden that was enclosed by a high wall. It was just as hot as any other part of the city but here there was no coal-dust. We would sit at dinner on the veranda and our talk would be accompanied by the music of insects, frogs and toads.

The following Saturday we were back at Princeps Ghat, loading for Trinidad, Barbados, Guadeloupe and Martinique. Then we shifted ship to Garden Reach for embarkation and so down the river, on our way.

It was two years since we had sailed from Barry but it seemed much longer. We were constantly on the go, always at work. Wonderful for the Owners, the ship never idle; and wonderful for us, too. The "gratuity" for coolies landed safely, averaged, in my case, about £30, for a round voyage when we carried coolies on both the outward and the return passage. They were good ships and, on the bridge, we had all served the company long enough to have the sense of belonging together, so they were happy ships. And I had been happy. I had every reason to be. I was within two months of my twenty-second birthday and, already, for eighteen months I had been Second Officer of a fine steamer.

But there was something that was not quite right. Discontent was creeping in, born, I am sure, of the ceaseless routine of duty and the absence of any recreation. This was the start of the seventh voyage out of Calcutta. Sea-watches of four hours on the bridge and eight hours below suggest that on long passages such as ours, there would be much time for sleeping, reading, pipe-smoking and loafing. But that was far from being the case. I was able to sleep for only three hours before midnight and for three hours after 4.00 a.m. My only exercise consisted of pacing to and fro across the narrow confines of the bridge when on watch. My leisure was a couple of hours before noon and before dinner in the evening. The food inevitably became monotonous and, just as inevitably, included frequent hot curries.

Our voyaging was almost constantly in the heat of the tropics and, excepting for two occasions, we were always in Calcutta at the hottest time of the year—between the months of April and September. Sweating profusely, one was tortured by prickly heat and drank more iced lime-squash than was good for the stomach. The stifling humidity made the day's work so exacting that one had neither energy nor inclination to go on shore in the evening.

There was nothing unusual in all this. Many sailors had to work and live under similar conditions but they were often dyspeptic as a consequence and perhaps that was the foundation of my own "bellyaching".

Farrow and I spent many a dog-watch discussing the hardship of our service. By the time we arrived in the West Indies I had worked myself up into the belief that there were many things that the Owners had not thought of, and that it was up to me to inform them. So I put it all in a letter, with respect, drawing their "esteemed attention" to the unusual nature of our service, the insanitary discomfort during long periods at sea in a ship crowded with emigrants, the hazard of contagious disease, the long voyages, the absence of any provision for paid leave and, in view of all these things, the inadequacy of the rates of pay. To all of which I concluded by remaining their obedient servant.

It was a foolish letter. There was nothing in it that the Owners did not know. After all, they had been running coolie ships for more than fifty years. And the rates of pay must have been alright because there were always men glad to sail in them, just as I was. And, too, there was that gratuity, so thoughtfully paid by the Crown Agent for the Colonies. As for leave, all I had to do was wait another year and the Articles of Agreement would expire. Then they would have to pay me off and send me home and I could take as much leave—without pay—as I liked, or could afford. But, in the pig-headed state of mind into which I had argued myself, I was not capable of such mature thought. Another year, when one had already served two, seemed a terribly long time.

We were at anchor at Barbados and I took my letter to the Old Man who sat, smoking a cheroot and reading, in his sea-cabin on the lower bridge. He read it twice, very slowly, and then looked at me, his face expressive of great concern. One did not write that kind of letter to the Owners. Indeed, a Second Officer did not even write to them at all. He did not say this but it is probable that it was what he was thinking. What he did say was that he understood my feelings but advised that I should not send the letter. It could do me no good and might do me much harm.

The next morning I took the letter ashore and put it in the box at the General Post Office. I could see nothing wrong with it, nothing offensive; apart from its element of lese-majesty, it should do me no harm.

Three weeks later we were again at Torrevieja for a cargo of salt. A new Chief Officer was waiting there to relieve Potter who was promoted to Master, and Captain Brown left us to go on leave. He was very happy. It was more than two years since he had seen his wife. I was sorry to see him go, the ship would not be the same without him. He was most cordial at parting and his reference was all that I could have wished.

In January, four months later, having repeated the previous voyage, we were back in Torrevieja and I received a letter from Captain Brown. It had been posted at Gibraltar, on his way out to India to take command of one of the other ships. It was a very nice letter, more friendly and less reserved than he had ever been with me aboard ship. He began with the quotation about the wonders of the Lord seen by those who "go down to the sea in ships", which he attributed to the many parsons on board and with which he was consoling himself for the mischance that he had not been able to spend Christmas at home. The Owners had not liked my letter and thought that it should be withdrawn, but they were not inclined to view the matter seriously. A relief would be sent out to Calcutta and, he said, when I got home I should go and see them. A new ship was building and she would be needing a Chief Officer.

It was a very nice letter and the Owners were kind. There was also a letter from my father. My three years' Agreement would be up in a few months and he thought it was time that I came home. He suggested that I get my Master's ticket in Calcutta and then go up for Extra Master in England.

I had much to think of as we went on our way towards Port Said: a couple of months' leave, a Master's ticket and to go as Chief Officer of a new steamer. And all before I was twenty-three years old. The *Dewa* would be the Owners' sixth ship and they would be building more. I might well be in command before I was thirty, might even command this very *Sutlej*. My mood varied between happy castle-building and gloomy uncertainty. I knew every course and distance from every point of land between Calcutta, the Fijis, the West Indies and the Mediterranean by heart. It would be wonderful to have your own ship. Then the gloom would descend. Know it all by heart! And have to do it year after year for thirty years or more; those long, long voyages in the cloistered loneliness of the Master of a cargo-steamer. For a young man with an active mind, it was a terrifying prospect. I decided that I would be a liner officer, go for the P & O or the Orient Line, always meeting different kinds of people on the run out to China, India or Australia. It would take many years before I got command but, at that age, money did not matter very much.

On Thursday, February 6th, we arrived in Calcutta. Seven days later I sent a cable to my father, signing it "Master Mariner". On the Monday I had driven away from Princeps Ghat in jaunty mood, with none of the usual pre-examination qualms. All that studying could do had been done and, if I did not succeed, I could always go up again when I got home. Such thoughts were going through my head while I stood, with a handful of change, paying the gharry-wallah outside the Port Commissioner's office. I gave him double the normal fare; it was that kind of day. In voicing his thanks he called me *Huzur* —Highness or Excellency.

When I turned to go into the building, I almost collided with a sadhu—a holy man. He was as tall as I, broad of shoulder and completely naked. His entire body, including his face, was smeared white with the dust of ashes. Some of his hair was tied on his head in a "top-knot", the rest hung in oily strands down his back. In one hand he held a staff that was surmounted by a small trident, garlanded with marigold flowers; in the other he held the dull black calabash shell in which he received the food offered by the pious. From his neck hung long ropes of carved brown beads. On his forehead was painted the emblem of Shiva, the bright yellow stripes, like an open *V*, rising from the bridge of his nose, with a crimson stripe in the middle. He wore his nakedness with such dignity, so naturally, that one was not even slightly conscious of it and he smiled gently as he gazed fixedly at me.

"*Ram, Ram, sita Ram, garib-log ka bhaiya,*" he cried. "*Bahut dur se aiya*"— "Greetings, brother of the poor. I have come from afar." In the circumstances the appeal was not to be refused. I dropped a silver rupee into his bowl and went into the Port Commissioner's office with his blessings ringing in my ears. That completed my confidence.

A few days later, I was among the second-class passengers on the poop of the steamer *Golconda*, looking at the *Sutlej* as we passed Princeps Ghat. "Chips", Tudor Cunningham and Yussuf were on the fore-deck, Captain Potter and Farrow on the bridge, waving their good-byes. It had been an affecting leave-taking. In the two years that we were shipmates Farrow and I had become like brothers. For nearly three years the *Sutlej* had been my home and I had been happy. She had steamed just about 170,000 miles and for one third of that distance had been in my charge, I had been her officer on watch. Now I was going down the Hughli for the last time.

The British India Company ship *Golconda*

13   *Brother Max*
of the Barque Engelhorn

The happiness and excitement of my own homecoming were greatly heightened by the arrival, a few days later, of my young brother Max, at the end of his first voyage in the large four-masted barque, the *Engelhorn*, of Liverpool.

Young Max had been away nearly two years. Good winds and the stout canvas of his lofty ship had carried him around the world and the schoolboy had become six foot three inches of brawny, bronzed and very happy homeward-bound sailor.

There followed six wonderful weeks, some of them spent in North Wales, in the glorious weather of May and June. We made excursions over the mountains, through the lovely valleys where the streams bubbled and chattered their way into the little lakes that nestled among the hills and looked like fugitive pools of celestial light. We got about the countryside on foot, by rail or a combination of both, and even by water, as on a day when, with my father and sisters, we travelled by a diminutive paddle-steamer up the Conway River to Trefriw— pronounced *Trev-ree-oo*.

It was an enchanting voyage of ten miles. Up with the flood tide, under the bridge, past the Castle, and then the beautiful vista of the meandering, silver stream lipping the meadows that covered the narrow floor of the valley where cattle stood knee-deep in the lush pasture.

On either hand, and in front of us where the river turned, densely wooded hills rose steeply to a sky of wind-torn cloud and patches of deep blue firmament. The whole scene was enlivened by the play of shafts of golden sunlight and swiftly fleeting shadow, by the glitter of water, the violet-hued mist of bluebells and ragged robin in the lower woods, the scatterings of primroses on the banks, and the scent of sweet-briar and hawthorn.

We were carefree and gay in the joy of being together, especially my father for whom such days were very rare. And our high spirits did not fail even when a large black cloud burst over our heads. For the others there was some shelter but Max and I remained on the fore deck, he sitting with shoulders bowed, the rain streaming from the peak of his cap, but still chuckling over some yarn of ship and shipmates.

At the end of June Max's holiday was over. He rejoined the *Engelhorn* and, with another cargo of coal, sailed from Port Talbot in the Bristol Channel for the winter passage around Cape Horn to the west coast of South America. When he had gone, I went to Liverpool and entered nautical school.

Ten weeks later I had done it. I was an Extra Master. Here was something to think about, to marvel over. Back in my lodgings, I did indeed think. Of the ship *Main* passing the Terschelling lightship five years earlier, while I was still an apprentice, and Captain Hatch puffing his pipe and saying to me with high, homeward-bound humour, "There you are, m'son, Hamburg tomorrow. The ship will be sold. You'll go in steam and one day I'll read of Commander de Mierre, Royal Naval Reserve, Extra Master."

He had almost laughed outright at the expression of surprise and apprehension with which I received his remark. And now, at least part of it had come true. I also thought of Jim Roberts whom I had met a few weeks later in the bar parlour of *The Swan*, in Wilmslow. He had recently completed a voyage as Second Mate of the *Avon*, a sister ship of the *Main*. That was our point of contact. He had worked his way to the quarter-deck from the fo'c's'le and had just passed for Master.

"I suppose now you'll go up for Extra," I suggested—perhaps with Captain Hatch at the back of my mind.

Jim Roberts turned his head to look squarely at me, with an air of such

The *Avon*, a sister-ship of the *Main*

affronted astonishment and for so long that I was startled and the match that he was holding over the bowl of his pipe burned his fingers.

"Extra Master!" he exclaimed, and then added in a final burst of indignation, "*Extra bloody fool!*"

His vehemence was, no doubt, in part a rebuff for my temerity—after only three years of seafaring—in suggesting what he, a qualified Master Mariner, might do.

"I don't have to have an Extra Master's ticket. I wouldn't get paid more, if I had one. It's just a damned luxury for those who can afford to stay ashore, swotting at nautical school, doing all sorts of fancy figuring that they'll never use at sea, just to get a piece of paper to tell the world how very bloody clever they are. That they're something different . . . the elite!"

In some degree he was right. With his Master's ticket he could command anything that floated, of whatever size. An Extra Master's certificate was optional, a distinction, indeed, to show that you had qualified in the more advanced and wider studies of your profession.

All the problems of navigation had to be worked out by spherical trigonometry and this included some methods used by the eighteenth-century navigators who were not able to rely on a good chronometer. Given a sheet of blank paper, one had to make a chart suitable for accurate coastal navigation. There were papers on magnetism and the compass, ship stability under various conditions of loading, meteorology and a short but penetrating paper on naval architecture that, in addition to questions of theory, required mechanical drawings of types of ship construction varying, in my case, from the double-bottom ballast tanks of a steamer to the amidship section of a sailing-ship.

I had enjoyed it all; the weeks at school and the company of other young sailors, the visits to the building berths at a local shipyard and even the examination. This lasted a whole week. On the Saturday morning, the examiner, Captain Keating—the same man who had passed me for Second Mate four years before—put me and my imaginary ship through a succession of serious situations until, finally, he relaxed.

"That'll do, Extra Master," he said. "I've got you through with a good average. The best this year, so far."

I was the only candidate for "Extra" that week, and in a daze of happiness I was making for the door of the empty room when he hailed me from his desk where he was putting a match to a well-filled pipe and blowing clouds of smoke.

"If you're thinking of joining the Cunard Line—and you couldn't do better —please give my compliments to Captain Dodd. He's the Marine Superintendent."

The Cunard Line. Not the P & O or the Orient. Not long, fair-weather voyages through the tropics to India, Australia, China and Japan but the Atlantic, the "Western Ocean", with its winter gales, its snow and freezing fogs. But home again every two weeks, perhaps, certainly every month.

I liked the look of the Cunard ships. When the state of the tide was such that they sailed in the evenings I had spent many hours on the landing-stage marvelling at their magnificence, at their glossy black hulls, immaculate white superstructure and those great, red funnels with their shining brass sirens and black tops, the smooth, almost gracious way in which they came alongside, the absence of confusion, the smartly uniformed sailors and . . . the officers! These, of course, excited my admiration with their frock-coats, their white kid gloves and the utterly unselfconscious manner with which they wore them. I was unable to leave a scene so fascinating until every line had been cast off and the great ship, now a blaze of lights, like a floating city, moved slowly into the dusk and headed for the sea.

But, until Captain Keating's remark, I had never thought of serving in that kind of ship. There was something awe-inspiring, even a little frightening, in their air of superior efficiency and their size. Most of them were twice the size of the ships that I was used to and ten times their tonnage. However, it was a challenge, too.

Captain Dodd was the Chief Marine Superintendent. He greeted me with a hand-shake and motioned to a chair across the desk from his own. His keen face was that of a sailor but his dress and manner were those of a business executive. His questions about my experience were many and searching but at last he was satisfied. With a friendly smile he told me that my appointment would be confirmed after I had been interviewed by the Chairman, Sir Alfred Booth.

That occasion was exciting in more ways than one. There was, of course, my youthful nervousness at meeting such a great man but, as I stood by the window of an ante-room, awaiting my summons, there was the view of the river to bring me some assurance. It was a blustery day in early October with a fresh north-westerly wind whipping against the ebb-tide bringing it to life with little white wave-crests and driving ragged clouds across the sky. The kind of wind that brought me the call of the sea so insistently when, as a school-boy, I stood on the balcony of the Town Hall clock-tower high above the smoke and roofs of Manchester. Almost as far below me now was the same scene that had entranced me when I saw it from James Nourse's rather dingy office when I was applying to be indentured as an apprentice in one of their sailing-ships and being told by their kindly old Liverpool manager that I might as well poison myself as go to sea.

That was eight and a half years before and now I had an Extra Master's ticket in my pocket. Out there, anchored in the stream, was the beautiful *Mauretania*, "Queen of the Merchant Service", and one day I might serve in her, might even have her in my charge.

Sir Alfred was slender and clean shaven, perhaps in his early forties. At first, to put me at my ease, he talked of a variety of things, calculated to bring me into conversation. Then he delivered a brief lecture about the conduct that the company expected of its officers. I listened with becoming attention and the comfortable realisation that it was, in fact, confirmation of my appointment.

A high proportion of the company's officers were commissioned in the Royal Naval Reserve. I, too, made application and, after an interview with the Commander of a local Coast Guard Station—who wanted to see "the cut of my jib"—I duly received my commission as Sublieutenant.

There was a total of about one hundred and twenty officers serving afloat plus a small unattached group on the dock to provide reliefs aboard the ships in port for those who had been given leave. This is where I started. For my first duty, I went on board the *Carmania* to keep the night-watch with another officer who was to show me what to do. She lay in the Huskisson Dock and, as I stood on the wharf, she towered above me, blotting out a large part of the night sky and looking enormous. I felt like a pigmy and was just about as confident as I walked across the gangway, through a door in the ship's side that admitted me to "E" deck. It was in the bowels of the vessel. I found myself standing in a small clear space in the neighbourhood of miscellaneous store-rooms and pantries now all silent and deserted. The only sign of life was an old Quartermaster who, when I asked him the way to the officers' quarters, came to attention and saluted before telling me what to do.

I had a long way to go. Across 'thwartship alleyways, turn left at fore and aft alleyways, then a sharp turn to the left and I would find a stairway leading to "D" deck, just abaft the first-class dining-saloon.

"Go through that, sir, and you'll find the main square and stairway that'll take you right up to 'A' deck. Then, if you walk along the alleyway, at the for'ard end you'll find the door marked 'Officers Only'. Open the door and you'll find another set of stairs that takes you right into the officers' quarters. I'm sorry I can't come with you, sir, but you'll have no trouble."

He was right. I had no trouble. There was emergency lighting everywhere and on each deck there was a steward-watchman. But it was a long way and there were a lot of stairs and there was something a little eerie about the deserted ship. Much like a theatre in the middle of the night when the stage is bare and everybody has gone home. Not an impossible parallel; the theatre

R.M.S. *Carmania*

sparkles and lives while the show is on, as the passenger liner does when she is at sea, but in the intervals both are cold and lifeless.

So it was good to reach the officers' quarters, the bright light and the "lived-in" atmosphere and to hear movement in one of the cabins. That would be my watchmate. I went over, treading quietly on the thick carpet runner, and arrived at an open door just in time to see a once familiar face staring at itself in a mirror while in the act of lighting a cigarette.

Speaking loudly, I rapped smartly on the bulkhead.

"One bell, sir. Time to turn out for the middle watch. Seaboots and oilskins. All hands wear ship at eight bells."

He was so startled that his cigarette fell into his washbowl. It was Arthur Platt who had been Second Mate of the ship *Main* for the last year of her three-year voyage, while I was still an apprentice, and we had not seen each other for five years.

It was a happy reunion and, before any talk of my duties, we spoke of our doings and the ships we had sailed in. Platt was a Senior Third Officer, thoroughly content with life and his prospects. In the Cunard you were an officer; and treated like one. You dressed for dinner and took your meals in the first-class dining-saloon. The pay was good, you got three weeks' leave

213

with pay. The average time to command was eleven years, if you behaved yourself, and there would be quite a decent pension at retirement age.

That was the burden of his lay and it was all very encouraging. I changed into uniform and we got down to business, spent some time studying a plan of the double-bottom and the system of tanks for fresh water and ballast, and the "chits" from the Engineer Officer on watch, advising what pumping was going on, so that we were warned of any effect on the ship's trim and the mooring-lines.

Then we made our rounds, a long walk through all the decks of the ship, checking that all fire appliances were ready for use and all watchmen at their points of duty. At our approach, each of these—usually seated on a camp stool, under a light, reading—got to his feet, saluted and reported: "All correct, sir." Platt solemnly returned the salute, said, "Thank you," and we continued.

All this quasi-naval formality was strange to me, as I remarked when we were back in our quarters drinking tea and eating the sandwiches that had been sent on board for our supper. Platt laughed; then, more seriously, he explained that such naval courtesy was observed in all the ships of the fleet.

During the next two months I kept watches in a half a dozen of the ships from the proud, 33,000-ton *Lusitania* to the humble 3,000-ton *Lycia*. It was an excellent way of getting to know the ships and the kind of men I would be sailing with, for in the daytime the senior officers also had their hours of duty.

There was a camaraderie that I found delightful. All were experienced sailors. All had Master's or Extra Master's tickets and, although a proper respect for rank was observed, there was no weight-throwing by seniors or sharp distinction between seniors and juniors in their conduct with each other. Having in retrospect the limited or non-existent fellowship of the ordinary, three-officer, cargo steamer, it was a little like those early days in the half-deck of a sailing-ship where a community of purpose produced such unaffected companionship.

The weeks were full of interest and taught me many things about this new manner, this new chapter in my seafaring, from the latest appliances for navigation on the bridge and for the pre-determination of ship stability, to a fuller knowledge of the etiquette on which Platt had been so insistent. This last I gained when I was keeping the night-watch in the *Campania*. On my rounds one of the stewards when making his report, stood to attention but did not salute.

"Shouldn't you salute an officer?" I asked.

"Yes, sir, but only when wearing a cap."

He was a nice young man, about my own age, and I could see that he was having difficulty in keeping a straight face. So was I: and at last we both laughed and I saluted again while he stood to attention and then went on my way. That was one of the things Platt did not tell me.

At last I got my sea-going appointment as Junior Third Officer of the *Carmania*. I had been spending the days, when not on duty, at my home in Cheshire and now, in order to get on board in time to sign the Articles, I had to take a train that left at 4.30 a.m. It was a bitterly cold, wet morning in late December. I sat in the corner of the third-class compartment with my feet on a flat hot-water cannister that was the only form of heating and that I shared with the only other occupant who sat opposite.

He was a comfortable-looking middle-aged man who had beside him a small oblong leather case, the kind of thing carried by businessmen. At first we did not speak but when we were well on our way, he opened the attache case, took from it a clean white napkin which he spread across his knees, and a large packet of sandwiches. There was also a thermos of hot tea.

It looked wonderful and I could not help smiling at his enjoyment. That brought a smile in return, and an appreciative word about his "missus" who would not let him leave home without a bite to "stay the stomach". Getting up so early he had not been able to manage more than a cup of tea and a piece of toast. It had been the same with me and I was easily persuaded to accept a cup of tea that was as strong as it was hot and sweet, and one of the ample sandwiches.

That brought us to life. We lit our pipes and fell to talking while the rain beat noisily against the windows and on the roof. The wind roared and hit us such violent broadsides that the train shuddered in its progress. My fellow-traveller shuddered, too, humorously, and remarked that it was no kind of day to be going to sea. I was surprised. He looked more like a prosperous merchant than a sailor, although he was old enough for his face to show some signs of wind and weather.

"What ship?" I asked.

"*Carmania*," he replied and asked in his turn, "What's yours?"

"*Carmania*. I'm Junior Third Officer."

"I'm the Senior Butcher," he returned with a smile and, indeed, with such a whimsical emphasis on the word "Senior" that we found the coincidence very amusing and enjoyed a good laugh.

On board, the whole ship's company assembled in the third-class dining-saloon to be entered on the Articles for the voyage. Their numbers and diversity were impressive. It was in truth like going to sea in a floating city. Deck officers and sailors were a quite small minority.

It was a lively scene and a busy day. Each member of the ship's company had to have a place in a life-boat and had to know where it was and in which boat. When the Articles were completed I took a crew-list up to our quarters where we got to work. We had thirty-two boats, a life-boat and a collapsible boat at each of the sixteen pairs of davits on the boat-deck. For each boat there was a pocket-size notebook in which we wrote the names of those assigned to it. Departmental lists of boat-stations were also made and distributed so that everyone could be told which boat he had to go to.

At midnight we unmoored and, with the help of tugs, passed into the lock. There we had to wait until the tide was high enough for the gates to be opened and it was about 3.00 a.m. when we anchored in the river, in midstream.

When the others left the bridge and went off stations, I remained, keeping anchor-watch. I wrote up the log, entering the times of engine movements, and then paced the bridge and looked around. The wind was strong, south-westerly, and it brought with it the chimes of the clocks striking the half hour. Then I looked down to the water that was so far below me. If the *Sutlej* had been alongside I would have been looking down her funnel.

The *Carmania* seemed immense. At four o'clock I was relieved and I went thankfully to my cabin for two hours' rest. It was more than twenty-four hours since I had left my bed at home and I would be on duty again at six o'clock.

When I turned out again the whole ship was alive. Both watches had hoses rigged and were scouring the decks, fore and aft. By 7.30 a.m. the dirt of dock-land had gone.

Then the siren emitted a series of piercing, falsetto wails, alarm bells rang, loud and insistent, throughout the ship and everyone dropped what he was doing and went to his fire-station. At all points, fire-hoses were manned, and fireproof doors in the alleyways closed, as well as the watertight doors below in engine-room, bunkers and collision bulkheads. The Surgeon, orderlies and nurses were on the alert in the hospital and bedroom stewards and stewardesses assembled in the squares by the first- and second-class dining-saloons, each bearing a supply of blankets in case the imaginary emergency should lead to taking to the boats. A tour of inspection by the Chief Officer and the Board of Trade Inspector ended the parade and we went to breakfast.

Breakfast. No time to dawdle. Just a brief and delicious interval. Then, again, the alarm signal sounded. This time a succession of short, very deep rumbling bellows from the steam-whistle and we all ran to our quarters to get life-belts and then up the stairway that gave the shortest route to our stations on the boat-deck. At each boat the person in charge checked in his boat-book that all who should be there were present, and in my boat I was pleased to see the smiling face of my friend of the previous day, the Senior Butcher. After we had swung out a couple of boats and got them inboard again, back on their chocks, the Inspector was satisfied.

Sailing-days from Liverpool were busy days. Hardly was the boat muster over than tenders came alongside bringing the parcel-post mails in great bags and hampers, and the third-class passengers, most of them from faraway countries in all parts of Europe. And, of course, there were many from Britain. In 1913, there were no immigrant quotas in the United States and the cost of a third-class passage to New York was very little. A few years before one could cross the ocean for only sixty shillings—a seven- or eight-day passage, with three good, substantial meals a day, and all for £3.

At that time, with no curbs on immigration, or from trades unions, men of the building trades would travel to the U.S.A. each Spring, work there at high wages, as much per day as they could earn per week in England, and then come home for the Winter.

As soon as the tenders were away we hove up anchor and, with tugs fast at bow and stern, and the help of the last of the ebb-tide we dropped astern and came gently to rest alongside the landing stage. Our Pilot handled the great ship with calm ease in spite of the gale-force south-westerly wind that bore us down to our berth.

We were to sail at 2.00 p.m., and there began a period of intense activity. The first- and second-class passengers embarked and their heavy baggage was hoisted aboard, received by stewards and trundled away to the owners' cabins. There were Post Office vans alongside discharging a small mountain of mail that was carried through the side doors to the mail-room where, bag by bag, it was checked against the way-bill by the Second Officer and an official of the Post Office. With so much to be done, with the ship so suddenly full of excited new arrivals, one could have excused confusion, but the stewards, Bos'ns and deck-hands were, in their own way, just as expert as the Pilot. Fifteen minutes before sailing time all gangways had been landed and we were ready to leave the landing stage and go to sea.

And that is what we tried to do. Promptly, at two o'clock, our mooring-lines singled up, the tugs strained with all their power, the Pilot used the engines as much as was possible so close to the stage but could not get her away. The pressure of the gale on our broadside was too great and it was decided that we would have to wait until it eased off, perhaps towards sunset, at about four o'clock. The Pilot and Captain Barr left the bridge and at the suggestion of Carr (the Junior First Officer) I went to my cabin for a fifteen-minute spell— a smoke and, as he put it, to take the weight off my feet. This was no Summer's sailing with frock-coats and white kid gloves.

Like everyone else, I had been moving about the decks and up and down a seemingly endless succession of stairways since the previous midnight. It was a relief to sit on the settee, ease the weight of my great-coat from my shoulders and light a pipe.

I had been there only a few minutes when there was a sharp rap on the door.

"Come in," I shouted heartily, thinking that it would be our steward.

The door opened quietly. Taking the pipe from my mouth I jumped to my feet. It was the Chief Officer and I half expected a reproof because I was away from my station on the bridge. But his ruddy face was lit by a kindly smile.

"No, no. Please sit down and carry on smoking."

He took off his cap and stood leaning against the door, then he continued.

"This is your first voyage in the Cunard, de Mierre. I just wanted to tell you that I made a first voyage myself, nine years ago, and I still remember what it felt like. If there's anything I can do to help you at any time, day or night, do please come to me. That's all."

The door closed and he was gone, leaving me dumbfounded but very happy, marvelling that he, with all the responsibility that he was carrying on such a day, could still remember that there was a first-voyager among the officers and could find the time and have the kindness to make him so welcome.

That was Bob Irving, a man beloved throughout the company. As modest as he was gentle, he was Laird of an estate in Dumfriesshire where his family had been living in the ancestral home of Bonshaw Tower for more than eight centuries. That was the background he had stepped out of to go to sea as an apprentice in a sailing-ship, and he was a fine sailor. Many years later, when he was in command of the *Queen Mary*, he arrived in New York to find all the tug-boats on strike. So, the first Captain to do this, he put the great ship in her berth alongside the pier without their assistance.

Captain R. B. Irving, Cunard Line

We got away two hours later. A sharp squall of heavy rain had sent all but the most affectionate of the farewell-wavers to their homes. It was a final blast from the gale, for the wind moderated. It was a grey winter's day. We had seen nothing of the sun that was now below the horizon, but in the brief twilight the swollen river, moving slowly seawards with the turn of the tide, took on the subdued, yellow glow of the western sky.

Once clear of the landing-stage, the tugs left and, on the alert for the Pilot's orders, I stood by the engine-room telegraph.

"Half ahead port. Half back starboard. Port your helm."

The *Carmania* swung to starboard just as handily as the impudent ferry-boat that nipped across our bows.

"Stop starboard. 'Midships your helm. Half ahead starboard. Steady, steady as you go."

Now it was dark and the lights of street-lamps and buildings on both sides of the river slipped rapidly astern as we headed for the sea, for the lightship on the Bar that we could see flashing thirteen miles away. By 6.30 p.m. we were clear of the river, off stations, on sea-watches and Carr and I were relieved by Bob Irving and Platt. We would be back on the bridge again from eight o'clock until midnight.

We made our way to the dining-saloon by the same route that I had followed when the ship was dark and lifeless. Now the alleyways were covered with runners of red carpet, globes of light overhead brought out the silky sheen of the long vista of mahogany bulkheads. In the square, or landing at the head of the main stairway, on each deck, were large stands of flowers. Beside each one a small bell-boy stood on duty, white gloves tucked under the braided strap on his left shoulder, buttons shining, chest out, very proud of his job.

The dining-saloon was beautiful. The ceiling, or deckhead, was open to a round gallery in the centre. It was supported by carved wooden pillars and these, the ceiling and the panelled sides of the saloon were painted with white enamel and picked out with gold. The main source of light came from the pink-shaded lamps on the many tables that were now covered with gleaming napery, glass and cutlery, and decorations of fresh flowers.

Intense competition between the fleets of trans-Atlantic liners of all the European countries caused them to provide an extravagance of luxury, comfort and attention. They catered for an exacting and extremely wealthy clientele, for impoverishing wars had not yet eroded vast private fortunes and the ships had become like magnificent sea-going hotels.

Our table was not just inside the door, where we could have come and gone unobserved; to reach it we had to walk the length of the saloon between tables now occupied by excited passengers who effervesced with the happiness of

219

being on board, on their way home, or perhaps, just because they were in such delightful surroundings. Eager but unobtrusive stewards stood at their elbows and a suave personage, the Head Waiter, in black tail-coat and high, stiff collar and shirt-front that creaked with the brilliance of their laundering, alternately hovered over, or skimmed through the folio that was the menu and ended up by arranging a most satisfactory meal and leaving them with the feeling that they had done it all themselves, wines and all.

My previous experiences of feeding at sea, and even the Continental variety and plenty of my home, were no sufficient preparation for the epicurean profusion that now faced me. There were five of us: the First Officer, an excitable, talkative Scot named MacLellan; his watchmate, a quiet, scholarly Welshman, Griffith Roberts; Carr and myself; and a handsome young Irish officer in mufti, named Robinson, who was taking passage with us to Queenstown where he was to be married. Everyone was hungry but four of us had to be discreet because there had been very little sleep during the last thirty-six hours and we still had several hours to go, on the bridge.

So we avoided such fripperies as mousseline de foie gras, caviare, stewed frogs' legs and even oysters and ate an honest and sustaining dinner of thick soup, roast meat and a savoury. Under the lee of the land the ship did her nineteen knots with no noise of engines, or from wind and weather. The orchestra was making merry music and, in their smart uniforms, their faces ruddied by the keen December wind, my new shipmates seemed to be very nice people. It was a gay scene of warmth and well-being.

For the benefit of our guest, the conversation, led by MacLellan, turned on matrimony and the misfortune of one so young and hearty in being brought to forsake the freedom of bachelorhood. To this the Scot added whimsical, salty advice, cloaked in nautical allegory.

"Don't let her make heavy weather of it. Reef her well down, and whenever you decide that it's time for a cast of the lead, luff carefully. Put your helm down and back your main yard; shake her a little but don't let her get taken aback."

Carr was himself newly married. Joining the game, he came in on Robinson's side. The freedom and joys of the single man were wildly overrated unless you happened to be an unprincipled Highlander, reared with nothing below the belt but kilt and "sporrrran". That brought a laugh. When it died down, Carr went on, "And even he got married. Never fear, Robbie. Being married is wonderful." With sailorly sentimentality he added, "Your own cosy home for the little woman. No more lonely lodgings to come back to."

"Aye, that's what all you young fellows think," said MacLellan—himself not more than thirty years old. "But wait till the babies come. You get home from sea, all set to help the little woman so you can take her out for a meal, or tea and cakes with music and, instead, you spend all your spare time washing diapers."

Above our mirth Carr exclaimed that MacLellan was exaggerating; it couldn't be like that, he said.

"It couldn't, eh?" said MacLellan. "Well, I'm telling you. Our Sandy had me washing ninety-two diapers a day! That is, until he reached the farting stage."

At this we all laughed so heartily that the passengers at the nearby tables joined in, even though they had no idea what it was all about. Still laughing, Carr and I left the saloon to prepare for our watch; to smoke a brief pipe, wind mufflers about our necks, don greatcoats and be up there five minutes before the hour to have a look at the chart and then give our eyes time to get accustomed to the darkness.

Carr went over to the Chief Officer who was amidships, in the wheel-house, talking with Captain Barr, and I went to the port wing of the bridge where I found Arthur Platt.

"That's Point Lynus abaft the beam. We passed it seven miles off. There's the Skerries on your port bow, about twelve miles away. Another hour and you'll be off the South Stack."

He told me the course and speed, gave me a few words of warning of the kind of things that the Old Man would want, and then went below. The ship was only eight years old and completely up-to-date for her times, but mechanical gyro-compasses and radar had not yet made their appearance. We had to depend on our own eyes, like good, old-fashioned sailors. As soon as Platt had gone, I went on top of the wheel-house and looked about me, trying to take it all in. Enjoying the moment and the retrospect.

On a blustery December day, four years before, we had stopped the rusty old *Highland Scot* off Point Lynus to pick up our Liverpool Pilot. And how glad we were to have the Pilot aboard after that near disastrous passage from London.

And four and a half years before that, one of six tired, hungry and rather bewildered first voyagers, I had spent a warm summer's day beating between the Isle of Man and the Welsh coast to get around these same Skerries. That was the year of the *Carmania*'s own first voyage. We took the water together. And now, here I was, the most junior of her seven officers, perched above her bridge, a very small speck in relation to her great bulk, enjoying the moment and the comfort of self-confidence as I took successive bearings of the light on the Skerries and made a quick mental calculation of the distance at which we would pass it when we had it abeam, half an hour later. I got down to the bridge, to make my report to Carr and came face to face with the Old Man who stood blocking the wheel-house door. I saluted and made my report to him and in return got a gruff, "Thank you."

It was very dark, with a clear atmosphere. Good weather for watch-keeping; the kind of night when the lights of lighthouses were seen at the maximum range of their visibility and those of other ships shone against the blackness with remarkable brilliance. There was a good deal of traffic but there was no occasion to alter course to keep clear of ships we were overhauling or meeting. We were lucky. There would have been an unpleasant mess of crawling at slow speed among the noise of sirens, whistles and fog-horns had the sou'wester backed to the south-east, throwing down a blanket of rain and drizzle as thick as any fog.

Shortly after two bells—nine o'clock—we had the South Stack light and the loom of the town of Holyhead on our port beam and were heading south-west down the St. George's Channel on a course that would take us past the Tuskar Light, eighty-six miles away. The Old Man had gone below and the Pilot had gone to his dinner with the Chief Officer. Normally, he would have left us off Point Lynus, the end of his pilotage, but he was coming to Queenstown where, after a wait of a few hours he would pick up the *Lusitania* for the inward pilotage to Liverpool.

The rest of the watch was uneventful. Carr paced the starboard side of the bridge and I did the same to port, going into the wheel-house now and again to watch the steering—the habit of any good officer but, in these ships, rather a matter of form because the Quartermasters were so expert. It did not take long for the good north-westerly wind to tear the clouds apart when I was able to get a star azimuth and check the compass deviation. This I reported to Carr. Then I went into the chart-room to enter it in the Deviation Log and to write up the Bridge Log, recording the times and distances of passing the various lights, the courses steered and the meteorological details of the watch.

Five minutes before midnight our reliefs were there and, after leaving the bridge, I made my rounds of third class and steerage while Carr did the same in the parts of the ship reserved for first- and second-class passengers.

All was quiet below; everyone fast asleep, nobody smoking and the watchman at his post. I climbed the many stairways up to our quarters and, a few moments later, was in my bunk. I had not had my clothes off for more than forty hours and for every one of those hours I had been busily occupied. I lay thinking of all that had happened during that long day; of how, as soon as the ship was fast alongside the landing-stage, one of the first things we had done—Carr and I—had been to plot the position of the centre of gravity of the combined weight of everything that the ship was carrying, and the extent to which this was below the normal centre of buoyancy. This (like the length of a pendulum) and the way the ship sat in the water—her trim—usually a little deeper at the stern than at the bow, governed her stability, her behaviour at sea. I was tired but very happy. I had joined a company of keen, conscientious sailors, good shipmates, in a ship where nothing was left to chance.

At daylight we anchored in Queenstown harbour where, in due course, a tender came alongside bringing more passengers and mails. At ten o'clock we were away again and three hours later we passed the Fastnet, heading into the broad Atlantic on our way to New York.

That was a typical sailing day out of Liverpool, for me the first of nine such voyages made that year, none of them remarkable but seven of them noteworthy because they were the last to be made with that graciousness and observance of the fitness of things that were destroyed for ever or changed beyond recognition when the world plunged into the madness of war. Life aboard a Cunarder of those days bore about the same relationship to its conduct today as the sedate photographs in a family album bear to the "girlie" pictures that frame the doorways of cabaret and night-club in any large city.

There were no public address systems or piped music invading every corner of the ship, no perpetual itch for jungle music and twitching limbs, no "Bingo" or other organised, general gambling. The lovely drawing-room was reserved for the same decorous use that it would serve in any leading hotel or large country mansion. In the winter months a bright coal fire burned in the fireplace and at various times during the day the orchestra gave concerts.

The warning to dress and the time for dinner were given by a bugler blowing the merry notes of *The Roast Beef of Old England*. Smoking in the dining-saloon was not permitted at any time. Once during the voyage there was dancing in the dining-saloon, after dinner had been served but there was no "Captain's Dinner" with absurd paper hats and spurious gaiety. The only thing that remotely resembled this happened every voyage on the night before arriving in New York. Then, half-way through dinner, the orchestra, playing very spiritedly, would strike up *Dixie*. This always brought a burst of applause and little cries of joy from our passengers whether Yankees from New England, Southerners from the deep South, hyphenates of recently acquired citizenship or just plain Mr. and Mrs. Morris Bernstein.

There must have been something very compulsive in the melody, with the drums and fifes that were part of its arrangement, with its rhythm suggestive of marching feet and waving banners, demanding that all patriotic citizens rejoice in their American nationality.

The smoking-saloon was reserved for gentlemen. Ladies were not allowed in there. At 11.00 p.m. it was closed for the night and, if any of the passengers could not be persuaded to leave at that time, the Steward reported to the bridge and the Junior Officer of the Watch came down to ensure that, as far as possible, the ship's rules were complied with, without unpleasantness. But this action was taken very rarely.

On Sunday mornings, the following notice was displayed:

> DIVINE SERVICE WILL BE HELD IN THE
> FIRST-CLASS DRAWING-ROOM AT 11.00 A.M.
> A MASS FOR ROMAN CATHOLICS WILL TAKE
> PLACE AT THE SAME TIME IN THE SECOND-CLASS
> IF THERE IS A PRIEST AVAILABLE AMONG
> THE PASSENGERS.

"So one's divine and the other's not. One's first-class and the other's not."

The elderly Irish priest who said this had come aboard in Queenstown. Musingly, he rubbed his chin as he chuckled over the wording of the notice. Then he caught my eye and said, with a broad smile, "Well. With the help of Saint Patrick, it's meself'll go down there and make the second-class first-class—and Divine, too, I'll warrant."

The service was staged with considerable formality. Five minutes before the hour the bell was tolled. The reading-desk was draped with the British and American flags, a choir of stewards sat behind the desk. Outside, on the promenade deck, the Intermediate Third Officer, wearing frock-coat and white gloves, inspected the church-party of able seamen and ordinary seamen, all wearing their best uniforms. When the Captain arrived, with the Purser or the Second Officer, they were marched into church by the Bos'n, the Officer bringing up the rear.

All this ceremony was taken for granted and even enjoyed by the seamen. Most of them had spent years in the Royal Navy and it was the kind of thing they were accustomed to. And for them, too, it was a satisfying show to be seated in softly upholstered chairs, among all the sweet-smelling pretty ladies and opulent male passengers. These often included one or two parsons but I cannot remember any occasion when any of them accepted the invitation that he should conduct the service. It seemed that, like all the other passengers, they were there to enjoy the novelty of seeing this done by sailors.

And the sailors did it extremely well. In his trim frock-coat with its brass buttons and gold-braided sleeves, with his grey hair and rugged, weather-beaten face, Captain Barr looked the prototype of generations of gallant, resourceful shipmasters. He intoned the prayers and canticles in his deep voice with clerical eloquence, for all that on the bridge he could produce such wide-ranging flights of profanity. And Second Officer Fall—himself to be Commodore at a later date—read the lessons with a reverence equal to that of any churchman. The music of the orchestra was good, so was the singing of the choir and the congregation responded generously in the collection that would benefit the Missions to Seamen and other maritime charities.

Executive authority over passengers and crew lay with the navigating officers. Of this there was no doubt; it was recognised throughout the ship. The Junior Third Officer received as much respect from the Chief Steward—and gave as much in return—as did the Chief Officer. Whatever the emergency or unusual circumstance, the "bridge" was always immediately informed and called on for help when necessary.

That could sometimes be quite unpleasant, as on one bright, sunny morning when an agitated steward came running to the bridge to report that one of the second-class passengers had gone mad and was roaming about the promenade-deck, aft, flourishing a large knife and talking gibberish.

"Had some kind of a brain-storm, sir. Looks like a big lumberjack. Never stopped drinking since we left New York."

With a worried frown, Carr listened attentively and then turned to me.

"Alright, de Mierre. You'd better go along and see what it's all about. He seems to be bigger than you so you'd better pick up a saloon-deck man on your way in case you need any help."

It was another time of swallowing hard and trying to look composed but I am sure that the steward was not more frightened than I was. Aft, the promenade-deck was deserted and looked as though a miniature riot had been in progress; rugs, books and overturned deck-chairs lay scattered about. But there was no sign of the madman. Presently, a Master-at-Arms—a kind of ship's policeman—came out of the entrance and reported that the man had gone to his cabin, close by, on the same deck.

We went there, the steward, myself, the Master-at-Arms, the saloon-deck man and stood in the alleyway, outside the cabin, listening to a mixture of raving and shrieking laughter that ended in moans and sobbing.

"Come on," I said. "We've got to stop this before he slits his throat or starts shrieking again. Master-at-Arms, you go and get the Surgeon." Then, to the other two, "We'll go inside."

I opened the door and went in. To my horror, the steward promptly pulled the door to again, leaving me in there, alone. I do not like madmen. This one was sitting on the edge of the lower berth, elbows on knees, holding his head, his fingers buried in a mop of black hair. A heavy, horn-handled hunting-knife lay on the deck by my feet. Instinctively, I kicked it under the bunk where it clattered noisily against a tin trunk. The man jumped to his feet, startled. He stood, arms aloft, gazing wildly about him. I was thoroughly scared and took refuge in tough-sounding bombast.

"What the devil d'ye mean, making such a noise aboard my ship. Running around like a crazy man. If there's any more of it I'll have you clapped in irons."

The louder I shouted, the more my self-assurance returned and, to my relief, the clutching hands that looked as though they were about to grab my throat, fell to his sides.

"I'm sorry, Captain," he said. "There ain't nobody speaks my language round here. I jest cairn't make 'em understand."

"Understand what?" I asked.

"That we're all *dead*," he exclaimed, vehemently.

"You mean that I'm dead and you're dead?"

"Yes, Captain. That's it." He shouted excitedly, as if delighted that at last he had found somebody who understood him.

"Well," I replied, as though studying the matter, "but if we're both dead how can we talk to each other and hear each other speaking?"

At this he sat down again on his bed, let his great hairy hands hang loosely between his knees and looked at me with an expression of bewilderment that, at any other time, would have been comical.

"It do seem strange, don't it?" he replied.

Now Dr. Mackenzie arrived with his orderly and I remained only long enough to hear him say, "Drink that my man, and you'll be fine . . . when you wake up, tomorrow . . . or maybe the day after."

My first voyages in the Cunard were made in the depth of winter and I learned that large, fast ships had ways of their own and that mere size and power did not always make them superior to the weather. They presented such vast surfaces of hull and superstructure that, when they ran into the hard gales of the North Atlantic, they had to be kept going at a speed at which they would answer the helm and hold to their course against the contrary pressure of wind and sea. That could mean as much as eight to ten knots. Meeting seas that might be racing towards you at twice that speed frequently put the bows under and jarred the ship from stem to stern. When she rose again, the water poured noisily from her fore-deck, much of it being caught by the wind and flung in masses of heavy spray over the bridge and against the forward funnel.

Our passengers of the first and second class, on the upper decks amidships and aft, were cosy and dry, but those in the steerage, whose deck space was constantly swamped and no longer safe for them, had to remain below.

That was the kind of weather we had for practically the entire crossing on my second voyage in the *Carmania*. Already off Queenstown it was so bad that

Captain Barr would not go in to pick up the mails and passengers that awaited us; and Collins, the Liverpool Pilot, had to make the round voyage. South of the Newfoundland Banks we struck the tail-end of a hurricane, with vicious seas running on top of a mountainous swell. It came out of the south-west, dead ahead, and was so furious that once, when her bows were rising but were not yet clear, a second great sea came along and totally submerged the forward end of the ship and smashed most of the glass in the wheel-house on the bridge, sixty feet above the water. Then "Jimmy" Barr hove her to and she lay until daylight, pitching and rolling as wildly as a vessel one tenth her size.

That happened shortly before we reached the end of the long, curving track that had been followed since leaving the Fastnet, the "corner", the point where we made a major alteration of course, from south-west to west, and steamed on a straight line that would, if our reckoning were correct, take us to the Nantucket light-vessel, some 1,200 miles away.

There was, of course, no reason to doubt the correctness of our reckoning. We had seen very little of sun or stars, but the *Carmania* had made upwards of one hundred round voyages to New York, and in the Deviation Log could be found the error of her compass at practically any position along the track. If you are sure of the course you are steering and know your speed and distance since leaving the last position, it is a simple matter to calculate the change in latitude and longitude and arrive at the new position. "D.R."—Dead Reckoning, they called it. I mention it only because in those days, if you were not able to get an observation of sun or stars, that was the only way you had of finding your position.

The weather moderated but continued thick with patches of freezing fog that persisted until we were about one hundred and fifty miles east of Nantucket when it turned to snow, falling heavily, driven by a northerly wind. So on the lower bridge we swung out the boom, hauled the deep-sea lead out to its end where it would drop well clear of the ship, and took a cast getting no bottom at one hundred and fifty fathoms.

Actually, for all its rugged winter weather, its fog, ice and snow, the eastern American coast is otherwise not so inhospitable, because when you are still far from the land you suddenly strike soundings of reasonable depth. Where we took our first cast there are about 1,200 fathoms of water but, two and a half hours later, with still one hundred miles to go to the lightship, we got bottom at fifty fathoms and were sure that we had made a good cast because the "arming"—the lump of tallow that filled a cavity in the heel of the lead—was encrusted with a sample of grey sand and small fragments of broken shell. Three hours later another cast gave us thirty fathoms and after that the lead was dropped every ten miles so that our line of soundings could be compared with the depths of water given on the chart, thus verifying our position. And so we continued until, at last, in an interval between our own bellowings, we heard the deep roar of the lightship's fog horn, distant but unmistakable. We swung in the boom, put the lead back in its locker and headed for the Ambrose Channel light-vessel, off Sandy Hook, upwards of two hundred miles away.

At Ambrose you got your Pilot and went into the quarantine anchorage off Staten Island where, on that particular voyage, we lay throughout the night.

Large slabs of ice drifted by. On shore, the snow was deep. About a mile away was Brady's wharf where, seven years before, at the same time of the year, we had worked so hard in the ship *Main*, shovelling the mud and rubble ballast out of her hold. And, up harbour, near the Statue of Liberty, was the spot where the *Main* had anchored while waiting for a loading berth and where I had fallen over the side for a freezing dip among the chunks of ice. The wind was now blowing from that direction and brought with it that all-pervading smell of kerosene from the oil berths at Tidewater and Constable Hook. The air was full of the noise of bells and whistles: mournful tinkling notes and despairing, asthmatic, abbreviated toots from the channel buoys; the sharp, hard clanging of the nearby railway; the multi-toned whistles of the ferry boats. It was all very familiar. I missed only the company of the few square-rigged sailing-ships that had shared the haven with us.

In good weather conditions, entering and leaving New York was a simple business. There was sometimes a fair amount of traffic in the channel but the pilotage was straightforward. There were no tidal locks to bother about. The piers were built at right-angles to the Hudson River and all you had to do was to get your ship up there on the last of the flood-tide so that she could make a ninety-degree turn in slack water and then steam gently into her berth. Tugs were fast at bow and stern to give a pull, or push, if necessary.

On that second voyage, we landed our passengers on the Saturday morning and, after two days of ceaseless work—filling the coal bunkers, discharging and loading cargo, taking aboard stores, clean laundry, mails and, finally, cleaning ship—sailed again on the Monday evening. On the pier a multitude of people, gay and noisy or tearful and silent, watched us go. It was a thrilling moment when the deep roar of our whistle split the frosty air and echoed loudly from the nearby buildings. The ship trembled as the propellers, going full speed astern, drove the river water with its flotsam and lumps of ice up into the berth that we were leaving. We backed swiftly into the stream, stopped and remained motionless for the few moments before the ship gathered head-way and moved slowly past the lower end of Manhattan where, in the dusk, the tall, black shapes of the buildings were perforated by hundreds of lighted

228

office windows where land-bound midgets scratched away with pen and ink in dog-eared ledgers, while we headed for the broad, free ocean.

It was an agreeable life. One accepted the gales, the cold, wet fogs and even the occasional near presence of drifting icebergs as the normal daily round. On my next two voyages in the *Carmania*, having been promoted, I went on duty with the Senior First Officer, Peter Murchie, keeping the middle watch. This was not the usual torture of broken sleep, because when we turned in after leaving the bridge at 4.00 a.m. there was no turning out again at 7.30 a.m. to wind chronometers. We could sleep until ten o'clock when our steward gave us breakfast in our cabins and there was still plenty of time to get ready for the bridge and the afternoon watch.

Murchie was an Edinburgh man, tall and slender and with a lively, elfish humour that was delightful. He was one of the few who had known what he was letting himself in for before he became a sailor. He was thought to be delicate so his father sent him away as a passenger in a sailing-ship for a voyage to Australia and around the world. From the comparative luxury of the saloon table, sleeping all night and enjoying the dry comfort of the poop, he had seen the hardship of little sleep and meagre food, and of work aloft in wild weather that was the lot of apprentices and seamen. And that, he decided, was the life that he wanted.

His natural bearing was that of polite dignity. I so well remember the occasion when we met on our way to dinner, in the main square outside the dining-saloon, three gentlemen who were having a rather noisy, good-natured argument. As we approached, one of them, thinking perhaps to have a bit of fun at our expense, waved an arm and addressed Murchie.

"Here's the man who can settle the matter. We're arguing about the word 'bunt' and what it means in English, and I'm sure that you can tell us."

Without a moment's hesitation Murchie replied, "Well, sir, in English the bunt is the middle part of a square sail as any sailor will tell you. Then there's bunting, also familiar to seafaring men—the many-coloured stuff that flags are made of. And that word comes from the German word 'bunt' "—he pronounced it *boont*—"and I think that'll be the one you are wanting. Do you not remember Goethe's *Erl-king* that you learned at school?" Then, with a nice cadence and in perfect German he quoted: "*Manch' bunte Blumen sind an dem Strand*," and followed with the English, "Many motley flowers are on the bank."

Peter Murchie had said all this with his hands clasped behind his back and the sober air of a schoolmaster. Indeed, the three jovial German-Americans were so astonished that they looked like schoolboys, as they stammered out their thanks.

In the last week of July, 1914, I left the *Caronia* where I had been for three pleasant summer voyages on the Boston service. She was so popular that Boston society regarded her almost as their own. They were very hospitable and some of us were often invited ashore to dine, or to spend a Sunday at one of the beach resorts. On that last voyage we brought the Harvard boat and its crew who were going to Henley. With their families, sweethearts and glee-club they seemed to fill the ship, and life on board was a gay round of sport during the daylight hours, and of merry laughter, flirtation and beautiful singing on the boat-deck in the evenings.

I had not wanted to leave the ship but a toe, mis-shapen through having once been broken, was so uncomfortable as I went about the decks in the heat of American summer, that I decided to get rid of it and was given a few days' leave. It was quickly done but when, on August 4th, the war broke out, I was still in a nursing-home, chafing at my temporary disability and hourly expecting my mobilisation orders.

A week later, I was back in Liverpool. In the Huskisson Dock both of my ships, the *Carmania* and the *Caronia*, were being converted into armed Merchant Cruisers, painted battleship grey, already under naval command. Several of their officers were appointed to them as Lieutenants, R.N.R., and I was chagrined not to be one of them.

Instead, I joined the *Campania* and, on August 15th, sailed for New York with every available square foot of passenger accommodation, including the third-class and steerage, occupied by people who were so delighted at having the means of getting home again, that the occasional discomforts of an over-crowded ship were not noticed. For them, the ship was a haven of refuge after a nightmare fourteen days in a Europe that was suddenly smitten by a terrifying epidemic of war madness.

Within a period of seven days the headlines had screamed of declarations of war: Austria against Serbia; Germany against Russia; Germany against France and Great Britain against Germany.

And then there had been the difficulty of making their way to the Channel and to England by transport systems that gave priority to troops and military equipment moving in the other direction. No wonder they were well satisfied to be on board the *Campania*. She was a grand old ship that could still do her twenty-one knots and if everything else in the world was hideously ugly that summer, the Atlantic weather was perfect. We were back in Liverpool in seventeen days and sailed again for New York four days later.

An old Atlantic greyhound – the *Lucania*, *Campania*'s sister-ship

In New York the first person to come aboard was a telegraph messenger with a cable that my father had sent the previous day. My orders had come. Immediately on arrival in Liverpool I was to report to Devonport Naval Barracks for active service. I was glad. The suspense had not been agreeable; five weeks had gone by and one wondered if there were something that one had omitted to do.

And I was excited. I stood by the gangway watching the equally excited passengers going ashore, when a plump and very pleasant little lady, a Miss Collison of Germantown, Pennsylvania, and her pretty young niece came to say good-bye. The crossing had been so pleasant and she hoped that next time we were in port, when they were settled down again after their travels, I would come and see them. Thanking her, I explained why this would not be possible. Immediately, Miss Collison invited me to dine with them that same day.

The Astor was a gracious hotel. There were four of us, the other being the niece's grandmother, a Mrs. Wheeler, who was deaf. It was an enjoyable evening. The only uncomfortable moment came when it was time for me to go. The old lady, speaking rather loudly, as so many deaf people do, said good-bye in a voice that must have been heard by most of the people in the drawing-room.

"Good-bye, my boy. Take care of yourself. And mind you kill plenty of Germans."

I felt conspicuous and foolish. I had not yet thought of killing anybody. Not even Germans. And there were probably many Germans in the room, within earshot.

Then little Miss Collison very sweetly kissed me on both cheeks, while she held my hand. As she did so, I realised that between our palms was something small, flat and very soft to the touch. It was a beautiful, miniature, suede-bound volume, about the size of a large postage stamp. It was . . . it is . . . *The Gospel According to Saint John*. It is in my pocket now. I have carried it ever since.

On the fly-leaf Miss Collison had written:

> *God bless and protect you*
> *is the wish of a friend.*

14 *Devonport and Gibraltar*

When the *Campania* arrived in Liverpool I left her at the landing-stage. I had received the mails on board, in New York, and had to deliver them to the General Post Office. On the way, I took my uniforms to the tailor who would change stripes and buttons. Then I went home. It was late evening on Thursday, September 24th. My father was already there, waiting for me with a cigar and a glass of wine.

"Ho ho, my boy. You got my cable in New York?"

"Yes, thank you, Dad. And another when we arrived this afternoon."

"When are you going?"

"By the train at midnight on Saturday."

"But they sent for you two weeks ago. You're late. Can't you go tonight?"

"Yes, I could. But I've got to be in naval uniform and I'll not get that till Saturday morning. That's the best the tailor can do. He's swamped by people like me, all wanting to be first."

The old man was satisfied but still a trifle disgruntled. Like everyone else, he was infected by the prevailing war-fever. My older brother was already a private in Kitchener's army. It did not seem right that I should spend forty-eight hours doing nothing. Had it been in any way possible he would have gone to war himself.

At midnight on Saturday the station was but feebly lit and was practically deserted. My father, sisters and fiancée were the only ones on the platform. It was not a cheerful moment but, as the train started to move and I leaned out of the window, my father took off his hat and gave three hearty cheers.

At Devonport Naval Barracks—H.M.S. *Vivid*—a Sunday stillness lay overall. Even the sentry at the gate spoke almost in a whisper when he directed the cabby to the office of the Captain Superintendent. There a Writer ran his finger down the pages of a large folio, finally wrote the time of arrival against my name and then answered my questions.

"Yes, sir. There's a cabin for you in the officers' quarters. No, there's no need for further report. The O.O.D.—Officer of the Day," he explained with a smile—"will give you all necessary instruction and information in the morning."

In the morning the only instruction I got was to don the "rig of the day" which was white flannels, white sweater, jacket and cap, and then to take my place in the ranks of a squad of sublieutenants. The O.O.D. who had charge of us was a Lieutenant, R.N.R., who had just completed his twelve months' training in the Navy and was quite at home in his job. He spent a few moments looking us over and for another few moments had us jumping to attention and standing at ease. Then he marched us into a large drill-shed. In there, as we proceeded down its length, we were individually detached from the squad and each stationed at the end of two long files of about sixty men.

There had been no previous warning of this parade and I had not the slightest idea what was going to happen. And, for all that we were in an enormous drill-shed, probably about one thousand of us, there was a solemnness in the air that did not encourage any informality. I could not catch the eye of some other officer who knew the ropes, stroll over and ask what it was all about. Each stood, wooden-faced, at the end of his company of men, and these in turn were just as rigid. Then, in the distance, with a reverberating prelude of drums, the band of the Royal Marines played the National Anthem. This was followed by prayers, said by a Chaplain who was so far away that his intoning could only be faintly heard. However, it must have come to an appropriate ending for it was replaced by the band playing very loudly and merrily, *A Life on the Ocean Wave*.

Officers began shouting orders and, to my consternation, I realised that the noise of this was moving in my direction. The officer of the third company in front of me, quite a small man, let out a bull-throated roar: "A Company, SHUN. Form FOURS. QUICK march. Right WHEEL." And away they went. Then came "B" company, and "C". Then it was my turn. I shouted the commands that I had picked up from my predecessors. They were most satisfyingly obeyed and, feeling a little better, I marched my men down to the parade-ground.

There I was in trouble again. The first thing we met was a flag-pole and a purple-faced Warrant Officer who addressed me as follows:

"Stand here, sir, and when the last file of your company is in line with this flag, shout 'D Company, right turn.'"

Hardly had he finished speaking than it was time for me to act.

"D Company," I yelled, "RIGHT TURN."

Not only was the order obeyed but, to my alarm and astonishment, my men, marching in a compact body, four abreast, changed formation when they turned right, strung themselves out into two long files and went marching

234

briskly down the parade-ground, with me in the rear in a state of sweaty apprehension, with no idea where I should be but quite certain that it was not there. And this was confirmed by an agonised yell from the Warrant Officer.

"D Company OFFICER. Get in FRONT of your men, sir. PLEASE."

I doubled round to the front of the company, picked up their step and was marching, still rather bewildered, on their right wing, when a ventriloquial cockney voice came over my shoulder.

"Hit's a march past, sir. Ye'll be more comfortable amidships."

A few rapid steps to the left put me in the centre and, once more, by listening to the officer of the company in front of us I was able to give the "Eyes RIGHT" and attempt a smart salute when we came to the saluting base and the "Eyes FRONT" when we had passed it. And what a relief that was.

That was the manner of my introduction to the Royal Navy and it was probably a very satisfactory one. It certainly brought home the fact that you did not "know it all" and, also, that there was nothing reprehensible in feeling foolish. So long as one tried and learned. Some of this may have been appreciated by the men. My awkwardness was very obvious but, whatever may have been their inclination, none smiled. And there was the kindly cockney whose advice surely saved me from disgrace.

I was to be in barracks for only six working days but, in spite of this inauspicious start, I enjoyed them and was disappointed when they ended. It was only a brief glimpse of the Navy that had been, for so long, so exclusive a society. I use the word society because there was a cohesiveness between officers and men, much like that of a closely united family, and the exclusiveness embraced the men as completely as it did the officers.

The days were spent in the gunnery school where I marvelled at the Petty Officers and their smooth-flowing, verbatim instruction from the gunnery manual. We stripped and reassembled the breech mechanism of light and heavy guns and, as I became more accustomed to the jargon of gunnery, I could feel only respect for their dedication. They belonged to the Service and, just as truly, the Service belonged to them.

At the end of the week, on the Sunday afternoon, I was resting in my cabin when a messenger came to say that I was wanted in the wardroom. There I found a Lieutenant Commander and three Sublieutenants, all that could be found in the barracks. Two Sublieutenants were wanted for H.M.S. *Pelorus*.

"Yes, I know. You'll all go," said the Lieutenant Commander. "But she only wants two. Let's get the dice box."

And that is how it was done. Sublieutenant Thompson and I won. We began our active service on a throw of the dice.

The following morning we were in Queenstown, looking for our ship. We were expected. One of her whalers lay at the steps of the quay, waiting for us. The ship herself lay to a buoy in mid-harbour where she had been coaling. The crew were washing down and the water poured from her scuppers, but the quarter-deck, where we both came to attention and saluted smartly, was already glistening and clean. The Corporal of Marines on gangway duty brought his heels together and stood stiff as a ramrod while the First Lieutenant, who was there to receive us, returned our salutes. Then he introduced himself, learned our names, and with a warm handshake welcomed us on board and took us aft to the Captain.

That night the *Pelorus* was buffeting a lively sea, making her way against a fresh head wind for the patrol station off the Scilly Isles, about one hundred and thirty miles away. She would cruise back and forth along a line that ran sixty miles south-west from the Bishop Rock light and do so for ten days. Then she would run up to Bantry Bay, in the west of Ireland, and for two days would lay snug in Bear Haven. Snug, but all hands busy coaling ship and taking stores aboard. Then to sea again, for another ten days' cruise, this time on a line running sixty miles south-west from the Fastnet. After that, back to Queenstown for coal and stores and start the round all over again.

Ten days at sea, two days in port with coal-barges alongside, port and starboard, and everyone, excepting only the Captain and Surgeon, shovelling coal, filling wheelbarrows, trundling them along the decks, tipping and shovelling coal down the bunker manholes. Starboard and port watches in sharp competition, to be the first to finish. It was hard, dirty work but also good fun and officers and men evidently enjoyed doing the same kind of work at a common level. There was little opportunity for going on shore, either in Bear Haven or Queenstown. On the second day, if we did not go to sea immediately, when ship and guns were clean, the men were piped to "make and mend"—that is, do their own bits of sewing and wash their clothes.

In her day, the light cruiser *Pelorus* had been a smart little ship. Now she was rather old. When the war broke out she was in Devonport, on the point of paying off, after three years on the Persian Gulf and Western India station—waters for which she was well suited. She was only 305 feet long but carried six four-inch guns, with their heavy, armoured gun-shields, six three-pounders and two fifteen-inch torpedo tubes on deck. That was a lot of weight for such a small vessel to carry in the stormy weather of the Western Approaches, in winter. There were, of course, good days, but when it blew hard she would shovel the solid water over her bows and fill the decks. There were many times, when it blew a whole gale, that we would have to run for it and take shelter in Crow Sound, Scillies, until it became fit to resume patrol.

There was a lot of that kind of weather and sometimes it provided very

H.M.S. *Pelorus*

picturesque contrasts. I so well remember one morning when, on a day of brilliant sunshine, the wind fairly screamed out of the north-west and the green seas of the shallow water came rushing at us, flinging their dazzling white crests aloft and deluging the fore-bridge. There was not a part of the ship that was not swept by spume and spindrift, all of it gleaming in the sun. The hollows between the seas were streaked with foam and the almost cloudless sky was that lovely blue of northern winter. And, close at hand, to leeward, was a goodly fleet of small steam trawlers, out from the fishing-ports of the west country—Bideford, Penzance and Mevagissey—little, round-bellied vessels built of wood, as buoyant as seagulls, rising to allow the seas to pass under them and never the smallest gobbet of spray going aboard.

As cosy as a bevy of fishwives, they looked to us. And I suppose that the *Pelorus*, bucking the seas and throwing up fountains of spray, with the smoke streaming from her two funnels and the white ensign flying in the gale, stiff and quiet, from her gaff, must have looked very businesslike and comforting to them.

Captain of the ship was Commander Ernest Stevenson, R.N. In the wardroom were three Lieutenant-Commanders: the First Lieutenant, the Chief Engineer and the Surgeon; five Lieutenants: the Navigator, a Lieutenant R.N., and four R.N.R.s, Thompson and I having been promoted; a Paymaster Sublieutenant and the Captain's Clerk, a total of ten. The domestic side of the wardroom was looked after by the Paymaster Sublieutenant who also ran the wine accounts. Officers' servants and waiters were chosen from the detach-

Officers of *Pelorus*

ment of Royal Marines that was part of the ship's company. We ate our meals in the wardroom and spent our leisure there. It was our only place of recreation but it was comfortable, well-furnished and heated by an efficient coal-stove. Another important item of creature comfort was a large barrel of excellent Irish stout, well chocked off, and that we could drink at a cost of a penny the pint. This, with liberal helpings of shrimps and prawns, farm butter and fresh, crusty bread, gave us many a delicious lunch when we were coaling ship in Bantry Bay. So while life on patrol in the Western Approaches in winter was sometimes a bit rugged, it had its compensations and there was nothing monotonous about it. We kept watches on the fore-bridge, looking out for vessels that perhaps should be stopped and interrogated, perhaps boarded, and also taking it in turns to decipher, by means of the special secret codes, signals from the Admiralty or other H.M. ships. At night, guns were loaded, ready for instant use and the guns' crews, in thick duffle clothing, slept by their guns.

238

By day, such extreme vigilance was relaxed but there would he occasional surprise bugle calls to "General Quarters" when everyone ran to his station for action.

Lieutenant Rutherford Collins, R.N.R., and I were the boarding officers. No matter who was on watch, or if we were off duty, at any time, night or day, and in any kind of weather, if a vessel had to be boarded we were turned out to go away in the boat. Always the same two officers and always the same coxswain and boat's crew. We came to know each other and did what had to be done by instinct and, even on the blackest of nights, without fumbling. Like everything else in the Royal Navy, the drill was exact and efficient. When the boat had to go away, Collins and I and the boat's crew would "fall in" on deck by the davits. The Warrant Gunner issued our arms of revolvers and ammunition belts, with the addition of cutlasses for the men. When these had been buckled around our waists the Gunner gave the order to load. Each drew his revolver from its holster, pointed it outboard, opened the breech, took six cartridges from the belt with the left hand, loaded, closed the breech, and only then was the right arm lowered and the revolver dropped, out of harm's way, into its holster.

Then we took our places in the boat, ready for lowering. On our return to the ship, as soon as we had been hoisted out of the water and the boat had been secured, we jumped down on deck, fell in under the watchful eye of the Gunner, and unloaded by the same drill, in reverse. I give the procedure in detail because I found such precaution surprising but it taught me that no loaded weapons are left lying around in the Navy.

Our Montagu whalers were wonderful sea-boats and I enjoyed boarding. It was always thrilling and was sometimes amusing. One Sunday afternoon, on one of the good days, with moderate wind and sea and bright sunshine, I was on watch when a deeply laden, dirty-looking tramp-steamer came up on my starboard quarter, steering to cross my bow. She was doing about eight knots and we were loafing along at our patrol speed of five. As our courses converged I hoisted signals asking for her name and destination but they were ignored. Captain Stevenson was walking the poop, watching all this, and now he came to the bridge.

"Alright, de Mierre. Make 'stop instantly'. We'll board him."

We hoisted this signal and it, too, was disregarded. By this time we were so close that, through our binoculars, we could see that the only person on deck was the man at the wheel.

"Well, I'm damned," said the Captain. "There's a man who's not bothering his head about submarines or anything else. No look out. Put a shot across his bows."

From the three-pounder gun on the fo'c's'le, immediately below us, came an ear-splitting crack that almost took the cap off my head. The little shell raised a mighty splash about one hundred yards ahead of the tramp. Doors were flung open and her people came tumbling out of their cabins. Someone ran up to the bridge to stop the engines and she lost headway.

Collins and I climbed her coal-begrimed rope-ladder to her equally dirty deck where we were received by a grey-haired, unshaven man. He wore a dingy, collarless flannel shirt, old trousers that hung from once white but now badly stained braces, and carpet slippers. Collins was normally a Chief Officer in the Royal Mail Company. He had a precise, rather dandified manner of speaking.

"Will you kindly take us to the Master."

The grubby-faced man was so surprised by this request that he glanced quickly around and over his shoulder, as though startled into looking for the Master, until he regained his self-possession.

"The Master," he exclaimed, "why, that's me. I'm the Master. What is it ye'll be wanting of me? Maybe we'd better go to my quarters."

He said this advisedly for a small crowd had gathered about us. The saloon, his quarters, was aft, in the poop, for the *Killin*, of Glasgow, was an old-fashioned ship. We sat at a red baize-covered table, under an ornamental sky-light, and the following conversation took place.

"Ahem!" from Collins, "I'm not going to ask you, Captain, *why* you ignored our signals and made it necessary for us to waste good ammunition, because the reason is, ahem, only too obvious. Nobody on the bridge and nobody keeping a look-out anywhere else and, apparently, the only one who was not in his bunk, fast asleep, was the man at the wheel. And even he must have been dozing. A German submarine wouldn't have to waste a torpedo on you. He could come quietly alongside and take you by boarding."

The old man listened with wrinkled brow, eyes blinking, but said nothing and Collins continued.

"Where're you from?"

"Left Cardiff yesterday morning, bound for Savona wi' a cargo of coal for the Italian State Railways."

"Well, before leaving didn't you go and see the naval officer, the Routing Officer?"

"Aye. I did."

"Didn't he give you a book, a *T357*, telling you where you might meet our patrols, in case you took to the boats, and a lot more very confidential information?"

The Captain remained silent, looking so puzzled that Collins went on.

"Didn't he give you a small, green canvas bag, with the *T357* inside it, pierced with brass eyelet holes, with weights stitched into it so that it would sink if you had to throw it over the side to prevent it falling into the hands of the enemy?"

"Aye, he gave me that. But I never looked inside it."

"Where is it?" said Collins. "Let's see it."

"Nay. I canna do that. I hav'na got it."

"Not got it!" Now it was our turn to be puzzled.

"Nay. Yon Routing Officer said it would be sae terrible if the Germans got it, or some spy stole it. An' I've nae safe place to hide it. I did'na get a wink o' sleep the night, for worrying about it. An' I know I wouldna' hae slept any other night. So, this morning I put it over the side."

On another such day of moderate weather, when we were standing in toward the Irish land, I sighted a small steamer on my starboard bow, steering to the southward. I altered course, bringing her right ahead, and was examining her through binoculars when the Captain came on the bridge.

"What is she, de Mierre?"

"Either Dutch or Danish, sir. Can't be sure yet."

"Well, close her. Close her. Stop and board her," he said.

Then, looking me full in the eyes, but with a twinkle in his own, he added, "I don't trust these foreigners. Do you, Hans?"

"No, sir," I replied, with a grin, "not one of them."

But she was a friendly little vessel, carrying a cargo of dried salt cod from Iceland to the Mediterranean. Her Captain did not in the least object to being stopped and, indeed, insisted on giving us a bottle of Swedish punch that was much appreciated in the wardroom.

That night, during my decoding watch I translated an urgent signal from the Admiralty. It instructed us to be on the look-out for a vessel flying the Dutch flag that was suspected of meeting German submarines in one of the many bays of the Irish coast, and supplying them with provisions and fuel. I took the message down to the Captain's cabin and stood, waiting, while he read it.

"Thank you," he said, handing the signal back to me.

Before leaving his cabin I said, "More foreigners, sir."

"Yes . . . Hans," he replied with a pleasant smile.

That was the only suggestion that was ever made, that I was not as English as any other Englishman. And it was a very genial one.

My Lords Commissioners of the Admiralty were broadminded, provided they were satisfied regarding origin and loyalty. The Navy List contained several officers with foreign names, even German names. And, what's in a name, anyhow? One of the most distinguished German submarine commanders was a man named Arnaud de la Perriere.

People on shore were not so reasonable. Our family name, although spelled exactly as at present, was then written in one word, with a capital "D". Its unmistakable French origin should have been apparent to anyone, but evidently this was not so with the provincial authorities in the Manchester area. Although one of his sons was with the Manchester Regiment, fighting in Flanders, and another was at sea as an officer in the Royal Navy, my father— a proud man—suffered the annoyance of having to prove that he was not, by origin, an enemy alien. He therefore reverted to the present form, which is one that has been used by some families of the name ever since the thirteenth century.

At the close of a cold, blustery day in the last week of November, we were approaching the western, or seaward, end of our patrol from Bishop Rock, making rather uncomfortable weather of it. We rolled heavily to an unusually high westerly swell and, at the same time, punched and plugged away against a short, brisk sea that came out of the south-west. There had been a lot of rain and the barometer was very low—all the earmarks of heavy weather approaching from the west, driving up that big swell, and we were all looking forward to turning our backs on it and making for Bantry Bay. The ten days were up and they had been very busy. We had been away in the whaler so frequently that we began to feel like real whalemen. The sun had gone down but it was not yet dark and we were on the point of making our turn, when a medium-sized passenger steamer came up from the southward. She was flying flags that were the code signal meaning, "Send boat, I have something important to communicate."

She lay, stopped, to windward, rolling heavily. The *Pelorus*, also stopped, had altered course, putting wind and sea on her port bow to make a lee for the whaler when it was launched from the davits on the starboard side. However, she lay head on to the swell. It ran along her flanks in tall hummocks and steep valleys. The whaler had been lowered well below the rail and hung there waiting for the First Lieutenant's order, "Let go!" When that came, one of our crew would give a sharp pull on the release tackle and the boat would drop into the water.

It was now quite dark and, although the First Lieutenant could not see the swells, and had to be guided by the motion of the ship, when he gave the order we landed fair on top of a swell and were water-borne without feeling it. Then, out oars, and pull for the steamer, seeing neither steamer nor *Pelorus* when we were in the troughs. Finally, we got alongside. They threw us a line and, when the vessel was at the depth of her roll towards us and the rope ladder hung plumb from her rail, we leapt on to it, swung against her side when she rose to roll in the opposite direction, and then climbed on board.

An officer took us through a crowd of excited passengers, up to the bridge where the Captain was waiting in the chart-room. She was one of the Yeoward Line, had come from the Canary Islands and was bound for Liverpool. That morning she had spoken the German sailing-ship *Melpomene* which, being 116 days out from Mejillones, knew nothing of the war. After verifying her longitude, she had asked the steamer to report her "all well" to her owners in Hamburg.

This was great news. She would be carrying about three thousand tons of nitrate and would be a valuable prize. We took note of the course and distance steamed since speaking the sailing ship, gave the Captain profuse thanks and hurried down to our boat.

Eight hours later, at two o'clock in the morning, we saw her—a black shadow against a still blacker background.

"Stop her," whispered Captain Stevenson.

In our excitement we all spoke softly, as though she might overhear us and mysteriously take flight. Then the spell was broken.

"Searchlight," said the Captain, sharply.

The brilliant white beam shot forth, lighted on and completely embraced the *Melpomene*. She was hove to under three lower topsails and fore topmast-staysail, waiting for the "blow" that all the signs foretold. She had almost no way on her and was rolling heavily. But she looked beautiful and I remembered that I had seen her five years before, leaving Melbourne, homeward-bound.

Now she was homeward-bound again, had come round Cape Horn and had been nearly four months at sea. She was within two hundred miles of Falmouth and orders that would probably tell her Captain, Captain Imelmann, to bring his ship home to Hamburg. They might be home, with wives, sweethearts and families, within the week, and would surely spend Christmas with them, sing the season's songs and hymns around the Christmas tree, and hear the children singing *Stille Nacht—Silent Night—*before going up to bed. That was something to look forward to, to think about in the night-watches, when all was, indeed, so silent. A year and a half since you had seen them last; and what fun you would have, spending that "pay-day". If you had no family St. Pauli would take you to her ample bosom.

Such would have been their thoughts for days, for weeks, until that dazzling shaft of light came so suddenly and so mysteriously out of the darkness. Out of the darkness, to paralyse them with astonishment, to blind them so that they did not see the boat-load of armed men until it was alongside and our bowman jumped aboard with the end of our painter and Collins and I got into her main shrouds and dropped to her deck. Then the searchlight was switched off and we stood in the centre of a group of shaggy-haired, young sailors. The only light came from a hurricane-lamp, held aloft by the Captain, a slightly-built man with a long, black beard.

"Captain Imelmann," said Collins gently, "we are truly sorry to interrupt your voyage. We are at war with Germany and you are our prisoners."

"*Grosser Gott!*" exclaimed the Captain, so shocked that he let the lamp fall into the water that swirled about our ankles.

For what seemed like a long minute, the others stood in stunned silence until the Mate, who resembled a skinny, ginger-haired Irishman rather than a German, came out of his trance and took charge of the situation. He was a bit of a buffoon, but he spoke in English—the lingua-franca of sailing-ships—he turned to the Captain, "Wek up, Captain. Der officer want all your papers."

"That's right, Captain," said Collins, "Official Log, Certificate of Registry, Articles of Agreement, Bills of Lading and Manifest of your cargo and clearance papers from Mejillones."

Back on board the *Pelorus*, Collins and I were hoping that we would have the fun of sailing the ship into Falmouth, but a signal from the Admiralty instructed that she be towed to Queenstown. It was decided that a wire towing-hawser should be shackled to the chain cable of the *Melpomene*'s port anchor. Then, we would heave out forty-five fathoms of her chain-cable. The ship would thus be towed from her windlass and the weight of all that chain, hanging from the end of the towing-wire, would act as a spring, if it really did come on to blow. Before entering harbour we would make the towing-wire fast aboard the *Melpomene*, and get both anchors ready for letting go.

All went with great despatch. We returned to the *Melpomene* with our prize-crew of twelve seamen, a signalman and two marines, their hammocks and a week's rations of potatoes, bread, fresh and preserved meat. Within the hour we had our men, mixed up with the German seamen, walking round the windlass capstan, heaving out the chain. There was one amusing moment. The German Mate and carpenter were very co-operative but, at first, the seamen would not turn out of their fo'c's'le that was in the forward deck-house. Some sea-lawyer among them declared that they were finished. The ship was a prize and the prize-crew should do the work.

The man appointed Bos'n in charge of our men was a brawny, bearded Leading Seaman named Hewitt. He was quite capable of tucking one of the Germans under each arm and not bothering about it.

"Hewitt," I said, "these lads think they're passengers. Turn 'em out, please."

Hewitt was a man of parts. His eyes twinkled as he said, "Ay, ay, sir." He walked to the weather-door of the fo'c's'le, which his bulk completely filled; and, with a wonderful imitation of gutteral German, yelled, "*RRRAUS*," as he stepped inside. The strike was over. The young sailors leapt to their feet and ran out of the lee door.

When the chain was hove out, and the windlass screwed up, I turned to the Mate.

"Alright, Mister. Clew up your tops'ls and make 'em fast."

There was no more hesitation. The sailors ran smartly to clew-lines and bunt-lines when the topsail sheets were let go. When they ran aloft to make the sails fast, some of our men would have gone up with them, had they not been stopped by Hewitt.

"Come on . . . Down, out of that. Yes, I know . . . I know. Ye reefed and double-reefed an' handed topsails in the brigs. But ye didn't do it with a cutlass and a pistol hanging on yer backside, banging yer brains out."

The tow to Queenstown took two and a half days and was without incident. Collins and I kept four-hour watches, with our men posted in pairs for two-hour spells of sentry duty, by the three hatches. A Marine, with his rifle and bayonet, was stationed on the poop. The German crew showed not the slightest wish to make trouble. Most of them were quite young and more inclined to yarn, joke and argue with our men than anything else. Each group seemed curious about the other and the Germans enjoyed the fresh food that we shared with them.

It was early afternoon when we entered harbour. The *Pelorus* left us and went on to her own buoy. She sent her whaler for Collins but I was left in charge, with the prize-crew, until the military should come and relieve us. There was not long to wait but, in the meantime, a boat came alongside with a fat, jovial-looking man in the sternsheets. Speaking with a strong French accent, he asked if he might come aboard. He was Captain of a large French barque that lay close by, the *Eugene Schneider*. She had been together with our ship in Mejillones, and Captain Imelmann was his friend. Could he come and see him. And, of course, I gave permission.

"You'll find him in the saloon," I said.

Shortly afterwards, a launch came along with the soldiers: an officer, a sergeant and six privates.

The officer, a Lieutenant, came to attention and saluted.

"Alright, sir," he said, "we'll take over."

"Thank you," I replied, returning his salute. I went into the saloon where I found the two captains discussing the situation, over a glass of whisky, from a bottle that the Frenchman had brought with him. I was glad to sit down, be rid of my cap and light a pipe. I sat yarning with them about the ships they had been in company with on the west coast, seeking news of the *Engelhorn* and my young brother. The *Engelhorn* was a smart ship; deeply laden with coal, she had sailed from the Bristol Channel to Mejillones, made the winter passage round the Horn and arrived there in 101 days. Now she was homeward-bound from Valparaiso and could not have been very far behind the *Melpomene*.

Our talk was interrupted by the military officer. He marched into the saloon, brought his heels together and saluted.

"Captain," he said, "your ship is anchored under the guns of the fort. If you attempt to move you'll be sunk." Another salute, a smart about-turn, and he left the cabin.

Captain Imelmann looked puzzled, as well he might be. With no power but his sails, which were furled, he had not the means of attempting to move. The Frenchman, who had regarded the martial performance with open-mouthed astonishment, looked at me in dismay. Although I could think of nothing to say, I felt apologetic.

Aboard the *Pelorus* everyone was keenly interested in our prize. In the ward-room we were besieged by questions. How had we been treated? Where had we slept? What had we eaten? What had they eaten? What were they like? Did we have any trouble with them?

We could only reply that we had been well treated and that they seemed like a decent set of people, just like any other merchant seamen. They were all disappointed but the ones most deeply affected were the Second Mate and the Captain. The Second Mate was bitterly sorry and kept muttering, "Prisoner of war, prisoner of war. *Mein Gott!* When it is finished and they say what did I do, I say . . . prisoner of war." The Captain, like any good shipmaster was upset that he had not been able to complete the voyage, but there was an added reason for his dismay.

"Tomorrow is his birthday."

This created a sensation. "His birthday! Has he got any bubbly?" said one, "or anything else to drink? And how about tobacco? Do you think he'd like some cigars?" said another. And so it went on. Each had his own ideas and in the end we filled a couple of pillow-cases with all these things as well as some tins of fancy biscuits and a freshly-baked cake, several loaves of white bread and some rock-buns.

Then occurred a near mutiny. According to the regulations, if more than five men fall in at one time with a request it constitutes a mutiny. Now the whole prize-crew had fallen in on the quarter-deck. When I went out to see about it, Hewitt stepped forward.

"Sorry about this, sir," he said, with a grin. "Please don't clap us in irons. We've heard you're going aboard the prize. Do you think the First Lieutenant would let us come too, sir? We'd like to take them German chaps a few bits and pieces to eat and drink, out of our canteen. They've got no soft bread, nothing to smoke and they've been on salt provisions for nigh on four months."

We all went away in the cutter. The men had two large gunny sacks containing soft bread, tins of sardines, sausages, tobacco, cigarettes and some slabs of cocoa and chocolate. We climbed the accommodation-ladder looking like a lot of naval Santa Clauses. The military guard was dumbfounded; the Germans were also, but they were touched. Much of the over-hearty hand-shaking, back-slapping and laughter disguised moist eyes and a lump in the throat.

Aft, Collins introduced Edmunds, our First Lieutenant, to the Captain.

"Sorry about this, Captain," said Edmunds. "Silly to wish you a Happy Birthday. How the devil can you be happy? But, cheer up. When you write your family they'll know you're safe and you can tell them—with our compliments, please—that you drank their health on your birthday."

We were in the saloon and while he had been speaking the steward placed the contents of the pillow-cases on the table. In addition to several other bottles, there were three full-sized bottles of champagne.

"Open those, steward, please," said Edmunds. And then, to the Captain, "If you would like to invite your Mate and Second Mate, sir, please do, so that we can drink your health before we go."

This was done and really enjoyed. The Captain, in spite of a most natural tear glistening on his cheek, made an attempt at a happy smile. The Mate flourished his glass with a touch of comedy and the Second Mate, unintentionally even more comical, brought his heels together, stood stiff as a ramrod, threw his head back and cried, "*Unserem deutschen Kaiser!*" And, when he had swallowed his wine, he emitted a hollow, ironical laugh and a lugubrious, "Prisoner of war."

When we left, Captain Imelmann said, "We shall see you again?"

"'Fraid not," replied Edmunds. "We sail tomorrow, and I don't think we're coming back."

In the late afternoon of the following day, we sailed. The sun was down but it was not yet quite dark. The *Melpomene* looked grey and lifeless. Four months earlier, on the night before she sailed from Mejillones, she had hoisted four bright lights in the form of a cross—the Southern Cross—to show that her loading was finished. One after the other, every sailing-ship in the roadstead had cheered her: French ships, British ships, Norwegians, Swedes and Finns. Each had shouted: "Three cheers for the homeward-bounder. Hip-hip hurrah! Hip-hip hurrah! Hip-hip hurrah!"

To each she had cheered in reply and then boats from the other ships brought friendly sailors aboard to drink some beer, sing with them, wish them good-bye and good passage home.

Here was a sad ending to it all. Now she seemed forlorn and deserted. But when we steamed slowly by, her crew lined her rail and, as we headed for the sea, thirty German voices rang over the water giving us the honour of a traditional west coast farewell.

"Three cheers for H.M.S. *Pelorus*, Hip-hip hurrah! Hip-hip hurrah! Hip-hip hurrah!"

It was the first week in December and it seems, in retrospect, from a naval point of view, that a phase of considerable activity had ended. In September, a German submarine had torpedoed the cruisers *Aboukir*, *Hogue* and *Cressy* in quick succession, being able to do this because two of them stopped and put their boats in the water to rescue the survivors of the first to be stricken, thus presenting themselves as sitting ducks for the next two shots. That was something of a shock but it was digested as an act of war.

In the North Sea British ships destroyed the German battle-cruiser *Blucher*. At the other end of the world, off the coast of Chile, at the end of October, the German cruisers *Scharnhorst*, *Gneisnau*, *Leipzig* and *Dresden* met a small British squadron and sank the *Good Hope*, the *Monmouth* and the armed merchant-cruiser *Otranto*. One month later they were themselves destroyed by a British battle-cruiser squadron off the Falkland Islands. The German cruiser *Emden* had been sunk by the Australian cruiser *Sydney* in the Indian Ocean, the *Koenigsberg* had gone into hiding, up a river in East Africa, the German merchant-cruiser *Cap Trafalgar* was destroyed by H.M.S. *Carmania* in the South Atlantic, and other German merchant-cruisers such as the *Kronprinz Wilhelm* and the *Prinz Eitel Friederich*—normally liners of the North German Lloyd—interned themselves in Norfolk, Virginia.

The German battle-fleet was bottled up in Kiel and Wilhelmshaven, dominated by a superior British fleet that was based on Scapa Flow in the north of Scotland. There were no enemy naval forces at sea in the world's oceans. By the end of 1914 it looked as if the naval side of the war might have been won. It was surely well under control. And, up to that point, the opposing sides, while taking advantage of every chance to blow each other to bits, had observed the rules and still preserved some vestiges of respect for each other.

A great change took place in 1915. Out of her own seaports Germany no longer had any means of access to overseas trade or supplies and, on March 1st, Great Britain declared a complete blockade against Germany. This meant that any merchandise—whether of a warlike nature or not, whether solely for civilian use, nourishment or benefit or not—carried in neutral ships, destined for or coming from Germany were regarded as contraband of war and could be removed. Enemy nationals travelling in neutral ships were also subject to arrest.

Germany retaliated by declaring a blockade against Britain and France. The submarine, with its limited range in its early stages, had been regarded as a weapon of coastal defence. Now it was developed to the point where it could keep the sea for weeks and cruise over great distances at a speed which enabled it to overtake all but the fastest merchant vessels. It very soon became an effective weapon of attack, especially in those early months of its raiding when merchant-ships were permitted to make their voyages singly, unescorted, and depth charges and electronic underwater listening devices had not yet been invented.

Vessels bound for Allied ports were torpedoed or sunk by gunfire, often in the darkness of night, or in weather so bad that boats could not be launched, and passengers and crew were left to drown. On April 27th, 1915, the Cunard liner *Lusitania* bound from New York for Liverpool with a full complement of passengers, including many women and children, was torpedoed by a German submarine off the Irish coast, near the Old Head of Kinsale, and sunk with the loss of some 1,198 lives.

The Germans justified this by declaring that well before she left New York they had given warning of their intention to sink the ship. But, in the eyes of the world and particularly in the United States of America, that did not make the callous brutality of the act less heinous. In the same week, the Germans sprang an equally horrible surprise by releasing clouds of poison gas against the Allied troops on the Western Front.

These acts of appalling savagery caused an intensity of hatred on both sides that was to remain for many years. There were still thirty years to go before the unrestrained barbarity of "total war" was universally accepted, before the most civilised nations would slaughter each other's civilian population by dropping thousands of tons of high explosives on open, congested cities; before, indeed, two lumps from the very fires of hell would be let fall from the skies and two whole cities and nearly half a million people consumed in an instant, literally in a flash.

I cite the few important events of the opening months of 1915 to explain the change that took place. Our departure from Queenstown, followed by the cheers of the *Melpomene*'s crew, marked the end of a chapter.

We had left under sealed orders which, when opened, directed us to proceed to Gibraltar. There, we reinforced the small flotilla of torpedo-boats that patrolled the Straits. We had exchanged the winter gales and wild seas of the

Western Approaches for Mediterranean sunshine but it was very monotonous. For periods of ten days we steamed at slow speed, to and fro, east and west, in mid-Straits, for a distance of about thirty miles. There was no boat-work, no boarding. We were like a policeman on his beat, making sure that the traffic did what it was told and that, unless there were special circumstances, no vessel passed through the Straits without first being sent in for inspection or instruction by the officers of the Examination Service. These were stationed in the Bay, just inside Europa Point.

The periods of coaling ship in the naval harbour, with the two or three days' rest that followed were welcomed by all hands. Unlike Bantry Bay or Queenstown, here there was everything for us. We indulged in all kinds of physical exercise and sport, piped the hands to bathe, sailed whalers and cutters, got together teams of sailors and Marines for hockey and football matches. And in the evenings there were all the amenities, the drink-pots and flesh-pots, of an ancient and well-established naval base.

It is not surprising that we enjoyed these things to the full and, in the case of some of our men, to overflowing. Our sailors were thoroughly seasoned, professional blue-jackets, who knew all the tricks and dodges of the service. They were a fine body of men, of the breed that a hundred years before had taken enemy ships by boarding and hand-to-hand fighting; wonderful men under discipline and, of course, some of them with a remarkably facile capacity for attracting trouble in their occasional hours of freedom.

I think of able seamen Benson and Noblet, to each other and to their chums, Jerry and Nobbler, and their return from shore leave with the last liberty boat, at midnight.

Before describing the events of that occasion it is necessary to mention that sailors of the Royal Navy, in those days, chewed tobacco and the equipment of a well-found cruiser included a supply of small, wooden tubs. For me, one of the most appealing, most sympathetic naval commands was the Bos'n's pipe after "Evening Quarters" when the ship was in harbour.

"Twee-oo-twee-oo-wee-wee. All the starboard watch place spit-kids. Carry on smoking."

Then the spit-kids would be placed about the decks, filled with clean salt-water, all convenient and ready for use.

Jerry was tall and thin. Nobbler was short and fat. They came over the gangway, saluted the quarter-deck, then automatically raised their arms, sideways, to shoulder level so that the Corporal of Marines could run his hands over their clothes to make sure that no liquor was being smuggled on board.

They were not merry in their cups. Grimacing and blinking, they swayed like saplings in a high wind. A large basket of strawberries hung from Nobbler's left hand. They made a comical sight. But they survived the ordeal, made a smart left turn and were moving away when Thompson, who was Officer of the Day, said, "Corporal, search those strawberries."

The Corporal's arm shot out and he grasped Nobbler's right elbow so suddenly that, thrown off his none too steady balance, Nobbler sat down in the spit-kid but managed to hold the basket without spilling. In the same instant, Jerry hauled off and punched the Corporal on the nose and in return got one that seated him in the scuppers.

The strawberries concealed two flasks of whisky so Jerry and Nobbler were in serious trouble. Without further ado they were put down below in the cells. Next morning they came before the First Lieutenant, with the Corporal of Marines in attendance, while the Master-at-Arms read the charge.

"Able Seaman Noblet did bring spiritous liquors aboard in time of war. Able Seaman Denson did strike Corporal of the Gangway while latter was in execution of his duty."

Little Nobbler, of course, had nothing to say. But when Jerry was asked by the First Lieutenant how he could so far forget all discipline as to strike the Corporal of the Gangway, his face took on a deeply aggrieved expression.

"Well, sir. 'Ow would you like it if you came aboard and the Corporal pushed your pal in the spit-kid?"

The First Lieutenant's air of bewilderment at such an idea was comical. He contained his laughter, and the two men were sentenced to six weeks' detention in the Naval Barracks on shore.

Next to the cell was the Paymaster's office where I sat yarning when we heard the cell door open. There was the noise of a metal dish sliding over the deck, then the loud bang of the door being closed.

"What is it, Nobbler?" we heard Jerry ask.

"Same old bloody stew."

"Could do wiv' some o' them strawberries now, couldn't we, Nobbler?"

"Ay," groaned Nobbler in reply. "Seven pahnds o' strawberries and forty-two bloody days to eat 'em in."

Our rare days in harbour were not all so gay and frolicsome. At one time the scourge of influenza swept through the base and we lost three of our best seamen; they died on the same day and were buried on the same day. On board the *Pelorus* we, officers and men, carefully rehearsed the manner in which we would pass through the town with the flag-draped gun-carriage, in slow march, with arms reversed. And the firing party was drilled by Petty Officer Hewitt, in the melancholy part that they would have to play. With rifles and ammunition belts and wearing gaiters, the men stood at ease, listening to his instructions.

"When ye arrive at the gate of the cemetery, the right file takes the right gatepost, the left file takes the left gatepost, and with a smart right and left turn ye faces the roadway. Ye place the muzzle of yer rifle on the toe of yer boot, ye folds yer hands across the butt, ye sinks yer chin upon yer chest and assumes a mournful aspect."

And, with arms reversed, the firing party did a slow march onto the quarter-deck where, with great earnestness, they carried out the mournful attitudes. I have often chuckled in sympathy and with respect for the memory of this day. It was surely another proof of the utter adequacy of the manual of drill, another strong fibre in the fabric that clothed officers and men in a common, a mutual loyalty to the Service, their Service.

In February, the monotony of patrol was relieved when we towed battle-practice targets for H.M.S. *Queen Elizabeth*. She was then the most modern ship of the Navy. The length of the tow was about six hundred feet and the *Queen Elizabeth* was so far away that we could only see the top of her funnel. Then there was a vivid, yellow flash, a raucous noise as though an express train were rushing across the sky, a thunderous roar and then a salvo of shells fell in a close cluster that threw up a lofty fountain of water just to the left of the target. It gave one an uneasy feeling of what it would be like to be on the receiving end of such shell-fire in battle.

On our return to harbour, wardroom and gunroom officers of the *Pelorus* were invited to dine aboard the *Queen Elizabeth*. This was another remarkable experience. I could not attempt a description of the giant battleship. There were as many young, keen-faced officers in her wardroom, so it seemed, as would equal the entire ship's company of the *Pelorus*. They included several R.N.R. officers and one of them, a Cunard Line Chief Officer named Hatcher, took me under his wing and made the evening just that much more agreeable.

Back on patrol, our little *Pelorus* seemed puny. She had been well looked after, and was as effective and as efficient as on the day when she had been built. But that was many years before. Now she was probably out of date.

A little later she was taken off active duty and stationed in a quiet bay in the eastern Mediterranean as a wireless relay ship, between the fleet in the Dardanelles and the Admiralty.

Captain Stevenson remained in Gibraltar as Captain of the Depot, John Rutherford Collins became Assistant to the Officer Commanding Patrols and I went into the Examination Service.

15   *Naval Control Service*

In the Examination Service we were divided into two watches, each consisting of a Lieutenant R.N.R., a Lieutenant R.N.V.R., an officer of the Gibraltar Port Service, one of their steam pinnaces with its Gibraltarian crew, and two signalmen. We did twenty-four hours' duty in the bay, when we lived aboard the Examination Vessel, but most of the time we spent in the pinnace, boarding the ships that had been sent in by the Straits Patrol or that were entering port in the normal course of their business.

Over the months one came to know every type of vessel that came into, or passed through, the Mediterranean. There were the regular traders to the Spanish and Italian ports—small, beautifully-kept British and Scandinavian ships. Then there were the colliers, frequently old and rickety, of all national-ities, bound from the Bristol Channel or the Tyne, to the many coaling depots and hulks that were dotted around the shores of the Mediterranean. These coal supplies were practically all British-owned and coal was an important factor in British power. If you were a neutral, you did what was asked of you, otherwise you might find it difficult to fill your bunkers. And, every so often, you took a cargo to Britain, usually pyrites and a deck-cargo of oranges, lemons, grapes or that most precious of all fruits—the onion. There were no oil-fired steamers or motor-ships in those days. You came back with a cargo of coal to replenish the stocks that you were consuming when you were following your own sweet will. It was surely a very equitable, a very fair use of power.

Then there were the distant traders, mostly Greek and Italian, from all parts of the western hemisphere, North and South America, the West Indies and Central America and West Africa, laden with all the things that a blockaded enemy most needed, most longed for—edible fats and oils, lubricating oil, cotton, copper, spelter, bacon, pork, meat, wheat, maize, linseed, sugar, cocoa, tobacco and coffee. And it was our job to see that he did not get them. Every-thing of enemy origin, or destined for the enemy, was contraband of war. Anyone who was trading with the enemy, or for his benefit, was blacklisted. The blockade of Germany had only been in force for about a month when I left the *Pelorus*, but already we had lists of the names of ships, shippers and consignees who were suspect.

The job was interesting and instructive. I saw, in practice, many phases of maritime commerce that I had so far only read about in my textbooks. It was difficult, too. Many vessels, in good faith or otherwise, declared that they had no knowledge of the restrictions at the time of loading. We scrutinised bills of lading, cargo manifests and insurance certificates, very often to no purpose because the name of the consignee or the persons who were to receive the merchandise was not stated. Everything was "To Order", like a blank cheque, with some marginal note that in case of need the Customs or Forwarding Broker at the port of discharge should be notified. It was sometimes unpleasant too. The neutral shipmasters wanted to complete their voyages and get home. But until we could find out from London whether or not the ship might be allowed to go on her way, she just had to lay in the Examination Anchorage. Several months were to pass before the neutrals learned how to conform to our regulations—or to get around them. After that, all was plain sailing. We were welcomed on board, given presents of bottles of vermouth, Swedish punch and occasional delicious lunches of spaghetti-hellenique.

Several small sailing-vessels passed through our hands and one, a two-masted schooner, a regular banksman, had made the passage across the Atlantic in twelve days. Her Captain was a good-natured, sanguine man, fat as a butter-tub. With his cargo of dried codfish he was bound for Piraeus and the only charts he had were the maps in the back of a large family Bible.

"Good enough for Saint Paul. I guess they'll do for me."

He was, of course, joking about Saint Paul but quite serious in his intention to navigate by the maps in his Bible. However, he gladly anchored for a few hours while I had some real charts sent out from the Naval Chart Office.

Danish topsail-schooners and barquentines brought their cargoes of dried cod from Reykjavik and would return to Iceland with salt. These did not take the interference with their voyages so gracefully but we understood their annoyance and always did our work as quickly as possible, keeping the little ship under way, our pinnace alongside holding her hove to, in the eye of the wind. We boarded one of these on a brisk day when there was a fresh south-westerly wind and a rough sea. Her papers were in order but, when I came to issue the clearance certificate, I found that the canvas bag that contained our official stamp had been left in the pinnace. The R.N.V.R. officer, a most eager and conscientious man, jumped to his feet, ran up the short companionway and immediately afterwards there was the noise of a considerable splash. The Captain of the schooner had been standing all the time, bouncing his backside, back and forth, against the mahogany panelling of the saloon. Now, he mounted half way up the stair, looked over the companion-hatch, came down and resumed his backside bumping.

"What's the trouble, Captain," I asked.

"Other officer," he replied, "fell into the water."

I rushed up on deck. My watchmate had indeed fallen over the side and the pinnace's crew was having a job getting him on board again. The phlegmatic Danes, however, thought it was none of their business and, in the case of their Captain, not worth a single word of any kind.

The passenger-liners, mostly Spanish and Italian, came from the American continent or the West Indies—from such places as Vera Cruz, Mexico, Havana or Puerto Rico—and, in addition to passengers of all nationalities, they carried large cargoes. It was the passengers who gave us the greater trouble. The Spanish ships would be intercepted by our patrols before they could enter Cadiz, the first port for which they were destined. They had to make the detour to Gibraltar and suffer our examination before being able to return there. I must say, however, that their very dignified Captains always received us with courtesy and often with an hospitable cup of excellent coffee.

Through our Intelligence Service we were often warned when to expect enemy nationals, or agents, and in what ships they were travelling, either as passengers or as members of the crew, sometimes, indeed, as stowaways. Three of these latter were taken out of a Norwegian ship coming from Barcelona. Two of them were found in the bilges, under the bed-plates of the main engines; the third almost got away. We were on the point of giving up when he was found hiding in the bunkers, covered with coal.

When necessary, we could get help with language problems at any time of the night or day. Mr. Higginson, Manager of Thos. Cook & Son, Ltd., was fluent in French, German, Spanish and Italian and would be with us within half an hour of receiving our call.

Some agents must have got through but many were caught without great difficulty. Unless they are unusually clever, it is not easy for a Frenchman, Englishman or German to pretend to be some other nationality without being found out. One of those who got through fooled us completely. We knew he got through because he sent us his kind regards.

He was a first-class passenger in the luxury liner *Tomaso di Savoia* that arrived in the middle of a wild, rainy night. We sat in the lounge, going over the passenger-list. The Purser had all their passports and brought before us those passengers whom we wished to see personally. We were almost finished when Higginson pointed out that there were still two, a man and his wife travelling with Swiss passports, whom he would like to see. The Purser looked at the Surgeon who explained that the man was very ill. He had warned him that there would be a visit by British naval officers and, if we had no objection, it would be more advisable for us to go to his cabin.

The man was in bed. His wife, haggard and careworn, wearing a faded flannel dressing-gown, was wiping his forehead with a handkerchief that was moistened with eau de Cologne. The moment he saw us, the man attempted to sit up, but he was seized by such a severe paroxysm of coughing that he fell back on his pillow, panting and struggling to regain his breath. His wife was beside herself with anxiety and we remained only long enough to assure them that they would not be disturbed any further.

The next time we boarded that ship we asked if the man had survived the voyage. "Survived!" exclaimed the Purser; his eyebrows went up. Not only had the man survived, in Genoa he had slapped his chest and said that in two days he would be with his regiment. He was a Major in the German army. And please would the Purser thank those British officers in Gibraltar for their consideration, next time he saw them.

Shortly after this, Higginson had his consolation. Among the passengers in another Italian liner was a Dutchman in the second-class who said that he had been working as a cook in one of the leading New York hotels, and was now on his way home. Yes, he knew that there were neutral vessels going direct to Holland but he preferred to travel through Italy, Switzerland and Germany rather than risk the German submarines and the mines in the North Sea.

He was too nonchalant. He spoke with an exaggerated American twang, chewed gum noisily and, for a cook, was too knowledgeable, too smooth in his talk of submarines and minefields. Although seated in the first-class drawing-room he had not removed his hat. That was a silly mistake. It was a neglect so un-European that it seemed to be deliberate, done with a purpose. It made Higginson suspicious.

Higginson was a mild-looking little man, with small, clerkly hands and large, soft eyes; his mouth was hidden by a moustache. He might have been a boy, made up as a man. Very quietly, he asked if the Dutchman would please take off his hat. Then he stared at him for a long moment, as though planning his next move. Then, from his papers he pulled out the front page of a German illustrated weekly. It bore a large photo of the Captains of the two armed merchant-cruisers that were interned in Norfolk, Virginia.

Holding out his fountain pen, Higginson placed the page in front of the "Dutchman", put his finger on one of the figures and said, "Would you please autograph this one for me, Captain Thierfelder."

The case of Elena Teodorini, a fat, elderly *prima donna*, was different. In a cabin de luxe on board the Spanish liner *Reina Victoria Eugenia*, she was travelling from Buenos Aires to Cadiz. In Buenos Aires, so we were informed,

XXIV. Jahrgang
Nr. 17

Berliner

25. April 1915
Einzelpreis
10 Pfg.
oder 15 Heller

Illustrirte Zeitung

Verlag Ullstein & Co., Berlin SW. 68
Copyright 1915, by Ullstein & Co.

Die Führer der erfolgreichen Hilfskreuzer „Prinz Eitel Friedrich" und „Kronprinz Wilhelm",
Korvettenkapitän Thierichens und Kapitänleutnant Thierfelder.

The front page of the German weekly, with its photograph of
the two merchant-cruiser captains

she had a studio of voice-culture and was intimate with German official circles. She was thought to be carrying despatches for the German Ambassador.

The liner was intercepted and we were all ready when she arrived. We had a couple of plain-clothes men from the Police Department to search her baggage and cabin, as well as a female officer for the personal search. It took hours. There was one enormous wardrobe-trunk full of sheet music and operatic scores and, in addition, the old lady had harvested quantities of note-paper from practically every hotel in South America and Mexico. Much of this was sent ashore for test, but proved negative. No documents were found, either in her baggage or in her cabin—where every fitting that could be un-screwed and taken off was unscrewed and taken off. The female officer did the same in the personal search. The old lady was stripped of clothes and of every cosmetic embellishment that could be removed. The result, the officer said, was awful. But it was also negative.

We had drawn blank. We could do no more; the vessel was allowed to go back to Cadiz which normally she would have entered fifteen hours earlier. She was on the point of going in when along came a small, armed, French trawler that was patrolling the entrance to the Straits. She, too, had information about Elena Teodorini. This time the Spanish Captain was justifiably indignant. He produced the certificate that we had issued but it was ignored. The Frenchman had his orders and he was going to carry them out. What the British might have done was none of his concern.

However, he would not delay the ship unnecessarily. All he wanted was Elena Teodorini and her baggage. So, out there, on the high seas, the Spaniard rigged a derrick and all the wardrobe trunks were landed aboard the trawler. Then, the poor old lady, weeping and very frightened, was placed in a large wicker basket, with two seamen to give her confidence, and swung over the side. The trawler then went off at full speed in the direction of Casablanca.

"Well," said Captain Harvey, R.N., our Flag Captain, when he heard of it, "kudos for them perhaps; or it could be an expensive case of compensation. Anyway, *vive l'entente cordiale.*"

The biggest haul, and perhaps the most interesting, came a few days later. The patrols sent in an Italian liner, bound from New York to Genoa. The weather was rather warm and, when the ship was anchored, we sat on deck with the passenger-list before us on a card-table. Instead of the Purser having to take time fishing it out, each passenger carried his own passport. The work went quickly and, when we had been through the list, six passengers had been kept to one side for further questioning, one from the first-class, one from the second-class and four from the steerage.

The first-class passenger had an Argentine passport. He was a tall, aristocratic-looking man and there was nothing to identify him as a German except his wardrobe of beautiful suits, all of which had been made in Germany. His name was Carl Bredo. He was arrested on suspicion. He did not object but he wept bitterly.

The second-class passenger was tall, broad-shouldered and square-jawed with a stern, weather-beaten face. A rugged seafaring type. In his plain double-breasted blue suit he looked like a typical Merchant Service officer of any nationality. He was, he said, a Dane and had been Mate of the Norwegian sailing-ship *Semantha* when she was sunk by the German armed merchant-cruiser *Kronprinz Wilhelm* off Cape Hatteras, on February 3rd. His passport was the only thing he had; all his other papers were lost in the *Semantha*. I expressed sympathy that he, a neutral, had suffered so at the hands of our enemy, but was sure that he would not mind taking me to his cabin so that I could see for myself.

It was a four-berth cabin. He went in before me and, as we entered, I saw in the top bunk, to my left, a cheap writing-pad. Whether or not it was his bunk, I did not know, but in that kind of work, one's eyes and fingers were everywhere. I quickly raised the cover of the pad and let it fall again, without his seeing that I had done so. But in the pad I had seen a piece of thin paper on which the name that was in his passport, Nils Chris Hansen, had been traced over and over again.

So I knew that my "Dane" was travelling with a false passport, one that did not belong to him, but which bore all the required visas, and in which his photograph had been substituted for that of the real owner. He had been tracing the name for practice, in case he should be asked to sign for comparison with the original.

He had very few clothes and no other papers. But, in passing an old felt hat from hand to hand, to lay it to one side, I noticed that the leather band inside was perforated with the initials "M.K.". I only glimpsed this and made no remark about it. I was sure that they were his true initials but I wanted to find some definite proof.

"Let me see your wedding-ring, please."

He took it off and showed it to me, but it told me only his wife's name and the date of the marriage.

"Have you a watch," I asked.

Yes, he had a watch, a very handsome one, a gold hunter. The cover was engraved with the initials "M.K.".

"Hullo!" I exclaimed. "Here's a funny thing. Your name is Nils Chris Hansen but your watch is marked 'M.K.'."

"Ach, ja!," he smiled expansively. "It was my grandfather's watch."

"And this, I suppose, was your grandfather's hat," I said.

He was silent, quite nonplussed, so I continued, "I'm sorry. Whatever your name is, it is not Nils Chris Hansen. Let's not waste time. Pack your things. You'll have to come with us. We are at war with Germany and you are my prisoner because you're a German."

"No, no, no," he said, excitedly. "I'm not a German. I give you my word of *honour* that I'm not a German."

"A German hasn't got a word of honour," I said.

"*What!*" he bellowed harshly.

Then he saw how completely he had fallen into my trap. He was crestfallen, every indignant hair back in its proper place. The game was up and he admitted that his real name was Max Kjer and that he was a lieutenant from the interned

Kronprinz Wilhelm. He was depressed over his failure to get through but seemed to feel a little better when he learned that his Captain had been taken a week earlier.

The four steerage passengers were poor, bewildered young men with rosy cheeks, blue eyes, yellow hair and Roumanian passports. Something seemed to have gone wrong with the legendary German thoroughness, for four young men less like Roumanians would have been hard to find. Their names, too, were a joke: Stefan Stefanovitch, Ivan Ivanovitch, Iannou Iannouvitch and Mihail Mihalovitch. And these were the only words of any language that they would utter.

We stood in the open steerage, surrounded by a crowd of Italians, all delighted to have this spectacle to beguile them. Talking to the young men produced only the parrot-like repetition of their fictitious names, so I hit on the following plan. While examining the contents of their bags I kept up a continuous chatter in German, about the things I was handling. Just a lot of nonsense.

"Let's see. What's this lot? Bar of soap. Shame that it hasn't been used more, all these shirts are dirty. A piece of chewing tobacco. No books, no papers. The poor man cannot read."

The four watched me keenly and listened to my every word with close attention. I did not know German naval commands, but assuming that they were similar to our own I suddenly stood upright and rigid and rapped out:

"*Achtung! . . . Muetze ab!*"

Four pairs of heels came together, old cloth caps were snatched from their heads and, in their nondescript, civilian clothing, four young seamen from the *Kronprinz Wilhelm* came smartly to attention. They had not been able to resist the voice of command and, just as spontaneously, the Italian steerage passengers burst into delighted laughter.

All that happened in 1915. The Mediterranean was now becoming one of the most active theatres of war. By the middle of the year Italy had joined the Allies. The task of detecting contraband and enemy nationals was simpler. It was also the year of the Dardanelles Campaign, the bombardment of the Turkish forts by French and British warships in March; the desperately brave landings of British forces on the Gallipoli Peninsula in April and August and the equally courageous evacuation; the complete withdrawal at the end of the year, and the continuation of the war against the Turks in Macedonia, Palestine and Mesopotamia.

A vast and varied procession of vessels poured through the Straits of Gibraltar, warships great and small and transports of all kinds, all hurrying eastwards. Handsome liners, their luxury left behind in many a dingy, dockside warehouse. Just one class now. A mass of young men—thousands of them —all with hot, flushed faces; the air of the troop-decks filled with their chatter and laughter, the stink of their new khaki uniforms and the smell of their sweaty bodies. I heard the accents of home aboard the Cunard *Franconia*. She was also carrying some of the Cheshire regiment. One of them touched my elbow as I was making for the side door, in the troop-deck, to go to my pinnace.

"Long way from Wilmslow, sir."

I halted and automatically put out my hand to have it firmly grasped and find myself looking into the face of a smiling, stalwart young man. It was Herbert Hankinson. He had worked in the shop of a grocer in the village but in the evenings he used to come to our house to teach young Max to box. The meeting was a brief backward glance at a carefree period that had gone for ever. Bert, wearing a sun-helmet, was on his way to fight the Turks. Max, the merry schoolboy, and all his shipmates had been taken by the sea.

Then there were the cargo liners, their holds filled with stores, explosives and ammunition; large, heavy ships with a dignity of their own. Many of them carried deck cargoes of field-guns or howitzers and the soldiers who would man them. We had much to do with them all, to give route instructions, information about minefields, patrols and the latest reports on the position of enemy submarines. In these unforgettable days one saw all kinds of ships and men, some of them acquaintances or old shipmates.

There was, for example, the steamer *Roman Prince*, bound for the Dardanelles. Her Captain was tall, broad and bearded, the double of Max von Kleditsch who had been our Second Mate in the ship *Main*. We went to his cabin where I noticed that the bookcase over the writing-desk was filled with German books. For a moment, I stood looking at them. Then I sat down with no doubts about what I was going to do but hesitating, nevertheless, while I thought of the strange fate that should send this man to sea as Master of a ship freighted so heavily with stuff that could blow him and his crew to bits if a German torpedo found its mark on the ship. There could be no question of this man's loyalty. My train of thought was broken by the sudden realisation that he was speaking to me.

"You were looking at my books, Lieutenant. Wondering if I'm a German, I suppose. Well, I'm not a German now. You can give me my route instructions and any other secret information that you have for me." His face took on a look of great sadness and his voice shook a little. He pointed to a framed photograph of a fine young man wearing bandolier, puttees and spurs—the uniform of the Field Artillery.

"That's our boy. Our only child. When I sailed, he'd been missing for six weeks."

He went on his way. His ship, a massive black shape on the brilliant path of early sunlight, swung east, past Europa Point and was quickly out of sight. A few weeks later we read that the *Roman Prince* had landed her guns, ammunition and stores in the face of heavy fire from Turkish shore batteries and that her master, Captain Andersson, had been decorated for his distinguished and gallant service.

A more light-hearted encounter took place on board another such transport, in the middle of a dark and windy night. When I had finished my business with the Captain, a military officer came into the cabin. He was in charge of the troops that accompanied the deck-cargo of field-guns and he wanted to know if I would take the mail that he and his men had written.

As I looked at his freckled face and ginger hair, I knew, in spite of the unfamiliar tooth-brush moustache, that I had seen him before. When I had come home from Calcutta in the *Golconda*, two and a half years earlier, as a second-class passenger, she had four cadets aboard—very superior young men who never on any account had anything to do with passengers of the second-class.

Here was ex-cadet King, his navy-blue uniform and brass buttons abandoned for khaki, with two "pips" on his shoulders—a Lieutenant of the gunners.

"Why, certainly, Mr. King. I'll take your mail."

He was astonished and delighted to be recognised and, for the remaining few moments that I was on board, the cabin rang with his laughter and exclamations.

"I say! How perfectly top-hole meeting again! Amazing show, what?"

All this for the benefit of the stolid, rather taciturn Captain in a sort of brisk volley of "one-up-manship" that was climaxed when I was a good hundred yards away in my pinnace and the whole ship's company got the benefit of his stentorian hail: "I say, Old Chap, any time you'd like to write, the R.A.C. in Pall Mall will always find me."

I had come up in the world. My Lieutenant's stripes were my cachet.

Twice my old ship *Sutlej* passed through my hands, once with Captain Brown on her bridge and at a later date with Harold Findlay as her Master and Morris her Chief Officer. I had been with Findlay in the ship *Main* and with Morris in the *Arno*. These were delightful reunions but the meetings with the old carpenter, Johanson, and with Yussuf, the officers' servant were just as happy. Tudor Cunningham had retired to his home in lovely Tobago.

A procession of ships: large troopships; hospital ships just as large and as crowded; the heavy, confident, cargo liners and then the little old tramps; slow ships, some of them not able to do more than seven, very few able to exceed ten knots. Plugging away on voyages to Malta, Mudros, or through the Suez Canal and up the Persian Gulf. Brave little ships that kept going through the long years of the war.

A completely new breed of craft breasted the ocean to go out for service on the Tigris River in Mesopotamia; all kinds of vessels of shallow draught, including one that had been a "penny-ferry" across the River Tyne. The kind of vessel with an open well amidships, for boilers and engines to work the paddle-wheels; her deck only about two feet above the water. When she arrived I could hardly believe my eyes.

Steamers had been coming in, showing signs of heavy weather damage and one had the bulwarks of his bridge-deck buckled by the weight of the seas that had come aboard. Then there appeared, coming into the bay, something that looked like a haystack. It was the "penny-ferry". She looked like a haystack because for a height of six or eight feet from her main deck a timber super-structure had been built for crew accommodation and to preserve the deck cargo of bunker coal. When I asked her Captain if he had experienced any bad weather in the Bay of Biscay or off the Portuguese coast, he answered by taking off his cap and asking in his turn, "Is my hair white?"

He had been through all the heavy weather that the other ships had seen and had realised that if he had attempted to heave to in the normal manner by bringing wind and sea on his bow, the first comber to come aboard would sweep everything away, put the fires out and that would be the end of them. So he put sea-anchors out—heavy canvas drogues that had been prepared for just such an emergency—and, attached to them by stout wires from bow and stern, he rode out the gale, broadside to wind and sea. Although the odd little craft, hanging from her sea-anchors, rolled with the motion of a swing-boat at a country fair, everything passed underneath her; and, said the old chap, "She never even shipped one drop of water, s'help me God."

When off duty I lived on board an old wooden frigate, the *Rapid*. She was also the depot ship for a small flotilla of submarines. Her cabins were pleasant and she was as cosy as an old-fashioned country inn. A little later, her name was changed to *Hart* and it seemed to me that whoever had chosen this name had been tempted to call her the *White Hart* but had lacked the courage.

On shore, there were many agreeable things to do. One walked the steep paths of the Rock to the summit to see, from that unusual height, the little town and harbour far below. To the east was the almost perpendicular drop of about one thousand feet, to the rain catchment. Below that was Catalan Bay with its colony of fisherfolk. Then the beaches, fringing the landscape, curving away to Marbella and Malaga. To the north were the rosy brown shapes of the Sierra

H.M.S. *Hart*

Madre and, across the Strait, to the south, the sombre peaks of the Atlas Mountains looked very close.

Then down again, to see, on the way, the apes gathering in the bushes near Devil's Gap battery where food was sometimes placed for them. It was advisable to give them a wide berth for some were large and vicious and of great strength. I once saw one perched on top of a sentry-box, jerking it back and forth as though riding a rocking-horse. And the sentry-box was bolted down on two heavy railway-sleepers that had been dovetailed together in the form of a cross.

Past Devil's Gap and on to the Garrison Library for tea and toasted muffins. This became one of my favourite haunts. It was a kind of United Services Club and had a large collection of fascinating old books including, of course, many naval books of seamanship, block- and mast-making, rope-work and sail-making. The very paper they were printed on was a joy to touch. The authentic accounts of early voyages of privateering and discovery held me spellbound as did, also, the bound volumes of newspapers going back to the days when the fleet came in after the Battle of Trafalgar to bury its dead, land its wounded and set shipwrights, riggers and sailmakers to work repairing the prizes and restoring their own ships to fighting trim.

On certain days, in the little square below the terrace of the Library, the Military Band of the Garrison would play those old favourites of all military bands of that era: brisk Naval and military marches, wistful Irish or Scottish folk-music, merry English country dances and popular tunes from the musical comedies such as *The Country Girl* and *The Geisha*.

By the time the concert neared its end it would be dark and the music would have carried me ten years back and ten thousand miles away to the Eden Gardens in Calcutta where the band of the Northumberland Fusiliers served up the same musical menu.

I spent many happy afternoons with the family of my watch-mate, Captain Noble of the Port Service, and sometimes went with the children for picnics and bathing or took them to a confectioner's for tea and cream-buns when young Charlie, "Wee McGuffie" as he was affectionately called, would get cream all over his face. He was only about five years old but even at that tender age his sang-froid, his mastery of the situation, revealed his innate executive ability. With calm deliberation he passed a pudgy forefinger over each cheek, scooped up the errant cream and popped it into his mouth. Now he is a person-age in London shipping circles, with three sons of his own. It was always a breath of home-like sanity to be with old "Jock" Noble, his wife and the three children—John, Mabel and wee Charlie. And I write this not in any nostalgic sense. It is just good to recall, and to be with again, a truly happy family of kind people. Simple things gave great contentment and I treasure the memory of Jock's pleasure when they were able to leave their flat because a house had been allotted to them. A real house! Of two storeys! And with fireplaces!

"Man! It'll be grand," said old Jock. "I'll be able to see the bairns on the hairth-rug before the fire. And," he exclaimed, his eyes sparkling, "they'll gae upstairs to their beds."

Much could be written about the Rock of Gibraltar and its people. It had been in British hands for more than two centuries and the hundred years that preceded our arrival in H.M.S. *Pelorus*, in December 1914, had been years of peace. Neither it—the Rock—the Navy nor the Army had been engaged in any war that they could not handle on their own. That is, without the assistance of thousands of other individuals who came from all the varied civilian walks of life, and with the great majority of whom the gentlefolk of the naval and military services, completely immersed as they were in the preoccupations of their own orbits, would never come in contact. What! Never? Well, hardly ever!

There was nothing brahminical, or caste-like, in this exclusiveness. It was just the way in which their lives had been shaped and, in the Navy, it was shared by Petty Officers, seamen and Marines.

The result was to give Gibraltar society a tenacious, lingering flavour of Jane Austen and Anthony Trollope. There were the concentric circles that revolved around the Admiral, the Governor and the General Officer Commanding Artillery and their staffs, with their At Homes, garden parties, receptions, amateur theatricals, riding to hounds with the Calpe Hunt, their polo and race meetings.

Then there were the Senior Officials of the Civilian Services—the Secretariat, the Treasurer, Naval Constructor, Army Ordnance and Supply. Then came the general populace which at that time may have numbered twelve to fifteen thousand. Here, too, there was an aristocracy of old families who were also drawn into the vortex of the concentric circles. Like so many Gibraltarians, most of them were of Genoese or Maltese origin.

In times of peace the commercial life of Gibraltar was chiefly concerned in supplying the needs of merchant ships, including many passenger liners of all nationalities. When one was sighted, a flag would be hoisted at the signal station on top of the Rock. Then, the Agents jumped into their launches and put out into the bay. The shopkeepers made the most attractive display of all the goods that were hardest to sell. And the apes, who could also read the signal flag, would come scampering down into the town, to sit on the wall of the Trafalgar Cemetery because they knew that that was the one place that all the passengers would be sure to visit. The one main street would be crowded with passengers happy to break the monotony of their voyage and eager to spend their money. With the coming of darkness they went on their way, the little town went to sleep again and the apes returned to their lairs.

Something of that pattern still remained when we arrived but it was rapidly fading. Every passing month saw its further obliteration. The major naval actions had been won but the ever-growing menace of the German submarine called for more and more swift craft to hunt them, and fleets of trawlers were requisitioned for mine-sweeping. The dockyard grew ever more busy with the work of conversion and repair. When we arrived, the work on board the *Carmania* was still not completed. I went to have lunch with Peter Murchie and, when I went to pay my respects to Captain Barr, I found him standing in the remains of his once sumptuous quarters.

With the march of the months through 1915 and with such a great concourse of fat ships in the eastern Mediterranean, the German submarines were never short of easy targets for their torpedoes and mines and the amount of work at Gibraltar made it necessary to bring a large number of ship-repairers, welders and shipwrights out from England.

266

P. A. Murchie, 1915, H.M.S. *Carmania*, Gibraltar

So the people milling about the main street and the little alleys that crawled up the slope of the Rock, were just as gay as the visiting tourists had been, just as willing to spend their money and even more constant. Indeed, they were always there. And that was something of a mixed blessing. The bars and gin-shops had their work cut out to satisfy the thirst of the dockyard-mateys and the shoals of young fishermen whose normal playgrounds were the chill, grey streets of Thurso, Wick, Aberdeen or Grimsby.

All of these very soon dispersed the few remaining sedate wisps of early-Victorian air. The trawlermen were now under naval discipline, the Skippers having a kind of Warrant rank and uniform. The deck-hands wore the usual bluejacket's rig. But these things only served to increase the anonymity that being so far from home gave them. The streets rang with Scottish, Geordie and West Country voices, shouting to make themselves understood. The heavy red wine—in some places laced with potato spirit—went quickly to their heads and the patrols on picket duty had much to do to keep the peace, to give assurance, by their noisy tramping, in the streets where dwelt the dark-eyed damsels of joy—assurance to both damsels and their clients; but the two files of the picket kept close to the walls on each side of the street because that was the best

267

way to avoid the occasional chamber-pot that some playful young seaman might toss through the window.

Yes. Things had changed and that very rapidly. And, like all the change that has been going on ever since, it was not all good. There was more of everything in circulation—more people, more money, more food, more drink, more unattached young men from all walks of life, and plenty of unattached young women. As the grey-haired, Belgian refugee comedian had sung in a Plymouth music-hall, when he made up an impromptu verse for an encore, in his delight at the tremendous applause and sympathy that his songs in French had received, "We all fight togezaire in ze gran cose. We catch ze blooming Kaiser an we punch 'ees bleddy nose."

It was all in a grand cause and easy to understand, easy to justify. But in taking up so bravely, in giving up so much, in offering life itself, to fight for King and Country, much that was very good was also discarded. On board the *Hart*, too, things were different. The flotilla of submarines had gone to the Dardanelles and never returned and now she acted as a receiving ship. She gave shelter and food to me, to a few Paymasters of the Naval Base, Officers passing through to other appointments or who had come in, in charge of enemy ships taken as prizes.

Then, in 1916, the Royal Naval Air Service arrived. Gallant, light-hearted young men who flew their primitive aircraft over the Straits and out over the Atlantic, trying to spot German submarines. Few of their machines were seaplanes, able to land on the water and all were very slow. No doubt, the prevailing fresh westerly winds made all the difference in bringing them safely back again. They lived aboard the *Hart* and, since they were the most numerous body of permanent residents, took over the mess.

These young men wore on their sleeves the two gold stripes of Lieutenants of the Royal Navy, surmounted by the Air Force wings. Those were the days when every flight was an adventure—the internal combustion engine was not all that reliable—so it is not surprising that during their hours off duty they were possessed by such intense feelings of well-being, such euphoria, that their general behaviour and deportment was quite unlike that of the mature, regular naval Lieutenant. Their service was in its infancy; it was a game that had just begun, too young to have bred traditions of its own or to have learned those of the Royal Navy.

And, when ignored or not respected, some of these traditions acquired a ritualistic importance, a power as of things of the spirit. And that, I am sure, is just what they are. That is the invisible substance of tradition; that is its unifying strength, its richness.

Our mess was very social. We were often visited by senior officers of the

The author, 1916, H.M.S. *Cormorant*, Gibraltar

Navy or the Marines, either as a change from domestic environment or because they chose that way to entertain some visitor. There were thus some interesting evenings when we listened to the talk of war correspondents or artists. I remember especially Norman Wilkinson and Montagu Dawson. At dinner, the scene in the old wardroom was pleasant; the long, highly polished mahogany table with its shaded candles and, over it, the poop skylight. It was easy to imagine, as I often did, that up there, a ghostly officer of the watch, wearing a three-cornered hat, cocked an eye aloft to equally ghostly topsails. We were waited on by six privates of the Marines under the supervision of old Corporal Fairall. To a young man of twenty-six Fairall seemed old but he was really a man in the prime of life, broad of shoulder and straight-backed, with thick ginger-coloured hair, sprinkled with grey. If it had not been for the war he would have taken his pension and been at home with his family, his wife and a youngster of sixteen, who was also headed for the Royal Marines.

One Saturday night, a guest night, was something of a gala occasion. Our airmen had been roundly entertained in the mess of the Garrison Artillery and the hospitality was being returned. My guest was Peter Murchie, now in command of H.M.S. *Grangemouth*, an armed escort vessel. Many pink gins were consumed and by the time we were half way through dinner and these had been fortified by a little sherry with the soup, some Chablis with the fish and a fine claret with the saddle of mutton, faces were glowing, tongues were wagging and everyone was enjoying himself hugely; the evening was a great success.

At this point, it is necessary to mention that all civil gatherings and all other services of the Crown toast the Sovereign while standing to attention. In the Royal Navy one remains seated. I have heard various reasons for this but do not know which is authentic. One explanation is that on board the earliest naval ships, there was not enough head-room below decks to allow a man of average height to stand upright. Other accounts, more frivolous but also plausible—or, let me say, possible—say that one of the Hanoverian Kings was dining on board the flagship and that by the time glasses were filled for the loyal toast, everybody had already drunk so much that none could trust his legs. The King was in the same condition and whatever the King does is right, and as right as right can be. So He graciously decreed that in His ships His health should be drunk without rising.

Another version has it that the Monarch, a tall man, also rose to his feet, while his officers were drinking the loyal toast, and bumped his head painfully against one of the beams. Whether he swore in German or in English is not recorded, but then and there he declared that in the naval service, whether in ships, in boats or on shore, the health of the monarch should be drunk while seated.

The moment arrived that stilled all tongues. Our waiters had swept the crumbs from the gleaming table, had placed large bowls of fruit, nuts and raisins in the centre, and a plate and finger-bowl before each place. Then they stood to attention while the decanters, following the path of the sun, made their round of the table. And, when all glasses were charged, the Mess-President— the Flight Lieutenant at the head of the table—tapped with his gavel and, while raising his glass, said to his opposite number at the foot of the table, "Mr. Vice, the King."

The Vice-president, in his turn, raised his glass and said, "Gentlemen, the King."

To my astonishment, President, Vice-president and all the guests rose to their feet and my instinct was to rise, too, but Murchie placed his hand on my arm and we remained seated, drinking our port and feeling rather uncomfortable. Indeed, for some moments everyone, including the waiters, looked uncomfortable.

After dinner Murchie and I, smoking our cigars, left the wardroom to go up on the poop. Near the poop ladder an officers' cabin that opened on to the quarter-deck had been converted into a pantry and, in there, I was very concerned to see the figure of old Fairall. His arms rested on top of a cupboard, his face was buried in his arms and he was shaking with the violence of his sobbing.

"What's the trouble, Fairall?" I asked. "Is there bad news from home? Has something happened to the youngster?"

For some moments there was no reply but, at last, he straightened up, reached for his handkerchief and, struggling to regain composure, he answered, "Sir. I've been twenty-five years in the Navy and that is the first time 1 ever saw the King's health drunk standing up."

Talking of the cause of his woe increased its poignancy and again he fell to weeping softly. So we left him, knowing that there was nothing that we could do about it but feeling a bit sad. There was nothing funny in it. Fairall had not been nipping at the drinks that had flowed so freely that evening. He was keen and conscious of his duty. It was quite clear that, for him, there had been a desecration of one of the things of the spirit, a fraying of the cords that bound them all together in such magnificent selfless loyalty to their service.

And who shall say that he was not right.

It is not surprising that naval tradition was strange to the newcomers. Like a whirlwind, the war had gathered to itself countless thousands of all kinds. They came from all the varied layers of society and from every part of the world.

Lieutenant Mostyn-Lloyd, R.N.V.R., came from Mexico where, excepting for the years spent at school in England, he had lived all his life. He was, of course, completely at home in English and Spanish. He was rather short and broad-shouldered. Under his thick, brown hair he had a merry face with moist, long-lashed, brown eyes that in their mildness were at variance with a nose that gave every evidence of having been frequently broken. Whatever may have been his early ambitions, he was a rolling stone, a willing victim of the easy, bountiful life of Mexico where food, wine and strong drink were cheap and plentiful, and the women as beautiful as their lovely country, and as agreeable and hospitable as its climate.

Never intended for the sea, when the war broke out he was, nevertheless, in command of what he called a small, steam coasting-vessel. By his account, it was a steam-lighter in which he followed the coast, stopping as necessary at all the small ports to land or take on board a few bags of coffee or beans, demijohns of wine, bales of hay, mules, sheep, goats and some deck-passengers. He knew nothing of navigation and had no need of it. He followed the trend of the land. Any tricky ship handling was done by the Bos'n. He arrived in his own good time and sailed again when he felt like it or, having regard to the diversions on shore, when he was able to do so.

To join the Army, he went to Canada. It was a long way from Mexico, but it was easy to get a job looking after the mules aboard a ship bound for Montreal. He went straight to the recruiting office and must have carried with him a powerful smell of the stables.

"Where're yer from?" asked the Sergeant.

"Mexico," replied Mostyn-Lloyd.

"Right!" returned the Sergeant. "Cavalry fer you."

So he went to a cavalry regiment but they left their horses in England and went across to Flanders as infantry, he as a machine-gunner. For a year and a half they were in the front line, living like rats in the mud of the trenches about Ypres and Dixmude and a place that he called Plugstreet. With his machine-gun, Mostyn-Lloyd was always on the firing-step of the trench, firing with intense and murderous deliberation at the waves of grey-clad Germans who rushed at them through the grey mist and fell in the bloody quagmire of no-man's-land. That he might get hit himself never entered his head. And he never did. But one day, suffering great pain at the back of his head, he fell to the ground, unconscious, and was carried away to hospital. A severe case of cerebro-spinal-meningitis, the old spotted fever.

For a long time he remained unconscious, in a critical condition. But he recovered and, after a short spell of sick-leave, during which he married the nurse who had looked after him, he was sent back to the Army, not to Flanders but to the Curragh, in Ireland, for permanent duty at the base. This was not at all to his liking, working as a kind of "blasted peon", handling at the railway station the baggage and equipment of troops who were leaving for the front. Three times he smuggled himself away with them, on each occasion being reported absent without leave, until arrested by the Military Police in France. Once, he even got as far as Belgium. In the end, a medical board decided that he was no longer fit for service and he was discharged from the Army.

He went to London and, for a few weeks, while his money lasted, seems to have had a taste of cosy, English, domestic happiness. He had a warm-hearted, devoted wife who, when not on duty, was a good cook and an excellent provider as well as a most light-hearted companion. When his money was gone, the problem of earning his living arose and for that he did not have much to offer except his knowledge of Spanish. None of the jobs advertised in the papers matched his kind of experience—or lack thereof—so he made the rounds of the Government departments thinking that he might get work as a censor, or perhaps in the Military Intelligence Service. With this in mind, he was being interviewed at the War Office and had hardly done describing the kind of life that he had led in Mexico when the gallant Colonel facing him, threw up his hands.

"Why, my dear chap, you're just the kind of man they are looking for in the Navy. Here, take this chit and go round to the Admiralty. That officer's a friend of mine. I know he'll fix you up. Right-ho. Good-bye."

What a celebration there was when he went home with the news: a commission as Lieutenant, R.N.V.R., and a uniform allowance. In no time, he was wearing a monkey-jacket with brass buttons and two marvellous, gold, wavy stripes, looking every inch a sailor, swinging his arms athwartships and rolling when he walked. All to the huge delight of his wife. And the night he left home, before taking the train for Liverpool to join a transport that was to carry him to Lagos in West Africa, they went to the Café Royal and did themselves proud, and got just a little tight. There was something about Lagos that was not quite right. After a few weeks they decided that they did not need him in their Examination Service. He was transferred to Gibraltar and posted to duty as my junior officer.

For a couple of months he was a pleasant watch-mate, keen to learn the ropes. With his happy-go-lucky temperament and fluent colloquial Spanish, he was popular with the Gibraltarian crews of the Examination Vessel and the boarding pinnaces. He was never tired of talking about his past life in Mexico and of all the fun that he had had in the Army before he was struck down with the fever. Oddly enough, although his subsequent behaviour might suggest that his life in the trenches in Flanders and the terrible sickness might have affected his brain or contributed to his alcoholism, he spoke of it as though it were one of the happiest times that he had known.

There was a positive nostalgia in his stories of life in billets, behind the lines, during the rest periods. Of the rich comradeship that existed between them all. And even of the weeks in the line, the bitter cold hours of sentry duty, on the firing step, in the long winter nights when all was quiet and, by contrast, the luxury and warmth of the dug-out with its brazier of glowing coals and, above all, the superlative savouriness of the maconochie stew.

His descriptions were so vivid that the things he was talking about were, indeed, conjured up to life. He was transported. For a few moments one lived it all with him, in a sort of hallucination, even sitting behind a machine-gun, pumping a stream of lead into "the bastards", mowing them down.

Hallucination or not, his fervour at such moments was so great that, when he finished speaking and realised that he was standing on a clean deck and was not sitting behind a machine-gun, he would pass the back of his hand across his mouth, wipe away a trickle of saliva, then heave a deep breath and go below to his cabin. When next he appeared, there would be a strong smell of whisky.

Very soon we realised that he was a heavy drinker and we noticed that, when he came on board for his twenty-four-hour spell of duty, there was always a bottle of whisky rolled up in his oilskins. Like many habitual drinkers, however, no matter how much he took he never got drunk. So apart from admonishing him, we were never able to put him off duty. A few words of warning were sufficient. He realised that if he were sent away from Gibraltar, as he had been from West Africa, he would be out on the street again. The thought terrified him. That would be the end. He became very contrite and self-critical, relapsing into a gloom of despair. He was no good, never had been. And why had such a fine, good girl married him? Over and over again he spoke of this. Why, he would exclaim in exasperation, couldn't he have gone back to Flanders, as he tried to. Back into the front line, stick his head up and let a German sniper solve the problem. Then at least she'd have a widow's pension. He did not know how much but it must be something.

In the Spring of 1917 the fighting in Flanders was particularly bloody. Names that were then our daily diet but that are now almost forgotten, were constantly in the news: Bapaume, Peronne, Ypres, Messines. These had been retaken by the British Army but only after appalling losses of men, killed and wounded. And men includes officers of whom the losses were proportionately greater. There were fewer of them and they were easy targets.

One result of the terrible casualties was an Admiralty Weekly Order that invited naval officers who could be spared from their present duty and who were suitable for such service, to transfer to the corresponding commissioned rank in the Army.

When we received our copies of the A.W.O., Mostyn-Lloyd was so jubilant, so restored in his morale, that one would have thought that he had won the whole of the first prize in the Spanish lottery. With the fateful piece of paper on his knee, he slapped it with the back of the fingers of his right hand, in a typically Latin gesture.

"*Ai, Dios mio!*" he cried, "*Que suerte tengo!*"—"My God! What luck I've got!"

He ran down to his cabin and almost immediately reappeared with a full bottle of whisky under his arm. He took out the cork and—drank it? No! He emptied it over the side and then flung the bottle as far from him as he was able to. During the following week he did not touch a drop for, of course, he had applied for a transfer to the infantry. Within ten days he had been accepted and was on his way home to rejoin his regiment as a Captain.

And that is the full extent of my personal knowledge of him but we can be sure that in London there was, oh, such a happy reunion. That the missus, as he called her, would cook a dish of his favourite fish-pie; and, that when the time came to go, there was another supper at the Café Royal where a smart, pugnacious-looking, military officer, but one who had very soft, brown eyes, and his wife who was such a good companion, got just a little drunk.

In 1917 we had been at war for three years but the grim monotony of slaughter and destruction made it seem very much longer and there was no prospect of it coming to an end. It was as though the opposing armies would go on murdering each other, mutilating each other, and starving each other's civilian populations until all were prostrate.

Then the Americans arrived—Admiral Niblack and his staff and vessels of the United States Navy, the cruisers *Chester* and *Birmingham*, *Paduca* and *Yamacraw* and flotillas of destroyers and small craft joined ours in the work of convoy protection and U-boat hunting.

Metaphorically, they came with arms wide-spread, wanting to embrace everyone in good fellowship and to be loved. And what more effective ingredients for popularity could there be. They brought with them a freshness, an effervescence, that overflowed and penetrated every cranny of our little society, naval, military, civil and civilian. When my wife and I were announced at the garden party at his house, Admiral Niblack's welcome typified all that I have been trying to say.

"Lieutenant and Mrs. de Mierre," he repeated, with hands outstretched. "Come in. The water's fine."

We loved it and so did everyone else, civilians and all. They were equally taken to the hospitable American bosom and I treasure the memory of a dance at the house of the charming Parodi family, music by the band of U.S.S. *Yamacraw*. It ended at 2.00 a.m. when the band marched down the deserted Main Street playing *Roll down the field, Navee, sails set to the sky*, led by their Commander, Captain Wrigley, who flourished an empty violin-case as a Colour Sergeant's staff.

With this addition to the newcomers, our naval traditions became less crusty.

The Naval Chief of Staff was assisted by three officers of whom one was always on duty to carry out the responsibilities of that office. Shortly after the end of the year I was appointed to be one of these Executive Duty Officers, as they were called. I replaced Lieutenant Commander Joseph Kenworthy, R.N., and did two watches with him in order to learn the job.

Naval operations in the eastern Atlantic, south of Cape Finisterre and north of Lagos, and in the western Mediterranean, came under our supervision. In the office was a table, size about twelve feet by eighteen feet, on which was painted a chart of this area. A number of coloured strings denoted the tracks of convoys, each identified by a small paper flag that showed the convoy number and the position last reported by its Commodore. Other flags marked the whereabouts of our patrols, of other naval vessels and of any enemy submarines recently reported. All Allied ships were in wireless touch with the S.N.O.—the Senior Naval Officer, Gibraltar—and that meant our office.

The appointment was a welcome, gratifying change and my pride in it was not dampened by the deprecatory, superior attitude of my mentor. The Honourable Joseph Kenworthy was the heir to a Scottish earldom and in due course became Lord Strabolgi. He was tall, broad-shouldered and handsome, with regular features and thick, black hair. He had been some kind of boxing champion of the Navy, probably heavy-weight, and perhaps modesty was not prominent among his virtues.

In our day-time spell of joint duty, when the office had been full of people, reporting Convoy Commodores, the Chief of Staff, and even the Admiral, I had not given him much attention, as a person. However, when we did the night-watch together there was less going on. There was even a cot that had been brought into the office so that one might rest if possible. At about eleven o'clock the Yeoman of Signals brought us some supper. Driving rain drummed on the windows. A bright fire burned in the grate and we blinked at it while eating sandwiches and drinking cocoa. There had been no conversation of a personal nature but when he had finished, and replaced in his pocket the handkerchief with which he had been wiping his fingers, The Honourable Joseph broke his silence.

"You know," he said, "I'm leaving this office and going to another job."

"Yes," I replied. "I know. I'm taking your place."

"It's ridiculous," he continued, "sending a man like me to a job like this. It's just about like sending a landscape gardener to plant potatoes."

I had no such overweening self-confidence. My duties were challenging and the responsibility great but it was most interesting to be concerned with all naval operations in our own area and to be currently advised of events in all other spheres. There were many pleasant moments, some amusing and some exciting. One night, the Captain of H.M.S. *Adventure* sat in the office with me, chatting merrily, with great informality while he awaited his gig. That sounds a trivial thing to write down but his name was Evans—"Evans of the Broke". It was a terrific honour. This was the man who, while Captain of the destroyer *Broke*, met in the English Channel a German destroyer that he engaged. Fearing that the German might be of higher speed and so get away, he rammed her and, with his bluejackets, took her by boarding, in the Nelson manner. A romantic and adventurous character, he had been on an expedition to the Antarctic in the barque *Discovery* with Captain Scott. Like Admiral Togo of the Japanese Navy, he had begun his seafaring career as a cadet in the training-ship H.M.S. *Worcester*. If he had not passed the examinations for the Navy he would have gone into the Merchant Service. I think that this gave him a sympathetic interest in Naval Reserve Officers.

Anyway, there he sat, a man of medium height, with a lively, ruddy, smiling face and eyes that sparkled as much as the gold oak leaves of his "brass hat", talking with me as easily as though he were also only a Lieutenant, all about the sailing-ships that I had sailed in as an apprentice.

Another pleasant occasion was the arrival of a convoy from Oran. The Captains of the two escorts came in to report. Peter Murchie, now a Lieutenant-commander in command of H.M.S. *Grangemouth*, was one and Lieutenant-commander Poteet, U.S.N., in command of one of their new four-funnelled destroyers, was the other. Murchie was the first to arrive and was talking with the Chief of Staff and Admiral Grant when there was a smart *rat-tat-tat* on the door and Poteet came in. He whipped off his cap, tucked it under his left arm and greeted the little group.

"Good morning, Admiral." Then, to Murchie who, though only a Lieuten-ant-commander, was Captain of his ship, "Morning, Cap'n." And, lastly to the gaunt, austere, Chief of Staff, Captain Denis Crampton, R.N., "Morning Mister."

Murchie's red face scarce concealed his delight. The Admiral chuckled a cordial "Good Morning" in reply, and the Chief of Staff, after a grimace of affronted surprise that lasted but a fraction of a second, smiled broadly and responded with a hearty, "Captain Poteet, good morning, sir." Then all four laughed with unaffected warmth.

Another of our escorts was H.M.S. *Chrysanthemum*, a sloop. We liked her and her Captain, Lieutenant-Commander Poer de la Poer. Her first arrival was in the middle of a black, blustery night and there was difficulty in the Examina-tion Anchorage in understanding her name until, at last, her Captain shouted, "Chry . . san . . the . . mum. The autumn flower, you know."

One of her officers, Lieutenant Flowerdew, later to command one of Elder Dempster's West African mail steamers, was a friend of ours. Bert Flowerdew was another of those lucky men who never lost his appetite for his job, or his sparkle, for whom the occasional drudgery and danger of seafaring passed un-noticed. The only time that I ever saw in him any sign of concern was when he left with me his sextant and the gold watch that had belonged to his father.

The *Chrysanthemum* had just got in with the remnant of a convoy that she had escorted from Algiers. She was the only escort as it was a small convoy of but three ships. During the day she had towed a blimp—kite-balloon—from which an observer officer could scan a wide expanse of the sea. All went well until the night before arrival in Gibraltar. Then they ran into a thunderstorm, with torrential rain and vivid flashes of forked lightning. Suddenly, the balloon, hauled down for the night and floating only a few feet above the poop, was struck. It exploded with a loud report and disappeared in a ball of fire.

At that moment a German submarine that had been stalking them fired two torpedoes in quick succession and simultaneously sank two of the merchant ships. So there was the roar of two further explosions and, during the few moments before they sank, of steam blowing off from the stricken ships. To this pandemonium was added the shock of the depth-charges that the *Chrysanthemum* launched. As far as I remember, there were no casualties, the crews got smartly away in their boats and were taken aboard the *Chrysanthemum*.

The Convoy Commodore, Commander Norman, R.N.R., was the only one who was at all upset. He was a short, rather pompous little man. He sometimes fixed a monocle in his eye but it usually hung from its cord, swinging about outside his monkey-jacket. He was on the bridge of one of the torpedoed ships. She was sinking rapidly so the naval signal-rating, who was one of his staff, thoughtfully dropped a cork lifebelt over his head and was hauling the tapes tight around the waist when Commander Norman said sharply, "Ho! As you were! Cast off that dam' lashing. You've got my eye-glass inside my life-belt. It's no use to me, in there."

The spring and summer of 1918 saw severe fighting in France and Belgium. In what proved to be a last great effort the Germans attacked and advanced but were then thrust back and, by September, were in full retreat. Four years of a war that could so easily have been avoided and which, in their first ruthless advance through Belgium, they had been so confident of winning, had brought only appalling slaughter of youth and manhood and a blockade that had reduced them to the brink of starvation.

And there was nothing to alleviate the bewildering hopelessness of their position. They had no gloriously powerful new ally to jump into the fight at their sides with hundreds of thousands of men, fresh and eager, and material resources, in great abundance, within easy reach. Their resistance became incoherent, their endurance as flaccid as the famished bellies of the families they had left in their homes.

The march of events towards their total collapse quickened. At the end of October Germany's only allies—Turkey and Austria—threw up the sponge. They were out of it. This meant that any submarines at large in the Mediterranean were faced with the choice of returning to their bases at Pola or Constantinople, which would amount to surrender, or of running the gauntlet through the Straits of Gibraltar and then making the long ocean passage of some two thousand miles around the north of Scotland, into Norwegian territorial waters, and so down the North Sea to Kiel or Wilhelmshaven.

It was a grave decision. When the submarines first came out, the Straits had not really been a problem. They had chosen the blackest part of a night when there was no moon, had kept close to the African shore and run on their electric motors. There had been no reverberating *oom-pah* exhaust of diesel engines and they were ready for an instant "crash-dive" if a British patrol came too near. Now it was different. They knew the Straits would be heavily defended.

Still, it was wintertime and, with thirteen hours between sunset and sunrise, there should be at least ten hours of darkness. They could again hug the African shore, and be invisible against the mountainous background. They could do a good fifteen knots on the surface, and might be clear of the narrows in a couple of hours. They would have to make the attempt on the surface because when submerged they had to switch from diesel to electric power for their propellers. With the entire bulk of the submarine immersed, they would have to thrust aside, to displace, a greater volume of water—lower power, a heavier load and their speed would be greatly reduced. In addition, a two- to three-knot current, that flows continually into the Mediterranean from the Atlantic, would be against them. Their submerged speed, over the ground, would be about four knots, perhaps less.

The narrowest part of the Straits, from Gibraltar to Cape Trafalgar, is thirty-five miles long. A submerged submarine would take eight hours or more to make the passage and, during that time, with such low speed and consequent sluggish ability to manoeuvre, would be an easy target for depth-charges. There was no doubt. Their decision would be to try the passage of the Straits, at high speed, when the night was at its darkest. This was confirmed when their sudden spate of night-time signals was picked up by wireless bearings and we were able to stick five small red flags in our table and watch them approach their rendezvous and then move in line ahead in our direction.

A warm welcome was prepared for them. Strung across the Straits, at intervals of a few miles, were small flotillas of some seven vessels in each line, of which the one in the centre was in wireless touch with our office. All were, of course, armed and most of them could drop or launch depth-charges. They were of various kinds, such as armed boarding-vessels, torpedo-boats, motor-launches, converted fishing-trawlers—normally engaged in mine-sweeping—United States submarine chasers and, at the western end of the Straits, beyond Cape Trafalgar, a few destroyers.

As things turned out, perhaps the welcome prepared was too warm. All ships had been thoroughly briefed and knew what to do: report to our office and, in the same instant, to attack. But there were so many of them, in such a small area, that it is surprising that they did not damage or sink each other by collision, gunfire or depth-charge.

It was nearing midnight on November 8th when the Signal Station reported a message.

"*York* to S.N.O. Two suspicious vessels moving from east to west at high speed. Am closing for attack if necessary."

In reply, while I still had the Yeoman on the telephone, I gave him for immediate transmission, as from the S.N.O., a signal to the *York* acknowledging, and signals to the senior ships in each of the other lines of the barrage, as we called it, repeating the information received from H.M.S. *York*. Then I telephoned the Chief of Staff and the Admiral.

Both arrived a few minutes later. The Admiral had evidently jumped out of bed for he was wearing slippers and had pulled a pair of trousers and a greatcoat over his pyjamas. The next two hours were tense, thrilling and frustrating. In our office, we were much like blind men at the theatre. All flotillas were continually in touch with us and "out there" it was evidently a complete scrimmage. Altering course to ram. Or firing point blank at something that promptly disappeared beneath waves so thoroughly churned up that no hydrophone ever invented could pick out the beat of a submarine's propellers from among all the other propellers that were thrashing the water over its head. There were momentary brilliant shafts of a searchlight, that showed up nothing and blinded everyone. Sometimes ". . . a bloody great conning-tower. Less than a hundred yards away. Got it fair amidships with our twelve-pounder. Went down like a stone." Or again, ". . . ran right over him. Didn't feel him touch but sure felt the scrape of his periscope. Gave him a couple of depth-charges, set so shallow, they dam' near blew my own propellers off. Didn't see any more of that particular Hun. If he got away, I'll bet he had an awful headache."

Those were the kind of comments that I listened to later but there had been so many participants, all "having a go", that we had no certain knowledge of the results. How many had attempted the passage? How many were damaged? How many, if any, sunk? The water of the Straits is quite free from obstructions, rocks or shoals. A skilful submarine Commander, when attacked, could dive as deep as he liked without fear of hitting bottom, come up again when the roar of the traffic over his head was far enough away, and resolutely pursue his way westward.

That is undoubtedly what the Captain of *U.B.50* did. Until, at last, he could get around Cape Trafalgar and set his boat quietly down on the shelving sands of Trafalgar Bay. At that time, the German submarine was regarded as a pestilent horror, always associated with the merciless sinking of the *Lusitania* and other acts of savagery such as firing on the open boats of survivors of vessels they had sunk. But there were also some humane submarine Commanders who, before leaving them, gave such boats advice about the nearest available help or shelter, sometimes offering medical assistance and even towing them long distances toward land and safety.

These had retained the decency of all good seamen. They would be the kind of German sailors who had risked their lives to rescue the crew of the ship *Arno*. After all, in that particular war, the submarine offered the only way by which a German sailor could fight for his country, as a seaman. Perhaps the Captain of *U.B.50* was that kind of man. When the motors were switched off, the engines at rest, he may have assembled his crew and thanked them for their skill and their prompt obedience to orders that had brought them all so far on their way home.

Then perhaps each man received a tot of grog and it is not stretching imagination too far to suggest that, when pannikins had been filled, the Captain may have told his men that they were laying in Trafalgar Bay where the British Admiral Nelson had gained his famous victory over the French. Perhaps he made a little joke and said, "I hope it's catching." Then he would cry, "*Unser Kaiser, hoch!*" Drams are drained, out go the lights and, but for those on watch, they are all soon asleep.

Before sunrise he was under way again, taking a cautious sweep of the horizon through his periscope. Against the brightening sky in the east there was nothing near enough to be troublesome. But the sight that met his eyes to the south-west must have made him exclaim aloud. It was a big, fat, British battleship of the King Edward VII class, a veritable floating fortress, with a crew of more than seven hundred officers and men.

Every detail of her silhouette, armament and construction must have been known to the submarine Captain, even the fact that she was protected by a belt of Krupp armour, nine inches thick, amidships. He planted his torpedoes with much skill. The first struck the torpedo store and the second the magazine where the 9.2-inch shells were stored. The explosions, deep in the bowels of the ship, were extremely violent. Then, we may suppose that after three rousing *hochs* for their Kaiser, *U.B.50* headed for the Atlantic.

That was the morning of November 9th, 1918. On that same day, their German Emperor, the arrogant, war-hungry, heroic image of 1914, picked up his skirts and fled to Holland, abandoning the country that he had brought to chaos, collapse and revolution.

The torpedoed ship was H.M.S. *Britannia*. Salvage tugs were sent as soon as her distress signals were received and, for some hours, it was thought that they might succeed in bringing her in. But she was too seriously wounded and sank within sight of the Rock. It was a sad loss. Built in 1904, she was still a fine man-of-war and it was a bitter blow for her complement because she had been based at the Cape of Good Hope and they were looking forward to seeing their families again. The explosions, which would have been below the watertight flat, caused only few casualties. But several of the survivors, landed in apparently perfect health, died suddenly a few hours after coming ashore, usually after eating. It seems that their deaths were a delayed reaction to the poisonous fumes from the exploded magazines.

It was a day of mixed emotions, sorrow over the loss of the *Britannia* and satisfaction over the news of the Kaiser's flight and the mutiny of the German Navy. That night we sent a signal to escorts and convoys, giving them permission to burn steaming lights. When I came on duty the following morning, I read the signal and thought of the vast relief that it must have brought to all the shipmasters. For the last four years they had steamed through the darkest nights, frequently in the middle of a convoy with other ships that they could not see, close ahead, astern and on either side. Submarines were a constant worry but so, also, was the ever-present risk of collision. Now, the Old Man would be able to stand in the lee of the wheel-house and put a match to his pipe without fearing that its light would betray his presence to an enemy.

That morning the *Yamacraw* brought in a convoy from the east and Captain Wrigley came to the office to make his report to the Chief of Staff. Afterwards, he remained seated by my desk, smoking some of my good, dark navy in an old corncob pipe, with much enjoyment. I mentioned the signal and asked if they had received it in time for it to be of any help.

"Help!" exclaimed Captain Wrigley. "Sure. We got it alright, some time before midnight. I've been on my feet ever since. I wished you'd never sent the blamed thing."

I was too astonished to say anything and, seeing this, Captain Wrigley continued, "It's all dam' fine for you Limeys. The war comes along and you've got such a big merchant marine that you can call on thousands of real sailors to help the Navy. My young men learned their rule of the road and whatever other seamanship they've got on top of Macy's building, right in the middle of New York City. As long as they couldn't see anything it was alright. Life went along all quiet and peaceful. But as soon as the convoy switched on side-lights, stern-lights and masthead-lights, they were so busy shifting the helm to avoid collision that we dam' near had three or four collisions every watch."

Armistice Day in Gibraltar was a day of melancholy. The water of the bay was dull as pewter, the puddles on the streets mirrored a sky heavy with clouds that wept ceaselessly as though moved by the mournful beauty of the funeral music, as though in concert with the slow, measured tramp of seamen and marines marching with arms reversed and of those who drew the long line of gun-carriages with their flag-draped coffins.

The war was over and the only shot that I had seen fired in anger had been the one that we put across the bows of a British tramp-steamer. No, that is not quite true. One night I had been in the field of fire on which just about every gun on the Rock, was concentrated. Their marksmanship was magnificent. If it had not been so, not only would Captain Noble and I and our boat's crew have disappeared in a cloud of bloody splinters but even the Rock itself would have suffered. It happened early in 1917, a period when German submarines were especially active. In the naval harbour, behind the boom-defences, were several crowded transports and some battle-cruisers.

Suddenly, all the lights of the town went out and in the same instant search-lights transformed the Examination Anchorage from dark night to brilliant day. Into this same area poured a terrific salvo of shells from the heavy batteries above the town and from the guns on the moles that enclosed the harbour. We were steaming about the anchorage in a launch that was our favourite. She was an old-fashioned naval steam-pinnace of the 1890s, with a comfortable cockpit, well-sheltered cabin and a nice bell-topped brass funnel that was always kept highly polished.

Somebody had seen a submarine in the anchorage. Whether or not there was one, we never found out. But, if so, she must have been blown to bits. One lot of heavy shells landed all at once on the same spot and there was a tremendous explosion that was accompanied by subsidiary explosions, some yards on either side, as though a submarine had indeed been struck and the torpedoes in her tubes had gone up in sympathy.

Our beautiful brass funnel twinkled in the searchlights so we stopped engines and lay still so that we could be clearly distinguished and might not bother the gunners—or be mistaken for a submarine by one who was over-zealous. We were witnessing a remarkable display of roaring sound and blazing light: vivid tongues of fire which darted from the guns; the crisp crack and resonant boom that was magnified by the great sounding-board of the rocky background, the whistling scream of the shells and the beautiful, sparkling masses of water thrown high into the air when they landed or exploded. And then, the relatively slow collapse of these fountains, the currents of cool air that they dispersed and the seething, pattering susurration as they splashed down into complete subsidence. Perhaps it was the only time in history when all the guns of the Rock blazed away at a single target.

Our real concern was for the American oil-tanker *John D. Archbold* that might have been the submarine's intended prey. She had on board fifteen thousand tons of aviation spirit. If she had been hit by torpedo, or by one of the guns, there would have been a blast that would have extinguished everything in the anchorage and wrecked a goodly portion of the town. We felt sorry for this American crew. But when we went on board at daylight they seemed to regard the whole thing as a rather fine show. Carrying all that high-test benzine through the danger zones had made them callous about the prospect or possibility of sudden destruction.

The skinny, little, leathery-faced Mate greeted us as we climbed over the rail. For him there had been no doubt at all. A submarine had been blown to smithereens less than a hundred yards away. He had two wicker coal-baskets full of ugly-looking shell fragments, any single one of which could have given a mortal blow. They had picked them up from the decks.

"Made a bit of a racket when they came aboard," said the Mate, "but nobody was hit."

"No good worrying, at this game," the Old Man chimed in. "If it's got your name on it, you'll get it. And," he drawled, "you wo-o-o-on't kno-o-ow a darn thing about it."

Now, everyone wanted to go home. Not only from Gibraltar, but from all the other bases in the Mediterranean and points east. It was the Sea Transport Officer who had additional worries. And, as the weeks went by and every homeward-bound transport that came along was crowded to the limit of her capacity, I decided to make my own arrangements and then get permission to leave when I had done so. I had many good friends in the Port Service and so had no trouble in picking out a cargo-steamer and then going on board to talk with the Captain. I chose the S.S. *War Pointer*, from Alexandria for Hull with a cargo of cotton and cotton-seed.

Her Old Man, Captain Melsom, was obdurate. He had no accommodation for passengers. And my wife! Absolutely out of the question. "The answer is *no*! And it's no good going to see the S.T.O. or anybody else." He knew what he could do and what he was going to do. And nobody was going to tell him any different. It was the natural reaction of somebody who was not going to submit any longer to his normal authority being usurped by some uniformed jackanapes on shore. There was no use trying to overcome it by argument or persuasion.

There was a ten- or fifteen-minute wait for my launch so, with his permission, I lit my pipe and remained seated on the saloon settee while he stood in a characteristic attitude, both hands stuck in the side pockets of his jacket, staring through a port hole at nothing in particular but with an air of inflexible truculence. Then I had the happy idea of asking whether he was related to Captain Melsom of the Cunard Line, adding that he had been very kind to me when I had been sent aboard his ship to help them in shifting her to a berth across the dock in Liverpool.

The effect was remarkable. The moody expression vanished and was replaced by a warm smile. That was his brother. Why hadn't I said that I was in the Cunard Line? He sat down in one of the swivel chairs and lit his pipe, too. After five minutes' talk about the Cunard and his own Donaldson Line, he suggested that I have a word with the Steward to see if he could perhaps do something.

And that is how it was done. For a few pounds the Steward let me have his cabin; my wife to sleep in the bunk, I on the settee. We made our good-byes and sailed just about three months after the date of the armistice. Except for a terrible smell in the cabin and a westerly gale with heavy seas as soon as we passed Cape St. Vincent, we had a good passage. The smell was so trying to my wife, who remained in the bunk during the first couple of days, trying to ward off seasickness, that, very apologetically, I spoke to the Steward about it.

"Oh!" he exclaimed. "I'm sorry. That's my hop pillow. Stuffed with hops, it is. To induce sleep, you know. So . . po . . rif . . fic. That's the word for it. And there's bin many a time, when we were in convoy, with ships being pipped to port and starboard, that it was a good bed-fellow an' kept my head down so that I didn't know a thing about it till the morning."

Its removal made all the difference. My poor Susan cheered up and was even able to stand in the lee of a deck-house and to admit that there was some beauty in the sparkling combers. For me, after four years of fair weather and office work, it was like coming to life again. It was a delight to see the breaking seas dancing in the sunlight, to watch the fleeting clouds, to feel the wind on my face and hear its song in my ears.

Four years and five months after I had left it, we arrived at my father's house—on February 21st, 1919. My Demobilisation Certificate was already there. It had been posted from the Admiralty while we were still at sea and was effective from the date of my arrival.

How fortunate I was to have come through it all physically intact and with a mind reasonably composed. The cast of dice that had sent me to the *Pelorus* had brought good luck. My name was listed among the officers mentioned in Admiralty Fleet Orders for valuable services rendered in the prosecution of the war.

The Imperial Merchant Service Guild.

(REPRESENTING THE CAPTAINS AND OFFICERS
OF THE BRITISH MERCHANT SERVICE.)

Solicitors at
Most Leading
Seaports at
Home and
Abroad.

Over 400 Agents
Ashore and Afloat.
Agents at Leading
Seaports throughout
the World.

TELEPHONE NOS.
8971 & 8972 BANK, LIVERPOOL.
3881 AVENUE, LONDON
1813 CARDIFF.
36 SOUTH SHIELDS.
52 CORPORATION, HULL.
4291 CENTRAL, GLASGOW.

ADDRESS TELEGRAMS
DOLPHIN, LIVERPOOL.
GUILDCRAFT, LONDON.
DOLPHIN, CARDIFF.
DOLPHIN, SOUTHSHIELDS.
GUILDCRAFT, HULL.
DOLPHIN, GLASGOW.

Secretary: Mr. T. W. MOORE, M.B.E., F.R.G.S.
Lieutenant, Royal Naval Reserve (Honorary).
Assistant Secretary: Lieut. G. B. SAY, R.N.V.R.
Cashier: Mr. C. K. MITCHELL.

HEAD OFFICES:

THE ARCADE, LORD STREET, LIVERPOOL.

OTHER OFFICES:

Dixon House, Lloyd's Avenue, London, E.C.
Colum Buildings, Mount Stuart Square, Cardiff.
Old Town Hall, South Shields.
41, King Edward Street, Hull.
Baltic Chambers, 50, Wellington Street, Glasgow.

781.

17th July, 1919.

To avoid unnecessary search and delay in reply, it is particularly requested that Members
when writing will give their Rotation Numbers.

Lieut. H.C.A. Demierre R.N.R.

Dear Sir,

It is with gratification that we learn that your name
has been brought to the notice of the Admiralty for valuable services
rendered in the prosecution of the war, and on this I beg to offer
you the hearty congratulations of the Imperial Merchant Service
Guild.

Yours faithfully,

T. W. Moore

Secretary.

I received a gratuity of £180 and, as I had not had any leave during the years of my active service, I was given pay, in lieu thereof, for 126 days. It produced £103. 19s. 0d. My share in the Naval Prize Fund came to £20. 5s. 0d., making a grand total of £304. 4s. 0d. For those days, it was a lot of money, a most welcome cushion between the demobilised servant of the Crown and the competitive civilian world. It was useful to me, too, but my father kept a warm hearth and I was still in the Cunard service.

16 *Back to the Cunard Line*

Liverpool was a grim place, not only for its heavy March skies, its rain and sleet, but also for the gloom that was everywhere present, like an air of grief for all the ships and men who had gone to sea and had not come back. Such a sombre pall of sorrow must have hung over every seaport in Britain and of every country in Europe.

The Cunard Line had suffered heavily, losing twenty-one ships, including ten of its passenger liners. The Marine Superintendents had had their worries but Captain Park, the one who was in charge of officer appointments, had shuffled things around so that none of us had the embarrassment of kicking his heels on the dock, drawing his pay, while knowing that there was no ship for him. He had all the pegs on his board in the appropriate holes and, after passing the Company Doctor to make sure that the war had really done me no harm, I was sent to London to join the *Saxonia* as Third Officer.

It was, in many respects, an interesting voyage. We went to Brest to embark American troops. They were so happy to be going home again that they were model passengers, obedient to their officers and the ship's regulations for safety below decks. I have good reason to remember the *Saxonia* but I never think of her without, again, seeing the contented face of a tall black soldier. I was making my rounds of the troop-deck, after leaving the bridge at four o'clock in the morning. In spite of the extraordinary hour, he was lying in one of the top berths reading a book entitled *What to Do When You Get Home*. As I stood there, my chin was just about level with his elbow.

"Well," I said, "what will you do when you get home?"

Without lowering his book, he turned a beaming face toward me and then replied, "Wall . . . sah." There was a pause for some heavy thinking, and then, "Ah guess Ah'll be jess gl . . air . . ud."

The welcome that awaited us in New York drove the troops into a frenzy of excited anticipation. Every vessel we passed tooted her whistle, ferry-boats, tugs, all shouted and waved and, to crown all, in the harbour, we were greeted by tenders that were decorated with flags and banners carrying the legend MAYOR HYLAN'S WELCOME COMMITTEE. The tenders were crowded with bonny young women, all dressed alike in blouse and skirt, long-sleeved, loosely

S.S. *Saxonia*

knitted black sweaters, fastened only at the waist, black stockings, black and white shoes and, literally to crown all, white straw boaters with broad black bands. It was quite definitely a uniform, and one that did nothing to mute the appeal that they made to the young soldiers who had been longing for this moment. The girls waved, blew kisses and shouted, so that the "doughboys" were quite beside themselves.

At the pier were long tables laden with ice-cream, doughnuts, cakes, piles of packets of cigarettes and a whole battery of urns of coffee. The young women were there to see that the boys were quickly served at the tables and that when they left, in spite of rifles, tin hats and other burdens, they might still carry a few packets of cigarettes, some candy-bars and a doughnut or two. I must say that it was a very happy scene, typical of the innate humanity and spontaneous affection of the American character.

One incident of spontaneous generosity that had nothing to do with the American character made me smile. Standing by the gangway, I was talking with the Marine Superintendent and was, apparently, being overheard by a Captain, U.S. Army, who was part of the disembarkation staff. Suddenly, on impulse, he went to the nearest table and came back with half a dozen packets of cigarettes.

"Take these, sir, and welcome," he said. "I'm an Englishman myself."

He thrust the cigarettes into my hands and before I could give any thanks he went away.

288

"There you are. See," said the Marine Superintendent. "You've heard all about those Germans who've got naturalised in England. They change passports but not their nationality. You know what they say at home," he grinned. "Once a German, always a German."

We sailed again for Plymouth, Le Havre and London, full of passengers and loaded with a cargo of thousands of tons of foodstuffs, much of it destined for central Europe, like so many of the passengers who, for five years, had been prevented from seeing their old homes and relatives. We arrived in the Thames, off Tilbury Docks, before there was enough water for us to get over the sill, so we anchored in the river. A tender came alongside for the passengers who would board the train that was waiting to take them to London. It also brought a telegram for me, urging me to come home as my father was critically ill with pneumonia. In my anxiety, I wished to leave immediately, to go with the passengers, and asked the Staff Captain, Gardiner, for permission to do so. To my surprise, he said that I should ask the Captain. So to Captain Diggle I went, feeling quite sure that he would allow me to go. However, the London

The author, on the bridge of the *Saxonia*

Superintendent, Captain Manley, had also come in the tender and, to my astonishment, Captain Diggle said that I should have to get *his* permission.

I had never before met Captain Manley. He was a tall man, broad of shoulder, and his face wore a stern, authoritative expression. He read the telegram, gave no word or gesture of sympathy but said, curtly, "You can't go till the ship's docked."

Now, I was not only anxious, I was furious. Without a moment's hesitation I went to my cabin, quickly changed my clothes, packed a small bag and went on deck, hoping to get the tender. But it had gone. However, we had hove up anchor and were moving towards the entrance to the lock that separated the docks from the river. The rope-ladder that the Pilot had used was lying on the fore-deck but was still fast to the rail. I called to Cadet Deane, who was standing close by, and told him to put it over the side.

All this was watched by Captain Manley who stood at the forward end of the boat-deck, at the head of the ladder that led to the fore-deck.

"You can't go till the ship's docked," he repeated.

"I'm going now," I replied.

Down on the fore-deck, I gave my bag to Deane, told him to bend it on to the bight of a heaving-line that he was to throw to me when I was on the dock. Then, I went over the rail and down the rope-ladder and, as the ship moved into the lock, I jumped ashore. I got my bag, ran around the stern, across the caissons that had just closed and over to the station where I caught the same train as the passengers.

At home, that night, I found my father delirious and two days passed before the doctor decided that he was out of danger. Then I bethought me of my own position. For the first time in my life, I had deserted my ship. I went to Liverpool to explain my behaviour to Captain Park. He listened in silence and, when I had finished, smiled and told me to go home again and to report for duty when it was certain that there was no longer any danger.

I next went away in my old ship, the *Carmania*, my favourite of them all. Our Captain was W. R. D. Irvine, tall and handsome with the dignity and bearing of an Admiral of the Fleet. He was nicknamed "Haughty Bill" and there were many stories about him, usually illustrating the triumph of his suave manners. One such occasion occurred on this voyage. It was the ship's concert with the usual appeal for seamen's charities. The Chairman, had gone to much trouble over his speech and, to give the statistics some human meaning, he concluded by placing before the audience a very small ship's boy.

The little chap was all scrubbed and rosy-cheeked and his wide, bell-bottom trousers made him look even smaller than he was.

"The only home he ever had," said the Chairman, "was in a Navy League

Orphanage. And now look at the little man. Clean, well-fed and some day, who knows, he may be Captain of a fine ship like this."

The simile must have been hard for "Haughty Bill" to digest but it was even more so for the "little man". Perhaps he was moved by the reference to his former condition as "a poor, little, hungry, orphan boy", but the surroundings were awe-inspiring and the proximity of the Captain was a new and quite terrifying ordeal. He burst into tears. The Chairman was disconcerted, thrown into confusion, but not Captain Irvine. He rose to his feet, a rather magnificent figure, picked up the small sailor boy and stood him on the chair in which he had himself been seated.

"Mister Chairman, Ladies and Gentlemen," he said, "of course, with your help, this young sailor . . . , and many more like him, will rise in the Merchant Service and perhaps I am indeed standing alongside the future Captain of a future *Carmania*. I am only sorry that I shall not be here to see it."

Exit tear-stained but smiling small boy, followed by a great burst of applause and a fine, fat collection for the charities.

Captain Irvine was as resourceful as he was good-looking. When one of his ships—I think it was the *Franconia*—was torpedoed, the submarine surfaced and called the boats alongside, intending to take the Captain prisoner. No Captain was to be found. The submarine was told that he had been lost. Actually, he was sitting at one of the oars, wearing a pair of greasy dungaree trousers, a life-belt and, around his neck, a sweat-rag. His face and head and bare arms were smeared with dirty bilge-water, like so many of the engine-room hands who were in the same boat.

The man I relieved was one of those types so ugly, in a rugged sort of way, that he was almost good-looking. I watched him closing his bags and marvelled at the dexterity with which he prevented a swinging monocle and its cord from getting mixed up with the straps that he was buckling.

"What's the Old Man like?" I asked.

"Oh," was the reply, "he's so stuck-up he can't ever remember your name."

This officer's name was Mordington-Jones so perhaps there was something to be said for "Haughty Bill". I always found him to be very considerate. Nearing the land, in fog, stations on shore were now able to give us the compass-bearing of our signals. It was Captain Irvine who explained the necessity of using a special chart to get a "fix" from these bearings and who showed me how to do it.

On that voyage, all the third-class accommodation was occupied by returning French-Canadian troops. They were tough and truculent and appeared to have but little regard for any authority. Their gambling gangs played all night if they wished and smoked when and where they felt like smoking.

Neither their own Military Police nor our Masters-at-Arms—the ship's police—could control them. All they could do was to see that there was no violence or damage. There was a general sigh of relief when they were landed in Halifax, Nova Scotia, and we were able to continue the passage to New York.

On our return to Liverpool I was sent to Southampton to join the *Mauretania* as Second Officer. She was a hive of busy workers, being restored to her peace-time elegance. Even in dry-dock her great size did not detract from her grace, so beautifully had she been designed. The knife-like stem, the hollow flare of her bows that came aft as far as her bridge and the clean run of her hull to the sternpost, to the four propellers and to the shapely, old-fashioned counter—these were the swift lines of a destroyer, of a clipper-ship.

On the water-line she was 762 feet long. On deck, her overall length was 790 feet. To realise the meaning of these figures, consider that if it had been possible to stand her on end in Trafalgar Square, she would have been as tall as five Nelson monuments. Placed on land, on an even keel, she would have covered the length of two full-size football grounds or six and a half baseball diamonds.

She had accommodation for 2,165 passengers and, when they were on board and she was stored with everything necessary for the Atlantic crossing, the *Mauretania* sat 33 feet 6 inches deep in the water, must have displaced about

R.M.S. *Mauretania*, Queen of the Atlantic

forty thousand tons of it and, above the water-line, her hull and superstructure rose as high as an eight-storied building.

Nine times as long as her greatest width, with her fine underwater lines, she was shaped for speed, like an eel. Her maiden voyage was made in 1907. She was now twelve years old but was to be active for another fifteen years. When she made her last Atlantic passage—on her sad way to the ship-breakers graveyard—she could still do better than her designed speed of twenty-five knots. When she came out, the birth and behaviour of such a vessel were indeed written, talked and boasted about, but publicity was restrained. It did not have those superb noise-makers radio and television and fell short of the world-wide shouting that greeted the later Atlantic giants. And yet, the *Mauretania*'s place is among these. She was only a little less in length than the *Aquitania* but was a good two knots faster. In 1919, and for many years thereafter, she held the record as the fastest ship crossing the Atlantic, the fastest merchant ship in the world. Another seventeen years were to pass before the *Queen Mary* appeared.

It was six weeks before the ship was ready for sea so there was ample time to get to know my way about, to become familiar with all the equipment of her bridge and wheel-house, her system of double-bottom tanks, and to meet new shipmates. The wardroom was mahogany panelled, lit by a skylight and surrounded on three sides by officers' cabins. The fourth, the forward side, was a thwartship alleyway on the other side of which were bathrooms, bridge pantry and, beyond these, the Captain's suite.

There were comfortable chairs and a square, red-baize-covered table, and the bulkheads were hung with signed photographs of the celebrities who had been entertained there from the handsome Marquis of Anglesey and Mark Twain to the most recent, less than three months old, Sir John Alcock and Sir Arthur Whitten Brown who had crossed in the ship before making their—and the world's first—Atlantic flight on June 15th.

None of us had sailed together before but the atmosphere was warm with that invisible link that exists between all sailors, with their talk of "last ships", in their search for mutual friends.

My wife and I lived in lodgings and when I was not on duty we made short excursions to Bournemouth or took the train to Lyndhurst Road and explored the New Forest. It was all very beautiful at that golden time of the year. We had a glimpse of a country life that has not survived the invading hosts of motors. Sometimes, our way took us along hot, white, dusty roads in the clearings, then through shady tunnels of rustling beeches to emerge on to a village green, as at Emery Down where, on a Saturday afternoon, we were lucky enough to see a rustic cricket match, complete with a keg of beer that had been placed in the shade, close at hand. The players were mixed sides of yokels and gentry with two supplementary young boys whose part was to do the running for two who were not able to run for themselves: one because he was too fat and the other because he had a wooden leg. All this we saw through the window of the thatched cottage where we ate our tea.

We sailed on September 21st and made our way to New York—this time via Halifax—in glorious summer weather, with smooth seas and balmy southerly winds. It was, however, the season of the autumnal equinox and on the homeward passage, instead of gentle breezes, we ran through a south-easterly gale of such violence that one big sea came over the bridge on to the boat-deck where it swept four life-boats over the side and smashed a couple more in their chocks.

Writing of my first Cunard voyages in the *Carmania*, I mentioned the un-wieldiness of a large liner navigating in heavy weather at reduced power. Here was something quite different. Power was not reduced. Captain Rostron handled his ship as though she were a destroyer and so had others before him. She stuck her nose into the oncoming seas with such impetus and so frequently carried such a weight of water over her fo'c's'le head that the steel bulkheads below the fo'c's'le head were buckled to a vertical arc, like an archer's bow, and the beams that supported the deck of the fo'c's'le overhead were shored up by baulks of heavy timber.

The *Mauretania* held the Blue Ribbon and was meant to keep it, come fog, mist, falling snow, heavy rain-storm or hard weather. Her twenty-five knots transformed a fresh breeze into half a gale and when it really did blow and she was plunging, then leaping up and smashing down, cleaving her deep furrow across the ocean, she throbbed to racing propellers, shuddered in her striving and panted as her pliant hull responded like a springy plank. Then the whole fabric of the acres of wooden panelling groaned and creaked in a succession of wavering moans.

Speed was reduced only when, in the Captain's judgement, to continue at full power must result in serious damage, or when it was so thick that you had to start the whistle going—the fog siren. Those early western ocean Commanders carried a tremendous burden of responsibility. So did the Officer of the Watch in the middle of the night, when all were in their beds, fast asleep. Patches of mist drift over the stars, then settle on the water.

"Hmmm," he says to his watch-mate, a Third Officer. "Not really thick enough to start the whistle, is it?" That is a rhetorical question. He expects no answer and gets none but strokes his chin and asks himself how far can he really see. Is it a mile or only two hundred yards? "We're doing a mile every two and a half minutes. And, by crikey, if the other fellow is coming along at fifteen knots, we'll cover that mile in ninety seconds! If it is a mile! If I put the engines on the 'Stand By' they'll let the steam go back, down below, so that they can handle their damn' reversing gear more promptly. And we'll slow down. And the racket of the telegraph'll bring the Old Man up! Oh hell! If there is another chap coming along from the east'ud he'd be eighty miles to the south'ard. That's what tracks are for. Isn't it?"

"Yes, indeed," replies the Third Officer primly. And then, reverting to the argot of the half-deck, he added, "Unless the sonofabitch is cutting corners."

So they keep on going!

It was not always like that. Sometimes, in mid-winter, we voyaged under skies that were the clear, cold blue of new ice, with smooth seas that glittered in warm sunshine. It all depended on where the wind came from. New York is, after all, in the same latitude, as close to the sun, as Naples.

The *Mauretania* and Captain Rostron were both very popular. The ship was always crowded and it seemed to me that embarking and landing so many people at such short intervals, having them on board for only five and a half days, of which they spent two days unpacking and packing, caused them, with few exceptions, to lose any individual significance. Every new batch of passengers seemed to be the duplicate of those who had just left the ship.

Six years had brought great differences. The war had caused much social change. There were not so many moneyed sportsmen taking a luxurious route to play polo in the Argentine, or to go after tarpon off the Florida coast or to fish for over-size trout in New Zealand. But there were more commercials, bagmen, afloat on generous expense accounts. More of them? Well, they were more in evidence than formerly. Much of the Victorian country-mansion atmosphere had gone from Atlantic travel.

For a part of my time in the *Mauretania* I carried out the normal duties of Second Officer, responsible for mails and specie and acting as a kind of Flag-lieutenant to the Staff Captain; supervising passenger protection against the weather on deck, and safety below in the matter of life-belts, fire-hoses, hydrants, extinguishers and fire-proof doors; joining the procession of Captain or Staff Captain, Surgeon, Purser, Chief Steward, etc., in rounds of inspection.

For all its importance, I found it dull, monotonous and pettifogging.

Then the Senior First Officer, Rodgers, went on special leave to sit for an examination, to qualify as a Nautical Surveyor. The Junior First Officer, Gale, took his place and I took over from Gale, as the Senior Officer of the 8 to 12 watch. Of the Queen of the Atlantic! For eight hours out of every twenty-four, she was in my charge. Doing her twenty-five knots. And, deep down inside of myself, I was so proud that I could scarcely stand my own company. That voyage was really the high point of my service in the *Mauretania*.

All through that winter, from September to March, we hurried back and forth between Southampton, Cherbourg and New York on round voyages that sometimes included Halifax and averaged eighteen days. Every homecoming meant a few days in some furnished rooms, or in an hotel if we felt that we could afford it; then, away again. Rail travel for my wife and the sea for me. We had been married three and a half years. It was time we had a house of our own. But where? One sailed out of London, Liverpool or Southampton. We had just about decided to look for something in a part of the country that was convenient to all three places, when I was taken out of the ship and posted to the *Pannonia* as Junior First Officer, to do a year's service between New York and the Mediterranean.

Our thinking had to be adjusted. Looking for a home of our own would have to be postponed. It was a bit of a blow but somebody had to sail in that service and it would have been worse if we had been unable to move because we owned a house and furniture. The company would give my wife a first-class passage to New York for £10, if we decided that I could support her there. My pay was about £33 per month—say, $160. We had the great advantage that we knew nothing about the cost of living in New York, so we thought that we might manage. As things turned out, the move could not have come at a more opportune time in our lives.

I went out in the *Carmania* with Captain George Melsom. He bore a close resemblance to his brother of the *War Pointer*, he was as forthright and devoid of "airs and graces". In command of a twenty-thousand-ton liner, when we entered Halifax, instead of shouting his orders from the wing of the bridge— or from anywhere else—he came into the wheel-house and handled the engine-room telegraph himself and put the ship alongside the wooden pier, with its rickety-looking piles, with as little fuss and as gently as though she had been a tugboat.

In New York, only the width of the pier separated us from the *Pannonia*. She had only arrived the previous day but, already, cargo was coming out of all her hatches. It was a blustery March day and the spicy smell that came from the contents of the baskets, bags, bales, barrels and butts that were going over the side—such as currants, raisins, figs, tobacco and white cherries that would one day be turned crimson, bottled with maraschino liqueur and popped into insidious cocktails and through equally crimson lips. There were olives, too, in butts of brine. It was slightly reminiscent of the bustle of the Salthouse

Dock in Liverpool that, sixteen years before, had held a romantic, sea-hungry schoolboy spellbound.

Going aboard the *Pannonia* was a little like going back to sea again. How can I express it? Perhaps my old sailing-ship Master, Captain Hatch, put his finger on it when we sat drinking a reviving cup of tea in the wardroom of the *Mauretania*, after a fatiguing tour of the ship.

"I'm glad I never had to go to sea in anything like this," he had said. "She's a lovely vessel but so big that she's . . ." he paused, searching for the right word ". . . so big that she's impersonal," he concluded.

That may seem to be a lot of nonsense to those who have only known big ships, but I came to realise that he had put my own feelings into words. You never felt that you "belonged" to such large ships, you just served in them; took them to sea and brought them back again. As a Junior Officer, you would sometimes, when in port, be asked by a Boss Stevedore or someone from the Wharfinger's Office to "go and have a look at No. 3, sir, so that we can start loading". Then, in company with an Engineer Officer you went down into the hold and saw that the well and the rose-box on the suction-pipes were clear. The result of the inspection was entered in the log-book and that was the sum total of your concern with any cargo carried.

It was the same with ship's husbandry—to give care and maintenance its good, old-fashioned nomenclature. The Bos'n came to the First Officer every morning for orders regarding the day's work but with passengers on board that meant very little. Everything was done by shore gangs, supervised by shore Bos'ns.

Big, fast ships meant keen watchkeeping and meticulous navigation. A good officer did both instinctively. That came of his years of training and with the same instinct and without especial mental effort, he conned the ship in coastal waters or in traffic and cared for her in heavy weather. And as you were ceaselessly going back and forth, along the same track, it soon became monotonous and very boring.

So I was content to go aboard the smaller *Pannonia*. I reported to Captain Gronow, his name as Welsh as Wales itself, and he was as kindly as its lovely countryside. He greeted me quietly as "my new navigator" and gave me welcome on board. I had met the Chief Officer seven years before when he was First Officer of the *Lycia*, one of the "brigs", as we called the small Mediterranean cargo-ships. I had been sent on board to help them shift ship and, sticking my head in his cabin door, asked where I could find Captain Hall—a notoriously religious man—to report on board.

With one foot on his settee, elbow on knee, John Chaworth Musters buried the fingers of one hand in a yellow, torpedo beard and he looked so much like

S.S. *Pannonia*

the fictional Captain Kettle that I would not have been surprised if the other hand that was in the pocket of his monkey-jacket, had gripped a revolver.

"Captain Hall," he snorted, "I don't know where he is, the devil-dodging, Bible-punching . . . !"

Remembering this, I was surprised to meet him again as a mild-mannered, clean-shaven, gently-spoken man who, as I soon found out, had some pretty rigid religious convictions of his own. The Senior First Officer was my old shipmate Arthur Platt. The first time we had sailed out of New York together was thirteen years before, in the sailing-ship *Main* where he was Second Mate and I an apprentice of two years' standing. The other deck officers were Ivan Thompson, Miles and a quiet young man named Simmonds.

After dinner that evening, I telephoned some friends to let them know that I was in port, but no longer in the *Mauretania*, and, as I expected, they asked me to go ashore that very evening, if I were free to do so, to give them my news. They were a family of Quakers with whom I had become very friendly after a chance meeting—a rather unusual one.

One voyage in the *Mauretania*, when the Staff Captain, R. D. Jones, and I were on our way back to the officers' quarters, returning from a fire drill, we were halted by a smiling little woman who stood determinedly in our way. She was evidently the kind of person who brimmed over with enthusiasm for whatever was her purpose of the moment. Now, it was the piano. There was one in the dining-saloon for the ship's orchestra. She mentioned it as being so far from any part of the ship where people might wish to be quiet that perhaps she could be permitted to play it in the middle of the afternoon, when she would be in nobody's way.

"But," said R.D., "there's a wonderful Bechstein grand in the drawing-room. Just waiting for you."

"Yes, Captain, thank you. But we don't want an audience. It's really for my friend. He wants me to play some Debussy for him."

The friend was an earnest young Frenchman who smiled, blushed and nodded in support. Of course, permission was given. She was an accomplished musician who could play anything at sight and transpose with ease. Debussy's *Arabesque* sounded as though the notes dripped from her fingers. The Frenchman was delighted. And so were we, especially the Staff Captain. Bob Jones had first seen the light of day on the coast of Caernarvonshire and was as musical as most Welshmen; in fact, rather more so. He had a voice of professional quality and loved to sing.

Arthur Platt, 1916, H.M.S. *Europa*, Gibraltar

With no disrespect, I would say that the ability to utter without effort the complicated sounds of their own language, accounts for the beauty of Welsh singing, for the purity of their vowel sounds, for such good, round *O*s and the second vowel *E* that seems to be produced in that part of the mouth where a horse carries his bit. It has an exact purity of timbre that I have also noticed in Russian singers.

Very little urging by me was necessary. He sang the Toreador song from *Carmen* with much vigour and dramatic feeling. Then he sang a sweet little English ballad *I know of two Bright Eyes*, which he almost whispered—as though we were being allowed to share a rather precious secret. The third treat was *All through the night*, sung with reverence, in Welsh.

R. D. Jones and I were good friends. We had been shipmates before the war in the *Campania*. After that musical occasion, every time we arrived in New York, the post would bring a note inviting us to go and dine with the Pusey family in their home. That was the name. The enthusiastic little woman was Elizabeth H. Pusey, of whose life a really interesting book could be written. That is also true of her father, W. W. Pusey who was one of the last of the Puseys of Pusey & Jones, shipbuilders of Wilmington, Delaware. They came on such hard times that the old gentleman took a job in a bank at less dollars per month than he had been accustomed to spend per day.

They had moved to New York and Mother Pusey with her daughters Elizabeth and Mary worked at dressmaking in an attempt to increase the meagre family income. It must have been, it was, for them a torturing slavery after their past life of society and holiday resorts. One day, Elizabeth straightened her back, stretched cramped fingers and announced, "Mother, I'm not going to sew another stitch."

"Well, dear," replied Mother, "if thee doesn't thee'll starve."

So far from starving, it was Elizabeth who by means that are not part of this story, let us call it pulling hard on her own boot-straps, lifted the family out of depression and penury. She was now running the luxury gift business that bore her name, assisted by her mother and sister. Now first-class passengers, she and her mother were returning from a buying trip to Paris, Brussels, Florence and Britain.

These good people, when told that I was to spend a year in the Mediterranean service and during all that time would not see my wife, were as truly distressed as though it was to happen to some member of their own family. With the impulsive kindness that is so much a part of the American character, they urged that I should not hesitate.

"Get your Susan out here. We'll see that she comes to no harm."

It was Mother Pusey speaking and I was so moved by such spontaneous warmth that only with difficulty could I stammer some words of thanks. At least, that is what I was trying to do when the old lady broke in.

"My boy, I know what thee would say. But there's no need to say anything. Nice people, thee knows, meet nice people."

This simple philosophy and the compliment that it implied, brought such a lump into my throat that I could not, indeed, have said another word.

We sailed for Patras, Trieste, Palermo, Naples and Gibraltar. The ship was deep with cargo and full of passengers who were going to all the countries of southern and south-eastern Europe to see again the families from whom they had been cut off by the long years of war. They were happy. There was much quiet, meditative singing of tunes so artless that they spoke of the simple pipes that had first given them voice from the lips of some shepherd on a Balkan hillside.

In the evenings they danced on deck; men and women, holding each other at arms' length by hips and shoulders, bobbed up and down in some gay czardas; or circles of Greek young men, with arms wound about each other's waists, stepped and stamped with much flourishing of feet and much perspiration and gaiety.

The weather was so warm that we were wearing white uniforms when we entered the Mediterranean and in the Ionian Sea and the Gulf of Corinth the heat was tropical; the sea, placid as though it had never known wind, was the same intensely bright, pale blue as the sky. We approached Patras at such an early hour that the Pilot must have been still abed. There was no sign of his boat so we moved slowly into the roadstead and anchored. Patras may have been asleep but not the *Pannonia*. The excited passengers who were to land there were up and about before dawn, dressed in their Sunday clothes which were of a superlatively American cut and a predominance of wide-brimmed, very pale-coloured felt hats, bright silver belt-buckles and shoes with high heels and toe-caps that rose to heights like miniature island peaks before they descended like vertical cliffs, all of an inch and a half, down to the tip of the shoe.

The Pilot came off with the Port Authorities—to get his note signed—and soon launches were alongside for passengers, and lighters for cargo. After forty-eight hours, we went on our way. The northern shore of the Adriatic Sea curves to the east and south until it meets the town of Trieste. At that point it makes a right-angled turn to the west, along the northern coast of the peninsula of Istria as far as Cape Salvore where it resumes its trend south-eastwards. The Italian Naval Officer in New York had said that we should not, on any account, make our turn and pass Salvore before daylight. When there was enough light we would see a buoy moored two cables north of Salvore Lighthouse. We were to pass between the buoy and the land and then lay a course for Trieste taking care not to go to the northward of the buoy because, if we did, we should steam right into a minefield.

We picked up Salvore Light at about 10.00 p.m. in my watch. I reduced speed and, just before coming up with the light, took a wide sheer to the west and south before turning north again when I turned the watch over to Platt at midnight. At four bells, 6.00 a.m., we had the Pilot aboard and were moving into our berth alongside the quay.

That part of the world was still smarting from the surgery that had carved up the Austro-Hungarian Empire. All kinds of peoples—Croats, Serbs, Slovenes, Jugoslavs and others from the bits of Ruthenia and Transylvania that were now attached to Roumania—smarted and all were politically articulate. Many were dissatisfied and nursed bitter grudges against the Roumanians and Italians who, as they saw it, had with such timely adroitness joined the winning side. Most of our Trieste passengers were destined for these areas and, before catching their trains, they went to stay at the Hotel Balkan.

On the previous day, a fanatical Jugoslav had walked up to an Italian Naval Officer in the town of Spalato and shot him dead. The news reached Trieste in the late afternoon on the day of our arrival. The Italian populace went wild, seeking Jugoslav blood. They wrecked cafés, making bonfires of great heaps of tables and chairs. Then they surrounded the Hotel Balkan, threw fire bombs through the windows and attacked the bewildered and terrified people who jumped or fled from the building. Troops and police arrived and dispersed the mob with a fusillade of rifle fire. The fire was soon put out and, now under military protection, our ex-passengers returned to the hotel to salvage the remains of their possessions. They had come a long way from the peaceful homes they had made for themselves somewhere in the U.S.A., but they still had far to go.

They were troublous times. Trieste was for us a terminal port. We remained there for a week or ten days and it was there that all personal laundry would be done—and there was a lot of it, including many white uniforms. However, the laundries were on strike. So, after a few moments of bad language, we realised that we would have to do it ourselves. We made our own soap-flakes by shaving blocks of soap into boiling water into which we put the clothes to soak; whenever the bath was not being used for its normal purposes some perspiring officer would be rubbing and dubbing, adding blue and starch and, eventually, even ironing. We became expert and thereafter, as long as I was in the ship, no laundry was sent ashore.

302

Troublous times indeed. Even our own medical department was affected. In compliance with Italian regulations, our two doctors, senior and junior, were Italian. They had come to hate each other. The younger taunted and ridiculed the elder until he could stand no more. With eyes blazing from his bony face, his teeth bared in an insane grimace above his sharply-pointed chin, the old doctor sprang at his junior and seized his throat determined to have done with him—to kill him.

In his struggle, the younger man found his face close to that of the old one. He fastened his own strong, white teeth on that pointed chin and bit it off. Bit it clean off, escaped through the door, spat the amputated chin out on to the deck and ran.

And ran. For the old man had produced a pistol—pulled a gun—and was close behind. After him. Stopping only to fire an occasional shot but trembling so much in his pain and passion that never once did he wing his bird. The first I knew of all this was when the young man, yelping with terror, dashed past me. I was in the line of fire. A couple of bullets whizzed by, humming like angry bees. Without waiting to see where they had come from, I stepped into a door-way—a refuge and an ambush. "I'll get him with a tackle from behind when he passes," I thought.

But he never did come past. Ivan Thompson—later Sir Ivan, Kt.B., Com-modore—but then a sturdy young man of about twenty-five, put out a brawny arm and brought the old man up, all standing. That ended the matter so far as the ship was concerned. They were sent ashore. For some days, Ivan Thomp-son kept the chin in a match-box in case it might be required in court but, finally, it was given to the fishes.

"After all," said John Musters, the Chief Officer, "proof that the old boy lost his chin is established by the fact that now, he hasn't got one."

"You leave-a Trieste," said the Naval Officer. "You pass-a that buoy. *Ecco!*" He pointed to the one I had drawn on our chart. "*Allora*, you go fifteen mi' *diritto* to *ouest*. You find *un altro*—'nuzzer' buoy. *Ecco!* You go sout'. Go Palermo." He wagged a warning forefinger and repeated, "Fifteen mi', *allora* go sout'. No before. All mines. Plenty mines."

So, ten days earlier we had idled away the hours before daylight, wandering about in a minefield. Our luck was great or the mines very few—if indeed they existed at all.

The *Pannonia* was a happy ship and Captain Gronow a most amiable commander. He had greeted me as his navigator and that was more than a mode of speech. He left the navigation to his officers. He had six of them and they were all Master Mariners. He satisfied himself on the agreed result of their observations and the course to be steered but he left the determination of these things to his navigator. When making and leaving port, with the Chief Officer on the fo'c's'le head, the Senior First on the poop, I was—under his eye—in charge on the bridge. It was wonderful to feel and to know that one had his confidence.

In Patras, he came into the chart-room just as I was putting in a convenient place the charts on which I had laid down the courses that we should steer through the islands, into the Adriatic and up to Trieste.

"And now," he said, "go ashore, Mr. de Mierre. Go and have a good tramp in those hills and don't come back till you feel like it. There's nothing to keep you aboard, here."

I have always thought of Captain Gronow as one of the most understanding and reasonable men I ever sailed with. Without losing a whit of his dignity or authority, he shared his command with us. We were all better for it and life was a little less monotonous.

Our call at Gibraltar was brief but I went ashore for an hour to see old friends. One of these suggested that I apply for the post of Captain of the Port which, he thought, might soon become vacant.

At that moment I had no thought of leaving the sea. Not because I was so supremely contented, but because I had no idea how to go about it or what there was that I could do on shore. Superintendents' jobs were few and far between and were usually given to officers who were quite senior—Chief Officers or even Captains. And now, prospects for promotion were not what they had been when I joined the company seven years before. Too many ships had been lost. But to be Captain of the Port at Gibraltar! The thought of it was like a dream of an unattainable paradise.

But why not try? Some day it undoubtedly would become vacant and the post was usually given to an officer of the Merchant Service and Royal Naval Reserve. When stationed in Gibraltar I had been friendly with the Colonial Treasurer. Now, I wrote to him and also to Admiral Heathcoat Grant under whom I had served there. Very promptly and with great kindness, they gave me excellent recommendations. The Colonial Treasurer wrote that he would have no hesitation in recommending me for any post where tact, common sense and thoroughness were essential qualifications. Admiral Grant wrote:

Lieutenant H. C. de Mierre during the two years he served under my command was intimately connected with all the duties of the Port at Gibraltar. I can confidently recommend him in every way as an officer suited for the post of Captain of the Port of Gibraltar.

Among the people waiting on the pier when we got back to New York was Susan, looking very bonny and very excited. She had come out in the *Carmania*, the week before; with eager interest, she was enjoying everything about her new surroundings. The Pusey daughters were in Europe so Mother Pusey had met Susan on arrival and taken her home with her. The problem of supporting life—Susan's life—financially, in New York, was therefore still just below the horizon but it had become immediate because it was no part of our thinking that kind friends, or anyone else, should shoulder our burden.

We took a modest room in a quiet little hotel on Eighth Street, just off Fifth Avenue! It was reasonably close to the ship and the weeks until our next sailing passed pleasantly but very quickly. Only too soon were we going full speed astern, backing into the river and among those on the fast receding pier was Susan, waving her handkerchief. She was soon indistinguishable among the crowd and, anyhow, I was too fully occupied to have time to look.

But I was not happy. Apart from missing her dear companionship, this time the ache of separation was more acute because, instead of taking a train and returning to her family, she was going to live by herself in the Laura Spellman Home—a sort of hostel for women. She had discovered it on her own initiative, found it very clean and reassuringly austere. And, quite importantly, it would be within our means. Sometimes she would visit the Puseys but it would be a lonely life. I was rather sick at heart on this occasion of putting to sea.

Indeed, my sense of values, had been upset by the interruption of four and a half years of active service. This was true of so many of us. I had been lucky, never in danger of death or mutilation. But, when it was all over and one attempted to take up again the threads of normal civilian life, one found that everything was different.

"Oh, most magnificent the youthful sea . . . the sea of the young heart!" It had gone. To breathe and sparkle again only in memory. The ocean had become a road of traffic. Not a dusty road but a road of interminably monotonous length. With years of going away and wanting to get back. And year after year pacing the bridge, back and forth, with nothing to occupy your mind but your own thoughts. Everything you did professionally was done with such unvarying repetition that it was done by instinct.

But what could I do? I was a sailor. Such thoughts had been with me very much when I was in the *Mauretania*. I used to look down from the bridge, at young men of about my own age, and say to myself that surely I had as much in my head as they, but my pay would not do much more than buy shoes and gloves for their womenfolk.

And, at home, before coming out to the *Pannonia*, my father had sat muttering mild swear-words as he wrote out a cheque.

"Look at that, my boy," he said. "It's for income tax!"

The figure was such that I could only exclaim, "Well, Dad, if I ever become Commodore in the Cunard, my pay won't be even half as much."

That had never seemed to matter, before. Money was not all that important. And the strange thing was that now that one had so much more—I started in the Cunard at £9 per month and was now getting £33—it mattered still less. There was nothing you could do about it except do your job conscientiously and wait for promotion.

After a voyage of two and a half months, we were back at the Ambrose Channel light vessel and my mind was made up. When we went alongside the pier, I received two further stimuli.

Across the dock lay the *Vennonia*, one of the Cunard cargo ships. She was discharging coal into lighters that would go to bunker the express steamers— the *Mauretania* and *Aquitania*. There was some kind of strike going on in New York so the coal had been brought down from Halifax. I could see Charles Ford and Gilbert Woollatt, the Senior and Junior First Officers, trying to keep clean while they walked about the decks in white uniforms. Many years later they were to be, respectively, Commodore in command of the *Queen Mary* and Captain of the second *Mauretania*. The *Vennonia*'s Master was Captain Hatcher whose guest I had been on board H.M.S. *Queen Elizabeth* when I was in H.M.S. *Pelorus*. "That," I thought as I looked across the dock, "might be my first command, in about another twenty years!"

The other stimulus was my Susan, waving on the pier. This time, not a handkerchief but a cheque book. The money I had left with her was practically untouched and she had a bank account.

It had come about like this. For the summer season, following society up to Cape Cod, the Elizabeth H. Pusey business opened in Hyannis. To have their company and to escape the heat of New York, Susan had gone there also and found a room for herself with a plump, comfortable, New England widow. Working with the Puseys for the summer were two young women just out of college—Molly Tolman from Smith and Helen McGlade from Wellesley. Highly educated and literary, they were young ladies of good family. Unfortunately, the younger daughter, Mary Pusey, took a dislike to Helen. Eventually, there was a flaming row and as a result both girls left.

It was the height of the season and this made things difficult for the Puseys. So Susan, who was doing nothing but pass the time as pleasantly as she could, immediately offered to help. She did not think of being paid for her work but rather of making some return for all the kindness she had received. However, being by nature very energetic and efficient, her help was so effective that they insisted on paying her a salary of $25 per week.

One hundred dollars—£20 per month. How we chuckled over this good fortune when we sat, that evening, on a bench in Washington Square. Susan had treated us to dinner at a rather smart Italian restaurant. It had been a celebration, with a whole bottle of Asti Spumante and I was smoking an excellent cigar that had cost all of twenty-five cents. Dear Susan. So forthright, so sensible with her rock-like integrity. Of course they were glad to employ her, and so would anyone else be. "Now," I thought, "I can do the same and, together, we shall have £40 per month."

But how? That moment in our lives we call the Battle of Washington Square. My thinking was not so incisive, so crystal-clear all of the time. There were many moments of sickening, bowel-griping, wavering doubt whether I could do it. Throw away all the fifteen years of hardship, of toil and achievement. Only I could decide; but, whatever my decision, I knew that Susan would be firmly with me.

It was a very hot summer in New York. The season of vacations, slow-downs and strikes. These prolonged our discharging and loading and gave me more time. I went to the Public Library, looked at the most promising periodicals that dealt with shipping, export and import, and made a list of addresses. I really did not know where to start but import and export sounded right and, at least, I could recognise a bill of lading or a cargo manifest when I saw one. When off duty, in the forenoons, I went ashore to look for that job. Dressed in my best, as I would have done in the City of London—grey suit, grey felt hat, a wing collar and white-spotted, blue bow-tie, yellow washleather gloves and a walking-stick. My black shoes twinkled and looked terribly smart with pearl-grey spats. But it was so hot that I could not wear these. As it was, I went ashore looking like the Marquis of Marshmallow.

The first call I made was chosen for its convenience—Broadway near 14th Street, just a few blocks from the ship. Importers and exporters, world-wide shippers and brokers. A designation so wide that, like the firm's name, it meant very little. The man who received me was genial and heard what I had to say without comment until I had finished.

"No," he rumbled in a deep, gravelly voice, "there's nothing for you here. I guess the name is a bit misleading. Our line is haberdashery and all kinds of trimmings for the garment trade. That's nothing for you." He grinned, sympathetically and went on. "Guess you'll do better away downtown. I should say you'd do well selling bonds or insurance." After a pause, and another smile, looking me up and down he said, "Too bad this ain't Los Angeles. There'd sure be a place for you in Hollywood. They're keen on

British types, just now." Another pause, staring out of the window and then, "Wait a minute."

He picked up his telephone and spoke with a friend called "Mac". I heard myself described as "a cleancut young man, just what you guys need, put some tone in your outfit. I'll send him down to you."

It was good of him to take so much trouble and all the others I met were as amiable, wanting to help. Not one threw up his hands and said, "We don't want sailors." They smoked their cigars, gave me cigars, listened, considered, then picked up the telephone and spoke with some other "Mac" and I went on my way.

It was warm work and, for several days, not encouraging. Then, one morning I passed a very dignified, dark-looking building on Broadway and noticed the name that was cut deep into the granite: GUARANTY TRUST COMPANY. "Frederic, Judson, Holden Sutton, Vice President," I said to myself. Who could forget a string of names like that? He and his wife had twice crossed in the *Mauretania* and he had brought an introduction from Geoffrey Duveen whom I had known as a Lieutenant R.N.V.R. in Gibraltar.

Rather automatically I went through heavy bronze doors. All was marble, bronze and gilt and there was an ornamental ceiling several storeys high. I stood holding hat, gloves and walking-stick, mopping my brow, looking up and around, trying to decide which it resembled more, a railway station or a temple. I was also a bit daunted. Then a man in uniform, with a large revolver at his waist, approached and put me on the way to Mr. Sutton. I went up in an elevator that moved so silently and so quickly that before I realised that it had started the attendant said, "Toid Floor. Trust Department. Here you are, sir."

Here was another marble hall, more conservative in appearance, less bustle, rather hushed. Behind a marble balustrade, on a raised, thickly carpeted platform were a few large desks, each splendidly isolated from its neighbour. In the middle was my friend. The armed guard of that floor took me to him, for which I was glad. I would not have had the courage to go behind that marble barrier and tread that carpet uninvited and unescorted. Mr. Sutton looked up from his papers, then jumped to his feet, hands outstretched.

"Why, bless my soul! What are you doing here? It's good to see you again."

After a mutually cordial shaking of hands I said that if he did not mind, I would just sit for a few minutes.

"I've covered a lot of ground this morning and it's good to take the weight off my feet. I noticed the name on the building as I went by. I'm on my way to see a man in Maiden Lane."

"Maiden Lane!" he exclaimed. "Then it must be about insurance."

"Must it?" I replied. "I don't know. I don't want any insurance. I'm going to see if he can give me a job."

"A job!" He was so surprised that he forgot to blow out the match with which he had lit our cigarettes and he burned his fingers. "You want to leave the sea?" he asked in a measured, earnest tone.

"Yes, indeed," I replied with a grin. "That's why I'm looking for a job."

"Would you come with us?"

"I'd come with anyone, thank you," I said.

He picked up his telephone. There was a brief conversation, very low, but I caught the now familiar "clean cut young fellow" this time with the addition, "trained mind".

We went up to the fifth floor where he left me with a Mr. Willer.

"My experience? Yes, sir." And again I repeated the long story of ships and navigation to far-off places with a little exaggerated embellishment of my knowledge of French, Spanish, German and some Hindustani. There was the usual quiet smile that got wider and wider until I had finished. Then he astonished me by asking, "And what do you want, Mr. de Mierre?"

"Want!" I replied. "I want a job."

"Yes, yes," he said. "I'm sorry. I should have said how much do you want; what salary."

That was a poser. My answer must reveal my utter ignorance of commercial life. But there was no use bluffing.

"What is your business, sir?" I asked in my turn.

At this, he almost laughed but, very courteously, kept himself under control. "We're a bank."

"Oh! Well, sir," I ventured, "I know rather less about banking than banking knows about me. What would be your minimum salary?"

"Twelve hundred," he replied.

"Dollars per annum," I elaborated.

"Yes, indeed," he said. Quite unable to restrain himself any longer, he laughed merrily and, with a considerable sense of relief, I joined in.

Now I was really face to face with that decision. The one that had been so finally taken—with clenched teeth and dogged determination, damn it—at the Battle of Washington Square. Now I had to cable the Cunard Line for permission to resign. It was Wednesday and the ship would sail on Saturday. There was no time for biting nails. This was zero hour. I was going to swallow the anchor. Join the midgets, the pygmies who wielded pens among dog-eared ledgers behind all those lighted windows that punctured the black silhouettes of the skyscrapers. I would fraternise, become familiar with the "fleshy fingers of finance". Me? So green that I did not know a bank when I saw one. So green that the sight of the financial page of *The Times* made me dizzy, "sick at the stomach" as the Americans would say.

It is not surprising that I suffered occasional bouts of cold perspiration and attacks by bellicose butterflies in my belly.

There could not have been a moment more timely for seeking encouragement and we were glad to go to Evensong with John Musters and Arthur Platt and afterwards to return with them on board the *Pannonia*. We sat on the boat-deck, outside my cabin, smoking and talking very little. It had all been said. And it had been in all respects a tiring day. When we got up to go Arthur Platt walked to the gangway with us.

"Good night," he said. "Get a good sleep and don't worry. You have thought about it quite enough. Just remember the lesson we had tonight and what old Saint Paul wrote to Timothy and, of course, to us. We have been given not the spirit of fear but of power and of a sound mind. And remember, too, that last hymn and don't think that you are doing it all yourself."

We walked down the pier, into 14th Street, to the Western Union office where I sent the cable. While I paid for it I was saying in my mind the words of the hymn:

Lord, my times are in Thy hand.
All my sanguine hopes I've planned.
To Thy wisdom I resign
And would mould my will to Thine.

On Saturday the *Pannonia* sailed. Susan had gone back to Hyannis; she had left on the Fall River boat for New Bedford, the night before. On Monday morning I would report at the bank as the most junior of four thousand clerks. I watched the ship back out of her berth and waved good-bye as my shipmates glided past—Arthur Platt on the poop, Captain Gronow on the bridge, John Musters and Ivan Thompson on the fo'c's'le head. It was a moment that stirred up deep memories and emotions. On a bitter February day, twelve and a half years before, I had stood on the same spot watching the *Etruria* sail with Max von Kleditsch, that rather tragic, conradesque Second Mate of my ship *Main*. It was Arthur Platt, the young man with a brand new Second Mate's ticket, who took his place and who was now waving good-bye, just as von Kleditsch had done. It was strange that our paths had crossed, converged so often. When he was in H.M.S. *Europa* he attended our wedding at the Cathedral in Gibraltar.

In the haze of the summer evening it was not long before they faded from view with the same finality as the *Arno* had done when she disappeared over the horizon on her way to Valparaiso.

Apprentice. Extra Master Mariner. What had I done!

For fifteen years so many seas had held me. As a boy, I had listened in shivering delight to their call when they crashed on the beach and then filled the air with their whispered chatter in the shingle and the scent that my romantic boy's mind translated into ships and distant shores.

I had rejoiced to see them leaping in gay, scintillating pursuit of each other in the glory of the trade winds; or gently heaving in a glittering expanse of silken, many-coloured tropical ocean.

Sometimes they had rushed into view with thundering noise and crested combers from behind a thick curtain of driving snow.

"As many seas as there are times and periods in a man's life."

They held me still. I would always hear their call. But another period of my life had begun. And I was young.

Appendix One

A GOOD PASSAGE

During the years 1873 to 1885, in six voyages, the Aberdeen White Star ship *Thermopylae* averaged seventy-one days from the Channel to Cape Otway, one day's sail from Melbourne. The famous *Cutty Sark* averaged seventy days to the South West Cape of Tasmania. This she would pass on her way to Sydney. It is about the same distance as to Cape Otway, actually seventy miles further.

In one of these years, twelve of the passenger clippers sailed out to Melbourne with an average of seventy-six days.

A better understanding of these passage times is gained if the voyage is divided into the three parts in which the ships would all experience the same conditions of wind and weather. The first part would be from the English Channel to the Equator—the "Line"; the second from the "Line" to the meridian of longitude of the Cape of Good Hope; and the third from the Cape of Good Hope to Cape Otway or to the South West Cape of Tasmania. (The passages of the fourteen ships are taken from *The Colonial Clippers* by Basil Lubbock.)

Vessel	Channel to line	Line to Cape	Cape to Otway or South West Cape	Total Days
Cutty Sark	22	23	25	70
Thermopylae	23	22	26	71
Twelve clippers	28	22	24	76
Average fourteen ships	24	22	25	72
Arno	36	23	28 (Adelaide) – 87	

Cape Otway is about 240 miles further than Adelaide, so a comparison with the *Arno* is only valid if the average time taken by the fourteen ships for the third stage, and the total for the passage, is reduced by one day. However, I put the *Arno* up there—among the stars—because this gives a better idea of what her passage time means. The figures show also that, in spite of being deeply laden, her passage to Adelaide might well have been under eighty days if she had not had the foul head winds after clearing the Channel.

Appendix Two

MAX KJER

Seventeen years after taking the six Germans out of the Italian liner at Gibraltar, my business took me to Bremen. The country was in a confused and depressed state; the year was 1932. Transfers of money abroad could be made, if at all, only by complicated and devious ways, generally at considerable loss, and I was examining possible investment in staple commodities as a more satisfactory alternative.

I had introductions to two of the nicest gentlemen that one could wish to meet, two partners—Herr Albrecht and Herr Mueller-Pearse, cotton brokers and merchants. They were elderly men and the troubled times that they had lived through since the collapse of their country at the end of the war seemed to have given them reserves of resilience and understanding that made them superior to the trials of the moment. So we drank sherry and smoked mild cigars and I learned much about raw cotton.

Back in my hotel, I was at lunch when I was called to the telephone. It was Herr Mueller-Pearse. He had enjoyed our meeting; Frau Mueller-Pearse was English and would I be free to dine with them?

It was a most interesting and agreeable evening—an excellent dinner deftly served by a manservant, and the appropriate wines. There were just the three of us and, when we sat in the drawing-room drinking our coffee, the talk quite naturally turned to the war. It was started by the old lady who had been so long in the country that she had a grown-up daughter who was married to a German officer. With her husband smiling at her so affectionately, she said how happy she had always been and that even during the worst days of the war, no one had caused any unpleasantness because of her English origin.

In my turn, to amuse them, I told them of our capture of the *Melpomene*, of her captain's birthday party, and then some of my experiences at Gibraltar. The story of Max Kjer caused quite a sensation. The old gentlemen's eyes blinked with rising interest and the moment I had finished he left the room.

When he returned, a few moments later, his face was alight.

"I think tomorrow you see your prisoner," he said, laying a finger along his nose, in his delight.

He had concluded that Max Kjer was an officer in the North German Lloyd and had telephoned his friend Captain Schluemann, the Marine Superintendent, to ask if they had an officer of that name. The answer was "yes". And when Herr Mueller-Pearse said that he had, in his house, the man who had taken Kjer prisoner, Captain Schluemann had exclaimed, "Na! Is that the story of the hat and the watch?"

Yes, he continued. Max Kjer was in their service, actually on board one of their ships in Bremerhaven. Without further ado, Herr Mueller-Pearse arranged that he should come to Bremen the following day, and meet us at my hotel at four o'clock.

One entered Hillmann's Hotel through revolving doors that gave immediately on to the hall porter's desk and into a roomy lounge. Here, on the next day, we sat awaiting the arrival of my prisoner. On the previous day Herr Mueller-Pearse had worn a comfortable, old lounge suit. Now, in honour of the occasion, he was dressed quite formally in black coat, striped trousers; and a narrow, white slip appeared over the neck-opening of his waistcoat. We sat watching the door and did not have long to wait. As the clock struck four, a burly figure, wearing a raincoat and felt hat came in and went to the porter's desk.

There was no mistaking him and while he stood there, waiting until he could get the porter's attention, I walked up and stood behind him.

"Well, Captain Kjer," I said, speaking in German, "you're still wearing the same hat."

Startled, he spun round. Then replied, with a smile, "No, it's not the same hat. But I've still got the watch."

"I'd like to have that in my hand for a second time," I said.

He produced the watch and put it in my hand, saying, "For a second time, yes." Then, waving a forefinger in front of my eyes, he added, "For a third time, no!"

The ice was broken. We laughed and shook hands heartily, got rid of the hat and the coat and joined Herr Mueller-Pearse who had been watching the little pantomime. Then came tea and toast and cakes and questions and answers, very many of these, some of which dampened the happiness of the moment, caused Herr Mueller-Pearse's brow to wrinkle and put him into a short meditative silence.

After all these years Max Kjer was still only a First Officer. The ship he was serving in was idle and laid up. He was getting only two-thirds of his normal pay. And, yes, they had children; three boys. His face lit up as he spoke of them. All were at school.

"Na!" exclaimed Herr Mueller-Pearse, "This won't do. I think we should go and see the Marine Superintendent. I'll do my best and you, Herr de Mierre, must also speak for your *Kriegskamerade.*"

Kjer and I both laughed, not only at the change in his designation, but at the very idea of bearding the lion in his lair. However, Herr Mueller-Pearse was serious. We got up from the table, got our hats and coats and walked round to the offices of the North German Lloyd.

With my memories of Captain Dodd, Sir Alfred Booth and the formal discipline of the Cunard Line, it was a little daunting for me. For Max Kjer it must have been something of an ordeal. But Herr Mueller-Pearse exuded good nature over all and from this we drew confidence. Even Captain Schluemann became less Marine-Superintendent-like and we were able to discuss the object of our visit in comfort and with coherence.

It was inevitable that Captain Schluemann's first interest should be in me. It was true, I was a real sailor and not only that, but a sailor who had left the sea and was achieving some success as a businessman? This opening proved to be to our advantage for, by the time I had told him of the ships I had served in, especially the sailing-ships of the distant past and my visit on board the school-ship *Grossherzogin Elisabeth* in Barbados—she was sponsored by the North German Lloyd—his mood was such that it was easy for me to express my disappointment that Max Kjer had not made better progress. With some emphasis, I said that had I not taken him prisoner in the war he would probably have fallen. I had not saved his life to have him remain First Officer. Smiling, I urged that Captain Schluemann should do everything possible to give him promotion and get him a command.

Captain Schluemann took it all in good part and then turned to Kjer. There followed a rapid conversation about his service, in which Kjer spoke with dignity and self-reliance.

We took our leave and returned to the hotel where, after drinking a glass of sherry with us, Herr Mueller-Pearse left us with many expressions of good will and optimism. Max Kjer and I dined well, drank some good wine, smoked a couple of cigars, talked much and then he got the train for Bremerhaven. It had been an enjoyable meeting and, when we said good-bye and wished each other luck, I did not expect to see him again or to hear of him again.

A few months later, the papers carried accounts of the plans to combine the fleets of the North German Lloyd and the Hamburg America Lines, to end unprofitable competition and to get rid of redundant and obsolescent ships. Redundant people, too, I supposed.

I thought of Max Kjer and wondered whether the meeting with Captain

Schluemann would help him to keep his job in such an emergency. I did not feel comfortable and was still thinking about him when the post, of that same morning, brought a letter from the benevolent but resourceful Herr Mueller-Pearse. He was terribly worried about my old *Kriegskamerade* and his family. Would I again intercede on his behalf and write to the Chairman of the North German Lloyd, Herr Direktor Stadtlaender, and seek to enlist his interest.

So, in my own hand, I wrote to this gentleman, begging his pardon for my presumption which I justified by my concern for the welfare of Max Kjer. I explained that when I had been a Lieutenant in the Royal Navy, it had been my good luck and Kjer's misfortune, that he should fall into my hands when, after serving in the German Armed Merchant Cruiser *Kronprinz Wilhelm*, he was trying to get back to Germany, to continue fighting for his country. That had been more than seventeen years before and now, as a First Officer, he was as loyal in his service to the Company. What was more, he had three fine sons who would, no doubt, also fight for their Fatherland some day. Would he kindly tell me that I had no cause for anxiety.

Herr Direktor Stadtlaender, also in his own handwriting, was kind and prompt with his reply. He appreciated my solicitude for my *Kriegskamerade* and was happy to assure me that I had no cause for anxiety regarding Max Kjer.

There was another pause of a couple of months until, one day, I received a large case containing twenty-five bottles of superlative wine and a letter from Herr Mueller-Pearse. He was delighted to say that my efforts had been successful, as I would see for myself from the enclosed letter from Max Kjer. A translation is given below.

Straits of Gibraltar.   *On board SS*. Aachen.   *24-4-33*

Dear Herr Mueller-Pearse,
Passing the Rock of Gibraltar my thoughts went involuntarily to our mutual friend Herr de Mierre. Therefore, I should not wish to have omitted to give Herr de Mierre, through you, news of my whereabouts at the moment. I am on the way to the Far East with the steamer Aachen *and expect to be back in Bremen about the end of August. Unfortunately there was no opportunity to call on you in Bremen this time as we sailed rather suddenly. On my return I hope, at last, to be appointed Captain and will let you know as soon as this happens. In the meantime, I am happy to be again in a ship that is under way on a nice long voyage. I beg that you will transmit my best wishes to Herr de Mierre and with kind regards to you dear Herr Mueller-Pearse, I am yours,*
M. Kjer

Höhe von Gibraltar, 21. 4. 33.

Norddeutscher Lloyd Bremen

An Bord des D. „Aachen"

Herrn

Müller-Pearse

Bremen.

Sehr verehrter Herr Müller-Pearse!

Beim passieren der Gibraltar-Felsens wurden meine Gedanken unwillkürlich zu unserem gemeinschaftlichen Freund Herrn de Mierre gelenkt.

Deshalb möchte ich nicht verfehlt haben Herrn de Mierre durch Ihnen berichtet zu haben wie ich mich z. Zt. befinde.

Ich bin auf der Reise nach Ostasien mit dem deutschen „Aachen" und gedenke ca Ende August wieder in Bremen zu sein. Leider bot sich mir damals in Bremen keine Gelegenheit Sie persönlich aufzusuchen, da die Abfahrt unseres Schiffes zumählst plötzlich vorgesetzt wurde.

Ich hoffe jetzt nach meiner Rückkehr vielleicht zum Vorgebirge befördert zu werden und werde die selbstverständlich sofort wieder in Bremen sein.

Einstweilen freue ich mich auf einer fahrenden Schiff zu sein und eine schöne lange Reise vor mir zu haben. Ich bitte Sie Herrn de Mierre meinen besten Gruß übermitteln zu wollen und bin mit den freundlichsten Grüßen von Ihr verehrter Herr Müller-Pearse, Ihr ergebener

M. Meyer.

A letter from my
Kriegskamerad

Appendix Three

BROTHER MAX

The *Engelhorn* sailed from Port Talbot, in the Bristol Channel, on July 1st, 1913, bound for Mejillones in Chile, with a cargo of coal. Her Master, Captain O. Olsen, had had her in his charge since 1907 and under his command she had made good passages of which those of her last voyage are typical.

Although she sailed around Cape Horn in winter—the hard way, from east to west—she arrived in Mejillones after 101 days. From Mejillones she sailed, in ballast, across the Pacific Ocean to Newcastle, N.S.W., in fifty-one days and came back to Valparaiso, again deep laden with coal, in only forty-five days. That is, twenty-one days less than the *Arno* and the *Comliebank* had taken in their "race" on the same passage.

Then, on August 26th, 1914, she sailed from Valparaiso, bound for Falmouth for orders. She should have arrived there in the first part of December but the months passed without news and the families of her crew had to accept

The barque *Engelhorn*

the grievous truth that neither their loved ones nor the *Engelhorn* would ever be seen again. She had "gone missing".

In my book *The Long Voyage* I wrote of the life of an apprentice in a sailing-ship and when it was first published, in November 1963, I was interviewed in the B.B.C. programme *In Town Today*. One result was that a gentleman who heard the broadcast, a Mr. Joseph Kyffin living in Lincoln, wrote to say that my name took him back to Valparaiso where he had met a young officer of the sailing-ship *Engelhorn* named Max de Mierre and, if there were any family connection, he offered to write telling me of his meeting with Max and his shipmates.

I replied that Max was my brother and Mr. Kyffin very kindly wrote at length. Below, I quote extracts from his letter.

It was through Mr. Hardy of our Valparaiso branch of the Missions to Seamen that I happened to be on board the Engelhorn. *One day in April 1914 Mr. Hardy called to tell me that the* Engelhorn *had anchored in the harbour, with some young men from Manchester aboard. So the following Sunday I accompanied him on his rounds in the bay, went aboard the* Engelhorn *and met Max and his shipmates. While the short service was to be held, the Captain invited me into his cabin and Max appeared with a message for him.*

After he had gone, the Captain told me of the splendid opinion he had of Max and of what a fine young man he was. He went on to tell me that during the voyage there had been trouble with some of the crew.

Two of them had attacked him and attempted to throw him over the side. One of his assailants had hold of his testicles and it was only by a superhuman effort that he managed to retain a grip on the iron railing which, as he showed me, was bent under the strain.

Fortunately for him, at this very critical moment, Max went to his aid and, as he said, saved his life. Remembering the size of Max's fists and his powerful build, I can well imagine that these two members of the crew did not escape without some pain for their trouble.

So far as I remember, it was the Third Mate who had gone sick and either left the ship or was unable to carry out his duties. However, the Captain told me that he had promoted Max to take his place and had been glad to do so. "A fine boy, only nineteen, but I promoted him".

Being one of the last to see Max, I was prompted to write to you and I am very glad that I did so because this letter will give you authentic details of an incident about which, perhaps, Max never told you. In any event, you will be still more proud of him and will have every reason to be.

Brother Max

The *Engelhorn* was loaded with barley and it is likely that a large proportion of it was carried in bulk because that would give a more economical use of space. It is a cargo that for safety depends on good shifting boards, some ballast, and careful stowage. But, in her twenty-five years of life, it was probably not the first time that she had made the winter passage homeward around Cape Horn with such a cargo; and her Master, Captain Olsen, was a man of great experience.

One can only think that the *Engelhorn* must have been overwhelmed by weather of unusual violence. But we can be sure that young Max met it with the heart of a man. And, who knows? Perhaps, in being so taken by the sea, he and his shipmates may have been spared an end less swift and merciful.